Praise for
Hebrew for the Rest of Us

"Among the plethora of available Biblical Hebrew teaching grammars, this second edition of *Hebrew for the Rest of Us* continues to fill a unique niche by introducing those who do not have the opportunity to study Biblical Hebrew formally to some of the insights that Biblical Hebrew can provide when studying the Bible in English. This new, thoroughly revised edition includes a separate workbook, improved charts, additional information for broad appeal (including curious facts about Hebrew and comparative notes on Aramaic), and assistance for teaching in an online mode. In addition, it provides a handy supplemental resource for college students who are struggling in their study of Biblical Hebrew grammar."

—Jacobus A. Naudé and Cynthia L. Miller-Naudé, University of the Free State

"Just because you don't know Hebrew doesn't mean that you can't benefit from the amazing tools created to illuminate the significance of the Hebrew language. In *Hebrew for the Rest of Us*, Fields provides the eager student with the essential features of the language with a view to mining those riches provided by the study of other original language tools. There is simply no better resource."

—Miles V. Van Pelt, Reformed Theological Seminary

Dr. Fields has filled an important resourcing gap in the training of future ministers. With astute attention to and engagement with modern electronic resources, Fields offers equipping for preachers, teachers, pastors, missionaries, and others to make responsible use of language tools in their ministry of the Word. Any materials that encourage and equip the church toward robust engagement with the Old Testament/Hebrew Bible are to be commended, and I am thankful for the work of Fields in developing this textbook and workbook targeted especially at this need within theological training and ministry preparation. My students have been well-served by the For the Rest of Us series.

—Allen Hamlin Jr., Cross-Cultural Worker Adjunct Lecturer in Biblical Languages (Trinity College Bristol), Author of *Embracing Followership*

T0244210

HEBREW
FOR THE
REST OF US

SECOND EDITION

HEBREW
FOR THE
REST OF US

USING HEBREW TOOLS TO
STUDY THE OLD TESTAMENT

LEE M.
FIELDS

ZONDERVAN
ACADEMIC

ZONDERVAN ACADEMIC

Hebrew for the Rest of Us, Second Edition
Copyright © 2008, 2023 by Lee M. Fields

Published in Grand Rapids, Michigan, by Zondervan. Zondervan is a registered trademark of The Zondervan Corporation, L.L.C., a wholly owned subsidiary of HarperCollins Christian Publishing, Inc.

Requests for information should be addressed to customercare@harpercollins.com.

Zondervan titles may be purchased in bulk for educational, business, fundraising, or sales promotional use. For information, please email SpecialMarkets@Zondervan.com.

Library of Congress Cataloging-in-Publication Data

Names: Fields, Lee M., author.
Title: Hebrew for the rest of us : using Hebrew tools to study the Old Testament / Lee M. Fields.
Description: Second edition. | Grand Rapids : Zondervan, 2023. | Includes index.
Identifiers: LCCN 2022039104 (print) | LCCN 2022039105 (ebook) | ISBN 9780310133995 (paperback) | ISBN 9780310136125 (ebook)
Subjects: LCSH: Hebrew language--Grammar--Textbooks. | Hebrew language--Textbooks for foreign speakers--English. | BISAC: RELIGION / Biblical Reference / Language Study | FOREIGN LANGUAGE STUDY / Ancient Languages (see also Latin)
Classification: LCC PJ4567.3 .F54 2023 (print) | LCC PJ4567.3 (ebook) | DDC 492.482/421--dc23/ eng/20220818
LC record available at https://lccn.loc.gov/2022039104
LC ebook record available at https://lccn.loc.gov/2022039105

Cover design: LUCAS Art & Design
Interior design: Kait Lamphere

Printed in the United States of America

---

24 25 26 27 28 29 30 31 32 33 34 /TRM/ 15 14 13 12 11 10 9 8 7 6 5 4 3 2

CONTENTS

Unit 4: Nominals

Unit 5: Verbals

Unit 6: A Method to Our Madness

PREFACE

There you are at your church carry-in fellowship meal. People rave about the carrot cake you always make; it's a special recipe with expensive ingredients and homemade frosting. You alone know that the cake only turns out right when you hand mix the ingredients—no electric mixer. It takes a lot of time and effort to make, but this is your church family. They are worth it. It gets your attention when little Johnny walks by with two huge pieces. A few minutes later he runs out to play, leaving his plate on the table. You notice that only a couple of bites are gone from the cake, and the remains are tossed on top of the other uneaten food on his plate. What sort of thoughts run through your head?

God used many authors and about 1,000 years to produce the Old Testament (OT). It makes up over 75 percent of the Bible. Yet, like little Johnny, some Christians take a few bites from the OT and leave the rest uneaten, together with a few remains from the New Testament (NT). Do you wonder what sort of thoughts run through God's head?

If the church is fed best when it feasts on all of God's word, then why do so many act like they are on a weight-loss diet? Perhaps a few Christians have an inadequate opinion of the OT, such as viewing the NT as Christian and relevant and the OT as Jewish and mostly useless. Probably most, who only dabble in the familiar passages, are intimidated by the OT. In comparison to the NT, people often feel that the historical, linguistic, and cultural gaps between the OT and the modern world require too much effort or expertise to bridge. True, it does take effort, but these bridges can be built, and the results will be well worth the effort.

Rationale for Mastering Tools for Old Testament Study

The first reason for mastering tools is to be able to mine the OT for the spiritual riches that lie buried but are accessible to those willing and able to dig for them. I assume that studying the OT is necessary and valuable, simply because it is God's word. It just requires a little more digging to reach the treasure. Obviously, knowing Biblical Hebrew is the most fundamental tool for OT studies, but not everyone is able to devote the amount of time required to learn the language.[1] Thankfully, more than ever there exists a greater number of original language tools, paper and electronic, to reduce the language barrier to the OT. Learning to use these resources, especially electronic ones, is like trading in a spoon for a shovel to do the digging.

Second, mastering Hebrew tools is not only valuable for studying the OT, it is also one of the most overlooked and valuable tools for studying the NT. This may surprise people at first, but it makes sense. All of the NT writers rely on the OT and base their arguments on it. The better a reader understands the OT, the better he or she can understand the NT.

I strongly believe that students of the English Bible who are able to use some of the original language tools to study the OT will both receive more benefit and joy when studying the OT and get even more out of their study of the NT. Using these tools to their greatest advantage involves some training.

The Purpose of This Book

Hebrew for the Rest of Us (*HRU*) is a companion to Bill Mounce's *Greek for the Rest of Us* (*GRU*, soon to be out in its third edition). These books are intended to equip English Bible students to maximize the benefit gained from using the many tools that exist to help bridge the language gap.

New resources are being published all the time and technology continues to grow. How can a person or a book possibly keep up? Mounce's solution is to teach a little about how the Greek language works so that the reader can more effectively use tools both current and those yet to be developed. In *HRU* I offer a similar solution. By learning some elementary facets of Biblical Hebrew, the English-only Bible student can maximize the benefit gained from these original language tools. This basic knowledge empowers an English-only student to refine study techniques on the Bible text itself and to read advanced secondary works such as dictionaries and commentaries that make direct reference to the original text.

The goal is to move toward greater independence in OT studies. No one on earth is totally independent in Bible study. The newcomer to the Bible is the most dependent. But even the most advanced scholars rely on the work of others. Translators rely on the editors of a printed text; those editors rely on the previous work of others in reading manuscripts; commentators rely on all of these plus grammarians, lexicographers, etc.

Once while I was on break from work at a public library, a woman with a heavy German accent asked what I was reading. When I told her it was a

---

1. Even here, don't sell anyone short. I once met a person who was teaching Biblical Hebrew to a class of about seventy members at a large congregation. I heard that people visited from the nearby major university to see how he was recruiting so many.

grammar of theological German, she said that was very good and it was good to read the Bible and compare versions. Then she added, "I never read any Bible study books; only the Bible." At first this sounds very pious. She meant well, but in reality it's as though she were saying, "There has never been a Christian born who has anything to teach me about God and the Bible." Dear reader, God did not design his church this way. This is why he gave apostles, prophets, evangelists, and pastors and teachers (Eph 4:11). God wants us to be interdependent. In this way we are connected to the church of every age. As we grow in knowledge and skill, we will grow in independence, but we will never be absolutely so.

The Style and Scope of This Book

My hope is that this book will appeal not only to college students but also to all people in the church who desire to study the Scriptures more deeply. Toward this end of a broad appeal, I have followed Mounce's example in *GRU* of adopting an informal, conversational tone. Also, I have limited footnotes as much as possible and included examples and illustrations that hopefully will be interesting and educational, sometimes even funny (if you laugh occasionally while you read, I will be happy—as long as we are laughing at the same things!).

I've also tried to match *GRU* in the depth of detail. For example, Mounce treats the grammar of cases and tenses pretty thoroughly for a book designed for English readers. When I treat sequences of Hebrew verbs, I go into about the same amount of detail. Because all languages have some things in common, there is overlap in some of the contents. I have tried to walk a fine line between making *HRU* a stand-alone book that doesn't assume students have gone through *GRU* on the one hand, and on the other hand avoiding unnecessary repetition.

Students of the English Bible can enhance their understanding of the Bible by knowing English grammar. In my years of teaching I have discovered that students exhibit an extremely wide range of knowledge of English grammar. I am no expert in English, but I have included items in the book concerning English grammar in an effort to provide a level playing field.

In order to make this book a useful resource after going through *HRU*, I provide numerous summarizing charts for convenient access which you can use in your own Bible study. I have collected several of them in appendix 3, titled "Action Figures," so that they can be readily found and repeatedly used. Eventually, though, you will learn the material so that reference will be ever less frequent.

What Level of Independence Can You Reasonably Gain After a Few Weeks of Study?

Here are some things you can expect. After studying the material in this book, you will (1) know the Hebrew alphabet, vowels, and how to pronounce the words; (2) learn some of the elementary features of Hebrew; (3) be able to perform word studies responsibly; (4) be able to use certain study techniques especially useful to the OT; (5) be able to understand your English Bible better, both because you will understand translation issues and because you will learn English better; and (6) be able to read the better commentaries and Bible tools that use Hebrew.

Here are two things you should not expect. (1) After you finish this book, you should never tell anyone that you know Hebrew. You will not know Hebrew, unless you take a full-fledged Hebrew course. (By the way, my ulterior motive in writing *HRU* is to inspire students to study full Hebrew.) (2) You will not be able to argue much with scholars on the basis of your knowledge of Hebrew, but you can ask questions and better follow the arguments of various scholars with different views, helping you to make an informed interpretational choice. As Mounce says in *GRU2* (p. viii), it's not a little bit of knowledge that is a dangerous thing, "it is a little bit of arrogance that is dangerous." Knowing everything in this book will not make you an expert Hebrew scholar.

How to Use This Book

My original intention was that *HRU* could be covered in one half of a three-hour semester college course. This would allow the other half of the course to be used for Bill Mounce's *GRU*, as I have done in my course, or to use an elementary book on interpretation, such as *How to Read the Bible for All Its Worth* (4th ed.; Grand Rapids: Zondervan, 2014) by Gordon D. Fee and Douglas Stuart.

Frankly, in my experience with undergraduates, getting through *HRU* in eight weeks is a pretty ambitious goal. That kind of rigor would discourage many people in churches who cannot find that much concentrated time. *HRU* does allow readers to go as far as they wish.

- **Chapters 1–4: A light snack.** Units 1 and 2 contain only four chapters. But because this material is so new to most people, it is better to spend extra time here to get these down well. Chapters 1 and 3 form the basis for the rest of *HRU. You really need to master the alphabet and vowels to understand and enjoy the rest of the material in the book.* Chapters 2 and 4 provide an overview of the history of the Hebrew language and the canon, text, and versions of the OT. These let students know what they are holding in their hands when they pick up a copy of the Hebrew Bible. Some readers may want to stop after units 1 and 2. Reading and using the words in other resources may be all they want to do. Just accomplishing this much is helpful. But I encourage you to go on.
- **Chapters 5–8: Heavy hors d'oeuvres.** For people who want to move beyond the alphabet and vowels, unit 3 teaches about roots and word formation,

clauses, conjunctions, and prepositions. Word formation in particular is quite different from English, and a knowledge of the workings of Hebrew will increase biblical understanding.

- **Chapters 9-17: Full meal.** Unit 4, chs. 9–12, explains nominals (nouns and words that act like nouns). Unit 5, chs. 13–17, explains the Hebrew verbal system. A course that ends here and includes ch. 18 in the next unit would make for quite a substantial course. But wait—there's more!
- **Chapters 18-21: Dessert.** Although each chapter applies the principles learned to practical Bible study, unit 6 is the real payoff. Chapter 18 presents how to perform sound word studies. Chapter 19 is advice on building a personal library. The final two chapters on OT narrative and poetry move the student to a new level of application for what has been learned in the previous chapters. Those who study these two chapters will be able to study the Bible at a pretty sophisticated level.

Other ways to use *HRU*:

- **For churches and do-it-yourselfers.** If working through all twenty-one chapters is too daunting, focus on just chs. 1–5, 9, 13, and 18. Chapters 1–5, 9, and 13 lay a vital foundation for doing the full word study presented in ch. 18. This skeleton will give an overview of the Hebrew language and teach you how to do proper word studies.
- **For college courses.** If time runs short in a semester, chs. 20 and 21 could be delayed and used in a course that studies OT prose or poetry. In fact, even if students have gone through chs. 20 and 21, a good review would be valuable at the beginning of course in narrative or poetry.
- **For students of full Hebrew.** Some have found that when full Hebrew grammars are too difficult to understand, *HRU* presents some things in a more understandable way.

What Other Resources Will You Need to Go Along with This Book?

If you were a professional construction worker, you would invest in many more tools than just a hammer, screwdriver, and a crescent wrench. If you really enjoyed hunting or fishing, you might be willing to spend hundreds or even thousands of dollars each year on tackle, boats, bait, and licenses. If you seriously want to study the Bible so you can understand and proclaim God's message to mankind more accurately, you will also want to invest in some tools of your trade, especially if you are in professional ministry.

Computer resources. Since the publication of the first edition, computer Bible programs have become commonly used by many Bible students. There are free resources available online, though there is often a reason why they are free. The serious Bible student will want to get something substantial, and each person will need to determine what they can afford and what best meets their needs. There is a list of some options in ch. 19.

I have chosen not to offer training in how to use specific software, because as soon as this book would be published, such instructions would be out of date. Instead, I present how to use the data that you can access in these programs.

I do make numerous references to Logos Bible Software, and I am grateful for their permission to use screenshots freely.

Print resources. If you wish to use paper resources, here are the bare minimum: an exhaustive concordance, an interlinear Bible, and a wordbook. I recommend the following:

- Lee M. Fields, *Hebrew for the Rest of Us Workbook* (Grand Rapids: Zondervan, 2023).
- Edward W. Goodrick, John R. Kohlenberger III, and James A. Swanson, *The Strongest NIV Exhaustive Concordance* (Grand Rapids: Zondervan, 2004).
- An interlinear Bible
    Either John R. Kohlenberger III, *The Interlinear NIV Hebrew-English Old Testament* (Grand Rapids: Zondervan, 1993)
    or Jay P. Green, ed., *The Interlinear Bible: Hebrew-Greek-English* (Peabody, MA: Hendrickson, 2005).
- William D. Mounce, ed., *Mounce's Complete Expository Dictionary of Old and New Testament Words* (Grand Rapids: Zondervan, 2015).

There are some other materials that would be nice to have access to. You will be unable to do some exercises without the information included in these works.

- An analytical concordance: Benjamin Davidson, *Analytical Hebrew and Chaldee Lexicon*, repr. (Peabody, MA: Hendrickson, 1981).
- A Hebrew concordance: John R. Kohlenberger, III, and James A. Swanson, *The Hebrew-English Concordance to the Old Testament* (Grand Rapids: Zondervan, 1998).
- A computer Bible program that deals with the Hebrew text of the Bible.

Why a Second Edition?

The number of chapters and all of the chapter titles are unchanged. Here is a list of many differences from the first edition.

1. **Thorough revision.** All the chapters have been edited, some more than others. In particular, the chapters on verbals include refined explanations and new examples. I have also incorporated more illustrations of flowcharting. The word-study chapter now includes a "shortcut" procedure along with the guide to a full word study. Discussions of key biblical passages have also been added. There are now indexes to Scriptures and subjects.

2. **Improved charts.** Since 2008, printing technology has advanced. Many of the charts as originally designed could not be replicated using the previous type-setting software. The charts have now been improved.

3. **Broader appeal.** One of the surprises in the feedback I have received over the years is that, though many were using *HRU* to teach the use of Bible study tools, some teachers were recommending *HRU* to students who were having trouble understanding their Hebrew grammars. Consequently, some of the new material mentioned below includes details that may prove more important to students of full Hebrew than to English-only Bible readers. I still worked at keeping footnotes to a minimum, but some references were important to make.

4. **Advanced information and curious facts.** This section occurs at the end of all chapters. I hope people read these; I tried to make them fun.

5. **What about Aramaic?** I thought some might wonder about Aramaic. I added a section at the end of each chapter. Mostly these deal with biblical Aramaic, but sometimes it is necessary to treat matters in other dialects of Aramaic found in targums and other Jewish literature.

6. **Additional resources.** The exercises and keys have been converted to a separate workbook. These exercises are invaluable to the learning process. Additional resources including audio files may be accessed by creating an account under Instructor Resources at zondervanacademic.com.

7. **Designed with online education in mind.** There are some new features that are present in *HRU2* and the accompanying *Workbook* (*HRUW*) that facilitate online learning. Chapter objectives are redone to conform to the revised Bloom's Taxonomy. Insets sprinkled throughout the book give teaching and learning ideas. Some supplementary materials will be available for phone apps and other electronic media. These include some audio files and flash-card materials for learning to read. A new edition of the video lectures may be done in the future.

8. **A separate workbook.** All the exercises have been removed from *HRU2* text. Instead, these have been thoroughly revised and expanded in *HRUW*. Review exercises occur at the beginning of most chapters in *HRUW*. A full key has already been prepared (available under Instructor Resources at zondervanacademic.com), so all the exercises "work." There should be more than enough here to enable readers to master the things covered in each chapter of *HRU2*.

xvi Hebrew for the Rest of Us

Why Go to All This Work to Study So Carefully?

B. F. Westcott, a famous NT scholar from the nineteenth century, wrote, "It is as perilous to live on borrowed opinions as to live on borrowed money: the practice must end in intellectual or even in moral bankruptcy."[2]

Christians ought to pursue better Bible study because ministry—service to others—demands it. If people want to speak about the meaning of passages and about theology only in vague generalities, if people want only to give pat answers memorized from what others have told them, they probably won't find this book of much value. But if you want to be careful and precise when you study and explain the Bible, if you want to be able to minister to others by having reasons for your interpretations, if you want to "own" your beliefs because you've studied them yourself, then you will benefit much from learning how to use the marvelous tools available to you today. You can only be as precise in your under-standing and explanation of Scripture or biblical doctrine as you are able to study Scripture closely.

Mid-Atlantic Christian University, where I taught for twenty-five years, is only about an hour from the Atlantic Ocean. A number of our students enjoy surfing. The goal is to skim across the top, not to go deep. Careful study of the Bible is the opposite. At first many Christians seem to avoid deeper Bible study because it involves too much effort. However, it is my experience in teaching groups from junior high on up that once Bible readers get a taste of deeper study, an understanding that is below the surface, they are never satisfied with "surfing" the Bible again.

Finally, we must never forget the reason we study at all: to be transformed into Christ's likeness by the renewal of our minds, until we all grow up into maturity. Deep study is no guarantee that mature faith will result, but shallow study guarantees that immaturity continues. Bible study is never complete until it results in worship. If, as a result of learning things presented in *HRU*, study and teaching of God's word becomes more dynamic and lives become more Christ-like, my prayers will be answered.

אַחֲלַי יִכֹּנוּ דְרָכָי לִשְׁמֹר חֻקֶּיךָ:
אָז לֹא־אֵבוֹשׁ בְּהַבִּיטִי אֶל־כָּל־מִצְוֹתֶיךָ:
תְּהִלִּים קיט ה–ו
—*Psalm 119:5–6*

Lee M. Fields

---

2. B. F. Westcott, *Lessons from Work* (London: MacMillan, 1902), 122.

ACKNOWLEDGMENTS

It is impossible to thank all who played a role in making this possible. I begin by thanking the many great teachers at Hebrew Union College-Jewish Institute of Religion and Cincinnati Christian University, of whom I am a humble beneficiary, plus those who have taught me through their writings. I thank my colleagues at Mid-Atlantic Christian University for encouraging me to pursue this project. Thanks also to my students over the years who helped improve this edition.

I am grateful to the many who have used *HRU* as individual students or as students at schools. I trust that the knowledge and skills learned by English-only users have led to a deeper relationship to the Lord and to his Scriptures. Reviewers and individuals over the years have kindly given me valuable feedback, and I am grateful.

I thank Verlyn Verbrugge, who made the first edition possible and whom I will see again one day! Thanks are due also to Nancy Erickson, Kait Lamphere, and the rest of the expert staff at Zondervan for the privilege to prepare a second edition of the text and a new workbook, especially to Michael Williams for his keen proofreading skills and invaluable suggestions. Thanks also to my friends Bill Mounce and Miles Van Pelt for encouragement and guidance over the years.

I thank my children, Brian and Beth, for encouragement during all the inconveniences my work caused to their busy schedules during the writing of the first edition when they were at home, and my wife, Julie, for listening to me talk through some of the writing process through both editions. Most of all, I thank God, on whose account this work was done. I pray that the readers will be drawn more deeply into relationship with him through a deeper encounter with his Scriptures.

ABBREVIATIONS

Bible Books

Gen	Genesis	Jonah	Jonah
Exod	Exodus	Mic	Micah
Lev	Leviticus	Nah	Nahum
Num	Numbers	Hab	Habakkuk
Deut	Deuteronomy	Zeph	Zephaniah
Josh	Joshua	Hag	Haggai
Judg	Judges	Zech	Zechariah
Ruth	Ruth	Mal	Malachi
1–2 Sam	1–2 Samuel	Matt	Matthew
1–2 Kgs	1–2 Kings	Mark	Mark
1–2 Chr	1–2 Chronicles	Luke	Luke
Ezra	Ezra	John	John
Neh	Nehemiah	Acts	Acts
Esth	Esther	Rom	Romans
Job	Job	1–2 Cor	1–2 Corinthians
Ps (Pss)	Psalm(s)	Gal	Galatians
Prov	Proverbs	Eph	Ephesians
Eccl	Ecclesiastes	Phil	Philippians
Song	Song of Songs/	Col	Colossians
	Solomon	1–2 Tim	1–2 Timothy
Isa	Isaiah	1–2 Thess	1–2 Thessalonians
Jer	Jeremiah	Titus	Titus
Lam	Lamentations	Phlm	Philemon
Ezek	Ezekiel	Heb	Hebrews
Dan	Daniel	Jas	James
Hos	Hosea	1–2 Pet	1–2 Peter
Joel	Joel	1–2–3 John	1–2–3 John
Amos	Amos	Jude	Jude
Obad	Obadiah	Rev	Revelation

Bible Versions

ESV	English Standard Version	NET	New English Translation
GNB	Good News Bible	NIV	New International Version (2011)
JB	Jerusalem Bible		
KJV	King James Version	NIV84	New International Version (1984)
LB	Living Bible		
MSG	The Message	NLT	New Living Translation
NAB	New American Bible		
NASB	New American Standard Bible (1995 revision)	NRSV	New Revised Standard Version
		RSV	Revised Standard Version
NCV	New Century Version		
		TEV	Today's English Version
NEB	New English Bible		

Grammatical and General Terms

(Not all of these are used in *HRU2*, but you may still find them helpful for your own study.)

1	first person	cj	conjunction/ conjunctive
2	second person		
3	third person	Coh	cohortative
A	active (used only in combinations)	cs	consecutive
		Cst	construct state
Abs	absolute state	d	dual
Acc	accusative case	D	*piel* stem
Act	active	Dat	dative case
Adj	adjective	Det	determined
Adv	adverb	DO	direct object
Ar	Aramaic	Dp	*pual* stem
Art	article	Emph	emphatic aspect
BA	Biblical Aramaic	f	feminine
BH	Biblical Hebrew	Fut	future tense
BHQ	*Biblia Hebraica Quinta*	G	gender, *qal* stem
		Gen	genitive case
BHS	*Biblia Hebraica Stuttgartensia*	H	*hiphil* stem
		Hp	*hophal* stem
c	common	HtD	*hithpael* stem

Imp	imperfect tense	Pret	preterite
Imv	imperative mood	Prg	progressive aspect
Ind	indicative mood	Prn	pronoun
Inf	infinitive	PrnSf	pronominal suffix
InfA	infinitive absolute	PrPtc	present participle
InfC	infinitive construct	Pst	past tense
Inter	interrogative	PstPtc	past participle
IO	indirect object	Ptc	participle
Juss	jussive	PtcA	participle active
Lex	lexical form	PtcP	participle passive
LXX	Septuagint	PtSp	part of speech
m	masculine	Q	*qal* stem
MnCl	main clause	RC	relative clause
n	neuter	Reflex	reflexive
N	*niphal* stem, Number	RhQ	rhetorical question
N^h	head noun	RPrn	relative pronoun
Nl	nominal	s	singular
Nn	noun	SbCl	subordinate clause
Nom	nominative case	Sbj	subjunctive mood
N^t	tail noun	SC	subject case
NV	nonverb	Smpl	simple aspect
OC	objective case	Subj	subject
P	person	Suff	suffix
p	plural	T	article (when a
Pass	passive		shorter abbreviation
PC	possessive case		than Art is needed)
Pf	perfect tense/aspect	TA	Talmudic Aramaic
PN	predicate nominative	targ	targum
Pp	preposition	U	undetermined
PPhr	prepositional phrase	V	verb
PPrn	personal pronoun	Va	verb active voice
Pr	present tense	Voc	vocative case
Pred	predicate	Vp	verb passive voice
Pref	prefix		

Secondary Resources

(Not all of these are found in *HRU2* but they are widely used.)

BDB   Brown, Francis, S. R. Driver, and Charles A. Briggs. *A Hebrew and English Lexicon of the Old Testament*

CHALOT	Holladay, William Lee, and Ludwig Köhler. *A Concise Hebrew and Aramaic Lexicon of the Old Testament*
DBLA	Swanson, James. *Dictionary of Biblical Languages with Semantic Domains: Aramaic (Old Testament)*
DBLH	Swanson, James. *Dictionary of Biblical Languages with Semantic Domains: Hebrew (Old Testament)*
DCH	Clines, David A., ed. *Dictionary of Classical Hebrew* (9 vols.)
GRU	William D. Mounce. *Greek for the Rest of Us,* 2nd ed.
HALOT	Koehler, Ludwig, Walter Baumgartner, M. E. J. Richardson, and Johann Jakob Stamm. *The Hebrew and Aramaic Lexicon of the Old Testament* (5 vols.)
IBHEG	Green, Jay P., ed. *The Interlinear Bible: Hebrew-Greek-English*
INIVHEOT	Kohlenberger, John R. *The Interlinear NIV Hebrew-English Old Testament*
LHEIB	van der Merwe, Christo. *The Lexham Hebrew-English Interlinear Bible; Bible. O.T. Hebrew*
LTW	Mangum, Douglas, et al., eds. *Lexham Theological Wordbook*
MCED	Mounce, William D, ed. *Mounce's Complete Expository Dictionary of Old and New Testament Words*
NETS	*The New English Translation of the Septuagint*
NIDOTTE	Van Gemeren, W., et al., eds. *New International Dictionary of Old Testament Theology and Exegesis* (5 vols.)
SNIVEC	Kohlenberger, J. R., and E. Goodrick. *Strongest NIV Exhaustive Concordance*
Strong's	James Arminius Strong, *Strong's Exhaustive Concordance*
TDOT	Botterweck, G. Johannes, Helmer Ringgren, and Heinz-Josef Fabry, eds. *Theological Dictionary of the Old Testament* (17 vols.)
TLOT	Jenni, Ernst, and Claus Westermann, eds. *Theological Lexicon of the Old Testament* (3 vols.)
TWOT	Harris, R. L., et al., eds. *Theological Wordbook of the Old Testament* (2 vols.)

CHAPTER 1

IT DOESN'T LOOK LIKE GREEK TO ME
The Hebrew Alphabet

Objectives
1. Write the letters of the Hebrew alphabet in order and out of order.
2. Name the letters in order and out of order.
3. Understand the two kinds of *dagesh*.
4. Transliterate the Hebrew letters into English letters and vice versa.

Introduction

If you have skimmed this book at all and found that these letters "do not look like Greek to you," that's a good thing! The Hebrew alphabet is quite different in appearance from the Greek and, even more, from the English alphabet. I have decided that the best thing to do is to jump right in to learning the letters and the vowels and to alternate chapters that supply background information. This will give you a little extra time to learn the shapes and sounds well.

If you have already learned the Greek alphabet from studying Mounce's *Greek for the Rest of Us,* you will note some similarities with Hebrew, because both the Greeks and the Israelites got their alphabet from the Phoenicians. The Greeks simply converted into vowels some of the Semitic letters that represented sounds that the Greeks didn't use and added a few extras for Greek sounds not represented in Hebrew. We in turn get the English alphabet from the Greeks through Latin. Watch for similarities in order and in the names of the Greek letters.

The Hebrew alphabet consists of twenty-two (some count twenty-three) letters with a total of twenty-eight forms. These twenty-two letters constitute the consonants alone. Originally the vowels, though pronounced, were not written. We will learn the vowels in ch. 3.

This chapter consists of two parts. The first is a writing guide teaching you the letters. Its purpose is to show you the proper order of strokes to write each letter. The letters are initially placed in an order to help you distinguish those that are similar in shape. After you master writing the forms, practice writing them in alphabetical order. If you want to, you can make flash cards with the letter on one side and the name of the letter on the other (see Supplemental Helps in *HRUW*

1

for pages that can be photocopied and enlarged or create an account under Instructor Resources at zondervanacademic.com for access to a Word document).

Remember three things: (1) Hebrew is read from right to left and anytime we write in Hebrew, it is in Hebrew order; anytime we write in English, it is in English order. (2) In this chapter we are discussing only the consonants. (3) *Have fun with this!* You will enjoy doodling in Hebrew and answering when your friends and family ask, "What's that?"

The second part is a chart of all the forms of the Hebrew alphabet in alphabetical order. Its purpose is to provide you with the necessary information to learn the names and the order of the letters, plus a few other things, just for reference.

You may find it helpful to learn the letters in groups: the first five, then the next five, then the last twelve in three groups of four. Many people learn them in a song, such as the one in the back of this book. Also, comparison with the order of the English alphabet will help in learning (e.g., נ מ ל כ ⟺ *k l m n*). The next-to-last column in the chart gives a guide to pronunciation. Since there were no audio recorders three thousand years ago, we cannot know exactly how words were pronounced. In fact, the Bible itself indicates that there were various pronunciations at different times and places, just as words are pronounced differently today in New York than in North Carolina. So, the pronunciation guide is approximate and designed mostly to be helpful for learning.

The Names and Shapes of the Hebrew Letters

The names of the Hebrew letters are simply words that start with that sound. So, the second letter *bet* begins with the sound *b*. As children we learn phrases like "A is for apple"; if we named our letters as the Phoenicians did, we might call the first letter *apple*. That's not really so strange, though, when you remember that we have a letter named "double-u."

Whereas we write our English letters sitting on the line, Hebrew letters sort of hang from the upper line. To learn the shapes, Hebrew letters may be categorized according to length and width. One letter does not reach the lower line; most do reach the lower line; a few extend below the lower line; one extends above the upper line. We treat narrow letters first, then wide ones, moving from simple to more complex strokes.

Directions
1. *Trace* the printed strokes starting at the top.
2. *Copy* the letters in the remaining space.
3. *Repeat* the name of the letter aloud each time you write it (a rhyming English word is in italics below the name of each letter to indicate proper vowel sounds; accented syllables are underlined). Note that the spelling of the names of the letters often differs from one writer to another. In *HRU2* the transliterated

spelling of the names of the letters (and of the vowels in ch. 3) follows the academic style presented in *The SBL Handbook of Style*, 2nd ed. (Atlanta: SBL Press, 2014), 5.1.1, except I use *waw* instead of the more modern *vav*.

FIGURE 1.1: Writing the Hebrew Letters

Narrow Letters

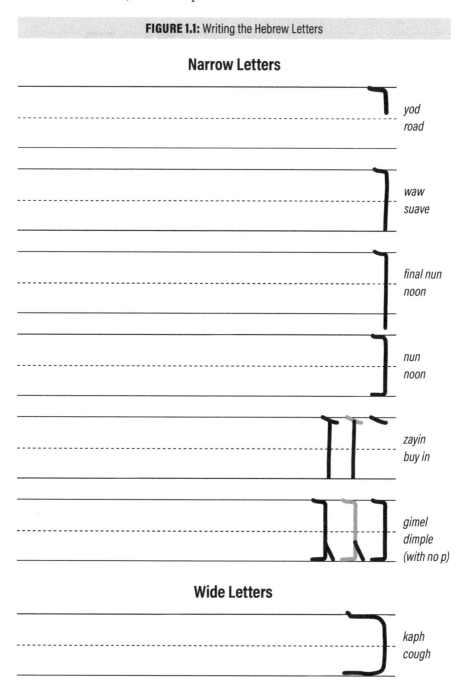

yod
road

waw
suave

final nun
noon

nun
noon

zayin
buy in

gimel
dimple
(with no p)

Wide Letters

kaph
cough

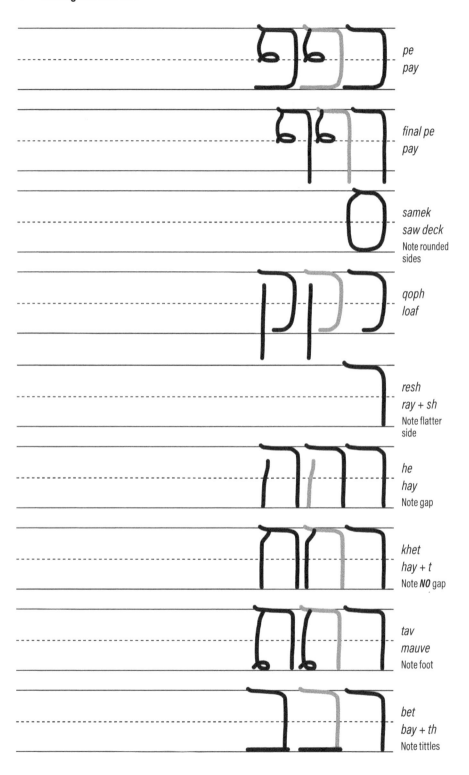

pe
pay

final pe
pay

samek
saw deck
Note rounded sides

qoph
loaf

resh
ray + sh
Note flatter side

he
hay
Note gap

khet
hay + t
Note **NO** gap

tav
mauve
Note foot

bet
bay + th
Note tittles

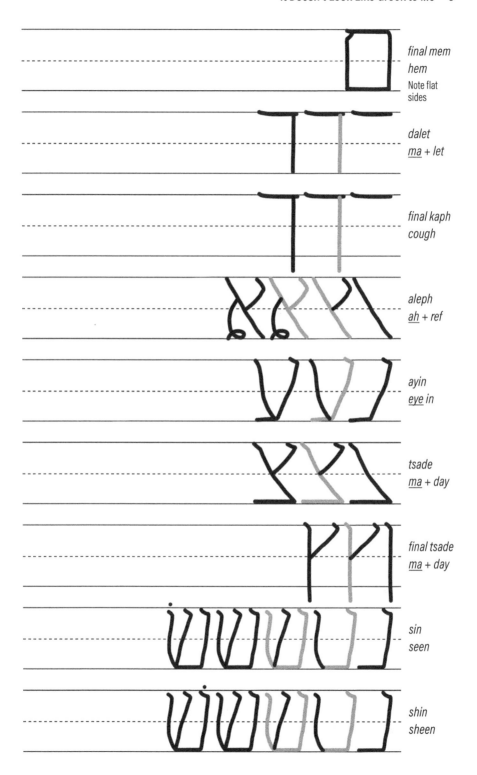

final mem
hem
Note flat sides

dalet
ma + *let*

final kaph
cough

aleph
ah + *ref*

ayin
eye in

tsade
ma + *day*

final tsade
ma + *day*

sin
seen

shin
sheen

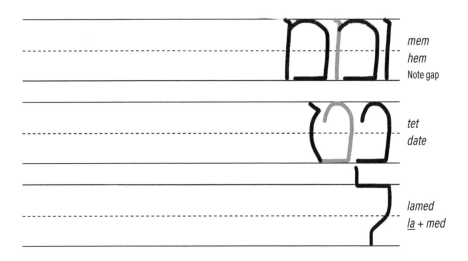

mem
hem
Note gap

tet
date

lamed
<u>la</u> + med

The Hebrew Letters in Alphabetical Order, Etc.

The chart of the Hebrew alphabet is given below. I include both academic and general-purpose transliteration styles. Let me point out some things.

> **Teaching/Learning Tip:** Learning the *aleph bet* song at the end of the book will aid in learning the alphabet. Start by singing the entire song one time even before writing all the letters. Then repeat singing a measure or two while giving students time to practice writing the alphabet in order. As singing goes faster, the rhythm will make the names stick.

1. The square forms of the letters given above are the shapes used in Jesus's day. There are six letters known as *begadkephat* (**bet, gimel, dalet, kaph, pe,** and **tav**) letters that may be written with or without a dot (called a *dagesh*) inside that letter resulting in a change in sound. The *dagesh* is present when these letters begin a syllable and serves to mark their sounds as hard (or plosive) rather than soft (or aspirated).
2. There are five letters that, when found at the end of a word, have a form different than when they are located elsewhere in the word. These are known as final forms.
3. Many works use transliteration instead of the Hebrew letters. So, you will need to be able to convert Hebrew letters into transliterated symbols and vice versa. Unfortunately, there are a number of different transliteration systems. The system used here is completely unambiguous and represents one Hebrew letter or vowel with one Latin character. For the aspirated *begadkephat* letters, many transliterate with two letters using an *h* to indicate the aspiration; so, *bh, gh, dh*, etc. We use underlining instead for the 1:1 character-correspondence goal.

4. Many commentaries use a general-purpose system of transliteration that avoids diacritical marks (i.e., dots, dashes, and other special characters added to English letters to specify characters in alphabets different from English). In *HRU2* you will learn a system with diacritical marks. In exercises to chs. 3 and 4 in *HRUW* you will be able to practice dealing with these to find the correct Hebrew word. A little practice doing this, and you will grow in your appreciation of diacritical marks.

5. The sounds of the Hebrew letters are approximated by similar sounds indicated by the **bold** letters in the English words listed in the "Sounds" column. Again, we don't know exactly how they were pronounced, but scholars can come up with a fair approximation by comparison of manuscript spellings, by comparison of words in cognate languages, and by seeing how other ancient languages like Greek transliterated Hebrew words. Follow the guidance of your teacher, if you have one.

6. Finally, the Hebrew letters were also used for numbers (the Greeks employed a similar system).[1]

FIGURE 1.2: The Hebrew Alphabet

Name	Square Forms	Final Forms	Academic Translit.	General Translit.	Sounds	Numeric Value
aleph	א		ʾ	ʾ or none	[silent]	1
bet	בּ		b	b	**b**oy	2
	ב		b̲	b, v	**v**ery	
gimel	גּ		g	g	**g**irl	3
	ג		g̲ or ḡ	g, gh	**g**irl	
dalet	דּ		d	d	**d**og	4
	ד		d̲	d, dh	**d**og (the)	
he	ה		h	h	**h**elp	5
waw	ו		w	v, w	**v**ery (**w**aw)	6
zayin	ז		z	z	**z**ero	7
khet	ח		ḥ	h, ch	**ch**emistry	8
tet	ט		ṭ	t	**t**in	9
yod	י		y	y	**y**ell	10

(continued)

1. The use of the letters as numerals goes back at least to the second century BC (Paul Joüon and T. Muraoka, *A Grammar of Biblical Hebrew*, rev. ed. [Rome: Pontifical Biblical Institute, 2006], 5f, citing G. R. Driver, *Semitic Writing: From Pictograph to Alphabet*, 3rd ed. [London: British Academy, 1976], 270).

Name	Square Forms	Final Forms	Academic Translit.	General Translit.	Sounds	Numeric Value
kaph	כ	ך	k	k	kit	20
	כ	ך	k̲	k, kh	chemistry	
lamed	ל		l	l	loud	30
mem	מ	ם	m	m	man	40
nun	נ	ן	n	n	noun	50
samek	ס		s	s	see	60
ayin	ע		ʿ	ʿ or none	[silent]	70
pe	פ		p	p	paint	80
	פ	ף	p̲ or p̄	f, ph	photograph	
tsade	צ	ץ	ṣ	ts	hits	90
qoph	ק		q	q	kit	100
resh	ר		r	r	red	200
sin	שׂ		ś	s	see	300
shin	שׁ		š	sh	shed	
tav	ת		t	t	tin	400
	ת		t̲	t, th	tin (thin)	

Observations on the Alphabet Chart

In these observations, I explain how I teach pronunciation to my students as well as how others teach. Let your teacher, if you have one, guide you. If you have Logos Bible Software, Hebrew pronunciation for every lexical form is available as an add-on. It is done by Randall Buth, and I prefer his system because it sounds like Hebrew to modern Israelis and the minor differences have pedagogical value.

1. **Number of forms.** If you count the number of letters in the chart, you might count twenty-nine instead of twenty-eight. I wrote the final *kaph* twice because of the five final forms; only the final *kaph* takes the *dagesh*. However, with or without the *dagesh* does not really matter; there is still only one final *kaph*. Noticing the *dagesh* in the final *kaph* is important for pronunciation and transliteration.
2. **Multiple transliteration systems.** There are almost as many systems of transliteration as there are published works. Most of the time you will be able to figure things out. Some simplified systems, though, do not transliterate *aleph* and *ayin* (and for these letter names I'm using this simplified

system!). This will make it a challenge for you to recover the Hebrew spelling for words. This is especially true for the vowels (ch. 3 below). The system in *HRU* and *HRU2* is perhaps a little overly precise, but it is unambiguous.

3. **Pronouncing *aleph* and *ayin*.** I teach my students to make a distinction between *aleph* and *ayin*. The *aleph* is a voiceless glottal stop that sounds like the beginning of the second word in the phrase "the end" (when the words are not run together as though it were "the yend"). So מַלְאָךְ (*mal* | *'ak̲*) is a two-syllable word, with *aleph* at the beginning of a syllable after a closed syllable (a syllable ending with a consonant instead of a vowel), and not silent as it is at the end of a syllable, as in מְלָאכָה (*məlā' | k̲â*). I teach *ayin* as a voiced glottal stop, even at the end of a syllable. This has pedagogical value when you learn about the furtive *patakh* (ch. 3). Teaching this is best done in person. Follow the direction of your teacher. If you are studying this book on your own, using Modern Hebrew silent pronunciation is probably the best option. If you ever go to Israel or speak with Israelis, pronouncing *aleph* and *ayin* with these distinctions will not sound strange to them.

4. **Pronunciation of the *waw*.** The *waw* was originally a /w/ sound. In fact, the title to ch. 7 is a play on this pronunciation of *waw*. However, most grammarians and all speakers of Modern Hebrew pronounce it as a /v/. Pronouncing the *waw* as /w/ does sound strange to the ears of native Hebrew speakers.

5. **Pronunciation of *begadkephat* letters.** As mentioned above, the pronunciation of these letters has changed from six to twelve sounds over the centuries. Evidently, when the Masoretes did their work (see chs. 3 and 4), they heard twelve sounds and represented those with the presence or absence of the *dagesh lene* (explained below). In Modern Hebrew, nine sounds are heard. Most teachers do not teach twelve. The simplest and best, in my opinion, is to follow the Israelis.

6. **Pronunciation of *resh*.** In Modern Hebrew, the *resh* is gutturalized, similar to French; this is what I teach my students. Other teachers pronounce *resh* like the English (with the tip of the tongue curled upward); others pronounce the *resh* as trilled or tapped (=a single beat of a trill). I accept all three from my students.

The Other Kind of *Dagesh*

As I explained above, the *dagesh* serves to indicate a hard (or plosive) sound in the *begadkephat* letters and occurs only in these six letters. This particular *dagesh* is called the **dagesh lene**. There is another *dagesh*, called the **dagesh forte**, that indicates the doubling of a letter. So, ט without *dagesh forte* is transliterated *ṭ*, and ט, with *dagesh forte* is transliterated *ṭṭ*. *Dagesh forte* can occur in any letter (including the *begadkephat* letters) except for א, ה, ח, ע, and ר. The first four letters are called guttural letters (because the sounds are made in the back of the throat), and none of the five can be doubled (though occasionally *resh* will take *dagesh*).

What about Aramaic?

The Aramaic and Hebrew alphabets are identical.

Advanced Information and Curious Facts

You may wonder how we know the order of the Hebrew alphabet. The answer comes from Hebrew poetry. There are a number of poems in the Bible that are alphabetic acrostic poems; that is, the first word of each verse begins with a successive letter of the alphabet. This is almost impossible to bring out in English. The best example is Ps 119. The reason it has 176 verses is because 176 is a multiple of 22 (by a factor of 8). Each group of eight verses begins with the same letter of the alphabet. Many English versions give the name of each letter at the beginning of each stanza.

One more interesting tidbit. Revelation 13:16 says the number of the beast out of the earth is the number of a man, 666 (six hundred sixty-six; note: this is not 6 + 6 + 6!). One of the ancient identifications of him was Nero. How did they come up with this? Someone realized that if you take the Latin name Nero Caesar and transliterate it into Hebrew (with an additional Hebraizing final *nun*), the sum of the numeric values of the Hebrew letters is 666. Here we go:

FIGURE 1.3: Hebrew, Nero, and Numbers

Caesar			Neron			
ר	ס	ק	ז	ו	ר	נ
200	60	100	50	6	200	50

= 666

An important public service announcement: Since we can calculate a numeric total for every word in the Hebrew Bible, some people imagine that these sums can yield a secret meaning. This scheme of interpretation is wrong. (1) It does not take into account textual variants (spelling or text-critical issues). (2) The OT does not use the letters as numbers; it always spells out numbers. (3) This method of interpretation actually draws attention away from the meaning of the words of the authors (both human and divine!).

If you hear or read someone teaching secret meanings in the numeric values of Hebrew (or Greek) words, run away fast!

And now, back to our regularly scheduled programming.

CHAPTER 2

WHOSE LANGUAGE IS DEAD?

The History of Hebrew

Objectives
1. Explain the periods of the history of the Hebrew language.
2. Type in Hebrew (and Greek) for use in papers and online.

Introduction

A "dead" language is one that is no longer spoken in a living people group. No one would think of English as dead, but English has changed over time. Words come into use and sometimes fade out of use. For example, if I describe something to my students as "groovy" (60s and 70s), they would think I was "wack, dude" (twenty-first century?). Sometimes words change meaning (*gay* meant something different in the 1890s than it did in the 1990s).

The history of English is organized into several periods by scholars. Old English is the name of the language from the fifth to the twelfth century. A little over a thousand years ago, the Model Prayer read like this:

> *Fæder ure Þu Þe eart on heofonum,*
> *Si Þin nama gehalgod.*
> *To becume Þin rice,*
> *gewurÞe ðin wila, on eorðan swa swa on heofonum.*
> *urne gedæghwamlican hlaf syle us todæg,*
> *and forgyf us ure gyltas, swa swa we forgyfað urum gyltendum.*
> *and ne gelæd Þu us on costnunge, ac alys us of yfele. soÞlice.*[1]

Though many might be able to make out a few words (e.g., *Fæder ure*), few people can understand it. Yet, it is English.

Similarly, Hebrew is a living language, though there are numerous differences

---

1. This text of the Lord's (Model) Prayer in the West Saxon literary dialect of the eleventh century is taken from https://www.ruf.rice.edu/~kemmer/Words04/history/paternoster.html.

between ancient and modern. Compared to English, however, Hebrew has remained generally the same over three thousand years![2]

Hebrew is a Semitic language. "Semitic" simply means a group of similar languages based on the names of the descendants of Shem as listed in Gen 10:21–31—languages such as Ugaritic, Akkadian, Aramaic, and Arabic. Semitic languages are divided geographically into East and West. West Semitic is subdivided into Northwest Semitic and South Semitic. Hebrew is a member of the Northwest Semitic group.[3]

In this chapter we will delineate the periods of Hebrew. It is placed here to give you some answers to questions you may have wondered about, without piling on to the work of learning the alphabet. The exercises in *HRUW* provide more opportunities for practice with the alphabet and transliteration that you learned in the last lesson.

The Periods of Hebrew Language

There is a long prehistory to Biblical Hebrew found in the archaeological remains of the cities where languages similar to Hebrew were spoken. As we mentioned above, Hebrew has enjoyed rather remarkable uniformity for over three thousand years. Scholars, however, have been able to identify some periods of development in the language.

The discussion below categorizes Hebrew into biblical and postbiblical. Some scholars refer to these categories as classical and non-classical.

Biblical Hebrew

The biblical texts themselves, assuming Mosaic authorship, were written over a period of about one thousand years. Remarkably, the language remained uniform enough that grammars of Biblical Hebrew can treat it as a unified language. The terms used to refer to this language, two found in the Bible and one that later came to be used most widely, are:[4]

"the language of Canaan" (Isa 19:18), *śəp̄at kənaʿan* (formally, "the lip [as an instrument of speech] of Canaan"), generally the language of people who occupied Israel and Judah during the first millennium BC
"(the language) of Judah" (2 Kgs 18:26, 28; 2 Chr 32:18; Neh 13:24); *yəhûdît* (formally, "Judahite"), specifically the language around Jerusalem in the sixth and fifth centuries BC

---

2. Bruce K. Waltke and M. O'Connor, *An Introduction to Biblical Hebrew Syntax* (Winona Lake, IN: Eisenbrauns, 1990), 4: "A well-educated Hebrew speaker can read and understand Hebrew literature from all stages, from the oldest portions of the Hebrew Scriptures to Modern Hebrew."

3. See J. A. Lund, "Aramaic Language," in *Dictionary of the Old Testament: Historical Books*, ed. Bill T. Arnold and H. G. M. Williamson (Downers Grove, IL: IVP Academic, 2005), 50.

4. See R. L. Heller, "Hebrew Language," *Dictionary of the Old Testament: Historical Books*, 380.

"Hebrew (language)"; *ʿibrît*, in the Bible is used only to refer to people (a Hebrew person), after the Enlightenment this term came to be used to refer to the language of every period[5]

Scholars identify two periods within Biblical Hebrew.

1. *Early Biblical Hebrew.* Hebrew has been in existence at least from the time of Moses, the middle of the second millennium BC. Scholars, even conservative ones, disagree over the date of the compilation of our OT. Most conservatives think that Moses wrote the bulk of the Pentateuch during the fifteenth century BC but that the text as we have it shows definite signs of later editing. The earliest extrabiblical Hebrew is found in inscriptions from the Iron Age (1200–540 BC). There is great similarity between these texts and Biblical Hebrew, but there is simply not much evidence on which to draw firm conclusions.
2. *Late Biblical Hebrew.* Still, differences can be identified between texts composed before and those composed after the exile in the sixth century BC. So, grammarians can describe those differences[6] and refer to the existence of Late Biblical Hebrew.

Postbiblical Hebrew

After Biblical Hebrew, changes do become more obvious and different periods can be described.

1. *Transitional period* is my designation for Hebrew after the Bible was completed (ca. 400 BC) and before the Mishnah was put into writing (ca. AD 200). The *Dictionary of Classical Hebrew* classifies all Hebrew before Mishnaic as Classical Hebrew. On the other hand, Segal, in his grammar on Mishnaic Hebrew,[7] includes Qumran literature within the Mishnaic Hebrew and dates the period 400/300 BC–AD 400.

   The writings of Qumran date from about 200 BC (the likely date of the foundation of the community) to AD 135 (the Bar Kochba rebellion). This important body of writings includes biblical texts, apocryphal texts, and sectarian writings, i.e., documents written by the community on various matters.
2. *Mishnaic Hebrew,* or Rabbinic Hebrew, is the language of the learning of Jewish teachers after the turn of the era. Mishnaic Hebrew is similar to the

---

5. See the entry עִבְרִי in Abraham Even-Shoshan, *Milon Even-Shoshan* (*Dictionary of Even-Shoshan,* in Hebrew, hereafter cited as Even-Shoshan, *Dictionary*), 6vols. (Jerusalem: Hamilon Hechadash [The New Dictionary], 2009), 1339.

6. Ohad Cohen, *The Verbal Tense System in Late Biblical Hebrew Prose,* Harvard Semitic Studies 63 (Winona Lake, IN: Eisenbrauns, 2013). See also Paul Joüon and T. Muraoka, *A Grammar of Biblical Hebrew,* rev. ed. (Rome: Pontifical Biblical Institute, 2006).

7. M. H. Segal, *A Grammar of Mishnaic Hebrew* (Oxford: Clarendon, 1927), 1.

language of Qumran,[8] and they probably overlap. But our evidence comes from the Mishnah, a document that was composed about AD 200 but preserves older material. It represents the written form of the oral Jewish law and was an attempt to apply and codify the Mosaic law in circumstances without the temple. Of the same dialect are other rabbinic works such as the Tosefta (ca. 300) and the Hebrew portions of the Palestinian Talmud (ca. 400) and the Babylonian Talmud (ca. 500 or 600). Perhaps the commentaries known as *midrashim* (which overlap these writings in time) should be included here, but some see their language as distinctive.

3. *Medieval Hebrew* is the period after the Talmudic period (ca. 500–600) to ca. 1700. This body of works is an ocean of materials written in many places by many Jewish teachers and includes all types of literature.

4. *Modern Hebrew* is the term for the language since ca. 1700. Its reemergence as a living language in Palestine is due to the efforts of Eliezer Ben-Yehuda beginning in the late nineteenth century. It is based on Biblical Hebrew, though there are differences, of course. It was made the official language of Jews in Palestine in 1921, and in 1953 the Israeli government founded the Academy of the Hebrew Language to make dictionaries, study the language, and direct its development by creating words, regularizing spelling, etc.

Figure 2.1 summarizes the periods of Hebrew and the scholarly discussions outlined above. The first column gives two major dichotomies according to the *Dictionary of Classical Hebrew*; the second is according to Segal. The third column lists the periods as described above, except that I've added a designation "Transitional" to label the six-hundred-year debatable period described above.

FIGURE 2.1: Periods of Biblical Hebrew

DCH	Segal	Periods of Hebrew	
Classical Hebrew	Biblical Hebrew	Early Biblical	before 540 BC
		Late Biblical	540–400 BC
	Postbiblical Hebrew	Transitional	400 BC–AD 200
Post-Classical Hebrew		Mishnaic	AD 200–500
		Medieval	AD 500–1700
		Modern	AD 1700–present

---

8. Segal, *Grammar of Mishnaic Hebrew*, 1.

Typing in Hebrew (and Greek)

Typing in Hebrew is a useful skill to learn, especially if you are a Bible college or seminary student and you must write papers. There are several programs available for typing in Hebrew. Also, there are two basic kinds of keyboard layouts. The first layout is an Israeli layout, which in principle is just like the English QWERTY layout. To use this requires that you learn the layout. I have found this to be a little difficult, especially in typing the vowels. The second layout is a phonetic layout. In this, the Hebrew letters are arranged to correspond most closely with the English letters (Q = *qoph*, W = *waw*, etc.). There are plenty of options, but I will offer one recommendation, and it is free!

1. Download bidirectional capability for free from Windows (or whatever operating system you are using) and a right-to-left paragraph icon will appear in your Home tab in the Paragraph panel.
2. Go to https://keyman.com/ (a.k.a. Tavultesoft) and under the Products tab download the latest version of Keyman for your operating system (Windows, Apple, etc.).
3. Under the Keyboards tab search for "galaxie" and download the "Galaxie Greek/Hebrew (Mnemonic) Keyboard Package."
4. If the fonts you need are not already loaded, you can download some from this site. Especially beautiful (and free) fonts for Hebrew are Ezra SIL and SBL Hebrew. For Greek, I prefer Gentium Plus (or the older Gentium Alt).
5. The Keyman site guides you to set up keystrokes to change language. So as not to interfere with other Windows settings, I use Ctrl+Shift+H to switch to Hebrew, Ctrl+Shift+G for Greek, and Ctrl+Shift+U for US English. I use Alt+1 for Times New Roman font, Alt+2 for Ezra SIL, and Alt+3 for Gentium Plus. You can make your own.

Keyman allows the bidirectional typing capability that you need, and the fonts include all the diacritical marks.

What about Aramaic?

Aramaic, just as Hebrew, is a Semitic language. Only a small amount of the OT is in Aramaic. However, Aramaic was the "big language," the lingua franca of the ancient Near East, used even into Roman times. Hebrew was by far the more obscure language. Here is a list of all the Aramaic passages in the OT:

1. Dan 2:4b–7:28
2. Ezra 4:8–6:18; 7:12–26
3. Jer 10:11

4. Two words in Gen 31:47, the place name "Jegar Sahadutha" (Hebrew "Galeed," NIV; both the Hebrew and the Aramaic mean "[stone] heap of testimony")

Aramaic is quite ancient, but pockets of dialects still exist in the present day. The history of the language is divided into five periods, all dates approximate:[9]

1. Old or Ancient Aramaic (850–612 BC, the Neo-Assyrian period)
2. Imperial or Official Aramaic (612–200 BC, Neo-Babylonian and Persian periods)
3. Middle Aramaic (200 BC–AD 250, Hellenistic and Roman periods)
4. Classical Aramaic (AD 250–1200)
5. Modern Aramaic

Some awareness of Aramaic is relevant to OT and NT studies. The Aramaic of Daniel and Ezra are Imperial Aramaic.

The targums are Aramaic translations of the Hebrew OT. These are from the Middle and Classical Aramaic periods. Some are basic formal translations but later became expanded translations or virtually commentaries on the Hebrew text, often only on key phrases rather than on every verse or word. They are important for understanding Jewish interpretation and at times can help in text-critical matters (determining what is the original reading of a text).

The legal portions (a.k.a., using a simplified transliteration, *halakah*, הֲלָכָה) of the Talmud are in Classical Aramaic. The story portions (a.k.a. *haggadah*, הַגָּדָה) of the Talmud are in Hebrew. The habit of the Jewish teachers was to tell their stories in Hebrew. For a little more on the Talmud, see the "Advanced Information and Curious Facts" section at the end of ch. 4.

Advanced Information and Curious Facts

What language did Jesus speak? This has been a matter of great debate. Many Jews in Palestine during the Roman period were trilingual: Greek, Hebrew (as a living language, not just the language of Jewish scholars!), and Aramaic. The Greek words *hebraïs* and *hebraïsti* always mean Hebrew; *syriakē* and *syristi* are used to refer to Aramaic.[10] The word *syriakē* does not occur in the NT.

---

9. See Lund, "Aramaic Language," 50, and Frederick E. Greenspahn, *An Introduction to Aramaic*, 2nd ed., Resources for Biblical Study 46 (Atlanta: Society of Biblical Literature, 2003), 6–7.

10. See Randall Buth and Chad Pierce, "*Hebraisti* in Ancient Texts: Does Ἑβραϊστί Ever Mean 'Aramaic'?" in *The Language Environment of First Century Judaea—Volume Two*, ed. Randall Buth and R. Steven Notley, Jewish and Christians Perspectives 26 (Leiden: Brill, 2014), 108–9. See also in the same volume, Marc Turnage, "The Linguistic Ethos of the Galilee in the First Century C.E.," 110–81. This book, edited by Buth and Notley, contains important articles on several relevant questions for understanding the linguistic environment of the Jews in the first century.

It is almost certain that Jesus and the Galilean apostles were able to speak Greek. Many Jews of Palestine were bilingual, at least enough to do business with a Greek-speaking world. In John 12:20–21, some Greeks come to the disciples requesting to see Jesus. It is unlikely that those Greeks would have known Hebrew, though it is possible that they knew some Aramaic. The disciples and Jesus would have to know Greek to understand them. Likewise, when Jesus heals the Gerasene demoniac (Mark 5:1–20), it is probable that he spoke to the man in Greek, since it was a Greek-speaking area.

Jesus clearly knew Aramaic. We see examples of Aramaic transliterated into Greek in the NT. When he healed Jairus's daughter, Mark 5:41 quotes the Aramaic and translates: "Taking her by the hand he said to her, 'Talitha cumi,' which means, 'Little girl, . . . arise'" (ESV). Although *cumi* might be Aramaic or Hebrew, *Talitha* (טַלְיְתָא), *talyətā'*, is clearly Aramaic; the Hebrew would be יַלְדָּה, *yaldâ*. Similarly, when Jesus was on the cross, he quoted Ps 22:1; Mark 15:34 reports, "And at the ninth hour Jesus cried with a loud voice, *'Eloi, Eloi, lema sabachthani'* which means in Aramaic, 'My God, my God, why have you forsaken me?'" (ESV). Omitting the vowels, the Hebrew of Ps 22:1 may be transliterated as *'ly, 'ly, lmh 'zbtny*.

Jesus also knew Hebrew. In fact, Hebrew was probably the common language of the Jews of Judea. We noted just above that Jewish teachers recorded in the Talmud a shift from Aramaic to Hebrew when they tell stories (*haggadah*, הַגָּדָה). It is a safe assumption that Jesus followed the patterns used by Jewish teachers and expected by their audiences, namely, that Jesus also spoke in Hebrew when he told parables.

CHAPTER 3

GET THE POINT?

The Hebrew Vowels

Objectives
1. Write the Hebrew vowels.
2. Pronounce Hebrew vowels, syllables, and words.
3. Transliterate Hebrew to English and English to Hebrew.

Introduction

So far, by learning the Hebrew alphabet, you have only learned the consonants. Naturally the question arises, "What about vowels?" As we mentioned in chapter 1, originally Hebrew was written with consonants alone. Of course when people spoke, they pronounced the words with vowel sounds; the vowels simply were not written. The vowel sounds of a written text had to be figured out from context. Scribes later developed systems of indicating vowels without having to alter the consonants. This was done by adding small symbols above or below the consonants. These symbols, arrangements of dots and short lines, are called *vowel points*, as opposed to the consonants, which are called *letters*. Vowels are not called letters as they are in English.

At first, trying to read consonants without any vowels may sound unbelievably difficult. But, if you know the language well (as an ancient native speaker would), it is manageable. You can do this in English:

Ths wh tk Hbrw lv t stdy th ld tstmnt.

This sentence is a pretty complex example for vowelless English, but you probably figured it out without much difficulty as "Those who take Hebrew love to study the Old Testament." In Hebrew, this works out a little easier in one way, since virtually no word or even a syllable starts with a vowel. However, because of Hebrew inflections (changes in form to indicate changes in meaning), there may be more variations than in English. Most Hebrew words are built on three-letter roots that have a basic meaning, to which are added vowels and various combinations of prefixes and suffixes that make meaning more specific. To illustrate, a sentence of unpointed Hebrew might include the word דבר, the root having to do with the formation of words. Without a context, the word might be pronounced in a number of different ways, depending on the intended meaning. In figure 3.1, I've put the three letters of the root in shaded type and the various vowel points in regular type to give only *some* of the possibilities. In the transliterations, I've shaded the English letters that correspond to the Hebrew consonants.

FIGURE 3.1: Be Grateful for Vowels!

Pronounced in various ways, the form דבר (without written vowels) might mean any of the following:

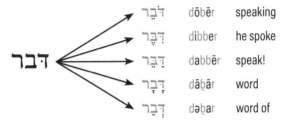

דֹבֵר	dōbēr	speaking
דִּבֶּר	dibber	he spoke
דַּבֵּר	dabbēr	speak!
דָּבָר	dābār	word
דְּבַר	dəbar	word of

Notice:

1. Remember that Hebrew reads from right to left, and English, even in transliteration, reads from left to right.
2. Vowel points are written above or below the consonant.
3. Every consonant in a word, except the last one, has a vowel point with it. The last letter only has a vowel point with it when the word ends in a vowel. The only time a consonant in the middle of a word will not have a vowel point with it is when the consonant is used to represent a vowel sound (see below) or when it is *aleph* at the end of a syllable. *Aleph* is always a consonant and is transliterated as such, but at the end of a syllable it becomes silent. In those instances, there will be no vowel point with it and the preceding vowel will be long. For example, in the second syllable of מְצֵאתִי (צֵא) the א has no vowel point with it because it is silent. However, the transliteration is still *māṣēʾtî*, with the א represented by the symbol ʾ.
4. The consonant is read first and the vowel is read after. The first word of figure 3.1 begins with the syllable דֹ. The little dot, or *point*, above the *dalet* is a vowel (a *holem* marks the sound *o* as in *hole*). To pronounce the syllable, the *dalet* is read first, then the vowel: *dō*. This syllable sounds just like the English word *doe* (there is, of course, no correspondence in meaning).

At first these "points" may seem confusing and intimidating. Do not become discouraged! You will soon become familiar with them. Besides, this is not the most important material to get right to the smallest detail. But being able to pronounce and transliterate with ease will make your experience with this book and with applying what you learn here more fun and rewarding.

Origins and Systems

The written system of vowels found in the Hebrew Bible is the culmination of many centuries of work. We may describe the development of written vowels as having taken place in three overlapping stages. The first stage is the period of **no vowels**, extending to the tenth century BC.

The second stage is the period of **vowel letters**, also known as *matres lectionis* ("mothers [aids] of reading"). During this period the consonants ה, ו, and י began to be added to indicate certain vowel sounds. The use of vowel letters generally increased through the biblical period, into the period of the Dead Sea Scrolls (ca. 150 BC–AD 70) and into the Mishnaic period (up through about AD 400).

The third stage may be called the period of **vocalization**. Vowel points began to be added to the consonantal text several centuries after the composition of the last book of the OT. Jewish scholars worked in three regions developing different systems of vowel pointing known today as the Palestinian, Babylonian, and Tiberian systems. These systems were designed in such a way that vowel sounds could be indicated by adding marks to the text without altering the Hebrew consonants in any way. The system that became standard is the Tiberian system developed by the Masoretes during the period AD 500–1000. This is the system that you will be learning.

English Vowels

A vowel is a sound made by passing air through the throat and mouth with no stoppage. The English alphabet contains vowels. Of the twenty-six letters, five are vowels. However, there are more vowel sounds than five and also more than five ways to write vowel sounds. We can speak of simple vowels, "vowel letters," and diphthongs.

Each simple vowel, *a, e, i, o, u*, has at least two sounds, long and short.

FIGURE 3.2: Simple Vowels in English

Simple Vowel	Short Sound	Long Sound
A	cat	cake
E	bed	complete
I	bit	bite
O	cot	hole
U	but	brute

What I'm calling "vowel letters" refers to those consonants that combine with a vowel to form a sound. You know of *w* and *y* used this way in English but there is also *h*. All three of these consonants combine with vowels to form a sound (in British pronunciation, commonly also *r*). Here is one example for each: bl**ew**, th**ey**, r**ah**!

English also has many diphthongs. A diphthong is two vowels used for one syllable, e.g., f**ee**t and f**ea**t. Hebrew tends to avoid diphthongs, though there is one important exception you will learn about below.

Hebrew Vowels and Sounds

Hebrew vowels are actually less confusing than English to pronounce. However, Hebrew has a good many more symbols.

> **Teaching/Learning Tip:** Teachers of Hebrew instruct students to pronounce the vowels in different ways. Students should follow their teacher's direction. I will present vowels according to modern Israeli pronunciation because it is simple and won't offend the ears of modern native speakers or scholars. You will learn to identify the symbols for the five vowel sounds. For a brief summary of the history of Hebrew vowel sounds throughout the biblical period and beyond, see Randall Buth, *Living Biblical Hebrew: Introduction, Part One* (Jerusalem: Biblical Language Center, 2006), 119. I realize that I am combining a modern pronunciation of vowels with a modified ancient pronunciation of consonants.

Whereas English only has five vowel symbols plus three "vowel letters" (not counting the numerous diphthongs), Hebrew indicates sounds using twenty different symbols, two of which represent two different sounds. This amounts to twenty-two different vowel symbols.

Classification of Vowels

Hebrew vowels may be classified according to a number of qualities. Figure 3.3 illustrates how I will present them. The numbers in parentheses give a count of each type. Two symbols can be long or short, and they will be counted as short in the chart. Hopefully this classification will help you learn the symbols quickly. (When we learn the vowels, we will use a slightly modified version of this chart.)

FIGURE 3.3: Classification of Vowels

Type	Simple		Composite	
	Short	Long	Short	Long
Full (17)	(5)	(3)		(9)
Reduced (5)	(2)		(3)	

Notice:

1. Vowels may be simple or composite. "Simple" refers to vowels written with a single symbol; "composite" refers to vowels written with combinations of two symbols. The areas with no number mean that those categories do not exist.
2. Vowels may be full or reduced. According to the Masoretic system, full vowels were required to form a syllable; and so a word has as many syllables as it has full vowels. Most modern grammarians treat all vowel points except silent *shewa* as syllables. I will teach the Masoretic system. You should follow your teacher.
3. Full vowels may be long or short; reduced vowels can only be short. The term *long* as opposed to *short* is thought by many scholars to refer to the vowel's sound quality (how the vowel sounds) instead of its quantity (the length of time a vowel sound lasts).
4. Reduced vowels are either simple (i.e., *shewa* alone) or composite (i.e., a *shewa* + a short vowel). Simple *shewas* are either silent (no sound) or vocal (with a very quick sound).

Before we get started on Hebrew vowels, you need to understand three things about transliteration. First, as we mentioned when discussing consonants, there are many systems of transliteration. When you are reading a book that transliterates Hebrew, there will usually be an explanation or key at the beginning. Some systems are detailed enough to enable you to transliterate back into Hebrew without any confusion, while other systems are simplified to enable people who don't know Hebrew to approximate the pronunciation of a Hebrew word, but transliterating from English back to the Hebrew may not always be clear. Most of the time you will have no difficulty. For Hebrew vowels, we are going to use a modification of the system of transliterations found in R. Laird Harris, Gleason L. Archer, and Bruce K. Waltke, *Theological Wordbook of the Old Testament* (Chicago: Moody, 1980), because it is complete and unambiguous.

Second, because English has only five vowels and three vowel letters, transliterating the twenty-two Hebrew vowel symbols into English means that in addition to English letters, extra marks are required, such as "long" marks (e.g., the line above the letter, as in $\bar{o}$). These are called diacritical marks.

Third, you will need to pay particular attention to the guides to pronunciation, because the symbols used for transliterating foreign languages are different than what you may have learned when you studied English. For example, in English the symbol $\bar{e}$ represents the vowel sound in **feet**; in transliteration this same symbol represents the vowel sound in **cake**.

We will treat full vowels and then reduced vowels. After that you will learn how to tell the difference between a pair of identical symbols that have different sounds.

Eight Simple Full Vowels

Similar to learning the consonants, we will move from simple to more complex. I'm also going to give you the names of the vowels. As non-Hebrew students, I don't think you need to memorize them, though your teacher may require it. I do not require my students to learn the names of the vowels, but I will sometimes use the names. It's easier to say *"qamets"* than to say, "that letter with the vowel under it shaped like a small capital T." You do, however, need to learn what sounds the vowels represent so you can pronounce Hebrew words.

> **Teaching/Learning Tip:** Using flashcards can be a helpful technique to learn and review letters, vowels, sounds, and transliterations. A document is available under Instructor Resources at zondervanacademic.com as a free download so you can print your own flashcards. It is easy to use; just be sure that the front and back match correctly.

There are eight simple vowel points. In most of the figures in this chapter I use a dotted circle (◌) to represent a given Hebrew consonant. This allows you to see the position of the vowel with a consonant. After the symbol I give the name of the letter, then the sound it makes by giving an English word that has the same vowel sound. The last three columns are transliteration and length (Long or Short). The ability to match the sound and transliteration with the correct vowel is important for you to pronounce the word correctly.

You may find it helpful to learn these eight vowels in two groups. Figure 3.4 gives the first five vowels comprised of dots only. I include both academic and general-purpose transliteration styles.

FIGURE 3.4: Vowels with Dots Only

Symbol	Name[1]	Sound	Academic Translit.	General Translit.	Length
◌	*hireq* (חִירֶק)	mach*i*ne	*i*	*i*	S, L
◌	*tsere* (צֵירֵי)	th*ey*	*ē*	*e*	L
◌	*segol* (סֶגוֹל)	th*ey*	*e*	*e*	S
◌	*qibbuts* (קִבּוּץ)	br*u*te	*u*	*u*	S, L
◌	*holem* (חֹלֶם)	h*o*le	*ō*	*o*	L

---

1. The Hebrew spelling is given here because the transliterated names of the vowels are not done in academic style and after you learn the material in this chapter you may find the Hebrew spelling aids in pronunciation. Spelling of the vowel names differs among authors, and multiple spellings are accepted. The spellings used here come from Even-Shoshan, *Dictionary* (in Hebrew), and where spelling variants were given, I selected those that matched the pronunciation I am most used to and is reflected in the simplified transliteration.

Notice:

1. *Holem* **with the *sin* and *shin* dots:** When *holem* is followed by *shin*, sometimes the dot on the right shoulder of the *shin* functions as both the marker for *shin* and *holem*. So the word Moses, *mōšeh*, may be written either מֹשֶׁה or מֹשֶׁה. Likewise, when the *sin* is followed by the *holem*, sometimes there are two dots above the *sin*, e.g., שֹׂבַע (*śōḇaʿ*), and sometimes the *holem* is included in the *sin* dot, e.g., שֹׂנֵא (*śōnēʾ*). This may seem confusing at first, but you will quickly learn to recognize when the *sin* dot has combined with the *holem*: in שֹׂנֵא it looks like the *sin* has no vowel symbol, which cannot be right. The only alternative is that the *sin* dot is also serving as the *holem*.[2]

2. **Reading the syllables:** Reading the letters and vowels is relatively simple. The consonant is read first and the vowel is pronounced after that. That means that every syllable in Hebrew begins with a consonant. There is one exception to this, which happens to occur quite often. We will get to that below.

   How to transliterate and pronounce the syllables in the "Syllable" column is presented below. After the written syllable comes the transliteration. In the final column I give an English word that has the same sound as the Hebrew syllable. NOTE: There is no correspondence in meaning; the Hebrew syllables are not words and have no meaning as they are and are totally unrelated to the meaning of the English word.

Syllable	Transliteration	English Word
הִ	*hi*	he
הֵ	*hē*	hay
הֶ	*he*	hay
הֻ	*hu*	who
הֹ	*hō*	hoe

Figure 3.5 shows the three vowels comprised of lines only.

FIGURE 3.5: Vowels with Lines Only

Symbol	Name	Sound	Academic Translit.	General Translit.	Length
◌ַ	*patakh* (פַּתַח)	f<u>a</u>ther	*a*	*a*	S
◌ָ	*qamets* (קָמֵץ)	f<u>a</u>ther	*ā*	*a*	L
◌ָ ◌ָ	*qamets khatuf* (קָמֵץ חָטוּף)	h<u>o</u>le	*o*	*o*	S

---

2. It is noteworthy that the printed Hebrew Bible called *BHS* (*Biblia Hebraica Stuttgartensia*) always

Notice:

1. *Qamets* and *qamets khatuf* are identical in form but distinct in sound and transliteration. The circle with the *shewa* follows the circle with the *qamets khatuf* to mark a closed, unaccented syllable. Later in this chapter you will learn that this is a silent *shewa*, and it is not transliterated. The syllable unaccented and closed with the silent *shewa* must have a short vowel. Therefore the vowel is *qamets khatuf*.[3] *Qamets* is much more common, so if in doubt, guess *qamets*.

2. It is not rare that the long *qamets* is followed by a syllable beginning with a vocal *shewa*. In these cases, the long *qamets* forms an open syllable (a syllable ending with a vowel). So, how can you tell this from the *qamets khatuf*? Worded another way, how can you tell if the word חָכְמָה should be pronounced מָה | חָכְ, *hok̲ | mâ* (a noun meaning "wise"), with *qamets khatuf* and silent *shewa*, or כְמָה | חָ, *ḥā | k̲əmâ* (a verb meaning "she was wise") with the long *qamets* followed by a vocal *shewa* that begins the next syllable?

   To clarify this, the Masoretes placed a vertical stroke after the long *qamets*. This mark is called a metheg, a Hebrew word meaning "bridle," and is used to mark the syllable as open. This gives the following, with syllables divided in the transliteration: חָכְמָה → *hok̲ | mâ* and חָכְמָה → *ḥā | k̲əmâ*.
   Problem solved!

3. Reading the syllables:

Syllable	Transliteration	English Word
הַ	ha	ha
הָ, הָ	hā	ha
הָ◌	ho	ho

At this point you may want to complete and read the corresponding exercises in *HRUW*. Practicing with a partner or a teacher is helpful.

Nine Composite Full Vowels

As we mentioned above, Hebrew began to use ה, ו, and י to indicate vowel sounds.[4] Many centuries later, the Masoretes incorporated their points into these vowel letters. Their system allowed them to mark vowels without having to alter the consonantal text (see ch. 4).

As for the sound these combinations make, the letter plus the vowel go together

---

edits so that a *holem* does not combine with the *sin* or *shin* dot. Other editions, such as text edited by Norman Henry Snaith, combine the *holem* with the *sin* dot. The manuscripts themselves differ on the practice. Other reference books, such as dictionaries and concordances, also differ in practice.

3. In case you are curious, *khatuf* (חָטוּף) is a real Hebrew word meaning "snatched" and by extension "abrupt" (see Marcus Jastrow, *A Dictionary of the Targumim, the Talmud Babli and Yerushalmi, and the Midrashic Literature* [London; New York: Luzac & Co.; G. P. Putnam's Sons, 1903] 1:450) and here refers to the brevity of duration: "hastened."

4. Some say א is also used as a vowel letter, but I disagree and will explain below.

to form one vowel sound. In transliteration the presence of vowel letters must be indicated. This is done in two ways: (1) placing a circumflex above the English letter (e.g., ô) or (2) transliterating both the vowel and the vowel letter (e.g., ōh).

FIGURE 3.6: Nine Hebrew Composite Vowels

Symbol	Name	Sound	Academic Translit.	General Translit.	Length
הֵ	tsere he	they	ēh	eh	L
הֶ	segol he	they	eh	eh	L
הָ	qamets he	father	â	ah	L
הֹ	holem he	hole	ōh	oh	L
וֹ	holem waw	hole	ô	o	L
וּ	shureq	brute	û	u	L
יִ	hireq yod	machine	î	i	L
יֵ	tsere yod	they	ê	e	L
יֶ	segol yod	they	ey	e	L

Notice:
1. All composite vowels are long.
2. The *he* occurs as a vowel letter only at the end of a word.
3. Except for *shureq*, the names for these vowels are the vowel name plus the letter name.
4. When reading the syllables, remember that these vowel letters are consonants functioning as vowels. All syllables still begin with consonants with one very common exception. The prefixed ו is one form of the conjunction most commonly translated "and" (see ch. 7). This ו forms its own syllable. These vowel letters merely represent one of the five vowels and are pronounced after the consonant that precedes them and form open syllables.
5. It is helpful to separate the syllables with a vertical stroke (|). So דָּ | בָר with simple vowels is pronounced *dā | bār* with each simple vowel point pronounced after the consonant above or before it. However, הוֹרִידוּ (the little arrow above the *resh* is an accent mark showing which syllable is stressed) pronounced *hô | rî | dû*.

Reduced Vowels, Simple and Composite

There are five reduced vowels. These are all forms of *shewa*. They are illustrated in figure 3.7. The word *khatef* (חֲטֵף, meaning the same as *khatuf* mentioned above) is a word that means "snatched" and by extension in this context "shortened" or "reduced."

Complexity	Vowel	Name	Sound	Academic Translit.	General Translit.
FIGURE 3.7: Five Reduced Vowels					
Simple *shewa*	֖	*shewa*	ba**na**na	ə	e
	֑	*shewa*	[silent]	[none]	[none]
Composite *shewa*	֖	*khatef patakh*	b**a**ll	ă	a
	֖	*khatef segol*	b**e**t	ĕ	e
	֖	*khatef qamets*	p**o**le	ŏ	o

Notice:

> **Teaching/Learning Tip:** Some teachers prefer to regard a consonant followed by a vocal *shewa* as a syllable. Follow your teacher.

1. Vocal *shewa* is transliterated with an inverted e: ə. Thus the word דְּבַר, with vocal *shewa*, is transliterated *dəḇar*.
2. The Masoretes viewed the reduced vowels as part of a syllable and not a separate syllable.
3. Silent *shewa* is not transliterated: דִּבְרֵי is transliterated *diḇrê*, not *diḇərê*.
4. The silent *shewa* can occur under any letter except *aleph*. Remember that an *aleph* (א) at the end of a syllable becomes silent and does not take a *shewa*; the syllable is regarded as open; e.g., קְרָאתִי, *qā* | *rāʾ* | *ṭî*. Notice that the *tav* does not have the *dagesh lene* (review ch. 1 on *dagesh* if necessary), since the syllable ending in *aleph* is open.
5. The vocal *shewa* occurs under any letter except for א, ה, ח, ע, and sometimes ר. These five letters normally get composite *shewas*.
6. A simplification would be to pronounce all three of the composite *shewas* the same, namely with a very short "uh" sound as in the first syllable of *banana*. However, it is better to make them distinct. Israelis pronounce them this way, and the vowels must be transliterated differently.

Final Steps for Pronunciation

You need to memorize the symbols, their sounds, and their transliterations. One way to do this is to make flash cards, putting the vowel symbol on one side with its name, sound, and transliteration on the other side. *Hebrew for the Rest of Us Workbook* has pages that can be photocopied onto card stock to make paper flashcards. For electronic resources, please see the introduction above.

In order to fine-tune your ability to pronounce Hebrew, you will need to know how to do four more things: (1) identify the function of a dot inside a Hebrew letter, (2) identify syllables, (3) distinguish silent *shewa* from vocal *shewa*, and (4) distinguish *qamets* from *qamets khatuf.* To do this quickly takes some practice, so be patient with yourself.

1. **Syllables and accents.** There are two types of syllables, just as in English: *open* syllables end with a vowel; *closed* syllables end in a consonant. That closing consonant will have a simple *shewa* under it except at the end of the word, in which case it is only written under a final *kaph.*

   A word has as many syllables as it has full vowels. Hebrew words are accented only on one of the last two syllables; in this book the accent is marked only when it does not occur on the last syllable. In דָּבָר there is no accent mark, so the accent is on the last syllable. In דֶּרֶךְ there is an accent mark on the next-to-last syllable. Most commentaries and other Bible study tools that you will use do not mark the accented syllable. When in doubt, accent on the last syllable.

   Composite *shewas* do not count as a separate syllable but are only part of the syllable and occur only at the beginning of a syllable. So, יַעֲשֶׂה has two full vowels and therefore two syllables. The syllables divide this way: *ya | ʿǎseh.*

2. **Furtive *patakh*** appears under final letters ה, ח, and ע when they are preceded by vowels other than *patakh* or *qamets.* Since pronouncing these letters requires the dropping of the jaw, one hears a short /a/ sound before these final letters. Here are three examples given in Hebrew followed by a transliteration with syllable divisions:

   גָּבֹהַּ, *gā | bōah*   לֹקֵחַ, *lō | qēah*   שֹׁמֵעַ, *šō | mēaʿ*

   Notice that the furtive *patakh* appears under these final letters and slightly offset to the right. It is transliterated with the regular *a* (some systems put this in parentheses) and is pronounced but does not form a separate syllable.

3. **Distinguishing silent *shewa* from vocal simple *shewa*.** There are two simple rules:

   a. Vocal *shewa* under a consonant begins (or is, if your teacher so leads you) a syllable. Silent *shewa* indicates the end of a syllable. In the word דְּבַר, the *shewa* is at the beginning of a syllable (obviously, since it is at the beginning of a word) and must be vocal. Composite *shewas* are always vocal. In יַעֲשֶׂה the composite *shewa* is vocal and begins the second syllable.

   b. *Shewa* after a short vowel in an unaccented syllable is silent. In מֶרְכָּבָה, the ר (*resh* + *shewa*) is preceded by a short vowel, *segol*, and there is no accent. Therefore, the *shewa* is silent and closes the syllable. The word מֶרְכָּבָה is a three-syllable word (three full vowels), and the syllables may be divided: מֶר | כָּ | בָה.

4. **Figuring out dots in letters.** Dots in letters occur in one of four circumstances:

Type	Occurrence	Function
Dagesh Lene	found only in *begadkepat* letters, בגד כפת	to indicate plosive sounds; transliterate as simple letters *bgdkpt*
Dagesh Forte	found in almost any letter (except ע, ח, ה, א), including *begadkepat* letters, ו, and occasionally ר	to indicate the doubling of a letter; transliterate with two of the same letter (e.g., *bb*, *zz*, *ll*)
Mappiq	ה at the end of a word	to indicate the ה is a consonant, not a vowel letter; transliterate with *h*
Vowel marker	in a *waw*: ו	to indicate the *waw* is a *shureq* vowel, not a consonant; transliterate *û*

Here is a decision tree to identify the dot:

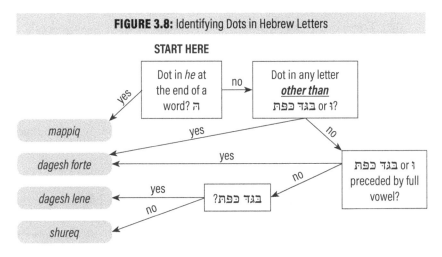

FIGURE 3.8: Identifying Dots in Hebrew Letters

Other Marks and Remarks

If you open a printed Hebrew Bible, you will notice that there are many more marks in the text than consonants and vowels. Many of these you can ignore. But some of them you will need to know about.

What You Can Ignore

Almost every word in the Hebrew Bible has some type of accent mark, sometimes even two. The accents, developed by the Masoretes, serve three purposes: (1) to mark the primary stressed syllable, (2) to divide the verse into logical phrases, and (3) to indicate musical notes (see Advanced Information and Curious Facts in this chapter). These accent marks come in numerous shapes and are very complicated, and detailed study is beyond the scope of what we are doing here. In commentaries and other materials that discuss the text of the Hebrew Bible, accent marks are rarely included, but sometimes commentators discuss them as a record of the interpretation of the rabbis.

What You Need to Pay Attention To

There is one accent mark you should pay attention to and some other marks occasionally used in the text that you might want to know about.

1. *Sof pasuq* (meaning "end of verse") is an accent mark found at the end of each verse. It looks similar to an English colon (but two diamond shapes): הָאָֽרֶץ׃. The Hebrew verse divisions are *almost* identical to our English Bibles.

   If you are saying to yourself, "I want more!," one more accent to note is the **athnach**. Most verses of the Hebrew Bible[5] are divided into two logical halves with the *athnach* accent. It is located beneath a letter with a long vowel, and in printed Bibles looks like a little wishbone or "v" pointing up: הַזֶּה. These can give you insight into how the Masoretes—who knew their Hebrew Bibles very well—made logical sense of each verse.

   Finally, these two accents and a few others are "heavy" accents that can affect the vowel on which they fall to change from the normal **contextual form**. These are altered patterns are called **pausal forms**. For example, the contextual form for "earth, land" is אֶרֶץ with the two *seghol* vowels. With a heavy accent, however, it becomes אָרֶץ with the first *seghol* changed to *qamets*. This vowel change has no effect on meaning. Lexical entries are given in the contextual forms.

2. *Mappiq* is an Aramaic word meaning "expressed." As explained above (p. 29 including figure 3.8) the *mappiq* looks exactly like a *dagesh*, but it only appears in the letter *he* at the end of a word to mark the *he* as a true consonant instead of a vowel letter: הּ. In this case the הּ is to be pronounced and is always transliterated with *h*. This makes a difference in meaning. For example, סוּס is the word meaning a male "horse." In the word סוּסָהּ, the *mappiq* indicates that the ending הּ is a suffix meaning *her* and the entire construction means "*her* horse." On the other hand, in סוּסָה, the הָ ending indicates that the noun is feminine meaning "mare" (a female horse).

3. *Maqqeph* looks like and functions similarly to a hyphen in English. The main difference is that it appears at the top of the line rather than in the middle; so:

   וּבְכָל־הָאָרֶץ   not   וּבְכָל-הָאָרֶץ

   Maqqeph indicates a close connection between two words.

---

5. In books other than Psalms, Proverbs, and Job, which have a special accenting system.

4. *Yod* **becomes silent** in the syllable יְ◌ at the end of a word. It is transliterated *āyw*, but pronounced /*āv*/. The *waw* is a consonant here and closes the syllable.

What about Aramaic?

The vowel names for Biblical Aramaic are the same as those in Biblical Hebrew, since the Masoretes developed the system for all of the Hebrew Bible.

Summary

It will be helpful to summarize and offer a word of encouragement.

Vowels

		Simple		
Type	**Sound Quality**	**(Short)**	**(Long)**	**Composite (all long)**
Full	f*a*ther	◌ (a)	[6]הָ,◌ (ā)	הֲ◌ (â)
	th*ey*	◌ (e)	◌ (ē)	יְ◌ (ê), יֱ◌ (ey) הֱ◌ (ēh), הֱ◌ (eh)
	mach*i*ne	◌ (i)		יִ◌ (î)
	h*o*le	◌◌ (o)	◌ (ō)	וֹ◌ (ô), הֹ◌ (ō)
	br*u*te	◌ (u)		וּ◌ (û)
Reduced	short sounds	◌ (ᵊ)		◌ (ă), ◌ (ĕ), ◌ (ŏ)
	silent	◌ ([none])		

FIGURE 3.9: Summary of Vowels

Syllables and Accents
1. A Hebrew word has as many syllables as it has full vowels.
2. All Hebrew syllables begin with a consonant except for one case that happens to be quite common: the prefixed syllable וּ, a form of the conjunction usually translated "and"; this forms its own syllable.
3. Closed syllables end with a consonant; open syllables end with a vowel.
4. An *aleph* (א) at the end of a syllable becomes silent and does not take a *shewa*; the syllable is regarded as open.
5. Composite *shewa*, just as vocal *shewa*, does not form its own syllable but always occurs at the beginning of a syllable.
6. The furtive *patakh* can appear under the final letters ה, ח, and ע. It is transliterated with the regular *a* and is pronounced but does not form a separate syllable.

---

6. I used a *he* instead of the dotted circle here simply to make the fonts arrange properly.

7. *Yod* becomes silent in the syllable יֹ at the end of a word. It is transliterated *āyw* but pronounced /*āv*/. Consonantal *waw* closes the syllable.

Simple Shewa

1. *Shewa* at the beginning of a word or syllable is vocal and is transliterated *ə*.
2. *Shewa* at the end of a syllable is silent and marks a closed syllable; it is not transliterated.
3. In words with simple *shewas* under two successive letters, the first is silent and the second is vocal, except at the end of a word, in which case they are both silent.

Dots (See Figure 3.8)

1. ה = pronounced /h/ at the end of a word and transliterated *h*.
2. *Dagesh forte* (doubling) = if there is a full vowel with the preceding letter.
3. *Dagesh lene* (בגד כפת) = if there is a simple *shewa* (at the end of a closed syllable) with the preceding letter.
4. ו = *shureq* (û) if preceded by letter with no other vowel.

An Encouraging Word

Now that you've made it this far, congratulations! This chapter on the vowels is the most challenging in this book. There will be more challenges in coming chapters, to be sure, but you do not need to master every detail. Just learning to pronounce and transliterate will give you the ability and confidence to read better Bible study resources with greater understanding.

Some of you may think that just learning this much is as much as you hoped for, and now you've accomplished what you wanted. Congratulations on meeting that goal! But I would encourage you to keep going. As you move through each chapter you will gain more insights and read your Bible better. But the main payoff comes in the final two chapters. The problem is that those chapters are difficult to appreciate fully without becoming familiar with the information in the intervening chapters.

So, I encourage you to be patient with yourself and to push through to the end.

Advanced Information and Curious Facts: A Synagogue Torah Scroll

In a Jewish synagogue, the Torah scroll (Hebrew text of the first five books of the Bible) is kept in an ark at the front of the synagogue, facing the congregation. The Hebrew Bible that people commonly buy includes vowel points and accent marks. An official Torah scroll, however, is written by hand in unpointed Hebrew text on meticulously prepared animal skin. Each copy has exactly the same number of "pages" and the exact same words on each page and on each line.

In the photograph below, a group assembles around an open Torah scroll. The reader does not touch the scroll but uses a *yād* (Hebrew for "hand") to point to the words in the text he is reading. The end of the *yād* is in the shape of a hand with the index finger pointing.

Incidentally, the reader in the synagogue memorizes how to pronounce the text and may even chant it in a worship service. The one who chants the text is called a "cantor." As mentioned above, one of the functions of Masoretic accent marks is to indicate musical notes. Actually, each one represents a series of musical notes or a chant. The ability to learn and perform the chanting requires a great amount of training and practice.

FIGURE 3.10: Reading a Torah Scroll

Photograph contributed courtesy of the Klau Library,
Hebrew Union College-Jewish Institute of Religion, Cincinnati.

THE SOUND OF TSERE AND SEGHOL IN MODERN HEBREW

These are signs for the changing rooms at the Dead Sea. The misspelling of the English illustrates that in Modern Hebrew the vowels Tsere (the long *e*) and Seghol (the short *e*) are not distinguished in vowel quality; they both represent a sound halfway between our *a* in late and our *e* in let. When diacritical marks are not used, both of these Hebrew vowels are transliterated into English with the *e*. So, the misspelling *ledies* makes perfect sense!

Photograph contributed courtesy of Lee Fields

CHAPTER 4

TABLETS OF STONE, JARS OF CLAY
Canon, Text, and Versions

Objectives
1. Take time to gain additional practice reading and writing Hebrew consonants and vowels in *HRUW*.
2. Explain the Hebrew canon of the OT, the text of the OT, and modern translations.
3. Explain *ketiv* and *qere* readings.

This chapter is added to provide some biblical data of interest to students of the Old Testament while they are learning the consonants and vowels.

Introduction: From Stone Tablets to Clay Jars

The story of how we got the Bible is fascinating and useful. I have enjoyed teaching a series I call "From Stone Tablets to Clay Jars" in several churches. One of the goals of *HRU* is to equip students to understand why English versions read differently. To do so requires that we understand how the Bible came to us.

This chapter serves two purposes: to help you understand terminology you may come across when reading books in the OT and to allow you to have some "lighter" reading while you are still learning the consonants and vowels.

Canonization

Have you ever wondered why the OT has the books in it that it does? Or why the Catholic and Orthodox Bibles contain books that the Protestant Bible does not? These are questions concerning the *canon* of Scripture. The area within biblical studies called "general introduction" deals with matters pertaining to the Bible in general: canon, text, and versions.

The English word *canon* comes to us in English through Latin and Greek ultimately from the Hebrew word קָנֶה, *qāneh*. This word first meant the "reed" or "stalk of a plant." Later it came to mean the instrument made from such a thing, "measuring stick, rule, straightedge." Eventually it was used metaphorically for a "standard" of any measurement. In our case, the term *canon* is used for a "standard" list.

It is essential to realize that the phrase "canon of Scripture" refers to the "list of authoritative books"; it does not mean an authoritative list of books.

Teaching/Learning Tip: While reading this chapter, learn the material that's interesting to you and that answers questions you would like to answer. Continue to learn the consonants, vowels, and transliteration, and practice pronouncing the Hebrew.

Several books that explore this issue are listed here:

Arnold, Clint. *How We Got the Bible.* Grand Rapids: Zondervan, 2008.
Beckwith, Roger. *The Old Testament Canon of the New Testament Church and Its Background in Early Judaism.* London: SPCK, 1985. Rpt., Grand Rapids: Eerdmans, 1986.
Geisler, Norman L., and William E. Nix. *A General Introduction to the Bible.* Rev. ed. Chicago: Moody, 1986.
Wegner, Paul D. *The Journey from Texts to Translations: The Origin and Development of the Bible.* Grand Rapids: Baker Academic, 1999.

Arnold's work is of a popular nature and contains lots of pictures. Wegner's book is a more substantial read and also well illustrated. Beckwith and Geisler and Nix are more technical but excellent standard works done by scholars holding to the inspiration and inerrancy of Scripture.

It is common to recognize three phases in the development of the canon: writing, collecting, and recognizing. These phases overlap in time and even in task, but it is still a helpful way to begin to understand the process. Figure 4.1 below gives an approximate timeline for these three processes for both testaments.[1] Following the chart, I will offer a few facts and a possible scenario for how the process of canonization of the OT took place.

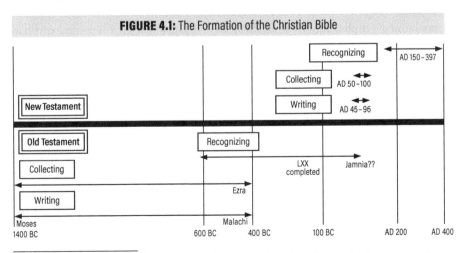

FIGURE 4.1: The Formation of the Christian Bible

---

1. I assume in this figure that Moses wrote the Pentateuch, without denying that there may have been later editing.

The Writing, Collecting, and Recognizing of the OT Books

There was a period when parts of the Bible were oral. The Pentateuch itself contains stories of events that occurred long before the books were written, and we have no indication that written records of them existed before Moses. We don't know how long God's words were only in oral form, but early on they were committed to writing. For example, Moses was commanded to write an account of the battle with the Amalekites as a memorial (Exod 17:14; see also Exod 34:27 and Deut 31:19).[2] This does give us an insight into the writing of the first five books: they were first composed in small parts.

Some seem to think that collecting the books was a process far removed in time from writing. The biblical evidence suggests, however, that this may not have been the case. The OT mentions that sacred writings were stored in Israel's sanctuary from the very beginning. So the books of Moses were collected immediately upon being written (Deut 31:24–26; cf. Josh 1:8; 2 Kgs 22:8).

Moses's successor, Joshua, also placed his writings near the sanctuary (Josh 24:26). This was also the practice of the judge Samuel (1 Sam 10:25). It is not to be expected that every book in the Bible explicitly says that it was put aside in the sanctuary, but it is very possible that this was a normal pattern followed.

If it's true that books of God's revelation were stored at the sanctuary, then was everything that was ever written by Israelites included in this collection? No. In fact, we know of twenty-five books named in the OT itself that were not included in Scripture, for example, the book of Jasher (Josh 10:13; 2 Sam 1:18).[3]

How did Israelites living during OT times know to include only the ones that eventually comprised our thirty-nine books? Deuteronomy 18:20–22 gives two tests. The first was doctrinal. Verse 20 mentions that those who speak in the name of other gods are not prophets of the Lord. This suggests that the standard for evaluating new purported revelation was the law of Moses itself. If a self-proclaimed prophet taught something that disagreed with what the Lord had revealed to Moses, he was a false prophet and was to be stoned.

The second test was fulfillment. Deuteronomy 18:21–22 says that the way to know whether a prophet was from God was to see if what he predicted came true. We see this same standard applied centuries later as recorded in the book of Jeremiah. Chapter 28 records a scene in which Jeremiah and another prophet, Hananiah, had a showdown. Jeremiah had been proclaiming that the Babylonian captivity would last seventy years, while Hananiah was saying it would last only two years. Both were claiming to be prophets of the Lord. How would the audience know who was right? In 28:9 we see that they determined reliability based on the same Deuteronomic test. Nobody, not even Hananiah, disputed

---

2. I am aware that some scholars do not believe that Moses even lived. For more information see Gleason L. Archer, *A Survey of Old Testament Introduction*, 3rd ed. (Chicago: Moody, 1994), 113–25.

3. See Lee M. MacDonald, *The Biblical Canon: Its Origin, Transmission, and Authority* (Grand Rapids: Kregel, 2007), 147–48, for a complete list.

the validity of this test. Clearly it was still in place. Over the next few years the readers would learn who was right.

It seems likely, then, that books that passed both tests were recognized to be the words of God. Those that failed one test or the other were removed from the sanctuary, though not necessarily destroyed or unused. Books that were unconfirmed in their prophecies were probably kept until they could be verified one way or the other.

The Closing of the OT Canon

When and why did the Jews recognize the canon of the OT as closed (i.e., no more Scripture was being written)? We can't set a precise date, but the Jewish sources indicate that they knew very well the difference between the writings of God's spokesmen (prophets) and those of other people. Two facts indicate this. First, the Jews during the intertestamental period recognized a "period of silence" when God was no longer speaking. Second, their writings reflect a known and commonly recognized body of literature.

Our first point, then, concerns the "period of silence." This is a modern term used to describe the roughly four hundred years between the writing of the last book of the OT, Malachi, and the appearance of John the Baptist. "Silence" does not mean that the Jews were not writing, just that what was being written was seen as not being direct revelation from God. We get clues that the Jews during the intertestamental period were aware of such a silence. This awareness may have been the result of the OT itself. Zechariah 13:3 seems to predict that a time of silence from God, a cessation of the prophetic voice, was coming in anticipation of the coming of the Messiah.

Second, there existed a recognized body of literature that was accepted as Scripture. Two books from the Apocrypha (Jewish writings written between 300 BC and 30 BC) use language referring to a set body of books. First, in the prologue to Ecclesiasticus (written ca. 130 BC) we read, "my grandfather Jesus, when he had much given himself to the reading of *the law, and the prophets, and other books of our fathers . . . the law itself and the prophets, and the rest of the books*" (KJV Apocrypha; italics added). Then in 2 Maccabees 2:13 (written ca. 100 BC) we read, "The same things [as in the writings of Moses] also were reported in the writings and commentaries of Nehemiah; and how he founding a library gathered together *the acts of the kings, and the prophets, and of David*, and the epistles of the kings concerning the holy gifts" (KJV Apocrypha modified; italics added).

More evidence for a set body of books comes from other sources. First, the Septuagint (abbreviated LXX), the Greek translation of the Hebrew OT prepared ca. 250–130 BC, included the thirty-nine books of the Protestant OT. Copies of the LXX from five hundred years later include the books of the Apocrypha, but we do not know when they were added.

The NT also indicates a known body of books, where we see both a twofold and threefold division as abbreviated references to the OT books. In the Sermon on the Mount, Jesus indicates a twofold division when he says, "the Law and the Prophets" (Matt 5:17; 7:12; et al.) and "Moses and all the Prophets" (Luke 24:27). In Luke 24:44 a threefold division is indicated when the OT is referred to as "the Law of Moses and the Prophets and the Psalms." These two designations follow the Jewish canonical order (see figure 4.3 below).

FIGURE 4.2: The English Arrangement of the OT Canonical Books

Division	Books	Division	Books
Law	Genesis Exodus Leviticus Numbers Deuteronomy	Major Prophets	Isaiah Jeremiah Lamentations Ezekiel Daniel
History	Joshua Judges Ruth 1 & 2 Samuel 1 & 2 Kings 1 & 2 Chronicles Ezra Nehemiah Esther	Minor Prophets	Hosea Joel Amos Obadiah Jonah Micah Nahum Habakkuk Zephaniah Haggai Zechariah Malachi
Poetry	Job Psalms Proverbs Ecclesiastes Song of Songs		

The Jewish arrangement of the canon is different, but it refers to the same books as and is the basis for the Protestant OT canon. The term *Tanak*, discussed below, is an acronym for the three parts of the canon. The oldest term used to refer to the collection of sacred books seems to be *Sefarim* (סְפָרִים, "[the] Books") found in Dan 9:2 and used by Jews thereafter, along with numerous other designations. Figure 4.3 below gives the names of the three divisions and of the subdivisions, where they exist. The "Prophets" includes works that Christian arrangement categorizes as history. These are called the Former Prophets, referring to Samuel, David, and Solomon, and the Latter Prophets, Isaiah, Jeremiah, Ezekiel, and the Twelve.[4] The word *Emeth* is the Hebrew word "truth" but is an

---

4. On the divisions and names, see Ludwig Blau, "Bible Canon," *Jewish Encyclopedia* (New York: Funk & Wagnalls, 1901–1906). Blau also discusses the fact that the order of books within divisions varies among ancient Jewish works.

acronym from the first letters of the first three books of the *Ketubim*. The "Five *Megilloth*" are grouped because each of these books is read at a different festival.

FIGURE 4.3: The Jewish Arrangement and Titles of the OT Canonical Books

Division	Subdivisions	Hebrew	Transliteration	Translation (Eng.)
תּוֹרָה (*Tôrâ*) Law		בְּרֵאשִׁית שְׁמוֹת וַיִּקְרָא בְּמִדְבַּר דְּבָרִים	*bərēʾšît* *šəmôt* *wayyiqrāʾ* *bamidbār* *dəḇārîm*	In the beginning (Genesis) The names of (Exodus) And he called (Leviticus) In the wilderness (Numbers) Words (Deuteronomy)
נְבִיאִים (*Nəḇîʾîm*) Prophets	Former Prophets	יְהוֹשֻׁעַ שֹׁפְטִים שְׁמוּאֵל מְלָכִים	*yəhôšuaʿ* *šōp̄əṭîm* *šəmûʾēl* *məlāḵîm*	Joshua Judges 1 & 2 Samuel 1 & 2 Kings
	Latter Prophets	יְשַׁעְיָהוּ יִרְמְיָהוּ יְחֶזְקֵאל שְׁנַיִם עָשָׂר	*yəšaʿyāhû* *yirməyāhû* *yəḥezqēl* *šənayim ʿeśer*	Isaiah Jeremiah Ezekiel The Twelve ("Minor" Prophets)
כְּתוּבִים (*Kəṯûḇîm*) Writings	*ʾEmeṯ* ("Truth")	תְּהִלִּים אִיּוֹב מִשְׁלֵי	*təhillîm* *ʾiyyôb* *mišlê*	Psalms Job Proverbs
	Ḥāmēš Məgillôt ("Five Scrolls")	רוּת שִׁיר הַשִּׁירִים קֹהֶלֶת אֵיכָה אֶסְתֵּר	*rûṯ* *šîr haššîrîm* *qōhelet* *ʾêḵâ* *ʾestēr*	Ruth Song of Songs Assembly Leader (Ecclesiastes) How! (Lamentations) Esther
		דָּנִיֵּאל עֶזְרָא נְחֶמְיָה דִּבְרֵי הַיָּמִים	*dāniyyēl* *ʿezrāʾ* *naḥemyâ* *dibrê hayyāmîm*	Daniel Ezra Nehemiah Accounts of the Days (1 & 2 Chronicles)

Most of the Hebrew book names are the names of authors (e.g., Isaiah) or main characters (e.g., Samuel) or are words that are found at or near the beginning of the text of the book (e.g., "In the beginning").

Summary

The fact that the term *canon* was not used until long after the death of the apostles does not mean that the church as well as the people of Israel before her had no concept of a list of authoritative books. That Moses was a prophet of the Lord was affirmed in the Pentateuch (Deut 18:15) and attested as such by many miracles. His writings were therefore authoritative. Subsequent writings were checked to see if they agreed with Moses and if their prophecies came true.

Meeting both of these criteria enabled these writers and their books to be recognized as having the authority of the Lord as well.

The Text of the OT

Perhaps you have wondered why your version reads differently from others—differences not just representing updating of language but substantively different words. For example, when reading the phrase "they have pierced" in Ps 22:16, what is the meaning of the NIV footnote, "Dead Sea Scrolls and some Hebrew manuscripts, Septuagint and Syriac; most manuscripts of the Masoretic Text *me,/like the lion*"? Or perhaps you had a night with nothing but time on your hands and you decided to read the preface to your NIV (seriously, it is valuable reading). You went along pretty well until the sentence, "The translators also consulted the more important early versions—the Septuagint; Aquila, Symmachus and Theodotion, the Vulgate, the Syriac Peshitta, the Aramaic Targums, and for the Psalms, the *Juxta Hebraica* of Jerome"—at which point you quit reading. These matters deal with the *text* of Scripture, the words of the Hebrew Bible themselves. Included here is the topic of ancient versions because they also are witnesses to the text.

Why is this question important for Bible-believing students? Because our service to others demands it. Dan Wallace is a top-notch conservative scholar of Greek and NT and has worked closely with "non-evangelical" scholars. In his contacts he has learned that most of them used to be conservatives. When confronted with challenges to the inerrancy of the Bible, the answers they received from their conservative friends were either simplistic or wrong. As a result, they concluded that there are no answers for the problems that can allow them to trust in the Bible. Evangelicals need to be able to face questions squarely and honestly, if we really have confidence that God's truth can stand up to close scrutiny. As Wallace has said in one of his lectures, "It would be better for us to have some doubts in our pursuit of truth than no doubts as we try to protect our certainties."[5]

Transmission of the Hebrew Text

The history of the OT text can be divided into five periods. Prior to AD 100, the books were composed, copied, and translated. The script changed from Paleo-Hebrew to Square Script. There were also changes in spelling and the use of vowel letters. The work of the "scribes," known from the NT, also took place. These men diligently copied and studied the Scriptures. Before 1900, we had no manuscripts from before AD 100. Since then, archaeologists have made several important finds of manuscripts from this period. Chief among these are the famous Dead Sea Scrolls (abbreviated DSS), discovered in 1948. Now we know of thousands of scrolls and fragments of scrolls going back to the second century BC.

---

5. Daniel B. Wallace, *Textual Criticism Series* (Bible.org, 2004), online video 1a, 35:40, http://feeds .bible.org/daniel_wallace/tc1a.rm. This was delivered at a church. For the quote, please go to the 12:10 mark.

Also during this period, the Hebrew OT was translated into Greek and eventually called the Septuagint (a Latin word meaning "seventy" and abbreviated with the Roman numeral LXX), completed at least by 130 BC. Studies in DSS, LXX, and other sources have led some scholars to believe that before AD 100 there were three main text families that all descended ultimately from the original text of the books. The original texts were copied and, while the recognition phase was going on, there developed what scholars call the Proto-Masoretic Text. From the Proto-Masoretic Text came three traditions, each associated with a geographical area: Palestine, Babylon, and Egypt.

FIGURE 4.4: Textual Families of the OT

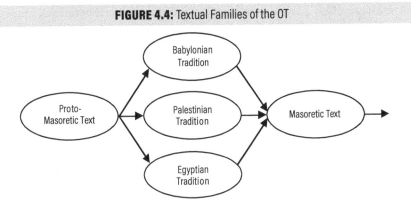

Because the DSS biblical texts, written before 100 BC, have more variants than later texts after the destruction of the temple in AD 70, scholars think that by about AD 100 the Jews of Palestine standardized the text from the various traditions. This important development means that all of our manuscripts after this time largely follow the tradition of this standardized text. This text was copied and preserved by later scholars known as Masoretes.

During the second period, AD 100–300, the Jewish scholars known as Tannaim (תַּנָּאִים) labored.[6] They were the successors of the Scribes (סֹפְרִים), ca. 500 BC to AD 100. The word *Tannaim* is an Aramaic noun with a Hebraized plural meaning "repeaters" or "teachers," since much of the learning and teaching they did was by repetition. An important product of their work is known as the Mishnah, which records some of the Jewish oral teachings aiming to apply Mosaic law to daily life in a postbiblical and post-Temple world.

The successors of the Tannaim were the Amoraim (אֲמוֹרָאִים), who worked during the third period, AD 300–500. The word itself means *speaker* and then comes to mean "teacher," much like the term *Tannaim*. These men taught and preserved the oral teachings for the Jews and were responsible for its written form in what we know as the Talmud. The Talmud consists of the Mishnah plus

---

6. Some scholars date the existence of the Tannaim to the third century BC.

additional teaching or commentary, known as Gemara. There are two versions of the Talmud: the Palestinian Talmud, put into writing about AD 450 in Tiberias of Galilee, and the more well-known and more extensive Babylonian Talmud, put into writing about AD 550. These two groups of Jewish scholars were largely responsible for copying the standardized text of the OT.

During AD 500–1000 (the fourth period) the Masoretes were at work. The word *masorah* probably means "tradition," most likely from a Hebrew root meaning "hand over." The Masoretic Text (MT) is the textual tradition preserved in manuscripts copied by these people. Besides copying, the Masoretes developed the system of vowel points and accent marks that are used universally in the Hebrew OT. They also collected and recorded special notations, known as *masorah*, to the text for accuracy. They noted variants and even errors, but they would not alter the received text, not even in the cases of obvious errors, though they did carefully note errors in the margins.

Finally, after AD 1000, manuscripts continued to be copied. Manuscripts continued to be produced for synagogue use, but they have little relevance for textual criticism, since their content was set. It is also during this period that chapter and verse divisions were added. The concept of verses is ancient. Rabbinic discussions at times concerned these divisions. These were standardized by the Masoretes about AD 900. Chapter divisions were added in the fourteenth century following the system derived from Stephen Langton (AD 1150–1228).

Sorting Out Three Ts

There are three words, each starting with the letter *T*, that people commonly confuse and that need to be distinguished: Torah, Tanak, Talmud. Along the way, we'll throw in Mishnah and Gemara.

> **Torah** (תּוֹרָה) is a Hebrew word used from the OT onward. It can mean "instruction" or "law." It is also used to refer to the five books of Moses.
>
> **Tanak** (תָּנָ"ךְ) is an acronym referring to the three parts of the Jewish arrangement of the canon as we saw in figure 4.3 above.
>
> **Talmud** (תַּלְמוּד) refers to Jewish teachings that began in oral form (often called the "oral law" or "oral torah") but were eventually put into writing. The oral law was basically an attempt to apply the teachings of Moses to times long after the Old Testament was completed.

The *Mishnah* (מִשְׁנָה) is the earliest surviving codification of these oral laws put into writing, which was done about the year AD 200.

Later comments on the Mishnah were made by scholars: how would they apply the teachings of the Mishnah? These also were originally oral and were known as *Gemara* (גְמָרָא), meaning "traditions," specifically referring to memorized teachings.

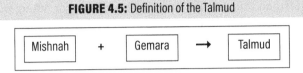

FIGURE 4.5: Definition of the Talmud

Mishnah   +   Gemara   →   Talmud

Talmud, meaning "instruction," is Mishnah + Gemara in written form. The Babylonian Talmud is much more complete than the Jerusalem Talmud. Both contain information from earlier periods.

Textual Criticism

Whenever some people hear the word "criticism" in the context of Bible studies, they think that the Bible is under attack from nonbelievers. This is not the only use of the term *critical*; here it means a careful analysis of the text of the Bible. Because the original manuscripts of the Bible no longer exist (these are called "autographs"), because there exist hundreds of hand-written Hebrew manuscripts, and because there are differences between them, scholars who print a Hebrew Bible cannot avoid making choices from among the different readings. What we see from the history of the Hebrew OT is that textual criticism has actually been in practice at least since the time of the Qumran community, who made corrections to the consonantal text of their copies of Scripture.

Editing and correcting certainly continued among the Jews. The Talmud records debates over how to pronounce (that is, what vowels to read in the unpointed text) certain words in the text. The masorah records various readings and textual difficulties that were known.

As we mentioned above, the Masoretes would not make any changes to their received text—not even to correct obvious errors. However, certain readings were written in the margin and marked *qere*. The word *qere* is a command to "read" the word in the margin instead of the word in the text. The word in the text is called *ketiv*, meaning "written." So it is not a question of whether textual criticism has been practiced, but how well, and the quality of the work is largely determined by the amount and quality of information possessed by copyists, printers, and translators.

Basically there are two kinds of variant readings: intentional and unintentional. By far the most common intentional changes have to do with spelling—remember the use of vowel letters beginning about 1000 BC and gradually increasing over time. The reason for these changes was almost always not to deceive but to clarify.

It is the unintentional variation that we may properly call an error. Sometimes when I try to copy something, I amaze myself with the number of errors I make. This is true especially when I'm in a hurry, but it even happens when I'm trying to be careful. Ancient copyists had the same difficulty, though they were trained and did far better than I do. Unintentional errors may result in omission of text, addition of text, substitution of text, or wrong word division. These errors can have many causes.[7] There may be mistakes of the ear. If a scribe is copying by listening to someone recite, he may mishear a word, or the reader may mispronounce. Much more common are mistakes of the eye. A scribe might mistake one letter for another. Sometimes when a scribe moves his eye back from his copy to the original, his eye may skip to the text in a different place, either above or below where he was because the same word is repeated, or even because another word begins or ends similarly.

So how do scholars decide which is the correct original text? They look at the evidence from Hebrew manuscripts and ancient translations and analyze it based on general principles. This evidence is summarized in some editions of the Hebrew Bible in notes at the bottom of the pages called a critical apparatus. Note that these principles are *not* strict rules.

1. *Manuscripts must be weighed, not counted.* Generally, it makes sense that the text of older manuscripts should be closer to the original than the younger. Since the older manuscripts are much rarer, we can't simply count the number of manuscripts for a given reading and expect to always have the answer. If a mistake occurred in AD 800 and most of the manuscripts after that (the vast majority of all manuscripts) copied the same mistake, then the majority reading would be wrong. This principle applies to the OT text, since the vast majority of manuscripts are all from the same (Masoretic) tradition. Though older manuscripts such as the DSS are therefore very important, still one should not automatically assume that they are always better than the MT.

2. *The best reading is the one that explains all the others.* In Gen 20 we read the story of Abimelech taking Sarah into his harem. The Lord appears to him in a dream and threatens him. In v. 4, Abimelech addresses the speaker as אֲדֹנָי. All English versions translate this passage as "Lord," because the Hebrew word אֲדוֹן means "master, sir, lord, Lord." The critical apparatus to the *Biblia Hebraica Stuttgartensia* (*BHS*), however, reports that instead of אֲדֹנָי, several manuscripts read יהוה, Lᴏʀᴅ, the actual name for God! It is much easier to explain how an original יהוה in the mouth of a Gentile might have been changed to אֲדֹנָי than it is to explain how an original אֲדֹנָי in the mouth of a Gentile came to be changed to יהוה. This suggests that יהוה might in fact be original.

3. *The shorter reading is to be preferred.* The tendency of scribes was to clarify by further explanation rather than by removing words.

4. *The most difficult reading is to be preferred.* Again, the tendency of scribes was to make a reading more understandable rather than less so.

---

7. For a nice list of nine types with OT and NT examples, see Paul D. Wegner, *A Student's Guide to Textual Criticism of the Bible: Its History, Methods and Results* (Downers Grove, IL: IVP Academic, 2006), 44–50.

Inspired Text

So here's the situation: no autographs (original manuscripts) exist, and the manuscripts that do exist show many differences. What do conservatives hold to be inspired? The preservation of God's Word involves two processes: inspiration and providence. Conservatives hold the autographs to be inerrant and infallible (see figure 4.6 below). God is absolutely perfect and, though infinitely beyond humankind in his being, is perfectly able to communicate to them in a way that they can understand. Human beings wrote as God miraculously directed them using whatever means he chose.

The other process is providence. Nowhere are we told that copyists or translators were miraculously and infallibly guided by God. Consequently, they were open to error. Yet, God works through his people, faithful and flawed though they be, to work to the best of their ability with the evidence that they have.

FIGURE 4.6: Textual Criticism and Inspiration

Or, God, Man, the Bible, and Inerrancy

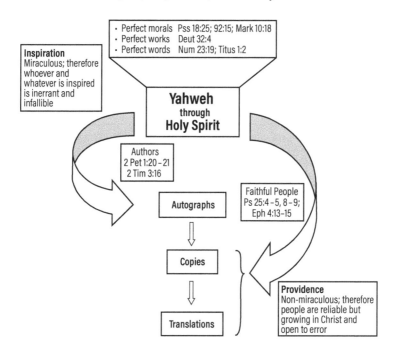

How can conservatives defend any claim to have God's very words? The situation is not as bleak as it first may appear. Two points are in order. First, the reliability of the OT text is extremely high. The MT and the DSS, roughly one thousand years older, are remarkably similar. Only about 10 percent is disputed at all, and we know where the rough spots are. Of that 10 percent, the vast majority of variations are matters such as spelling that have no effect on the meaning of the text. Second, though the study of textual criticism may affect the meaning of an individual passage, no major doctrine of Scripture rests solely on any disputed text.[8]

Versions

Many people find it confusing when the preacher or teacher they are listening to reads from a Bible version different from the one they are reading. Sometimes the versions are nearly identical. On the other hand, sometimes they are so different that it is hard to believe they are translated from the same Hebrew text. This is a question of the modern English *versions* of Scripture.

To illustrate the issue, compare the following versions of 1 Kgs 20:11.

FIGURE 4.7: Differing Renditions of 1 Kgs 20:11

KJV (1611)	And the king of Israel answered and said, Tell him, Let not him that girdeth on his harness boast himself as he that putteth it off.
LB (1971)	The king of Israel retorted, "Don't count your chickens before they hatch!"
NASB (1995)	Then the king of Israel answered and said, "Tell him, 'Let not him who girds on his armor boast like him who takes it off.'"
NLT (1996)	The king of Israel sent back this answer: "A warrior still dressing for battle should not boast like a warrior who has already won."
NET (1998)	The king of Israel replied, "Tell him the one who puts on his battle gear should not boast like one who is taking it off."
NIV (2011)	The king of Israel answered, "Tell him: 'One who puts on his armor should not boast like one who takes it off.'"
ESV (2016)	And the king of Israel answered, "Tell him, 'Let not him who straps on his armor boast himself as he who takes it off.'"

Here are some questions for you to consider and discuss:

Teaching/Learning Tip: These questions can lead to interesting group discussion.

1. What differences do you notice?
2. Which versions seem to be most literal/formal?
3. Which one changes the imagery? Is that significant?

---

8. Bruce K. Waltke, "The Reliability of the Old Testament Text," in the *NIDOTTE* (Grand Rapids: Zondervan, 1997), 1:65; the entire article, pp. 51–67, is recommended reading.

4. Which version is easiest for you to understand? Most interesting? Most easily memorized?

5. From which versions would you prefer to do detailed Bible study? Simple rapid devotional reading?

Remember: a version is rendering from one language into another and a paraphrase is rewording within the same language. To deal with this issue, we'll look at the task of translation.[9]

The Task of Translation

The process of translation is quite complicated (see figure 4.8). It begins with the original text and ends with a target text (the translation) in the language of the intended audience. In between is the original meaning the author intended. The black arrows track the translator's task. The first arrow involves the interpretation of the original text to ascertain the author's original meaning. The second arrow involves the interpretation of the target language (and culture) with the intention that the target text will communicate to the modern reader as nearly as possible the same meaning as the author intended. In the figure, the closer the two circles, the better.

FIGURE 4.8: Overview of the Translation Process

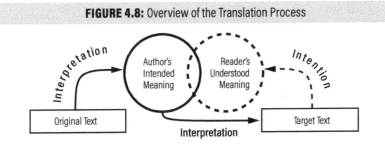

The process indicated by figure 4.8 points out some of the issues involved in translation. The first is the quality of the text. How close is it to the original? This is the issue of textual criticism. Second, there are always differences between the original language and the target language. Translators must make choices on how they are going to deal with these differences. What are the translation principles, more formal or more functional? How can the translator bring the circle of "Reader's Understood Meaning" to coincide more closely with the "Author's Intended Meaning"? Third, since the translator must interpret the original text to determine the author's intended meaning as well as interpret the language of the target text, *every translation is an interpretation.*

---

9. For a good analysis of this issue, see Gordon P. Fee and Mark L. Strauss, *How to Choose a Bible Translation for All its Worth: A Guide to Understanding and Using Bible Versions* (Grand Rapids: Zondervan, 2007). For a different view also held by evangelical scholars, see Wayne Gruden et al., *Translating Truth: The Case of Essentially Literal Bible Translation* (Wheaton, IL: Crossway, 2005).

This need not cause undue concern. First, our English translations are very well done; i.e., the centers of the circles in figure 4.8 are pretty close. Second, the difference in circles is true of all human communication. Think of the many times you and a friend or spouse have had a breakdown in communication.

This is also true for readers of the Bible. We would have the same problem even if we were studying full Hebrew—or even if God were speaking to us orally! The good news is that even though there is always a gap, communication still happens with excellent results. When a mom tells her three-year-old not to play in the street, the child knows what not to do. That doesn't always translate into obedience, however. How often God's people are just like children. We usually understand the Bible well enough to understand what behavior is pleasing to God, but that doesn't always translate into obedience.

Why So Many Translations?

We have an embarrassing wealth of translations of the Bible into English. What reasons are there for new translations?

- An improved Greek and Hebrew text base. As the results of textual criticism improve our original text, new translations or revisions may be called for.
- Different target audiences. Some translations cater to different English speakers: adults, children; long-time Christians, non-Christians; native and non-native English speakers.
- Different translation principles. Some translations strive to be more formal while others strive to be more functional. Formal translations (sometimes referred to as "literal" or "word-for-word" or "wooden") try to retain the structure (or *form*) of the original language as much as possible. Functional translations (sometimes referred to as "free" or "sense-for-sense") try to convey the meaning (or *function*) of the original text into the closest meaning of the target text.
- Increased learning about languages, ancient and modern. There has been progress just in the last few decades in understanding both Greek and Hebrew. This has an effect on the possible quality of translations.
- Changes in style and vocabulary of target language. For example, the word *conversation* now means interactive talking between people. Four hundred years ago it meant manner of life.
- Different intended use and audience. For example, is it intended for close study or for devotional use, public reading or private study, adults or children, more educated or less, the seeing and hearing or the blind and deaf?

One final question: Can we have confidence in our English Bible? Solidly, yes. The canon is well established. The text of the OT is preserved accurately.

Our modern English (the term *modern* includes the KJV) translations are very well done. The information in this chapter has explained why there are differences between translations: text base, target audience, translation principles, increased learning about Hebrew, changes in English, and intended use. The careful Bible student will compare versions. An awareness of the issues involved, such as we have treated here, should enhance such comparison.

The bottom line is that when people pick up an English Bible, they can safely regard what they hold in their hands to be the authoritative Word of God. Frederic Kenyon's oft quoted conclusion is still appropriate, "The Christian can take the whole Bible in his hand and say without fear or hesitation that he holds in it the true Word of God, faithfully handed down from generation to generation throughout the centuries."[10]

A Word of Encouragement

Congratulations, you have finished the first two units, the consonants and the vowels! Perhaps you are still feeling like these are confusing. That's okay. You know more now than you did before. *Hebrew for the Rest of Us Workbook* contains reviews on the consonants and vowels for several chapters to help you keep fresh and develop confidence.

Also, be encouraged knowing that these chapters are probably the most challenging in the book. There will still be challenges, but you do not have to understand every single detail. All you need to do is make advance over where you are today.

Some will be satisfied with just knowing these basics, and that's okay. I encourage you to keep going. There are payoffs along the way, but the main payoffs are in the final unit.

Advanced Information and Curious Facts

For more than two thousand years the Jews have not pronounced the name of the Lord. Jews today still used substitutes for the name of the Lord. For example, they commonly say "the Name," הַשֵׁם. In rabbinic literature a common expression is הַקָּדוֹשׁ בָּרוּךְ הוּא, abbreviated הקב"ה, meaning, "the Holy One blessed be he."

You recall that originally the books of the Bible were composed and copied without any vowels and the Masoretes preserved their received tradition of pronunciation with the vowel pointing system you have learned. So, what vowels did the Masoretes place within the letters יהוה, the Tetragrammaton,[11] in the Bible?

---

10. Frederic Kenyon, *Our Bible and the Ancient Manuscripts Being a History of the Text and Its Translations*, 3rd ed. (London: Eyre and Spottiswoode, 1895), 11.

11. This is a Greek word that means the "Four-letter (word)."

The Masoretes continued the long-established practice of substituting the word *Adonai*, meaning "the Lord." To record this tradition, they took the vowels from Adonai and placed them in the letters יהוה. Here is what that looks like:

Adonai with Points	YHWH with Points	Transliteration	Explanation
אֲדוֹנָי	יְהֹוָה	Jehovah	The composite *shewa* under the א becomes the simple *shewa* under the י as expected.

What makes the form *Jehovah* unlikely to be the original pronunciation is that the Hebrew יְהֹוָה is the letters of the Tetragrammaton receiving the vowels from a completely different word. (For the curious, the *J* developed from the letter *I* and came be used to distinguish the consonant sound of the letter from the vowel sound of the letter. So, you may find the Hebrew *yod* represented with *i, j,* or *y*.)

Elohim with Points	YHWH with Points	Transliteration	Explanation
אֱלֹהִים	יֱהֹוִה	"Jehovih"	This is an impossible form. Here the composite *shewa* under the א is retained under the י.

Sometimes the Tetragrammaton receives different vowels as follows:

The same process has been followed as before; that is, the vowels of another word were placed under the Tetragrammaton. In both cases the purpose of the vowels is not to provide a pronunciation for the Name but to give readers a visual clue to substitute the Hebrew words אֲדוֹנָי or אֱלֹהִים when reading.

One Jewish acquaintance of mine said that when he hears anyone say "Jehovah" or "Yahweh," it sounds like swearing. Of course in scholarship this may be relaxed in practice, and in my experience my Jewish friends are gracious to Gentiles, but I am aware of their sensitivity. Unless I'm engaged in a discussion about the Name or about matters in which specificity is needed, I tend to follow the NT and Masoretic practice of using the expression "the Lord."

For more on all this, please see the end of the next chapter.

CHAPTER 5

GETTING TO THE ROOT OF THE MATTER
Hebrew Word Roots

Objectives
1. Understand that most Hebrew words are formed from a three-letter root.
2. Understand how roots are altered to form different kinds of words.
3. Recognize and explain how different Hebrew lexicons are arranged.
4. Use the *Strongest NIV Exhaustive Concordance* (*SNIVEC*) or a computer Bible to access information.
5. Look up Hebrew words in wordbooks.

Tools Used: *SNIVEC*

Introduction

In ch. 3 we introduced the concept that most Hebrew words are built on three-letter roots that have a basic abstracted meaning. At that point we were talking about adding vowels to identify specific meanings or uses (see figure 3.1). In this chapter, I want to show you a little more about word formation and how this affects Hebrew vocabulary as well as some aspects of modern study (the arrangement and use of lexicons and their role in understanding biblical words). First, I need to introduce you to the Hebrew parts of speech and the qualities or characteristics of each.

Hebrew Parts of Speech

Below are two figures that we will use again in future chapters. The first figure lists the parts of speech in Hebrew. We can classify these into three basic categories: nominals, verbals, and function words. Within each class are various kinds of words.

Nominals and verbals are distinctive and have their own sets of grammatical qualities, which will be described in the next paragraph. Function words lack these grammatical qualities.

FIGURE 5.1: Hebrew Parts of Speech		
Nominals	**Verbals**	**Function Words**
Noun	Verb (Finite)	Article
Pronoun	Infinitive (Verbal Noun)	Conjunction
Adjective	Participle (Verbal Adjective)	Preposition
		Adverb

Figure 5.2 summarizes the grammatical qualities of verbals and nominals. If you were learning full Hebrew, you would learn to parse Hebrew words. "To parse" means to describe all the grammatical qualities of a word. We will expand the figure as our knowledge of Hebrew grammar grows. For now, it's enough to explain the elements of the chart. "Nn" means "noun" and "V" means a finite verb. The marks in the boxes indicate the features that nouns and verbs have. In the coming chapters we will cover these grammatical qualities in more detail and instead of simple Xs, you will actually be able to label specific information.

FIGURE 5.2: Parsing Information for Nominals and Verbals

PtSp	Word	Lex	Verbal Qualities						Nominal Qualities			
			Stem	Form	P	G	N	State	Det	Case	Suff
Nn						X	X	X	X	X		
V			X	X	X	X	X				

1. **PtSp**—stands for part of speech. This column is used purely for educational purposes. When I use a variation of this chart for my Hebrew students, I have students give the verse number instead of PtSp. They learn to complete this chart for every type of word. You, as a student of "pre-Hebrew," will gather most of this information from Bible study tools.
2. **Word**—the word as it actually appears in the Hebrew Bible.
3. **Lex**—stands for the lexical form, that is, the word as it appears in a dictionary. For verbs, the Lex is the root; for nouns the Lex is the singular form (very rarely a few nouns have only a plural form) as it would appear if it were the subject of a verb.
4. **Stem**—a characteristic of verbs; the different stems are patterns (see ch. 13).
5. **Form**—another characteristic of verbs. I use the term *Form* to include either the tenses/moods of the finite verb (chs. 14–16) or of the nonfinite forms, participles and infinitives (ch. 17).
6. **P**—stands for person, a quality of finite verbs connecting the action to the grammatical subject and, of course, personal pronouns.

7. **G**—stands for gender, a grammatical quality that is only generally related to sex. Note the overlap here of the Nominal and Verbal Qualities headings. In Hebrew, both nouns and verbs have gender.
8. **N**—stands for number. This also is a quality shared by both nouns and verbs.
9. **State**—is the quality of nominals; they are either absolute or construct (ch. 11).
10. **Det**—stands for determined. A noun is determined when it has the article, but that is not the only time (ch. 10).
11. **Case**—is the grammatical function of nouns or noun substitutes in a clause (ch. 11).
12. **Suff**—stands for suffix and refers to pronouns attached to the end of other words (ch. 11).

Triliteral Roots

Hebrew word formation is different from English word formation. Remember that most Hebrew words are built from triliteral roots. **Triliteral** means "three letter." The **root** is a theoretical reconstruction of the simplest part of a word that has meaning. It is what is left once all the vowels, prefixes, suffixes, and infixes are removed. So in the example we gave in figure 3.1, the root דבר often has something to do with making words. How a speaker pronounces the vowels or adds other things to the root determines whether the words are things (nouns) or actions (verbs).

Roots are theoretical in the sense that they are never found in a real text or speech. Even in unpointed texts the words must be pronounced with vowels. What we do see in a pointed text, of course, are the real words. Look at the following list of words:

FIGURE 5.3: Words Built from the Root לקח

לָקַח	take (verb)
לֶקַח	learning, teaching
מַלְקוֹחַ	booty, prey
מַלְקָחַיִם	tongs
מֶקַח	a taking of a bribe

These words all have in common the idea of taking or receiving something. They also all have in common the same three consonants: לקח, seen in black type. Because of this, scholars assume that these three letters form a root meaning common to all these words.

I need to point out one more thing: notice that in the last example, the ל

seems to have disappeared. Actually it has been replaced by a *dagesh forte*. There are a number of letters that do strange things in Hebrew. If you were learning full Hebrew, you would learn the ways some letters behave under various circumstances. Because of the tools that are now available to the English-only reader, you will still be able to find roots of words successfully. All you need to know is that sometimes letters may drop out; and when they do, they may be marked with the *dagesh forte*.

Hebrew Roots and Vocabulary

One way we change the meaning of words in English is by adding prepositions. Greek forms compound verbs similarly. For example, if we are simply moving, we use the word "go." If we are ascending, we add the preposition (used as an adverb) "up"; if we are leaving, we add the preposition "out," etc. Greek can accomplish the same thing by attaching prepositions to the beginning of words. At times Hebrew uses prepositions after words to specialize meaning, but much more often it uses completely different roots.

Below is a figure giving English, Greek, and Hebrew verbs of motion. The English dictionary form is "go" (the infinitive "to go" without the "to"); the Greek lexical form is "I go" (the present active[1] indicative first-person singular); the Hebrew lexical form is "he went" (the *qal* perfect third-person masculine singular; this will make sense later). I have put English and Greek prepositions[2] in bold type to define the preposition for you.

FIGURE 5.4: Comparison of English, Greek, and Hebrew Word Formation

English	Greek	Hebrew
go	ἔρχομαι	הָלַךְ
go **in**	εἰσέρχομαι	בּוֹא
go **out**	ἐξέρχομαι	יָצָא
go **away**	ἀπέρχομαι	עָזַב
go **near**	προσέρχομαι	קָרַב

I have simplified things somewhat. For example, a given Hebrew word may function in more than one category. But notice the way Hebrew uses completely different roots to indicate the different directions of movement.

---

1. Incidentally, readers who know Greek will observe that the verb in this example is actually "middle" in form. Some grammarians call this a deponent verb, i.e., a verb middle in form but active in meaning. But this does not concern us here.

2. Technically the English prepositions are adverbs in these examples.

Nominal and Verbal Formation

I use the term *nominal* to mean nouns plus anything that can substitute for a noun, such as pronouns, adjectives, participles, and even whole clauses. I use the term *verbal* to include not only finite verbs but the nonfinite ones, participles and infinitives.

Hebrew nominals and verbals can be derived from three sources (see figure 5.5).

Sometimes verbs are derived from nouns and are called "denominatives." An example of this in English is the verb "dust" derived from the noun "dust." (By the way, with respect to the verb, what is the difference between "dusting furniture" and "dusting roses"?) Occasionally nouns are derived from verbs and are sometimes called "deverbatives."

FIGURE 5.5: Hebrew Word Derivations

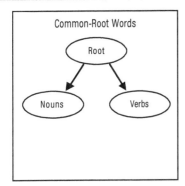
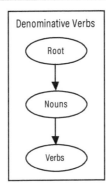
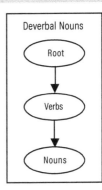

Most often nouns and verbs come from a common root. Basically, Hebrew can form new words either by changing only the vowels of a root or by adding prefixes and suffixes to the root. We do the same thing in English, though perhaps not to the same degree. Let's begin with English, then go to Hebrew.

Take for example the word *wind*. If it's pronounced with a long-*i* so that it rhymes with *kind*, it is a verb indicating an action you might perform with a string. By adding *-ing* it becomes a present participle; changing the vowel to *-ou* gives *wound*, which can be either a simple past finite verb or a past participle. However, if the root *wind* is pronounced with the short-*i*, then it is a completely different word, a noun referring to the movement of air molecules (there are other meanings). By adding an *-s* the noun becomes plural; by adding *-'s* it becomes possessive; by adding *-s'* it is plural possessive. But then, by adding *-ed*, it becomes a verbal adjective (past participle) referring to someone's condition who is breathing heavily after strenuous activity.

It's kind of funny when you think about it. We make jokes this way. A spam email making the rounds every so often and called "You Think English is Easy???" collects a number of these. One particularly funny one is, "The soldier decided to *desert* his *dessert* in the *desert* before he got his just *deserts.*"

This is the nature of language. Hebrew does the same thing. Figure 5.6 below reproduced from ch. 3 illustrates the first method, simple change of vowels (ignoring the *dagesh lene* in the first consonant of each Hebrew word). The first three examples are verbals: an active participle (in English a present participle), a finite verb (English simple past), and an imperative. The last two examples are nouns, both singular; translating the second one requires English to add a preposition such as *of*.

FIGURE 5.6: Hebrew Roots and Word Formation

Pronounced in various ways, the form דבר without written
vowels might mean any of the following:

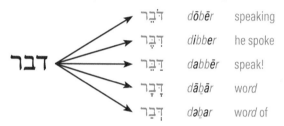

דֹּבֵר	*dōbēr*	speaking
דִּבֶּר	*dibber*	he spoke
דַּבֵּר	*dabbēr*	speak!
דָּבָר	*dābār*	word
דְּבַר	*dabar*	word of

Hebrew can also add prefixes, suffixes, infixes, or various combinations. Look at the examples in figure 5.7:

FIGURE 5.7: Hebrew Roots with Prefixes, Suffixes, and Infixes

Nouns	דְּבָרִים	words
	דְּבָרוֹ	his word
	מִדְבָּר	wilderness
	דְּבִיר	anteroom
Verbals	יְדַבֵּר	he will speak
	דִּבְּרוּ	they spoke
	דַּבְּרוּ	speak! (plural)
	מְדַבְּרִים	speaking (plural)

In this figure, the gray letters are root letters, in order to draw attention to the added features in black. Notice that the first noun is plural, the second is singular and requires the English possessive pronoun. Not only can a number of different words come from the same root, but sometimes there are two different roots that are identical. The third and fourth are from completely different roots with the same three letters, one with a prefix and one with an infix (an insertion in the middle of the root). Besides the root דבר having to do with words, there is another root דבר having to do with departing or destroying (G/K 1818; these "G/K" numbers identify individual Hebrew words and will be explained below), from which is formed the noun מִדְבָּר meaning "wilderness" (G/K 4497). As for the verbs, the first three are finite; the last is an active participle translated by the English present participle.

The point is that Hebrew forms its words differently than English. Still, it may form them by using similar processes (adding prepositions or prefixes), but they do different things. Some Hebrew words, which in an unpointed text would be identical, are distinguished in printed Hebrew Bibles by the vowel points. These points represent visually the pronunciations that the original audience would have heard in speech.

Lexicons, Lexical Forms (a.k.a. Lemmas), and Glosses

Dictionaries/Lexicons = Wordbooks. There are two terms that are often used interchangeably, *dictionary* and *lexicon*. For our purposes, it is useful to make a distinction: a lexicon is simply a dictionary between two languages. When we speak of "lexical forms," we mean the forms as they are entered in a lexicon. I think it is best to name the category of these reference works *wordbooks*, because this includes all works called either lexicons or dictionaries and because it does not get confused with Bible dictionaries or encyclopedias.

Newer Bible students must remember that Bible dictionaries are not the same as lexicons. A Bible dictionary is like an *Encyclopedia Britannica*, discussing concepts in articles dealing with many interrelated terms, whereas a dictionary/lexicon is like a *Merriam-Webster's Collegiate Dictionary*, defining individual words. An annotated bibliography of many of these is presented in ch. 19 below.

Lemma = Lexical Form. Another useful term is *lemma*. The lemma is the form of the word as it appears in a lexical/dictionary entry.

For example, starting out with English, again, if you read the sentence, "He wound the bandage around his arm with the wounds," to find the verb for *wound*, we would have to look up the entry for *wind*; in English the infinitive is the dictionary form for verbs. We would find *wounds* under the entry for *wound*; in English the dictionary form is the singular form. Now, imagine that you didn't know English well and read this sentence. If you picked up your lexicon and searched for the verb under *wound* and read the entry, "n. physical injury, emotional injury" and the next entry, "v. to injure physically or emotionally." Without knowing the dictionary form, you might become confused.

> **Teaching/Learning Tip:** Understanding the difference between a gloss and a definition is vital in thinking about how words and word studies work. Make sure this difference is clearly understood.

Glosses vs. Definitions. A gloss is the translation of a word to a near one-word equivalent of the original. A definition is a description of the meaning. Glosses are found in interlinear Bibles, in the lists of translations in concordances, or in the dictionaries found in some concordances, and in many other works, such as commentaries. A definition is a longer explanation that could not be used in a Bible translation.

The *Dictionary of Biblical Languages* (*DBL*) series nicely illustrates the difference. Below is an image from this work.

FIGURE 5.8: Glosses and Definitions in the *DBL* Series

3841 יֹשֶׁר (*yō·šěr*): n.masc.; ≡ Str 3476; TWOT 930b—**1.** LN 88.12–88.23 **uprightness**, i.e., the quality of conforming to a standard (Dt 9:5; 1Ki 9:4; Job 33:3, 23; Ps 25:21; 119:7; Pr 14:2; Ecc 12:10+), note: Pr 8:21 cj; **2.** LN 79.88–79.90 **straightness**, i.e., what is not crooked, or possibly a leveling or evenness of a path (Pr 2:13; 4:11+), note: the reference to an upright life; **3.** LN 88.39–88.45 **honesty**, integrity, i.e., honesty of words or actions to what is real (1Ch 29:17; Job 6:25; Pr 11:24; 17:26+)

The *DBL* marks glosses clearly with bolded type; e.g., "uprightness" is a gloss. Definitions follow; e.g., "the quality of conforming to a standard" is a description of the meaning (of the Hebrew and of the English gloss).

An important note: you must always remember that finding the root to a family of Hebrew words is **_not_** some secret to unlock hidden meaning. It is merely something later scholars have manufactured to help systematize grammar. As we shall see in ch. 18, *meaning is determined by usage in context.*

Other Roots

Though the majority of Hebrew words come from triliteral roots, there are a small number of common words that come from biliteral roots. Rarely quadriliteral (four-letter) roots appear. Here are a few examples.

FIGURE 5.9: Words with Bi- and Quadriliteral Roots					
Some Nouns with Biliteral Roots				**Some Nouns with Quadriliteral Roots**	
יָד	Hand	אָב	Father	עַקְרָב	scorpion
דָּם	Blood	אָח	Brother	אַלְמָנָה[3]	widow

Finding Roots

It is important for you to grasp the concept of roots because many commentators will make reference to them and there may be times when you will want to find the root of a word. Finding them is actually quite simple. Most of these resources include instructions for use in their introductions. I will summarize their use briefly below. Here are three ways to find roots.

Finding Words in Wordbooks

There are two basic types of wordbooks. First, lexicons, or dictionaries, which we've mentioned before. These works aim to exhaustively list and define all the words in a language or corpus. For our purposes, the corpus is Classical, or Biblical, Hebrew. This is primarily the OT. However, some works expand that to include later Classical Hebrew, such as the Dead Sea Scrolls, though not moving into the Rabbinic Hebrew of the Mishnah and beyond (see ch. 2).

The second type is theological wordbooks. These do not include every word in a corpus, but rather they focus on words whose meaning is significant theologically. They also tend to give extended discussions of word meaning. Common words without much theologically relevant content are not included. So, for example, whereas in a lexicon there will typically be detailed articles on הָיָה, "to be," or on prepositions, theological wordbooks typically do not have an entry for such words.

Here are some things to know:

1. **Using computer resources.** The simplest procedure is to use a computer program. The English words will be hyperlinked to original language words or to numbering systems (usually Strong's numbers) and to associated wordbooks.
2. **Dealing with homonyms.** Remember that some words and roots are homonyms, i.e., words spelled the same way, sometimes with the same vowels, but having a different origin and unrelated meaning. The lexicons will distinguish them using numbers, typically using Roman numerals. Also, different lexicographers sort (disambiguate) the words differently. Here is an especially complicated example from homonymous roots with the letters ענה. For the names of the lexicons, see the annotated bibliography in ch. 19. After the chart we'll make some observations.

---

3. The ה ending marks feminine gender and is not a root letter.

FIGURE 5.10: Disambiguating עָנָה[4]

English	Strong's	DBLH	BDB	HALOT	DCH[5]	TLOT	TWOT	TDOT
answer	6032	I, 6699	I	I	I	I	I	I
be afflicted	6031	II, 6700	III	II	II	II	III	II
be occupied		III, 6701	II	III	IV		II	
sing		IV, 6702	IV	IV	III		IV	

a. **Counting roots.** The last three columns are theological dictionaries and may or may not be making a statement about the number of words. The Strong's entries only distinguish two roots. In *DBLH*, Roman numerals are used, but words are listed following the Goodrick-Kohlenberger (G/K) numbering system.

b. **Distinguishing roots.** Notice that not only does the distinguishing of roots differ, but the Roman numeral designations are not always the same between the lexicons. When reading lexicons, you need to be careful that you are reading entries that truly correspond. Computer Bibles make this correlation for you for all the books in your library, but you should still read attentively.

c. **Categorizing occurrences.** Just as counting and distinguishing roots differ between the lexicons, so also the word count for each word may differ. This is also true for translations. When you do searches, even computerized searches based on the original language, word counts may differ, depending on how the editors of the Hebrew tagged words, and how this might be adjusted when that tagging is linked to various translations or textual traditions.

3. **Using paper resources.** Because you may at times need to do research in wordbooks that you do not have access to in your computer resources, it is useful to know how to look up words in paper resources. Here are some guidelines.

   a. **Identify your word accurately.** You will need to identify your Hebrew word (for details here, see ch. 18 below). If you are working from a specific passage, you can use your interlinear Bible tagged with Strong's or G/K numbers. You will also need to be able to read it in Hebrew, including the vowels. If you are working from a reference work, take note of the system of transliteration so that you can accurately determine the Hebrew letters.

   b. **Understand the arrangement of your lexicon.** Are the words arranged by the verbal root or in simple alphabetical order?

---

4. See the Abbreviations at the beginning of *HRU2* and ch. 19 for full bibliographic information.

5. *DCH*, the *Dictionary of Classical Hebrew*, actually distinguishes between thirteen different roots, noting that V–XIII are dependent upon scholars' research.

c. **Make sure that you have taken into account possible homonyms.** This can be verified by looking at the translations or glosses to see if they match, even if they are not identical.

Here are two examples.

Example 1. You are studying Ps 1, and you want to read wordbooks on the word translated "blessed," and you want to read BDB and *HALOT*.

1. An interlinear Bible tells you the following:
2. Strong's number: 835
3. G/K number: 897
4. Hebrew lemma: אַשְׁרֵי
5. Hebrew root: אָשַׁר
6. Searching for the Hebrew letters alphabetically in the *Enhanced BDB*[6] and knowing that the entries are arranged by verbal root, you find the following entries:

---

†[אָשַׁר] S833 TWOT183 GK886, 887] **vb. go straight, go on, advance** (Assyrian *ašâru* ZimSP 11; Arabic Aramaic in deriv.)—**Qal** *Imv.* אִשְׁרוּ Pr 9:6 אַשְּׁרוּ בְדֶרֶךְ בִּינָה *go straight on in the way of understanding.* Pi. *Pf.* אִשְּׁרוּ Mal 3:12 Gn 30:13; *Impf.* תְּאַשֵּׁר Pr 4: 14 + 4 times; *Imv.* אַשֵּׁר Pr 23:19; *Pt.* pl. מְאַשְּׁרִים Mal 3:15 + 2 times;— **1.** intensive *go straight on,* advance Pr 4:14. **2.** causative *lead on* Pr 23: 19 Is 3:12; 9:15. **3.** *set right, righten* Is 1:17. **4.** *Pronounce happy, call blessed* Gn 30: 13 (J) Jb 29:11 ψ 72:17 Pr 31:28 Ct 6:9 Mal 3:12, 15. **Pu.** *Impf.* Kt יְאָשֵּׁר Qr וְאֻשָּׁר ψ 41:3; *Pt.* מְאֻשָּׁר Pr 3:18 Is 9:15. **1.** *be led on* Is 9:15. **2.** *be made happy, blessed* ψ 41:3 Pr 3:18.

†[אֶשֶׁר] S835 TWOT183a GK890, or אָשֵׁר cf. LagBN 143] **n.[m.]** only *Pl.* cstr. אַשְׁרֵי **happiness, blessedness of** 1 K 10:8 + 32 times & c. sf., v infr.; abstr. intens. exclam. *O the happiness, blessedness of,* אַשְׁרֵי אֲנָשֶׁיךָ אֵלֶּה עֲבָדֶיךָ *happy thy men, happy these thy servants* 1 K 10:8 (= 2 Ch 9:7); אַשְׁרֵי אֱנוֹשׁ יוֹכִיחֶנּוּ אֱלוֹהַּ *blessed the man whom Eloah correcteth* Jb 5:17; אַשְׁרֵי תְמִימֵי דֶרֶךְ

The entry with the first three letters of your word does not seem to match exactly your target word. Turning to the introduction of the book you learn that the form or information enclosed in brackets, [ ], does not occur in Hebrew.

The next entry, however, matches the Strong's number of your word, 835, and the root you found. Your identification is confirmed when you note the glosses matching the meaning of the target word in your passage.

---

6. Francis Brown, Samuel Rolles Driver, and Charles Augustus Briggs, *Enhanced Brown-Driver-Briggs Hebrew and English Lexicon* (Oxford: Clarendon, 1977). For a more complete list of works and abbreviations, see ch. 19.

Example 2. You are studying the book of Proverbs, and you begin by reading the entry, "Proverbs, Book of," in the *Anchor Bible Dictionary*. The article mentions two terms, one of which is "*tĕbûnāh*," which you quickly and confidently transliterate back into Hebrew as תְּבוּנָה even though it is a slightly different style of transliteration than the one you have learned here. You want to read about this word in a wordbook. How can you do this?

1. **If you have a computer Bible or the Internet,** run a search for "*tebunah*." This should pull up the relevant information listed in the previous example. Also, an internet search of the transliteration will pull up some basic information, including the Strong's number and even the root, *byn*, בין.
2. **In BDB,** look up the entry for בִּין and beneath the root, find your word.
3. **In TLOT,** you notice that there is no entry for the word תְּבוּנָה, so you look up the root בִּין. You decide you still want more information and notice that at the beginning of the entry, *TLOT* gives cross-references to other lexicons with page numbers. One of particular interest to you is *HALOT*, "1:122a," meaning volume 1, page 122, column a.
4. **In HALOT,** you notice that the cross-reference took you to the root and you discover that words are in simple alphabetical order. You open the volume that includes ת and find the entry for תְּבוּנָה.
5. **In TWOT,** the introduction explains that entries are by the root but that derived terms are also found in alphabetical order with references back to the entry. *TWOT* has its own set of serial numbers for the roots, which are cross-referenced to the Strong's numbers in an index at the end. (In the Logos edition, the Strong's index is not included; searching can be done simply by typing the word in Hebrew or in transliteration.)
6. **In NIDOTTE,** you follow the same procedure. You look up the root and find it in volume 1, p. 652.
7. **In TDOT,** words are arranged under the root. After skimming technical language and discussion of the verb, you find the section focusing on "*tebunah*" on p. 106 of volume 2.

Obviously, few people have access to and time to comb through these many resources very often. But for key words, sometimes you may want to dig into the works of scholars. Knowing how to navigate them and learning what resources tend to be the most helpful will increase one's accuracy and efficiency in understanding and preaching.

There are so many good resources to use, and anyone studying the Bible seriously, especially preachers and teachers but even serious-minded lay people in a congregation, should routinely avail themselves of good wordbooks. And by the way, if a resource is available for free on the Internet, there is usually a good reason why it is in the public domain. It may be old or elementary. If you are serious enough about Bible study to be reading this page, you will want to avail yourself of the best word studies you can. We will return to these resources in ch. 18, where we learn how to do our own word studies.

THE VOW

I like to do an activity in fun with my students at this point. I have them stand, raise their right hands, and repeat the following after me:

I, [state your name],
will never,
never, ever,
use an English dictionary
to define a biblical word.

Using an Exhaustive Concordance

I am assuming that most readers of this book know what a concordance is and have used an exhaustive concordance at least a little. So, here I'm going to explain only briefly the *Strongest NIV Exhaustive Concordance (SNIVEC)* edited by Goodrick and Kohlenberger (G/K). Remember that every English concordance is tied to a specific version. If you study with the NIV, you must have a concordance to the NIV; if you study another version (ESV, KJV, NASB, etc.), you must have a concordance for that version. The G/K series of concordances are out in several versions. In my opinion, the G/K series is the best exhaustive English concordance one can purchase in paper. Though computer Bibles make use of paper concordances a bit passé, there is enough valuable information in the G/K series that you may want to buy one, if you haven't already.

The *SNIVEC* contains three main parts:

1. The main **concordance**, which is the bulk of the book, a listing of all the occurrences of each English word in the NIV.
2. The **dictionaries and indices** of original language words listed alphabetically and numerically and arranged in three sections: (a) Hebrew in regular type numerals, (b) Aramaic in regular type numerals beginning with 10,001, and (c) Greek in italic type numerals.
3. The G/K-Strong conversion **index** arranged in two sections: (a) Strong ⟶ G/K [Hebrew, Aramaic, Greek], then (b) G/K ⟶ Strong [Hebrew, Aramaic, Greek].

The dictionary section allows you to find both roots and derivatives from the roots. Here is an example using an entry from the *SNIVEC*. Suppose you are reading Gen 5:1 in the NIV, "This is the written **account** of Adam's family line."

So you look up "account" in the concordance section (p. 12), find the reference to Gen 5:1, and note the number identifying your Hebrew word, 9352. Next you turn to that part of the dictionary section that lists Hebrew words and find the entry with your number (p. 1507), which reads:

> **9352** תּוֹלְדוֹת *tôlēdôt*, n.f.pl. [39] [√3528]. account, record, genealogy, family line, records (14), account (10), listed genealogy (3), genealogical records (2), genealogy (2), account of line (1), account of the family (1), birth (1), descendants (1), family line (1), genealogical record (1), lines of descent (1), order of birth (1)

Following the G/K number, 9352, is the word in Hebrew (which you can now read), the transliteration (which you no longer need), then grammatical information (noun, feminine, plural), and frequency in brackets (the Hebrew word occurs thirty-nine times in the OT) and then also in brackets the root symbol, √, and the G/K number for the root. That's it!

Once you have found the root, you can now look up your word in Bible reference works that are not coded to Strong's or to G/K numbering systems. Also, just within the *SNIVEC*, you can now look up G/K 3528 in the lexicon section, p. 1416, and see that the root is יָלַד. There is no root symbol (because you've found the root), but in brackets an arrow, →, listing all of the words derived from the root יָלַד, or what we might call the word family. When you do word studies, you want to stick with your word. But when you want to study a word with too few occurrences to give you an accurate range of meaning, fewer than twenty or so, it may be helpful to study other words from the family. But even in this case, you will need to be very tentative in your conclusions and rely more on the experts. We'll discuss this more in the chapter on word studies.

In Logos, (a) open the Bible Word Study, (b) in the search box type "h:" and the transliteration to find the Hebrew word. The search results will include glosses; write the most common translation in the NIV and the G/K number of the word. (c) Scroll down to the "Root" section of the search results and the entry that matches the root (marked with the √ symbol). Use the *DBLH* to obtain the G/K number and the gloss of the root. For other computer programs, see the respective training materials.

Using an Interlinear Bible

The word *interlinear* means "between the lines." There are two kinds of interlinear Bibles: a traditional interlinear and a reverse interlinear. You will learn to use both of them.

A traditional interlinear Bible gives the text of the original language in the first line and below each original word the English equivalent. The result is that the English is out of order. A reverse interlinear gives the English text in the first line and the original language equivalent under each English word. In this case the original language text is out of order and some system is required to indicate the order of words.

There are two main books like this in print:

Green, Jay P., ed. *The Interlinear Bible: Hebrew-Greek-English.* 2nd ed. 1985; repr., Peabody, MA: Hendrickson, 2005. (*IBHGE*)
Kohlenberger, John R., III. *The NIV Interlinear Hebrew-English Old Testament.* 1985; repr., Grand Rapids: Zondervan, 1993. (*NIVIHEOT*)

Both give the Hebrew text according to the Masoretic tradition first and below the text a formal translation of the Hebrew. The chief differences lie in the Hebrew text base and in formatting details.

The Hebrew text base of the *IBHGE* is (presumably; Green doesn't actually state it) the Second Rabbinic Bible (1524–25), which was used as the text base for the KJV.[7] The base for the *NIVIHEOT* is the *Biblia Hebraica Stuttgartensia* (*BHS*), which is used as the text base for most modern translations.

In terms of formatting, the *NIVIHEOT* also gives the NIV in parallel. The *IBHGE* includes a parallel formal translation prepared by Green (for the NT he uses the KJVII, a version that was new at the time but never became popular and is not to be confused with the NKJV). In addition, the *IBHGE* places above each Hebrew word its *Strong's Concordance* number. This is a handy feature. Once you locate your Hebrew word in the interlinear, you immediately know the Strong's number, which gives you the lexical form and ultimately the root by means of an exhaustive concordance.

Using Electronic Sources

The *NIVIHEOT* does not give you G/K numbers, but you will still want to find that information. You can use the process described above for *SNIVEC*, or perhaps better, you can use an electronic Bible study program. There are several programs that provide this information in a reliable, usable format. In Logos Bible Software, simply hovering the cursor over a Hebrew word causes a pop-up window to appear that provides the root plus other information.

If you have already studied William Mounce's *Greek for the Rest of Us*, you probably used his book, *Interlinear for the Rest of Us*, which is a reverse interlinear.

Though there is no print reverse interlinear available, computer Bible software does have a reverse interlinear for the whole Bible for many versions. Figure 5.11 shows information taken from a display of the reverse interlinear in Logos Bible Software using the NIV. This feature allows the reader to display up to nine layers of information.[8]

---

7. So Geisler and Nix, *A General Introduction to the Bible*, 372, and the introduction to the NKJV.
8. For the NT, there is a tenth row, the semantic domain numbers in the Louw-Nida lexicon. For an OT counterpart, see the *Semantic Dictionary of Biblical Hebrew*, https://semanticdictionary.org/.

FIGURE 5.11: Logos Reverse Interlinear Data (Gen 50:5, NIV)

1	My	father	made	me	swear	an	oath
2	יְ₂	אָבֶ֫₁	הִשְׁבִּ֫יעַ₃	נִי₄	◄3	←	←
3	y	'ābi	hišbî'a	nî			
4	אֲנִי	אָב	שבע1	אֲנִי			
5	'ănî	'āb	šb'1	'ănî			
6	אֲנִי	אָב	שבעו1	אֲנִי			
7	'ănî	'āb	šb'1	'ănî			
8	RS1-S	NC-SC	VcP3MS	RS1-S			
9	589	1	7650	589			

The first line is English according to the version of choice (they are continuing to add more). The symbol ← indicates that the English word "oath" has no separate Hebrew word but is included in the word to which the arrow points, "an," marking a cluster of two words. Under "an" is another arrow pointing to the word "swear," forming a cluster of three words. Under "swear" is the symbol "◄3" meaning that the cluster is not grouped with the word under "me" but skips to word 3, "הִשְׁבִּ֫יעַ₃." So, the Hebrew word הִשְׁבִּ֫יעַ₃ is rendered by four English words, "made . . . swear an oath."

The second and third lines give the Hebrew text according to *BHS* in Hebrew and in transliteration. The fourth and fifth lines display the lemma, in Hebrew and in transliteration, respectively. Lines six and seven provide the lexical forms for each word. The eighth line is the grammatical labeling (tagging) for each word. The ninth line displays the Strong's numbers for each word.

Here is Gen 1:1 from the Logos Bible Software:[9]

FIGURE 5.12: The Logos NIV English-Hebrew Reverse Interlinear

In	the	beginning	God	.	created	the	heavens	and	.	the	earth.
בְּ₁	→	רֵאשִׁית₂	אֱלֹהִים₄	אֵת₅	בָּרָא₃	הַ₆	שָׁמַ֫יִם₇	וְ₈	אֵת₉	הַ₁₀	אֶ֫רֶץ₁₁
בְּ		רֵאשִׁית	אֱלֹהִים	אֵת1	ברא1	ה	שָׁמַ֫יִם	וְ	אֵת1	ה	אֶ֫רֶץ
P		NCFSA	NCMPA	PO	VaP3MS	A	NCMPA	C	PO	A	NC-SA

9. Chip McDaniel and C. John Collins, The *ESV English-Hebrew Reverse Interlinear Old Testament*, Genesis 1:1 (Bellingham, WA: Logos, 2006) containing The Holy Bible, English Standard Version (Wheaton, IL: Crossway, 2001).

Notice the following:

1. The dots (·) in the English text indicate places that have no English translation for the Hebrew word below.[10]
2. The Hebrew words have subscript numbers to indicate the word order of the Hebrew text. Further, the Hebrew words are sometimes divided into parts.
3. In the second line the arrow (→) under the first occurrence of *the* points to the Hebrew word that contains the notion of the English word, when there is no separate Hebrew equivalent.
4. The grammatical tagging in the fourth line looks complicated, but in Logos the definitions become visible in a box when the mouse is hovered over the abbreviations.

What about Aramaic?

Since Aramaic and Hebrew are both Semitic languages, they operate in many similar ways and share a lot of vocabulary. There are, of course, some differences.

1. Like Hebrew, Aramaic words are built from roots, most of them triliteral.
2. Much of the vocabulary is the same. For example, the word for "king" is מֶלֶךְ in both languages.
3. Some of the words that share an etymological origin are spelled differently. For example, *six* in Hebrew is שֵׁשׁ, but שֵׁת in Aramaic.[11] You do not need to know why, but in short it goes back to Semitic languages prior to Hebrew and Aramaic. Just knowing that there may be such connections can be helpful; many Bible wordbooks will point out etymological connections between Hebrew and Aramaic words. The most common consonant shifts are:

Hebrew		Aramaic
שׁ	=	שׁ
שׂ	⇔	ת
ת	=	ת
ז	=	ז
ז	⇔	ד
ד	=	ד

---

10. You should not worry that the translators left out something. We will learn more about this later, but for now it is enough for you to know that the Hebrew word marks the following word as the direct object and does not have any content. This Hebrew mark for the direct object is represented in English by word orderEnglish rather than by an English word.

11. For you linguaphiles out there, compare modern languages: six (English and French, though pronounced differently), sechs (German), seis (Spanish and Portugese), sex (Latin), šesť (Slovak), and ἕξ (*hex*, in ancient Greek; in Modern Greek it is ἔξι, *éxi*, to distinguish it from other words). These are all clearly etymologically related.

Hebrew		Aramaic
צ	=	צ
צ	⇔	ט
צ	⇔	ע
צ	⇔	ק

4. The patterns for word formation (vowels, etc.) have similarities but numerous differences. We will note some of these in future chapters.
5. Some very common words are different. Compare these:

Hebrew	English	Aramaic
בֵּן	son	בַּר
הָלַךְ	come, walk	אֲתָה
בַּעַל	lord, master	מַר

Sometimes the Hebrew writers used Aramaic words, especially in poetry.

And this is a free extra. In 1 Cor 16:22 Paul offers a one-word exclamation, "Maranatha" (μαράνα θά). The NASB simply transliterates the Greek. The Greeks transliterated two Aramaic words. The NIV translates the Aramaic, "Come, Lord!" The first word, *mar* or *maran*, is the word for Lord; the second one is the imperative for come! Fun, eh?[12]

6. There are also "false friends," i.e., words spelled the same but with different meanings. For example, both Hebrew and Aramaic have the word רב in common, and they are etymologically connected, but they mean something a little different.

Hebrew	English	Aramaic
רַב	many, much	שַׂגִּיא
גָּדוֹל	great, large	רַב

Some Payoff: Understanding Wordplays

By "payoff" I mean practical application. It is motivating to see how newly acquired skills can actually help in Bible study. Here is one illustration.

---

12. The Aramaic might also be translated, "Our [the *-na* ending] Lord, come!" Or the word might be divided *maran atha*, which could be translated the same as before or else "Our Lord has come!"

Suppose you are reading Jer 1:11–12, the vision Jeremiah has and his conversation with the Lord, but it seems a little opaque. Then you notice the NIV note in v. 12: "The Hebrew for *watching* sounds like the Hebrew for *almond tree*." Below is the NIV for these verses with bolding added. The note clears it up, and you might move on. But you have a lesson/sermon to prepare. So you decide to dig in just a bit.

> The word of the LORD came to me: "What do you see, Jeremiah?" "I see the branch of an **almond tree**," I replied. The LORD said to me, "You have seen correctly, for I am **watching** to see that my word is fulfilled."

Our recipe is simple: use an interlinear Bible to get the Hebrew word as it appears in the text, write a transliteration if necessary to clarify pronunciation, and check resources (*SNIVEC* or wordbook) to complete a table such as the following, and then write a simple explanation of what is going on in the text. The following chart uses data from an interlinear for the Hebrew text; and the lexical forms and G/K numbers come from *SNIVEC*. The Strong's numbers come from correlations in the *DBLH*.

In Logos, the Bible Word Study feature has a section devoted to the root and all words derived from that root. These are the results for שקד (the bar graphs at the end give frequencies and distributions):

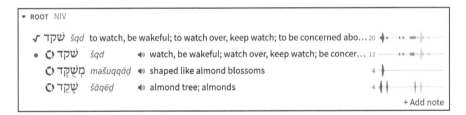

FIGURE 5.13: Words and Roots in Jer 1:11–12 Wordplay

NIV	Hebrew Text	G/K#	Gloss	G/K# of √	Str#
Almond tree	שָׁקֵד, *šā | qēd*	9196, שָׁקֵד	Almond tree, almond nuts	9195	8247
Watching	שֹׁקֵד, *šō | qēd*	9193, שָׁקַד¹	Be awake, watch, stand guard	√	8245

Explanation:	From the transliteration and glosses we conclude with the NIV note that the almond tree becomes a symbol of God's watching solely on the basis of similar sounds; there is no connection between the meanings of the words.

We have collected our data and understood the Lord's vision. In these dialogues with the prophets, often the vision evokes an utterance from the prophet. This utterance, then, becomes the prophetic pronouncement that results in the

Lord's taking action. Thus, the Lord actually involves the prophet in the prophetic pronouncement. In this case, the vision provokes Jeremiah to say *šāqēḏ*, and the Lord uses this as the ignition for his "*šōqēḏ*-ing" over his word to make sure that his words are accomplished, whether for good or ill.

Further Investigation

Figure 5.13 gives data for the words in the target verse. But why are there missing G/K numbers? Using the *SNIVEC* or other resources, especially those keyed to the G/K numbering system (such as the *DBLH*), can give answers.

9193 [1]שָׁקַד *šāqad*[1], v. [12] [→ 5481, 9195, 9196]. [Q] to be awake, watch, stand guard:–watching (3), did not hesitate (1), guard (1), have an eye for (1), lie awake (1), lie in wait (1), stand guard (1), watch (1), watch kept (1), watched (1)
9194 [2]שָׁקַד *šāqad*[2], v. Not in NIV. [Q] to be emaciated
9195 [3]שָׁקַד *šāqad*[3], v.den. Not in NIV [→ 5481, 9196; cf. 9193]. [P] to be shaped like an almond blossom
9196 שָׁקֵד *šāqēd*, n.[m.] [4] [√ 9195; cf. 9193]. almond tree, almond nuts:–almond tree (2), almonds (2)

The Hebrew to English dictionary and index of *SNIVEC* provide lots of information. The entry begins with the G/K#, then the lexical form with transliteration, grammatical part of speech, total occurrences, and a list of G/K numbers for related words (unmarked), derivative words marked with →; roots are marked with √, and words without the √ symbol are themselves roots. The entries conclude with glosses of definitions and then a list of translations used in the NIV with their frequencies.

Figure 5.14 duplicates the first two lines from the verse but adds information about the words referenced in *SNIVEC*. Also a quick check of the *DBLH* and one commentary note increases our understanding.

FIGURE 5.14: Words and Roots Related to שׁקד

NIV	Hebrew Text	G/K#	Gloss	G/K# of √	Str#
Almond tree	שָׁקֵד, *šā | qēḏ*	9196, שָׁקֵד	Almond tree, almond nuts	9195	8247
Watching	שֹׁקֵד, *šō | qēḏ*	9193, שָׁקֵד[1]	Be awake, watch, stand guard	√	8245
–		9194, שָׁקֵד[2]	Be emaciated	√	8245
–		9195, שָׁקֵד[3]	Be shaped like an almond blossom	√	–
	מְשֻׁקָּד, *mešuq | qāḏ*	5481, מְשֻׁקָּד	shape of almond flowers	9195, cf. 9193	8246

Note the following:

1. The G/K numbering system distinguishes three roots having the letters
   שׁקד; the Strong's system only one.

2. The *DBLH* for 9194 adds this definition after the gloss: "i.e., be physically wasted away, possibly implying
   loss of weight, and so in a weakened
   state (Ps 102:8[EB 7]+)."[13] Is this an
   outlier from these other roots or is it

   related? In the photograph a hand is holding some almonds. The nuts look
   shriveled. So, the "being emaciated" may well be equivalent to "looking like
   an almond."

3. Dyer comments, "The almond tree was named the 'awake tree' because in
   Palestine it is the first tree in the year to bud and bear fruit. Its blooms precede its leaves, as the tree bursts into blossom in late January."[14] On the other
   hand, Lipinski, שָׁקַד, *TWOT*, questions this connection.

4. Are all these words derived from a common root or are there different but
   homonymous roots? *SNIVEC, DBLH, CHALOT,* and *DCH* count multiple
   roots. Other wordbooks, such as BDB, *TWOT,* and *HALOT* treat them all
   as being connected to one root. Lexicographers and commentators do not
   always agree. That's okay. This is why there is not just one definitive wordbook or commentary.

Hopefully this example will motivate you to examine wordplays that you
read about so that your teaching of others can be enhanced. You won't have time
to investigate every question you might have. Just doing the first steps of the
example will do quite well.

Once again, there is more payoff in the final two chapters of this book. Keep
working!

Advanced Information and Curious Facts

Translating the Name of God

One of the challenges of translators is how to translate the name of the Lord,
the word *God*, and various combinations of the two. Now that you know the
Hebrew alphabet and vowels (and if you don't yet know the Greek alphabet, just
read the transliterations), and know what the LXX is, you can understand your

---

13. "EB" means English Bible versification. "+" indicates that Swanson, editor of *DBLH*, has cited
every reference in regard to this lexeme discussed under this definition.

14. Charles H. Dyer, "Jeremiah," in *The Bible Knowledge Commentary: An Exposition of the Scriptures*,
ed. J. F. Walvoord and R. B. Zuck, 2 vols. (Wheaton, IL: Victor, 1985), 1:1131.

English Bible better. Knowing this can increase your theological understanding as well.

FIGURE 5.15: The Lord and God in OT and NT, English, Hebrew, and Greek

English OT	← Hebrew →	Greek (LXX & NT) →	OT Quoted in English NT
1. Lᴏʀᴅ (note small capitals)	יהוה, *YHWH* = the personal name for God		
2. **Lord, lord** (note lower case letters)	אָדוֹן, *'ādôn* = "lord, master" either for YHWH[15] or people	κύριος, *kyrios*, = "lord, master"	Lord (= translation of Greek)
3. **Lord**	אֲדֹנִי, *'ădōnî* = "my lord" mostly for people, but can be used for God[16]		
4. **Lord**	אֲדֹנָי, *'ădōnāy* = perhaps "my lord"; used always and only of YHWH[17]		
5. **God, gods**	אֱלֹהִים, *'ĕlōhîm*	θεός, *theos*	God, god(s)
6. **Lᴏʀᴅ God**	יהוה אֱלֹהִים, *YHWH 'ĕlōhîm*	κύριος θεός, *kyrios theos*	Lord God
7. **Lord God** (NASB, ESV) **Sovereign Lᴏʀᴅ** (NIV)	אֲדֹנָי יהוה, *'ădōnāy YHWH*	κύριος θεός	[none quoted]

Here are two observations and one theological point:

1. Notice the use of small capital fonts when the name of the Lord is used in the OT.
2. The translators of the LXX, who were Jews, in order to avoid even accidentally taking the name of the Lord in vain, decided to substitute the word

---

15. Rarely used for YHWH, but see Ps 97:5 for a clear example: "the Lord (using the construct form אֲדוֹן, *'ādôn*) of all the earth." See also Ps 114:6 (Hebrew 7) in the absolute form.

16. Here we might include the majestic plural forms used for YHWH as in Ps 136:3, "the Lord of lords" (אֲדֹנִים לַאֲדֹנֵי הָאֲדֹנִים, *la'ădōnê hā'ădōnîm*). Numerous times "our Lord" (אֲדֹנֵינוּ, *'ădōnênû*) is used (e.g., Ps 8:2, 10) and may well be a parallel example, if אֲדֹנָי, *'ădōnāy*, is explained to be something other than *ādon* plus the pronominal suffix "my" (see next note).

17. For the analysis that אֲדֹנָי, *'ădōnāy*, is an emphatic form rather than a plural (honorific) of "Lord" plus a pronominal suffix "my" attached, see Waltke and O'Connor, *Introduction to Biblical Hebrew Syntax*, §7.4.3e, f.

There are some difficult passages. One such is Gen 18:3 in the theophany to Abraham (Gen 18:1 reads that יהוה, YHWH, appeared to Abraham and then proceeds with the story of the three men/angels). The MT reads that Abraham addressed his audience as אֲדֹנָי (with the *qamets* under the *nun*). This is the term usually reserved for YHWH. The LXX renders κύριε as a singular, but the identity is ambiguous. Jewish English translations differ. The *Tanak* (1917) renders "My lord," as though אדני is אֲדֹנִי, "my lord, sir," addressing only one of the three. The *Tanakh* (1985) renders as though אדני is אֲדֹנַי (with the *patakh* under the *nun*), "my lords," addressing all three. In Gen 18:13, one of the three visitors is identified as יהוה, YHWH.

Lord instead. In the LXX, they rendered this with the Greek word for *Lord*. The NT writers, writing in Greek, follow the practice of the LXX.

3. First Peter 3:14 clearly alludes to Isa 8:12b; the cross-references in ESV and NIV cite this. However, neither the NIV nor ESV cite Isa 8:13 as a cross-reference to 1 Pet 3:15a. Notice the parallels in the chart below.

FIGURE 5.16: Isa 8:13a according to MT, LXX and 1 Pet 3:15a

Hebrew	LXX	1 Pet 3:15a

[13] But
   the LORD **of hosts, him**
regard as holy.
	[13]
	   the Lord, **him**
	regard as holy,
		[15] but
		   the Lord, **Christ**
		regard as holy,
		    in your hearts

Note that the Hebrew יהוה (LORD) in Isaiah, rendered *kyrios* in both the LXX and in 1 Pet 3:15, is clearly applied to Jesus Christ. This equation of Jesus with the LORD of the OT is a clear equation of Jesus to the same personhood as the LORD. Some theologians have suggested that יהוה is the OT word that is broad enough to include the concept of the Trinity, since the NT applies it to both the Father and the Son. What do you think?

CHAPTER 6

YES, VIRGINIA, THERE ARE. . .

Clauses

Objectives

1. Distinguish various types of clauses.
2. Distinguish clauses from phrases.
3. Identify different types of clauses in Hebrew.
4. Flowchart subject, verb, indirect object, and direct object.
5. Be motivated to make flowcharts.

Introduction

Clauses are not difficult to understand. We use them all the time without need of explaining them. But when we study Scripture, we want to look at the text closely in order to understand and explain the meaning. Identifying clauses is an important part of this process. Explaining them can be tricky, though, when our memory of grammar gets a little foggy. Usually the main idea a writer wants to get across appears in a main clause. If our attention is misplaced in a secondary idea, we run the risk of misunderstanding exactly what the author intended.

In this chapter we will brush the dust off those parts of our brains that once learned clauses in English. Then we will move to the less familiar territory of Hebrew clauses. At this point we are just looking at the big picture of clauses. We will get to the finer points within the clauses in later chapters.

Finally, we will learn a system of flowcharting. Flowcharting is a simplified form of sentence diagramming. If you were one of the few who learned and loved diagramming sentences, I hope you will find this modified form still interesting and perhaps even more useful. If you were one of the many who hated diagramming sentences (I confess that I was), clear away your prejudices and give this a try. I use this all the time in studying Scripture. Sometimes meaning becomes clearer; sometimes other options of interpretation become apparent. In either case, the text comes alive.

Clauses

We need to start with some terminology. A clause is made up of a subject and a predicate (it contains a verb or finite verbal idea; more on this in the next chapter). The subject or the verb may be present or implied, but both are required. A phrase is a word or word group that does not contain a predicate, i.e., it has no finite verb.[1]

A sentence is made up of one or more clauses. There are two basic types of clauses: independent clauses and dependent or subordinate clauses. Just as the names imply, an independent clause can stand alone; a dependent clause "depends on," or hangs from, another clause.

An *independent clause* can be a complete sentence all by itself. Since a dependent clause by definition requires a main clause, it does not by itself form a complete sentence. When an independent clause has a dependent clause attached to it, this independent clause is called a main clause. The only difference between a *main clause* and an independent clause is that a main clause has one or more subordinating clauses modifying it, whereas an independent clause has no subordinate clause.

A *dependent clause* is introduced by a relative pronoun (who, which, that, etc.) or by a subordinating conjunction (after, although, because, if, except, etc.). A relative pronoun introduces a relative clause and functions like an adjective. Dependent clauses introduced by subordinating conjunctions are adverbial; that is, they modify verbs. This simple concept is important to grasp in order to understand the functions of clauses.

Study the examples below. I have numbered the sentences "S1," etc. Subjects are in bold type; the verbs or verb phrases are underlined; subordinating conjunctions and relative pronouns are in italics.

S1.   **Bill** <u>loves</u> Hebrew.
S2.   *Though* **Bill** <u>loves</u> Hebrew, **he** also <u>likes</u> food.
S3.   **Bill** <u>prefers</u> pizza, but **Jill** seafood.
S4.   **Bill** <u>will eat</u> seafood but <u>hates</u> raw oysters.
S5.   **Oysters** <u>make</u> Bill sick.
S6.   **Bill** <u>made</u> a strange facial expression *when* he <u>ate</u> raw oysters *because* **Jill** <u>dared</u> him.
S7.   **Jill**, *who* <u>should have been</u> sorry, <u>laughed</u> *because* **Bill** <u>made</u> a funny face.
S8.   **Bill** and **Jill** <u>are</u> still friends.

S1 is an independent clause. A sentence with only one independent clause is called a simple sentence.

S2 has two verbs and subjects. Therefore, there are two clauses. The first clause is introduced by a subordinating conjunction "though" and is dependent. If someone said to you, "Though Bill loves pizza," and stopped, you would be

---

1. Some people use the terms *clause* and *phrase* interchangeably, but it is useful and clearer to distinguish them.

waiting for something to complete the thought. The second clause is the main clause. A main clause plus a dependent clause forms a complex sentence.

S3 also has two clauses, but they are joined by a coordinating conjunction "but." Both clauses are independent; this is a compound sentence. You will notice that the verb in the second clause is implied.

S4 is another compound sentence, but in the second clause the subject is implied.

S5 has two direct objects (DOs) *not* joined by "and": "Bill" and "sick." Both words refer to the same entity. "Bill" is the DO and "sick" is the object complement: Bill became sick; the oysters made him that way.

S6 has three clauses. The main clause comes first. The first subordinate clause depends on the main clause, giving the time when Bill made the face. The second subordinate clause depends on the first subordinate clause (based on context), giving the reason why Bill ate the raw oysters.

S7 again has one main clause and two subordinate clauses. The main subject is "Jill," but the comma marks an interruption in the clause. "Who" introduces a relative clause, which functions like an adjective, describing the noun "Jill." Within the relative clause, "who" is the subject of the verb phrase "should have been." After a second comma the main clause resumes, and its verb is "laughed." The last clause is introduced by a subordinating conjunction "because" and is adverbial, giving the reason why Jill laughed.

S8 has two subjects and one verb. "Bill" and "Jill" form a compound subject. In this case, the "and" joins two nouns that both function as subjects of the verb. Notice that "and" is not a subordinating conjunction; it is a coordinating conjunction joining elements of equal weight in the sentence. The verb is a form of "to be." The subjects ("Bill" and "Jill") and the noun "friends" all refer to the same people. Bill and Jill are not doing something to the friends; they are the friends. So the word "friends" is not a DO; it is called a predicate noun in English.

Now that you have the general idea of how clauses function in English, you are ready to be introduced to Hebrew clauses.

Hebrew Verb and Noun Clauses

Hebrew clauses may be analyzed internally and externally. By externally, I mean how a given clause relates to surrounding clauses. By internally, I mean the nature of the verb within the clause itself. In this chapter we will look at clauses internally. There are two types of clauses based on the verb: verb clauses and noun clauses. The identity of the clause is determined by whether the verb is a form of "to be" or not "to be" (sorry, Shakespeare) in any tense.

If the verb is anything other than a simple "to be," the clause is a verbal clause. Sentences S1–S7 above are verbal clauses; in all of these a verb other than "to be" is either present or implied (S3). This is something so familiar, I don't need to give any biblical examples right now. As in English, the verb may be omitted, especially in poetry; but clauses in which this happens are still considered to be verbal clauses because some verb must be understood from the context. We will treat Hebrew verbal clauses in the unit on the verb.

If, however, the verb is a form of the verb "to be," the clause is a noun clause (or verbless clause). The Hebrew verb for "to be" is הָיָה, but it has a range of meanings. When it means anything other than "to be," the clause is considered to be verbal. Its most common meaning, though, is simply "to be." A peculiarity of Hebrew is that it regularly omits the verb הָיָה ("to be") unless there is some particular reason for including it, such as to specify time. English will almost always include it in translation. For example, if S7 were in Hebrew, the verb "are" would be omitted.

When Hebrew does omit הָיָה, translators must make a decision about the time frame (past, present, or future) based on context. I give an example of each time frame below with an English interlinear using marks to show where a verb must be understood and then the NIV with the verb in italics. (By the way, these examples all are in a traditional interlinear format, so the English word order moves generally from right to left with the Hebrew.) Notice that in each case there is no Hebrew verb "to be" and context determines the time frame; an "x" is used as a place holder to be filled by the bolded verb in the NIV.

PAST TIME (GEN 1:2)				
תְּהוֹם	פְּנֵי	עַל-	·	וְחֹשֶׁךְ
the deep	the face of	over	X	and darkness
darkness *was* over the surface of the deep				

PRESENT TIME (LEV 19:2)					
אֱלֹהֵיכֶם	יְהוָה	אֲנִי	·	קָדוֹשׁ	כִּי
your God	the LORD	I	X	Holy	because
because I, the LORD your God, *am* holy					

FUTURE TIME (RUTH 1:16)			
עַמִּי		·	עַמֵּךְ
my people		X	your people
Your people *will be* my people			

Flowcharting

Bible students may use various systems for flowcharting. I hope you will find the following presentation helpful. In this chapter I will give an overview of the process. Then in subsequent chapters we will add various features to it.

The task of flowcharting has three steps: (1) identify clauses and phrases, (2) indent clauses and phrases to show relationships, and (3) label the functions of clauses and phrases. In this chapter you will learn step 1: telling the difference between a clause and a phrase. A phrase will modify some element of the clause of which it is a part. At this point I want to make sure that you can identify the clause components of a sentence and isolate them.

In flowcharting, each clause and phrase gets its own line. There are four possible components of the clause line: subject (Subj), verb (V), indirect object (IO), and direct object (DO). As we mentioned before, the subject and verb are essential, whether they be expressed or implied (by context or the verb form itself). The indirect and direct object are optional. Anything that is not one of these four elements is either a conjunction or a modifier.

The only other things you need to know before getting started are (1) what an IO is and (2) how we treat subordinate clauses differently. First, the IO. Simply put, if a sentence has one, the IO is who or what receives the DO. English indicates the IO in one of two ways: word order or in a prepositional phrase with the preposition "to." If the clause order is Subj–V–IO–DO, the preposition "to" is not used. If the clause order is Subj–V–DO–IO, English uses a prepositional phrase with "to." In the following examples, again bold words are subjects and underlined words are verbs; in addition, I've used an arrow ($\rightarrow$) to mark the DO, a double arrow ($\Leftrightarrow$) to mark the predicate noun or adjective, and italic type to mark the IO.

S9.   **Bill** <u>gave</u> *Jill* $\rightarrow$ the money.
S10. **Bill** <u>gave</u> $\rightarrow$ the money *to Jill*.

In both cases the DO is "the money," and in both cases Jill receives the money. So Jill is the IO. Second, while main clauses are kept to the far left in the column, subordinate clauses are indented with their subordinating conjunction. Otherwise, they are treated in the same way as main clauses.

When we identify clauses and phrases, we want to keep subjects, verbs, and any direct or indirect objects on the same line. Any other component is a modifier. Modifiers are indented below the element that they modify.

Helpful Techniques

There are a number of ways to make flowcharting easier. First, you can save time in typing by downloading text from an electronic Bible or from the internet. Second, there are several ways of maneuvering words. You can print out the text on paper and use scissors and tape to group clauses and phrases, then physically move them around to the desired positions and tape them to a piece of paper. Far superior to this is to use a computer program that allows you to do diagramming (or flowcharting). I still like using Microsoft Word (MS Word) charts.

Notes and Reminders

1. Keep the Subj, V, IO and DO on the same line using tabs to separate them. This gives space to indent modifiers of the main line elements (S1–S10). Remember that IOs can be expressed either by word order (S9) or by a prepositional phrase (PPhr, S10).
2. Subjects (Subjs) are bolded, IOs are italicized, DOs are preceded by →; predicate nominatives (PNs, whether nouns or adjectives) are marked with ⇔ (S8).[2]
3. The parts of speech line up in all the sentences (S1–S10).
4. Subordinate clauses are indented and include their subordinating conjunctions (cj, e.g., *though*) or relative pronouns (RPrns) at the beginning (S2, S6, S7).
5. Clauses are separated by an empty line (S2–S4, S6, S7); phrases within a clause do not have an empty separating line (S8).
6. Coordinating conjunctions (e.g., *and*, *but*) get their own line and are indented between the words, phrases, or clauses they connect (S3, S4, S8).
7. Pronouns (Prns, including RPrns) are enclosed in boxes and arrows point to the antecedent (S2, S6).[3]
8. Modifiers, such as adverbs (e.g., *also*, *still*), are indented under what they modify (S2, S8).

What Good Is Flowcharting?

There are some limitations to flowcharting. It does not solve all exegetical problems, but it can help clarify the issues. Context is always the most important factor. The student of Scripture must learn to deal with other finer hermeneutical points as well. Flowcharts are least helpful (or necessary) for the simplest sentences and usually for narratives (stories). For example, no one would need to make a flowchart of S1. Even S2 through S8 are all very simple. But let me offer four reasons why flowcharts are helpful.

1. Flowcharting forces you to pay attention to relationships between clauses and phrases.
2. Sometimes flowcharting reveals options that you may not have considered. For example, in the Hebrew word order of Hab 2:4 and in the Greek quoted by Paul, the text reads: "The just by faith will live." The main clause is simple enough, but what does the prepositional phrase modify, the noun (subject) or the verb?

---

2. MS Word autocorrects --> to → and <=> to ⇔. If yours does not, look on the web for how to add autocorrects.

3. To box in a word in MS Word, double-click the word to select it and under the Home tab, in Paragraph field, select the Borders command and select Outside Borders.

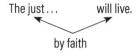

If it modifies the noun, then it means people, who are righteous by means of their faith, will live. It is similar to saying, "If people are declared just by faith, then they will live." But if it modifies the verb, then it means that those who are righteous (already) will live by means of a life of faith. The thought here is, "Those who are truly just will live lives by the principle of faith, lives characterized by faith." The student of Habakkuk and Romans needs to determine which meaning is intended based upon the context.

3. Another value is the ability to compare versions. Considering the various possible interpretations from all the translations boggles the mind and illustrates the difficulty of the text.

4. The greatest benefit, however, is for expository preaching and teaching. Once you have completed your flowchart and labeling, you can derive sermonic questions from the "answers" you have discovered and get points from the text. The thesis statement of a sermon or devotion might be derived from the main clause and its context. Subpoints might come from the subordinate clauses. Take Deut 32:46, for example. A flowchart might look like this (I have omitted the "Function" column for sake of space):

FIGURE 6.4: Flowchart of Deut 32:46

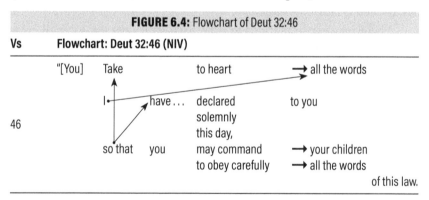

The main clause is a command by Moses to the people to take to heart his teaching. The implied subject of every command is *you*, which I have placed in brackets. This command answers the question, "What are we supposed to do?"

The second clause, a relative clause without a RPrn, explains "all the words" to mean the law that he had just recited to the people. It answers the question, "What words are we to take to heart?"

The third clause is introduced by the subordinating conjunction "so that" and gives the purpose. It modifies a verb in a previous clause. It might modify either of the two preceding clauses. If it modifies the main clause (option **A**), it answers the question, "For what purpose should we take these words to heart?" If it modifies the relative clause (option **B**), it answers the question "For what purpose am I declaring these things to you?" Sermonizing would develop the application of these points.

A teacher or preacher looking for a quick outline for a sermon or devotion could do worse.

What about Aramaic?

The function of clauses is the same as in Hebrew. We will make notes on verbs in later chapters.

Advanced Information and Curious Facts

Back to the alphabet! (You might do well to review; *HRUW* offers several reviews over time.)

The English Bible closely follows the Hebrew Bible in chapter and verse division (there are some differences). For the book of Psalms, the chapter divisions are the same. Psalms is divided into five "books," the first book consisting of forty-one psalms. Psalms 1 and 2 are thought to be later compositions and to serve as an introduction to the major themes of the whole Psalter. Except for two, all of the remaining thirty-nine psalms have titles with attributions to David; only Pss 10 and 33 are anonymous.

Further, the ancient psalm titles are included in the Hebrew verse numbering, but not in English.

In the LXX (Septuagint; see ch. 4 if you need a review), however, Psalms 9 and 10 are combined into one psalm. This throws off the numbering of the psalms (and it gets more complicated than that, but that is beyond our scope here). If they were one psalm, then David is the author of the anonymous Ps 10. The question is, on what basis did the LXX translators unite the two psalms? Here is what they saw:

Psalm 9	First Letter	Psalm 10	First Letter
1 (Hebrew 2)	א	1	ל
3 (Hebrew 4)	ב	—	מ
5 (Hebrew 6)	ג	—	נ
—	ד	—	ס
6 (Hebrew 7)	ה	—	ע

(continued)

Psalm 9	First Letter	Psalm 10	First Letter
7 (Hebrew 8)	ו	—	פ
11 (Hebrew 12)	ז	—	צ
13 (Hebrew 14)	ח	12	ק
15 (Hebrew 16)	ט	14	ר
17 (Hebrew 18)	י	15	שׂ
18 (Hebrew 19)	כ	17	ת

What do you think? Is this a "broken" acrostic demonstrating that these were really one psalm written by David, or are they two separate psalms, the second of which is anonymous? If they are one psalm, why do you think the poem was left broken and why were the two divided? For some suggested answers, see the "Advanced Information" in the next chapter.

CHAPTER 7

WOW!

The Conjunction *Waw* and Friends

Objectives
1. Identify English and Hebrew conjunctions.
2. Label the functions of conjunctions in flowcharts.
3. Compare versions' interpretations of Hebrew conjunctions.

Tool Used: Interlinear Bible (electronic or paper)

Introduction

We mentioned in the previous chapter that Hebrew clauses may be classified internally, i.e., by the type of verb in the clause, or they may be classified externally. By "externally" I mean how the clause in question relates to surrounding clauses. Languages that tend to link subordinate clauses to main clauses are called *syntactic* languages. English and Greek are syntactic languages. It is common in these languages to string together series of clauses using subordination. Paul is famous (or infamous among Greek students) for very long Greek sentences with all sorts of subordination.

Languages that link clauses together by coordination instead of subordination are called *paratactic*. Hebrew is paratactic. It does have subordinate conjunctions to introduce subordinate clauses, but more commonly Hebrew joins together clauses by a coordinating conjunction. The most common word in the Hebrew Bible is the conjunction *waw*. It occurs over 50,000 times in the OT! Interestingly, even though it's considered a coordinating conjunction, the *waw* can also mark structures that are subordinate. So even though Hebrew is paratactic, Hebrew uses various coordinating arrangements to communicate subordinate ideas. These will be covered in the coming chapters. You simply need to identify the three structures of Hebrew main clauses and the main functions of one of those structures.

In this chapter we will look first at English conjunctions and how they function. Then we will look at disjunctive clauses in Hebrew and the functions of the *waw* in these situations. Finally, we will look at labeling the functions of these clauses in flowcharts.

English Conjunctions and Functions

Conjunctions are words that join clauses, words, or phrases. As we've seen, there are two types. A coordinating conjunction joins clauses, words, or phrases of equal "weight" (see examples S3, S4, and S7 from the last chapter). Subordinating conjunctions introduce clauses that depend on another word or clause. The clause on which it depends may be either main or subordinate.

What you ultimately need to do is describe the function of clauses. These function labels are a shorthand for paraphrasing. To do this, you must familiarize yourself with conjunctions and what they mean. To aid you I have prepared three figures below. These figures list the conjunctions in alphabetical order and give their possible functions.

Figure 7.1 identifies the more common English coordinating conjunctions and places them in bold type. A popular acronym to remember seven of them is FANBOYS. I added *however* and arranged them alphabetically. Words that may be used either as conjunctions or prepositions are followed by an asterisk (*).

FIGURE 7.1: Coordinating Conjunctions and Functions

Word	Functions	Word	Functions
and	Continuation, Addition	nor	Negative Alternative
but	Contrast	or	Explanatory, Alternative (inclusive or exclusive)
for*	Cause, Explanation, Example	so	Inference
however	Contrast	yet	Contrast

When a word, e.g., *for*, can be either a conjunction or a preposition, how can you tell the difference? If the word is followed by a clause, it is a conjunction; if it is followed by a phrase, it forms a PPhr.

Figure 7.2 identifies the more common subordinating conjunctions. Some subordinating conjunctions may also function as adverbs; adverbial use is not marked. When you encounter a conjunction, simply find it on the list and write the function in the first column of your chart parallel to the conjunction. If there is more than one alternative, you will have to determine what the author meant based on context. That is part of the fun!

FIGURE 7.2: Subordinating Conjunctions and Functions

Word	Functions	Word	Functions
after*	Time—prior	as . . . as	Measure/Degree, Comparison
although	Contrast, Concession		
as	Comparison, Manner	as . . . so	Comparison

Word	Functions
as a result	Result
as if	Manner
as long as	Extent, Cause
as soon as	Time
as though	Manner
because	Cause
before*	Time—subsequent
besides	Continuative
both ... and	Addition
consequently	Result
even as	Comparison
even if	Concession
even though	Concession
except	Restrictive
for example	Example
hence	Result

Word	Functions
however	Contrast
if	Condition
in order that	Purpose/Result
inasmuch as	Cause
just as	Comparison
just as ... so	Comparison
lest	Condition (negative)
not only ... but also	Addition
now	Result
provided (that)	Condition
since	Time (inauguration), Cause
so	Cause, Result
so also	Comparison
so ... as	Comparison
so that	Purpose/Result

You might be wondering whether the function labels will mean anything to you. Hopefully you will understand most of the labels. Some of them, though, may not seem obvious. In order to clarify the less obvious labels, I have provided a third figure. Figure 7.3 is a reverse index of the first two figures. This figure combines both coordinating and subordinating conjunctions into one figure, then alphabetizes the items according to function, listing the conjunctions afterward. I provide a brief explanation for each function.

FIGURE 7.3: Function Explanations for Conjunctions

Function	Explanation	Words
Addition	Attaching of things or actions not in sequence; common in lists	and; both ... and; not only ... but also
Alternative	Alternative Exclusive: A or B, but not both A and B	whether ... or
Alternative	Alternative Inclusive: A and/or B. *Or* in English is ambiguous; context must decide	or, nor (negative)

(continued)

Function	Explanation	Words
Cause	The clause so introduced is the cause of the action/state of another clause	as long as; because; inasmuch as; now; since*; so; whereas; why; for*
Comparison	Marks an item as similar to a previous item	as; as ... as; as ... so; even as; just as; just as ... so; so ... as; so also; than
Concession	Introduces a clause recognized as compatible with the main clause, when at first glance it might appear that they are incompatible	although; even if; even though; though; unless; while; yet
Condition	Introduces a situation necessary for the fulfillment of another clause	if; provided (that); unless
Continuation	Marks a clause as sequential (in time) or consequential (logically)	and; besides; [untranslated]
Contrast	Marks a clause in opposition to another clause	although; but; however; whereas; yet
Example	Marks an illustration of a previous thought	for example; for*
Explanation	Introduces a clause that explains a previous clause	for*; or
Extent	Marks the limit of something	as long as; till; until*
Inference	Not to be confused with the adverb of time, the conjunction then marks the main clause, whose fulfillment depends on the fulfillment of a conditional clause	then, so
Manner	Marks the method or attitude in which an action was done	as; as if; as though
Measure/Degree	Marks or compares the quantity of something	as ... as; than; that
Place	Indicates the location of an action.	where(ever)
Purpose/Result	Introduces a clause indicating the intent of the agent of an action (Compare Result)	in order that; so that; that
Restrictive	Marks an item as excluded from the main clause	except
Result	Introduces a clause indicating the likely outcome of an action (Compare Purpose)	as a result; consequently; hence; so; then, lest (negative); now
Time	Marks the time of an action	as soon as; when(ever)

Function	Explanation	Words
Time (inauguration)	Marks the time of the beginning of the action in the main clause	since*
Time (prior)	Marks a clause whose action occurs prior to the action of the clause it modifies	after*
Time (simultaneous)	Marks a clause whose action occurs at the same time as the action of the clause it modifies	while
Time (subsequent)	Marks a clause whose action occurs after the action of the clause it modifies	before*
Time (termination)	Marks the time of the end of an action in the main clause, without indicating a resulting change in state	until*

First, do not memorize any of these figures (whew!). Second, skim over the list of conjunctions one or two times so that you can recognize them as conjunctions and know whether they are coordinating or subordinating. Third, when you are labeling the functions to your flowchart, consult the figures to put in the correct label and to understand the meaning of the label. These figures offer suggestive lists and are not exhaustive. If none of the categories above seem to fit a word, consult a good English dictionary.[1] Feel free to add your own categories. After using the figures a short while, you will find less need to consult them.

Waw: King of Conjunctions

In the last chapter we mentioned that clauses may be classified externally by the way they are joined together. There are two basic ways that clauses are joined: with a conjunction or without a conjunction. A conjunctive structure exists when two words, phrases, or clauses are joined by a conjunction. An asyndetic structure (the noun you are more likely to read is *asyndeton*) exists when two words, phrases, or clauses simply sit next to each other without a conjunction. (By the way, the word *asyndeton*, of Greek derivation, means "without conjunction"; the word *conjunction* is derived from Latin.) Asyndeton is less common than conjunction. It is found mostly in poetry or reported speech. In these cases, the writer expects the reader to understand the logical connection between clauses.

---

1. This does not violate "the Vow," because we are seeking to understand the functions of English words. Better would be to do this for the Hebrew conjunction and consult the *Dictionary of Biblical Languages*, because it provides both glosses and definitions.

Position and Appearance of the *Waw* Conjunction (*Waw* cj)

With only a few exceptions, anytime a Hebrew word begins with a *waw*, that *waw* is the conjunction. *Waw* is classified as a coordinating conjunction. But it may also introduce a subordinate clause. *Waw* is such a common and important feature of Hebrew that you will need to spend some time learning about it.

The *waw* cj never stands alone, but is always prefixed to a word, even before any other prefixes that might be attached. For example, דָּבָר means "word" or "a word"; וְדָבָר means "and a word"; וְהַדָּבָר means "and the word" (הַ [with a following *dagesh forte*] is the article; see ch. 10).

There are two classes of forms, *waw* as a consonant and *waw* as the vowel *shureq* (וּ). Normally the *waw* is a consonant and can have almost any vowel under it.

וְ, וַ, וֶ, וִ, ו

When *waw* cj is attached to a word beginning with the letters ב, מ, פ (oftentimes remembered with the acronym *bumaph*, or *bump*), or before a word whose first letter (other than *yod*—see "and Judah" in figure 7.4 below) has a simple *shewa*, the *waw* becomes the vowel *shureq*.

וּ

This is the only occasion when a Hebrew word or syllable starts with a vowel. As we mentioned in ch. 3, this lone exception just happens to be very common. As a composite vowel the *shureq* forms a long, open syllable. Therefore, when followed by a letter with *shewa*, that letter always begins a syllable and the *shewa* is vocal. Here are some examples to illustrate all of these forms of *waw*.

FIGURE 7.4: Attaching Conjunctive *Waw*

Hebrew	Transliteration	Translation
וְרוּחַ	wərûaḥ[2]	and a spirit
וְדָבָר	wəḏā | ḇār	and a word
וַיִּבֶן	way | yi | ben	and he built
וָאוֹר	wā | 'ôr	and light
וֶאֱמֶת	we | 'ĕmet	and truth
וֵאלֹהִים	wē' | lō | hîm	and God
וְהָיוּ	wi | hayû	and they shall be
וִיהוּדָה	wî | hû | ḏâ	and Judah
וּמֹשֶׁה	û | mō | šeh	and Moses
וּתְכֵלֶת	û | təḵē | let	and blue wool yarn

2. Remember that neither the vocal *shewa* nor the furtive *patakh* count as syllables. וְרוּחַ is a single-syllable word.

Range of Meaning for *Waw*

Waw is very flexible. The *SNIVEC* translates the *waw* conjunction well over fifty different ways! Because of this flexibility it is difficult to classify its uses. Figure 7.5 lists *some* of its functions. To get an idea of the English words that might be used to express these functions, I give a column of English glosses and a column of explanation. See also figure 7.3 above. The most common uses are addition and continuation. It is important to realize that ancient speakers of Hebrew did not go through this list of functions for the conjunction *waw* when they were speaking/writing any more than you as a speaker of English go through such a list when you use the preposition *of.* The purpose of this list is to give you language to talk about the meaning of a text when analyzing closely and when reading commentators. This same principle is true for the case functions and verbal functions.

FIGURE 7.5: Twelve Functions of Waw

	Functions	English Glosses	Explanation
Coordinating	1. Addition	and, also, while, both … and	Connects words in a sentence to form a list or connects sentences without any notion of sequence; this includes correlative uses
	2. Continuation	and, then, [untranslated]	Adds one expression to another with some notion of sequence
	3. Alternative	or, nor	May be inclusive or exclusive
	4. Contrast	but	The joining of a word or sentence to another from which it differs in some way
	5. Emphatic	indeed, even	Introduces an expression that restates the prior one without significant additional information
	6. Explanation	for	Specifies the meaning of a prior expression
	7. Hyphenating	and	Two words joined to form one idea (hendiadys) or two opposites joined to form a totality (merism)
	8. Introductory	now	Introduces a change of topic or focus
	9. Content	that	Introduces content after verbs of speaking; this actually marks the entire quotation as a substantive, the direct object of the verb of speaking or perceiving
Subordinating	10. Cause	because, for	Introduces the root or reason of a prior action
	11. Purpose/Result	so that, that, so, to	Introduces the intentional or likely outcome of a prior expression
	12. Condition	if, when	Introduces a circumstance necessary for the realization of a main clause

Here are some example uses. All English translations are from the NIV unless otherwise noted. The numbers of the functions in figure 7.6 correspond to those found in 7.5.

FIGURE 7.6: Examples of Functions of *Waw*

Function	Citation	Text
1.	Lev 19:36 Jdg 1:36 (ESV) 1 Kgs 13:24	Use … an honest ephah **and** an honest hin. **And** the border of the Amorites ran from the ascent of with **both** the donkey **and** the lion standing beside it.
2.	Jdg 5:8 1 Sam 5:11 Gen 49:10	but not a shield **or** spear was seen let [the ark] go back … **or** it will kill us[3] The scepter will not depart from Judah, **nor** the ruler's staff
3.	Lev 19:23 Gen 2:21 (NASB)	When you enter the land **and** plant any kind of fruit tree **Then** he took one of his ribs
4.	Prov 1:28	Then they will call to me **but** I will not answer;
5.	Jer 20:9	I am weary of holding it in; **indeed**, I cannot.
6.	2 Kgs 25:23 (ESV)	they came with their men …, **namely**, Ishmael son of Nethaniah,
7.	Gen 19:24 Gen 2:9	the Lord rained down burning sulfur [lit. sulfur **and** fire] the tree of the knowledge of good **and** evil.
8.	Gen 3:1	**Now** the serpent was more crafty than any of the wild animals
9.	Gen 8:13	Noah then removed the covering … and saw **that** the surface
10.	Gen 22:12 Gen 24:62	Now I know that you fear God, **because** you have not withheld Now Isaac had come from …, **for** he was living in
11.	Josh 9:20 Gen 19:32 (ESV) Exod 14:31 (ESV) Gen 18:21 (ESV)	We will let them live, **so that** God's wrath will not fall on us and we will lie with him, **that** we may preserve offspring Israel saw the great power of the Lord …, **so** the people feared I will go down **to** see whether they have done
12.	Deut 22:3	Do the same **if** you find their donkey

This list may not be exhaustive but it will cover most cases. See *HRUW* for more examples and practice identifying categories. The main purpose of figure 7.6 is to show that *waw* may introduce coordinating or subordinating clauses.

You need to realize that the *waw* in all of these cases might have been translated "and." The rendering "and" leaves the relationship between words or clauses vague, and the reader must still interpret the function. Translations that render other than "and" are trying to clarify those relationships.

---

3. The exclusive meaning of "or" is rare with *waw* and seems to be limited in Hebrew to the construction וְלֹא, formally, "and not," which might be understood as "so that not" (cf. ESV), which would be a negative purpose. The exclusive alternative in Hebrew is more common with אוֹ, "or," and פֶּן, "lest, so that not."

More importantly, *waw* is a structure marker. Its meaning is determined by structure and context. When a clause begins with 1 + finite verb, it is a conjunctive clause. When a clause begins 1 + nonverb (e.g., noun, pronoun, participle, etc.) the clause is disjunctive. We will look at these more closely in ch. 20 on prose.

Other Conjunctions

The *waw* conjunction is certainly the most common conjunction in Hebrew. There are other conjunctions, but none of them is prefixed; they are independent words or word clusters. The rest are subordinating conjunctions. Since you are learning pre-Hebrew, you don't really need to study the others. However, it might be helpful to see some examples. Here are some common conjunctions and their most common functions. For English words with the same function, compare figure 7.3 above. The translations are NIV unless otherwise noted.

> **Teaching/Learning Tip:** In flowcharting modifiers, original word order is often lost. Words moved out of order are indented under what they modify and marked with a ^ symbol. The places from which the words were removed are marked with ellipses.

אוֹ   Coordinating conjunction joining nominals
1. **Alternative.** Do you have a father *or* [אוֹ] a brother?" (Gen 44:19; this is an inclusive alternative)
Who gives them sight or [אוֹ] makes them blind? (Exod 4:11; this is an exclusive alternative)

כִּי   Either coordinating (1, 2) or subordinating (3–8); it may also be used as an adverb (9). Among the possible functions are the following:
2. **Explanation.** You will not certainly die. . . . *For* [כִּי] God knows that when you eat from it your eyes will be opened. (Gen 3:4–5)
3. **Contrast** (after a negative statement). You shall *not* call her name Sarai, *but* [כִּי] Sarah shall be her name." (Gen 17:15 ESV)
4. **Time**—simultaneous. *When* [כִּי] you work the ground, it will no longer yield its crops for you. (Gen 4:12)
5. **Cause.** Adam named his wife Eve, *because* [כִּי] she would become the mother of all the living. (Gen 3:20)
6. **Condition**—of a real condition (i.e., a situation that may potentially happen). *If* [כִּי] Cain is avenged seven times, then Lamech seventy-seven times. (Gen 4:24)
7. **Concession.** For you shall drive out the Canaanites, *though* [כִּי] they have chariots of iron, and *though* (כִּי) they are strong. (Josh 17:18 ESV)

8. **Result.** How have I wronged you *that* [כִּי] you have brought such great guilt upon me and upon my kingdom?" (Gen 20:9)

9. **Nominalizing.** This function causes a clause to be treated like a noun. You will not certainly die. . . . For God knows *that* [כִּי] when you eat from it your eyes will be opened. (Gen 3:4–5)[4]

10. **Emphasis.** This is really an adverbial function rather than a conjunctive function. I will *surely* [כִּי] bless you. (Gen 22:17)

אִם   Among the possible functions are the following:

11. **Condition**—of a real condition. *If* [אִם] you go to the left, I'll go to the right; *if* [אִם] you go the right, I'll go to the left. (Gen 13:9)

12. **Concession.** *Though* [אִם] I were innocent, I could not answer him." (Job 9:15)

13. **Alternative.** This is a coordinating function used in questions to mark the second question; sometimes left untranslated. Will a son be born to a man a hundred years old? Will [אִם untranslated] Sarah bear a child at the age of ninety? (Gen 17:17)

כִּי אִם This word cluster can work in two ways. First, each conjunction can work independently to introduce two clauses having the respective meanings listed above. Second, the two conjunctions can work together as one compound.

14. As **two separate conjunctions**, each introducing separate clauses. *For if* [כִּי אִם] you refuse to let them go and [וְ] still hold them, behold, the hand of the LORD will fall with a very severe plague. (Exod 9:2–3 ESV)

Notice in the ESV that the *For* (כִּי) introduces the main clause, which is found in v. 3: "behold, the hand of the Lord will fall with a very severe plague." The *if* (אִם) introduces the two conditional clauses in v. 2, which incidentally are connected by *waw* conjunction. Flowcharting this is quite helpful.

In the chart I have added elements that are assumed (a.k.a. ellipses) and enclosed them in brackets. I've also included function labels. And we can compare two versions. We will explain the labels in future chapters. For now, pay special attention to the conjunctions. In these charts, the conjunctions are bolded instead of the clause subjects.

---

4. To illustrate the "nominalizing" function, notice that if you replace the whole clause "*that* when you eat of it" with a simple noun such as "the man," the sentence still makes sense ("God knows the man"). The entire כִּי clause is functioning as though it were a noun.

FIGURE 7.7: Flowcharting Coordinating and Subordinating Conjunctions

Function	Vs	Flowchart: Exod 9:2–3 (ESV)			
Explanation		**For**			
Condition (1)	2		**if** you refuse	→ to let them go	
Addition			**and**		
Condition (2)				hold	→ them
Continuing				still	
Exclamation		behold,			
Anticipatory		the hand …	will fall		
Possessor	3	^of the Lord			
Instrument			with a very severe plague.		

Function	Vs	Flowchart: Exod 9:2–3 (NIV)			
Condition (1)	2	**If** you refuse	→ to let	→ them go	
Addition			**and**		
Condition (2)			continue	→ to hold	→ them back
Anticipatory		the hand …	will bring	→ a terrible plague.	
Possessor	3	^of the Lord			

In the previous verse, Moses is telling Pharaoh of the Lord's demand to let the Israelites go to worship him. The כִּי explains that judgment from the Lord described in v. 3 will come about if the two intervening conditions (v. 2) are met.

Notice that the NIV does not translate the כִּי but simply abuts v. 2 to v. 1 and does not include the exclamation at the beginning of v. 3. The logical connection to v. 1 must be figured out by the reader. The ESV, however, makes the connection with "For." Being able to identify the Hebrew behind the translations allows for more accurate interpretation.

Notice also that the *if* governs both of the first two clauses.

Being able to study the actual conjunction uses in a wordbook allows you to consider other options.

15. **Contrast** (compound conjunction indicating a stronger contrast than כִּי). This man will not be your heir, but [כִּי אִם] a son coming from your own body will be your heir. (Gen 15:4 NIV84)

The כִּי אִם marks a strong contrast.

FIGURE 7.8: Flowcharting the כִּי אִם Compound Conjunction			
Function	**Vs**	**Flowchart: Gen 15:4 (NIV84)**	
Anticipatory (neg)		This man will not be → your heir	
Contrast Anticipatory Description Source	4	**but** a son ... will be → your heir. ^coming from your own body	

Comparing Versions

At this point you are able to do some pretty sophisticated Bible study. You can compare versions and use a software interlinear for help. Because Hebrew uses the conjunction *waw* so often, and because its most common meaning is addition with the translation "and," translators into English face another challenge: style. Always translating the *waw* with "and" is poor style in English. To break up the monotony, translators will use different devices. Sometimes they will leave it untranslated; sometimes they will use a different conjunction. Since different conjunctions have different ranges of meaning, a reader of English paying close attention to the connecting words may infer a meaning from the English that is not intended in Hebrew.

For example, in Exod 3:16–17, the Lord tells Moses to speak to the elders of Israel the Lord's message. In that message is a series of clauses, which I summarize below.

KJV	I have surely visited you,	and seen that which is done	And I have said, I will bring you up
NIV	I have watched over you	and have seen what has been done	And I have promised to bring you up
ESV	I have observed you	and what has been done	and I promise that I will bring you up
NASB	I am indeed concerned about you	and what has been done	So I said, I will bring you up

There are several differences you notice, and we will come to these in time. Right now I want you to focus on the beginning of the third clause, which is the beginning of v. 17. Of the eight conjunctions, *and* is used seven times. The *and* used to introduce the third clause suggests to most readers the function of addition. The NASB translates the last one with *so*. When you check figure 7.2, you see that *so* may function as either cause or result. Checking the context, result is the more likely meaning of the NASB. The NASB makes explicit that the result of the Lord's concern was to say that he would bring them up. Checking an interlinear reveals that v. 17 in Hebrew begins with a ו conjunction. Figure 7.5 reveals that this meaning is within the range of *waw*. You have learned that NASB might well give the sense.

If you were reading a version other than NASB, you might not have been aware of the possibility of a cause-result relationship between God's concern (v. 16) and his taking action (v. 17). Since the other versions differ from the NASB on this point, you might be wondering how to check up on this interpretation. Of course, you may read commentaries, but in the coming chapters you will learn more to help you make a decision. This is when Bible study can be rich!

Conjunctions and Flowcharting

In the last chapter, I mentioned that I treat coordinating conjunctions differently from subordinating conjunctions. I do this because subordinating conjunctions define the adverbial function of their clauses. However, when coordinating conjunctions link clauses, they do not indicate the function of the clause; they describe the link between the clauses. Now you are ready to label the functions of both coordinating conjunctions and subordinate clauses. Here are some examples from the NIV.

FIGURE 7.9: Flowcharting a Coordinating Conjunction

Function	Vs	Flowchart: Gen 12:1 (NIV84)
Addition	1	[You] Leave → your country, → your people, **and** → your father's household
Addition		**and** [you] go

> **Teaching/Learning Tip:** The implied subject of every command is *you*. Inserting a "[you]" can hold the place of the subject and make connections to more obvious.

The first "and" connects nouns in a list of direct objects (DOs), so it is indented under the noun phrase it follows. I determined that it functions as "addition" and wrote "Addition" in the "Function" column parallel to its occurrence. The second "and" joins two main clauses, so it is indented above the clause that it introduces. Again, it functions as adding a command, so I wrote "Addition" in the "Function" column.

Function	Vs	Flowchart: Lev 19:2
Command		[You] be holy,
	2	↑
Cause		because I... am ⟺holy

FIGURE 7.10: Flowcharting a Subordinating Conjunction

This is a complex sentence with two clauses. The subordinating conjunction *because* introduces a subordinate clause indicating cause. The clause is indented and an arrow points to the modified word. In the "Function" column I wrote "Cause"; I also indented the entry because the clause is indented. This is not necessary. If you find this helpful to the eye, do it. These flowcharts are intended to be a tool for you, not a straitjacket. Feel free to modify the techniques presented here as you like.

Comparing Versions

Here is an example of the value of comparing versions. First, I display four common translations of Lev 19:5. Then I list all the Hebrew and English conjunctions and compare the translations, labeling the function below each. Finally, I explain the varying interpretations of the translations.

Comparing Translations of Conjunctions in Lev 19:5

Version	Lev 19:5
KJV	**And if** ye offer a sacrifice of peace offerings unto the Lord, ye shall offer it at your own will.
NIV	**When** you sacrifice a fellowship offering to the Lord, sacrifice it in such a way **that** it will be accepted on your behalf."
ESV	**When** you offer a sacrifice of peace offerings to the Lord, you shall offer it **so that** you may be accepted."
NASB	**Now when** you offer a sacrifice of peace offerings to the Lord, you shall offer it **so that** you may be accepted.'

Hebrew Conjunctions in Lev 19:5

Hebrew	KJV	NIV	ESV	NASB
וְ	And Addition	[none] —	[none] —	Now Result
כִּי	if Condition	When Time	When Time	when Time
[none]	[none]	that Result	so that Result	so that Result

Explanation of Translation Differences

All of these translations are valid. Remember from ch. 4 that we said, "every translation is an interpretation." Here are some observations on this challenging passage.

1. On וְ:
   a. The Hebrew connects v. 5 to what precedes, probably v. 4. The KJV translating with "and" is about as broad as the Hebrew but clearly marks the connection. The English naturally suggests addition, in which case v. 5 is adding to the prohibition of idolatry the offering of peace offerings in the correct manner. Checking the list of uses of *waw* allows you more options to consider.
   b. Neither the NIV nor the ESV explicitly translates the *waw*. This is equally broad to the KJV but adds one more option: without a conjunction the reader might think v. 5 starts a new topic unconnected to the previous.
   c. The NASB "now" shows a connection. *Now* might indicate result, in which case the offering of peace offerings is somehow the corollary of not turning to or making idols. It might instead introduce the first of a series of commands on correct worship.
2. On כִּי:
   a. The KJV "if" marks a condition, and the English implies the offering of a peace offering was optional.
   b. All the other versions have "when," which implies that the peace offering is assumed.

Interpretation of this verse involves more than just examining these two conjunctions, but we want to understand why the translations differ. Knowing how Hebrew conjunctions work enables you to understand and use information in interlinear Bibles and wordbooks and consider ranges of meaning more carefully. Now you are ready to read commentaries and better understand the issues and arguments involved.

What about Aramaic?

Aramaic conjunctions work the same way. Some conjunctions (cjs) are identical to Hebrew. The וְ is the same, until we get to the uses in the verbal system, as we shall see in unit 5 on the verbal system. Figure 7.11 is a quick summary of comparison of cjs not counting uses of וְ. Please note that this oversimplifies correspondences, but the aim is to show that some cjs are common to both Hebrew and Aramaic, but more often there are differences.

FIGURE 7.11: Common Hebrew and Aramaic Conjunctions

Hebrew	G/K	English	Aramaic	G/K
אוֹ	196	or	אוֹ	targ
כִּי	3954	since, but	אֲרֵי	targ
כִּי אִם	3954 + 561	but	אֱלָהֵן	targ
—	—	but, except	לָהֵן	10386
אַךְ	421	but, however	בְּרַם	10124
לָהֵן	4270	so, therefore	לָהֵן	10385
אִם	561	if	הֵן	10213

Figure 7.11 lists the Hebrew conjunctions discussed above with their corresponding G/K numbers and an English gloss. I've added לָהֵן, which occurs only twice in the Hebrew Bible but has a common Aramaic equivalent. The final two columns are Aramaic words corresponding to the Hebrew cjs. Accompanying them are G/K numbers. When there is no equivalent in Biblical Aramaic, targumic equivalents are given. Notice that in the targums there are no composite *shewas*, so אֲרֵי and אֱלָהֵן are spelled correctly (targums use different symbols for the vowels).

Advanced Information and Curious Facts

A little more on numbers. When you learned the alphabet, you learned that the letters were also used as numbers. The Greeks inherited this system and even retained some Semitic letters that they did not use except for numbers. Here they are:

FIGURE 7.12: Comparing Hebrew and Greek Alphanumerics

Hebrew	Number	Greek	Hebrew	Number	Greek	Hebrew	Number	Greek
א	1	α´	י	10	ι´	ק	100	ρ´
ב	2	β´	כ	20	κ´	ר	200	σ´
ג	3	γ´	ל	30	λ´	שׁ	300	τ´
ד	4	δ´	מ	40	μ´	ת	400	υ´
ה	5	ε´	נ	50	ν´		500	φ´
ו	6	ϝ´	ס	60	ξ´		600	χ´
ז	7	ζ´	ע	70	ο´		700	ψ´
ח	8	η´	פ	80	π´		800	ω´
ט	9	θ´	צ	90	ϟ´		900	ϡ´

For the number 6, the Semitic *waw* (transliterated into Greek as *wau*) was retained and the shape it took looked like two stacked gammas, so that the name of the letter was *digamma* ("double-gamma"). Notice that the Hebrew and Greek get out of alignment at number 90. The Greek letter is *koppa* and corresponds to the Hebrew *qoph*. Letters were added to the Greek alphabet to indicate sounds not in Hebrew. At 900 they added the letter *sampi* (i.e., *san* + *pi*; scholars suggest *san* was another /s/ or /ts/ sound). It corresponded either to the Semitic *tsade* or to the *shin/sin*.[5]

Bonus fun fact #1. If you have seen the series on the life of Jesus called *The Chosen* (I highly recommend it; at the point of this writing, season two, episode three is just released), perhaps you have noticed the name of the parent company, Loaves & Fishes. The logo for the company looks something like the figure below.

בה

Loaves & Fishes

What is the meaning of the Hebrew? It cannot be abbreviations for the Hebrew of the English translation; the word for "loaves" would be לֶחֶם (for the singular used as a collective plural, see ch. 9), and the word for "fishes" would be דָּגִים, and none of the letters match. Here's a hint: read the Hebrew left to right. Have you figured it out yet?

If you need it, here's another hint: think of the letters representing numbers (and ignore the *dagesh* in the *bet*).

Now you know it: five loaves and two fishes. The *he* and the *bet* are read left to right so that the numbers line up with the English words below them.

Bonus fun fact #2. In the "Advanced Information" section in the previous chapter, we asked questions about Pss 9–10. Here are two suggestions:

1. Ps 9:5 begins with ג, but there is no verse beginning with *dalet*. However, did you notice that the last letter of v. 5 is a *dalet*. Perhaps that is on purpose.
2. Ps 10:2–11 is a description of the wicked. These verses are excluded from the acrostic. Perhaps this omission is symbolic of their being excluded from the Lord's people and from his care.

---

5. Franco Montanari, "σάν," *The Brill Dictionary of Ancient Greek* (Leiden; Boston: Brill, 2015), for the *sin/shin* origin, and A. N. Jannaris, *An Historical Greek Grammar: Chiefly of the Attic Dialect* (London: Macmillan, 1897), §§2–3, holds to the *tsade* origin.

CHAPTER 8

LET'S NOT GET AHEAD OF!
Prepositions

Objectives
1. Identify a prepositional phrase both in English and in Hebrew.
2. Understand that Hebrew has prepositions that may be independent words or prefixed to other words.
3. Identify Hebrew prepositions.
4. Identify the functions of prepositions for English and Hebrew.
5. Compare and explain differences between English translations.
6. Flowchart prepositional phrases and adverbs.

Tools Used: Grammatically tagged computer interlinear or paper interlinear and Davidson

Introduction

Which word are you most likely to look up in a dictionary: "occlusion" or "of"? The answer is, of course, the word with which you are least familiar, probably "occlusion." But which do you suppose has the longest, most complicated entry in your dictionary? It may surprise you that it is the little word that has the bigger definition. The reason for this is because prepositions have such a wide range of meaning. The same is true in Hebrew. Translating them can be difficult and depends on a number of different factors. Not only that, but the range of meaning of a given English preposition is normally very different from the range of meaning of a given Hebrew preposition.

In this chapter, I want to show you a little more about word formation and how this affects Hebrew vocabulary as well as modern study, especially the arrangement of lexicons and the performance of word studies.

English Prepositions

Remember that a clause is made up of a subject and a predicate (something that contains a verb or finite verbal idea) and a phrase is a word or word group that does not contain a predicate, i.e., no finite verb (and therefore no grammatical subject). There are mainly three types of phrases: infinitival phrases, participial phrases, and prepositional phrases. In this chapter, we cover only the last of these.

The word preposition (abbreviated "Pp") means "placed (-position) before (pre-)"; i.e., a Pp is placed before its object (usually a noun or pronoun). A Pp plus its object constitutes a prepositional phrase (abbreviated PPhr) The symbol "(T)" refers to an optional article. This is illustrated in figure 8.1.

FIGURE 8.1: Structure of Prepositional Phrases

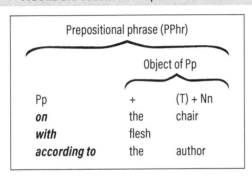

There are a few things to notice:

1. The article may be present between the Pp and the object of the Pp but is not required.
2. The object of the Pp is in the objective case. English nouns are not inflected for case, but pronouns are. "He" is a pronoun in the subjective case; the objective case is "him." The Pp is followed by the objective case, "him," rather than the subjective case, "he."
3. Sometimes a word group, such as "according to," functions as a Pp. We may call these *compound prepositions.*

The function of a Pp is to show the relationship between two words: the object of the preposition and another word outside of the PPhr. The other word may be either a noun or a verb. You need to conceive of the PPhr as an unbreakable unit. The role of the interpreter is twofold. You need to identify the word that the PPhr modifies, and you need to identify the function of the preposition; in other words, describe how the two words are related.

Below is a list of common English prepositions and the functions they can have. Words that may also function as conjunctions are marked with an asterisk (*). Note that the preposition "of" is so flexible that it is treated separately. See ch. 11 on the construct state.

The only way to become familiar with prepositional phrases is to work with them. You should read over the list of prepositions until you can identify them in a text. Some prepositions may be used as conjunctions. You can tell the difference by looking to see what comes after the word. If it is a phrase (without a verb), it is a preposition. If it is a clause (with a verb), it is a conjunction.

FIGURE 8.2: English Prepositions and Functions

Word	Function	Word	Function
about	Measure/degree	of	(see ch. 11)
above	Place	off	Place
according to	Cause	on	Place
across	Place	on account of	Cause
after*	Time	only*	Restriction
against	Dis/advantage, Place	out of	Cause, Composition, Source
among	Association	over	Place
around	Place, Reference/Respect	since*	Time
at	Place, Time	by means of	Agency/Means, Instrument
because of	Cause	contrary to	Dis/advantage
before*	Place, Time	down	Place
behind	Place	during	Time
below	Place	except	Restriction
beneath	Place	for the sake of	Cause
beside	Place	for*	Dis/advantage, Price
between	Place	from	Source, Separation
by	Agency/Means, Place	in	Place/Sphere
in accordance with	Cause	through	Agency/means, Destination
in front of	Place	to	Destination, Purpose, Reference/Respect
in regard to	Reference/Respect	toward	Destination
in spite of	Concession	under	Place
inside	Place	until*	Extent, Time
instead of	Alternative/Substitution	up	Place
into	Place	upon	Place
like	Comparison	with	Association, Instrument
near	Place		

Hebrew Prepositions

Structure of Hebrew Prepositional Phrases

The order of the words in a Hebrew PPhr is the same as in English: Pp-(T)-object of the Pp. However, there are two ways they appear, either as prefixes or as independent words. Prepositions that are prefixed are called inseparable prepositions because they never appear as independent words. Prepositions that are independent words are called separable prepositions.

Only three Pps are inseparable.[1]

בְּ "in, with, by"	כְּ "like, as, according to"	לְ "to, for"

FIGURE 8.3: Attaching Inseparable Prepositions to Nouns

Noun	Preposition	Prep Phrase	Transliteration	Translation
מֶלֶךְ	בְּ	בְּמֶלֶךְ	bəmelek	with a king
מֶלֶךְ	כְּ	כְּמֶלֶךְ	kəmelek	like a king
מֶלֶךְ	לְ	לְמֶלֶךְ	ləmelek	for a king

Most prepositions are "separable"; i.e., they stand alone. They may or may not be joined by a *maqqeph* (see example three below) with no change in meaning. Here are some examples:

FIGURE 8.4: Separable Prepositions before Nouns

Hebrew	Transliteration	Translation
לִפְנֵי מֶלֶךְ	lifnê melek	before a king
עַל בַּיִת	ʻal bayit	on a house
אֶל־בַּיִת	ʼel bayit	to a house

The Pp לִפְנֵי is actually a compound preposition comprised of לְ and פְנֵי meaning formally, "to the face of."

One preposition can be either inseparable or separable, again with no difference in meaning:

FIGURE 8.5: The Preposition מִן

Hebrew	Transliteration	Translation
מִן־מֶלֶךְ	min-melek	from a king
מִמֶּלֶךְ	mimmelek	from a king

In the first example, מִן may or may not be followed by a *maqqeph*. In the second example, notice that the *nun* of the preposition has been assimilated into the first root letter of the noun and is represented by the *dagesh forte*. There is no difference in the meaning of the preposition מִן with either spelling.

---

1. There are also long forms for בְּ, כְּ, and לְ: בְּמוֹ, כְּמוֹ, and לְמוֹ, respectively. בְּמוֹ and כְּמוֹ are prefixed Pps; לְמוֹ is an independent one.

Any of the Pps can have a pronominal suffix attached. The way these attachments are made is beyond what we are doing here. Books and computers that give you parsing information will identify these for you.

Looking into the future: In this chapter we are looking at prepositional phrases with nominals. In ch. 17 we will see how they can also function with Hebrew infinitives. It will be good to review these again there.

Some Functions of a Few Hebrew Prepositions

Of the top eight most frequent words in the Hebrew Bible, prepositions occupy five spots, a total of nearly 55,000 occurrences between them! This doesn't include the sign of the direct object, which has a structure like prepositions but basically has only one function. Here are the top five prepositions and a few of their main uses.

לְ

1. **Marker of Indirect Object (IO)**
   God gave [untranslated לְ; the NIV marks the IO with English word order] Solomon wisdom and very great insight. (1 Kgs 4:29 [Hebrew 5:9] NIV)

   Notice that what was given was wisdom and great insight. These are the direct objects. Solomon received them and is therefore the indirect object.

2. **Place** (אֶל [see below] is much more common to mark place than simple לְ, though לְ in compounds is commonly used for place or direction)
   He has just come *to* [לְ] our town today. (1 Sam 9:12 NIV)

3. **Dis/advantage**
   . . . for there is no pasture *for* [לְ] your servants' flocks. (Gen 47:4 ESV)

4. **Reference/Respect**
   Come, we must deal shrewdly *with* [לְ] them. (Exod 1:10 NIV; ESV also renders the preposition "with.")

5. **Time**
   Sarah became pregnant and bore a son to Abraham *in* [לְ] his old age, *at* [לְ] the very time God had promised him." (Gen 21:2 NIV)

6. **Possession**
   . . . the cupbearer and the baker *of* [לְ] the king of Egypt (Gen 40:5 NIV)

7. **Purpose**
   God intended it *for* [לְ] good. (Gen 50:20 NIV)

By day the LORD went ahead of them in a pillar of cloud *to* [לְ] guide them on their way and by night in a pillar of fire *to* [לְ] give them light, so that they could travel by day or night. (Exod 13:21 NIV)

In the first example, the Pp לְ is attached to a nominal (technically, this is an adjective being used as a noun), and in the second example the לְ marks an infinitive, just as *to* commonly does in English. Most often these expressions with the infinitive in both Hebrew and English indicate purpose. We will see more on this in ch. 17.

בְּ

1. **Place**

    They [the animals] are given *into* [בְּ] your hands. (Gen 9:2 NIV)

    . . . everything *in* [בְּ] it will be unclean. (Lev 11:33 NIV)

    See, the ark of the covenant of the Lord of all the earth will go *into* [בְּ] the Jordan ahead of you. (Josh 3:11 NIV)

2. **Time** [140 times]: "*in* [בְּ] the morning."

    Abram was seventy-five years old *when* [בְּ] he set out from Harran. (Gen 12:4 NIV)

    In the first example, the Pp בְּ is used with a noun that has to do with time. In the second example, the בְּ is attached to an infinitive. We will see more on this in ch. 17.

3. **Accompaniment**

    Arriving at Jerusalem *with* [בְּ] a very great caravan. (1 Kgs 10:2 NIV)

4. **Dis/advantage**

    . . . and, if war breaks out, [they] will . . . fight *against* [בְּ] us. (Exod 1:10 NIV)

5. **Instrument**

    With [בְּ] a donkey's jawbone I have made donkeys of them. (Judg 15:16 NIV)

6. **Agency/Means**

    Whoever sheds human blood, *by* [בְּ] humans shall their blood be shed. (Gen 9:6 NIV)

7. **Cause**

    Surely these things happened to Judah according to the LORD's command, in order to remove them from his presence *because of* [בְּ] the sins of Manasseh. (2 Kgs 24:3 NIV)

מִן

1. Separation

Wash me thoroughly *from* [מִן] my iniquity and cleanse me *from* [מִן] my sin. (Ps 51:2 ESV)

Depart *from* [מִן] me, all you workers of evil. (Ps 6:8 [Hebrew 6:9] ESV)

2. Source

Envoys will come *from* [מִן] Egypt. (Ps 68:31 [Hebrew 68:32] NIV)

3. Cause

I will multiply thy seed exceedingly, that it shall not be numbered *for* [מִן] multitude. (Gen 16:10 KJV)

The word *for* here clearly means "because of."

4. Comparison

Because the portion of the people of Judah was *too* large *for* [מִן] them, the people of Simeon obtained an inheritance in the midst of their inheritance. (Josh 19:9 ESV)

Better [טוֹב] is one day in your courts *than* [מִן] a thousand elsewhere. (Ps 84:10 [Hebrew 84:11] NIV)

A word-for-word translation of the Hebrew of Ps 84:11 is "Good is . . . from . . . ." This illustrates the most common way that Hebrew expresses comparison, i.e., an adjective followed by a מִן Pp.

5. Whole (a.k.a. partitive)

And they took them wives *of* [מִן] all which they chose. (Gen 6:2 KJV)

The "whole" is represented by the object of the Pp, *all*. The "part" is represented by the word "wives."

עַל

1. Place

God gave Solomon . . . a breadth of understanding as measureless as the sand *on* [עַל] the seashore. (1 Kgs 4:29 [Hebrew 5:9] NIV)

The [kings] . . . encamped *before* [עַל] Gibeon, and made war against it. (Josh 10:5 KJV)

More modern translations take this example as disadvantage. See below.

2. **Dis/advantage**

They, [i.e., the kings] . . . encamped *against* [עַל] Gibeon and made war *against* [עַל] it. (Josh 10:5 ESV)

Compare: They, [i.e., the kings] . . . took up positions *against* [עַל] Gibeon and attacked it." (Josh 10:5 NIV)

3. **Cause**

You are as good as dead *because of* [עַל] the woman you have taken; she is a married woman. (Gen 20:3 NIV)

אֶל

1. **Destination**

And [God] brought them *to* [אֶל] the man. (Gen 2:19 NIV)

2. **Place**

When I came *to* [אֶל] the spring today, I said (Gen 24:42 NIV)

3. **Indirect Object**

He gave them *to* [אֶל] two of his servants, and they carried them ahead of Gehazi. (2 Kgs 5:23 NIV)

Perhaps the most common occurrence of this use is in the expression: "[A] said *to* [B]. . . ," in which אֶל is commonly found after verbs of speaking indicating the person spoken to. The quotation of the words spoken actually functions as the DO of the verb, which the addressee receives.

4. **Dis/advantage**

Cain rose up *against* [אֶל] his brother Abel and killed him. (Gen 4:8 ESV)

Prepositions Changing the Meaning of Verbs

Some prepositions can be used in combination with a verb to change the meaning. When they do that, they may be understood as introducing a DO. English does this as well. For example, if you tell me, "I *worked* today," I imagine you going to a job. But if you say, "I *worked out* today," I know that you exercised. In such situations, I like to keep the verb and preposition together as the verb phrase; *work* and *work out* simply do not mean the same thing.

In Hebrew similar things happen. שָׁמַע is a verb meaning "to hear" and may take a DO. For example, in Gen 3:8, "The man and his wife *heard* [שָׁמַע] the sound of the LORD God as he was walking in the garden" (NIV). On the other hand, when this verb is followed by the Pp בְּ, as in שָׁמַע בְּ, the expression means "to obey," and the Pp בְּ marks the DO. For example, in Gen 26:5, "because Abraham *obeyed* [שָׁמַע בְּ] my voice" (ESV), "my voice" is the object of the Pp בְּ and is the DO of the verb "obeyed" (שָׁמַע בְּ).

Comparing Versions

Scholars sometimes interpret the Hebrew prepositions differently, and this is reflected in the translations. Figure 8.6 gives an example.

FIGURE 8.6: Translations of Prepositions in Josh 2:6

Translation	Hebrew	Function	Explanation
she had … hidden them **under** the stalks of flax (NIV)	בְּ G/K 928	Location	The spies were beneath the flax
she had … hidden them **in** the stalks of flax (NASB)		Location	The spies were surrounded by flax
she … hid them **with** the stalks of flax (ESV)		Association	The spies were hidden near the flax, though may be mixed in with it

This example has no theological import, but it is instructional for seeing how different interpretations may be represented in differing translations.

Adverbs

The word *adverb* (Adv) comes from Latin: *ad-* meaning "to" and *verbum* meaning "word"; here the meaning is limited to verbs. So an adverb is a word that modifies a verb; i.e., it describes it in some way. An Adv may also modify an adjective or another adverb. Adverbs give information about time, manner, place, and degree. English has many adverbs. Commonly these words are formed by adding *-ly* to an adjective: *quick–quickly*; *slow–slowly*. Many adverbs, however, don't end in *-ly*: *when, almost, there, fast, very*, including interrogative adverbs such as *how?* Even words like *yes* and *no/not* are adverbs. Adverbs also mark "degrees," for example, *very* and *rather*.

Hebrew differs from English in that it has relatively few adverbs and it does not form comparatives in the way English does at all. However, Hebrew does have ways of expressing these ideas. First, it may use an adverb. עַתָּה is a temporal adverb meaning "now"; מְאֹד is an adverb of degree meaning "very." Second, as in English, a Pp may be used. Third, as we will see in ch. 13, Hebrew very commonly uses a simple noun to express an adverbial idea.

One more thing. I mentioned that *yes* and *no/not* are English adverbs. Biblical Hebrew has two words for *no/not* (לֹא and אַל)[2] and no word for *yes*. Naturally, you are wondering how they answer a yes or no question positively. They would repeat the key word, usually the predicate. For example, in Gen 29:6, Jacob asks about the well-being of Laban. Compare the interlinear Hebrew and the NIV:

2. There are a few more negative adverbs but they are usually used with nonfinite verbs, as we shall see in ch. 17 on nonfinite verbals.

Interlinear	שָׁלוֹם peace."	· "(It is)	וַיֹּאמְרוּ And they said,	לוֹ to him?"	הֲשָׁלוֹם "(Is) peace	לָהֶם to them,	וַיֹּאמֶר And he said
NIV	Jacob asked them, "Is he well?" "Yes, he is," they said.						

The Hebrew with a formal equivalent would be, "And he said to them, 'Does he have peace?' And they said, 'Peace.'" Notice that where English uses *yes*, Hebrew repeats the word שָׁלוֹם. Incidentally, the ל in לוֹ is an example of a ל of possession.

Flowcharting Prepositional Phrases and Adverbs

There are two things to learn in this section. We have already studied how to flowchart coordinate and subordinate clauses, but in the last two chapters we ignored prepositional phrases. We are now ready to put these into place. Prepositional phrases may modify either nouns or verbs and should be indented .25 inches above or below the word they modify.

We've worked on Gen 1:1. Now we can complete it. "In the beginning God created the heavens and the earth" (NIV).

FIGURE 8.7: Flowcharting Prepositional Phrases

Function	Vs	Flowchart: Gen 1:1		
Time				**In the beginning**
Event	1	God	created	→ the heavens
				and
				→ the earth.

This is a simple sentence; i.e., one predicate with no coordinate or subordinate clauses. Notice that "in the beginning" is a Pp of time because *beginning* in this context refers to time. The interpreter must decide which element of the clause it modifies: subject, verb, or DO. Though all three are possible grammatically (remember that a PPhr may modify either a verb or a noun), the one that makes the best sense is the verb. Therefore, I indented the Pp about .25 inches to the right of the verb; I left it above the main clause, because doing that retains English word order.

FIGURE 8.8: Flowcharting Adverbial Phrases

Function	Vs	Flowchart: Gen 1:1		
Time				**In the beginning**
Event	1	God	created	→ the heavens
Addition				and
DO2				→ the earth.

Notice also that I've now added the functions in the first column. I indented "Time," because the Pp is indented. To the far left I assigned the function "Event" for the independent clause. You will learn more about functions in ch. 13.

Adverbial phrases are flowcharted the same way PPhrs are: indented .25 inches above or below what they modify.

What about Aramaic?

Prepositions in Aramaic function the same way as they do in Hebrew. Aramaic has the same three inseparable propositions בְּ, כְּ, לְ, and מִן functions the same way as it does in Hebrew. There are independent and compound prepositions, most of them identical to the Hebrew ones. Some are spelled differently. For example, the Aramaic אֲתַר, corresponding to the Hebrew relative pronoun אֲשֶׁר, is used in the compound preposition בָּאתַר meaning "after."

Adverbs also function the same way as they do in Hebrew.

Advanced Information and Curious Facts

Almost everyone knows that the Hebrew word הַלְלוּ יָהּ *hallelujah* (or *halleluiah* or *halleluyah*) means "praise the LORD." Perhaps you've noticed the spelling *alleluia*. Why?

The answer has to do with the Hebrew and Greek alphabets (you may wish to consult figure 7.12). Remember that all the letters of the Hebrew alphabet are consonants, and both the Hebrews and Greeks got their alphabet from the Phoenicians. The Greeks, however, turned some of the consonants they did not need into vowels and added some new symbols to signify sounds the original alphabet did not have.

The Hebrew consonant *he* became the Greek vowel *epsilon*. Except for archaic inscriptions, the Greeks rarely marked the /h/ sound with a letter. At times they used a breathing mark (later called a rough breathing mark) to indicate this sound. By the fifth century BC, these breathing marks disappear from inscriptions. By the beginning of the fourth century BC, the /h/ sound dropped out of pronunciation and soon ceased to be marked at all, except in historical spellings. The current system of breathing marks in printed Greek New Testaments originated in the Hellenistic period after about 300 BC and was fully developed in the Byzantine period beginning in the seventh century AD, including the rough breathing mark. [3] The Greeks transliterated halleluiah as ἀλληλουϊά, with the rough breathing mark (') above the first letter *alpha*. The English transliteration is *hallēlouia* with the *h* representing the rough breathing mark. Latin, which does have the letter *h*, transliterated the word *alleluja/alleluia*.

So, *hallelujah* is Hebrew. *Alleluia* is Greek before the Byzantine period and Latin.

---

3. See A. N. Jannaris, *An Historical Greek Grammar* (London: Macmillan, 1897), §§70–75.

CHAPTER 9

WHAT'S IN A NAME?

Overview of Nominals

Objectives
1. Identify various types of nominals.
2. Explain similarities and differences between Hebrew nouns and English nouns.
3. Use information found in analytical lexicons and exhaustive concordances.

Tools Used: Grammatically tagged computer interlinear or paper interlinear and Davidson

Introduction

Back in ch. 5 we categorized Hebrew words into three basic classes: nominals, verbals, and function words. For convenience, figure 9.1 reproduces figure 5.1:

FIGURE 9.1: Hebrew Parts of Speech		
Nominals	**Verbals**	**Function Words**
Noun	Verb	Article
Pronoun	Infinitive (Verbal Noun)	Conjunction
Adjective	Participle (Verbal Adjective)	Preposition
		Adverb

Unit 3 covered conjunctions and prepositions. This unit deals with nominals and the article. In this chapter we will study nouns; ch. 10 features the article and the concept of definiteness, or as we will call it, determination; ch. 11 gives more detail on nouns and pronouns; finally, ch. 12 covers adjectives.

Nominals and Nouns

A "nominal" is any word that functions as a noun. What besides a noun can function as a noun? Well, pronouns, adjectives, participles, infinitives, prepositional phrases, or even a number. Eventually we will understand that even clauses can function as nouns. For now, however, we will limit our discussion to the basic parts of speech.

A noun is the name of a person, place, or thing. In fact, the Latin word for *noun* is *nomen* (compare with the word *nominal* above), and the Greek word is *onoma*, both of which are nouns meaning "name." Names of persons and places are "proper nouns." We capitalize these in English; e.g., *Sam, Evelyn; Chicago, New York*. Names of things are common nouns. English used to capitalize these but no longer does. The "thing" may be either concrete (something you can experience with your senses, such as *flower* or *the sun*), or it may be abstract (something you can only think of, such as beauty or friendship). Note also that the thing may refer to a person, but the emphasis will be on what type of "thing" the person is: *police officer, teacher, preacher*.

Hebrew nouns have five basic qualities: gender, number, state, case, and definiteness. In this chapter we treat gender and number, in the next chapter determination (similar to definiteness), and in chapter 11 state and case.

Here I reproduce figure 5.2.

FIGURE 9.2: Parsing Information for Nominals and Verbals

PtSp	Word	Lex	Verbal Qualities						Nominal Qualities			
			Stem	Form	P	G	N		State	Det	Case	Suff
Nn						X	X		X	X	X	
V			X	X	X	X	X					

In ch. 5 we gave an overview of the meaning of the items in this figure. Let's look at these nominal qualities in more detail.

Gender

Gender is a categorization of the various forms of nouns. Various languages have three genders labeled masculine, feminine, and neuter (which means "neither" [masculine nor feminine]). The term *common* is used for words that can be any gender without distinction.

The English system of gender is not very well defined. English pronouns carefully preserve gender, but most native English nouns do not, though some words, mostly foreign, may retain a gender-distinctive ending.

FIGURE 9.3: Gender in English Nouns

Gender	Pronouns	Nouns
Masculine (m)	he	boy, stallion, waiter
Feminine (f)	she	girl, mare, waitress
Neuter (n)	it	house
Common (c)	I, we, you, they	horse, server

Some words maintain gender loosely. For example, *car* can be neuter ("That's my car; I just waxed *it*.") or feminine ("That's my car; boy, can *she* fly!"). *Hurricane* used to be feminine, but, because of recent gender sensitivity, now has a common gender (the proper names alternating between masculine and feminine).

Unlike English, Hebrew has a careful system of gender. A Hebrew noun is either masculine or feminine; there is no neuter (unlike English and Greek). A noun never changes gender, though there are a few nouns with common gender.

It is essential to realize that grammatical gender is a separate quality from biological sex. It is true that words referring to males are normally masculine (e.g., אִישׁ, meaning "man") and words referring to females (e.g., אִשָּׁה, meaning "woman") are normally feminine, but that is not always the case. For example, the word רוּחַ is usually feminine in gender and frequently masculine (e.g., 1 Kgs 18:12 in which Spirit is the subject of a masculine verb; see ch. 13 if you can't wait to find out what a "masculine verb" is). It most commonly means "wind, spirit, Spirit (as in "of the LORD")." Event though רוּחַ is usually feminine, in none of these cases is the entity female.

Number

Number is the grammatical quality of singularity or plurality. English nouns have two numbers: singular and plural, normally indicated by adding *-s* or *-es*.

FIGURE 9.4: Number in English			
singular	= one	noun + *no* ending	horse
plural	= two or more	noun + **s** ending	horse**s**

Words that come from foreign languages may retain their original plural form or they may eventually conform to English. For example, *index* is a Latin word that English adopted. The Latin plural is *indices* and English kept that. In recent years, however, English has brought *index* into conformity with the regular pattern and *indexes* is now an accepted term. Then English has its irregular plurals. The plural of *goose* is *geese*, but the plural of *moose* is not *meese*. The plural of *ox* is *oxen*, but the plural of *box* is not *boxen*. Furthermore, some English nouns do not have a singular form. For example, in the evening you might watch the news, but one story is not "the new." Then, if you're getting rid of odds and ends and you only have one left, what do you call it? (An old, corny joke, but I like it.)

Hebrew nouns have three numbers: singular, dual, and plural. The dual forms refer to two items as opposed to three or more items indicated by the plural. By the time of Biblical Hebrew, however, dual forms were restricted to things that come in natural pairs, such as eyes or ears. The plural forms, then, can refer to two or more, as in English.

FIGURE 9.5: Number in Hebrew

singular (s)	= one
dual (d)	= two
plural (p)	= two or more

Hebrew uses the grammatical quality of number in a couple of different ways.

1. **Numeric singular.** As in English, the Hebrew singular is commonly used for what we might call a "numeric singular," i.e., one individual.

2. **Collective singular.** Also, as in English, some nouns are collectives; i.e., a grammatically singular noun for a plural number. An example common to both English and Hebrew is *sheep*, צֹאן, which may be either a "numeric" singular or collective plural.

The plural number may be used in three ways in Hebrew.

1. **Numeric plural.** The plural number is used numerically like English, simply to mean more than one. This is by far the most common use, but there are two other uses that are important.

2. **Honorific plural.** The plural in Hebrew can be used to indicate majesty or some kind of intensive idea. Numerous examples exist, especially terms for God but also terms for humans. For example, in Isa 1:3, "the trough of its *master*,"[1] the word for "its master," בְּעָלָיו, is a grammatical plural, as though it were "its masters," but refers to one master. The most prominent example is treated in the "Advanced Information" section at the end of this chapter.

3. **Abstract plural.** Sometimes nouns are pluralized to convert them to an abstract idea. For example, נַעַר means "boy, lad, youth"; נְעָרִים can be a numeric plural, but is also used to mean the abstract idea of "youthfulness." In Jer 3:4 the Lord says to his rebellious people, "Have you not just called to me, 'My Father, my friend from my youth . . . ?'" (NIV). Using the electronic or book tools that we have studied reveals that the word translated "youth" is a masculine plural noun. If it were a numeric plural, then the meaning would be, "My Father, a friend from among my boys." Clearly the Lord is not one of Israel's young boys!

Now for the big question: how can you tell which function of the plural is being used? Most of the time the context makes this clear. But some passages are difficult and you as a pre-Hebrew student are not able to tell. You will have to leave this to the professionals. However, simple awareness of the concept makes it easier to comprehend differences in translations and discussions in commentaries.

---

1. This is my translation for sake of clarity, but this grammatical point is followed in published translations.

The Absolute State

Besides number and gender, Hebrew nouns appear in either of two "states," absolute or construct. Briefly, *construct* nouns are those that are constructed to or bound to a following noun; we will deal with this issue when we study noun cases in ch. 11. The absolute state is simple because this is similar to an English noun. Nouns are called *absolute* because they can stand alone; they are not bound to a following noun.

The lexical form of a noun is the singular, absolute form. This means that whenever you look up a noun in *SNIVEC* or other Bible study resources, the form that appears is the lexical form. On rare occasions the lexical form will be plural. This occurs because there are a few nouns that do not occur in the singular. So grammarians must decide whether to make the lexical form singular, even though it doesn't exist, or leave it plural.

Summary

1. Hebrew nouns have five qualities: gender, number, state, case, and determination.
2. Hebrew nouns are either masculine (m), feminine (f), or common (c).
3. Hebrew nouns are either singular (s), plural (p), or dual (d).
   a. Singular nouns may be numeric singulars or collectives.
   b. Plural nouns are usually numeric plurals. But two other important uses are the honorific plural and the abstract plural.
4. The lexical form of a noun is the singular, absolute form.

What about Aramaic?

The qualities of gender, number, and the absolute state are identical with Hebrew, though word formation may differ, as we will see in coming chapters. It is sufficient to show some examples of number. In the examples below, forms both with and without the article will be given (you'll learn why in ch. 12).

Singular

1. **Numeric:** מֶלֶךְ, מַלְכָּא *king*
2. **Collective:** אֶנֶב, אִנְבֵּה fruit[2]

Plural

1. **Numeric:** מַלְכִין, מַלְכַיָּא *kings*
2. **Honorific:** This is not as common in Aramaic. In Dan 7 עֶלְיוֹנִין, the honorific plural form, is used to refer to the one true God in vv. 18, 22, 25, 27.

---

2. In OT Aramaic, the form with the article occurs only in Dan 4:9[E12], 11[E14], 18[E21] and always as אִנְבֵּה with the *he*-form of the article (this form is also found in the DSS, e.g., 1QapGen ar [Genesis Apocryphon] XIII, 17). In the targums, however, typically this is אִנְבָּא with the regular *aleph*-form of the article.

Aramaic parts of the OT do not have any clear examples, but of course this is a small amount of literature. The plural forms אֱלָהִין, אֱלָהַיָּא, *gods*, do not occur as an honorific for the God of Israel in the Aramaic OT sections except perhaps for Dan 3:25, in the expression "Son of God" (KJV). However, most modern versions have "son of the gods," since the speech is from the mouth of Nebuchadnezzar. There is an example of an honorific plural in the targum to the Psalms at Ps 136:2 in the phrase אלהי אלהיא, "the God of [formally, the gods of] gods."

3. **Abstract:** רַחֲמִין, *compassion* (formally *wombs*)

Advanced Information and Curious Facts

Does the Word for God Teach the Trinity?

The most common word for *God* in the OT is אֱלֹהִים. It is clear that the ending on this noun is masculine plural (mp). Many Christians from the second century onward have argued that the plural form offers evidence for the doctrine of the Trinity.

Number, however, is a *grammatical* quality. We must still interpret its *function*. When אֱלֹהִים is used in passages referring to the one creator God, Jews and Christians are agreed that, since Scripture clearly teaches against polytheism, this is not a numeric plural. Nor is it an abstract. This is an example of an honorific plural, or the so-called plural of majesty. This is even more clear when the verbs used with אֱלֹהִים are verbs used with a singular subject. This conclusion rules out the possibility that the form אֱלֹהִים teaches the Trinity simply because it is a grammatical plural.

Arguments for the Trinity must be made on bases other than the fact that אֱלֹהִים is a grammatical plural form. Responsible Bible students and teachers must not take a shortcut by using inappropriate evidence to get to a desired conclusion, even if the conclusion is correct.

CHAPTER 10

BE SURE YOU READ THIS!
The Article

Objectives
1. Identify definiteness in Hebrew nominals.
2. Identify the presence or absence of the Hebrew article.
3. Identify functions of the presence or absence of the Hebrew article in English translations.
4. Distinguish between the Hebrew article and the marker for a question.

Introduction

I love old movies. One of my favorites is *The Bachelor and the Bobby-Soxer.* There is a running gag in the movie where one person (A) initiates a dialog with another (B), prompting predictable questions:

A1: "You remind me of a man."
B1: "What man?"
A2: "The man with the power."
B2: "What power?"
A3: "The power of Hoo-doo."
B3: "Who do?"
A4: "You do!"
B4: "Do what?"
A5: "Remind me of a man." .
B5: "What man?" . . .

Maybe it loses something in this book, but in the movie it's funny. In any case, this little routine illustrates one of the main functions of articles. At the beginning, A1, a character is introduced. Since his identify is not specified, he is called "*a* man"; it could be any man. But in A2 the speaker refers back to the "a man" of A1 and specifies which man. So he is referred to as "*the* man."

If a noun is indefinite, then there is no reference to a specific individual. Instead, the "thing" is viewed as any member of a class. If a noun is definite, it refers to a specific entity. The term *definiteness* is used interchangeably with the term *determination*. I will use "determination" because it refers to the quality of "definiteness" whether the article is present or not and avoids the possible confusion of "definiteness" with the presence of the "definite" article. In the parsing chart that we have seen, the presence or absence of determination is indicated in the "Det" column.

FIGURE 10.1: Parsing and Determination

| PtSp | Word | Lex | Verbal Qualities | | | | | | Nominal Qualities | | | |
			Stem	Form	P	G	N	State	Det	Case	Suff
Nn						X	X	X	X	X	
V			X	X	X	X	X				

What we will demonstrate is that, though there is overlap between the Hebrew and English definite article, the Hebrew article has additional functions.

Finally, it may seem strange that I've included the Hebrew marker for a question in this chapter (see "Objectives"). The reason for this is because Hebrew uses the consonant ה (prefixed) for both the article and the sign of the question, and this requires a little explanation.

The English Articles

English has both a definite article, *the*, and an indefinite article, *a(n)*. To express the idea of definiteness, English adds the definite article; the English article has additional functions as well. To mark indefiniteness, English may use the indefinite article for singular nouns or no article for plural nouns. Here are a few examples to illustrate.

1. I'd like to ride a bicycle.
   No particular bicycle is in view; the focus is on the action of riding.
2. I'd like to ride the bicycle.
   One particular bicycle is in view and the focus is on the individual bicycle rather than on the riding.
3. The bicycle is a cheap method of transportation.
   This is a generic use of "the"; no particular bicycle is in view, but bicycles as a class are distinguished from other types of transportation. The sentence would have meant the same thing if it had started out "A bicycle...."
4. I like to ride bicycles.
   Notice that the plural noun bicycles *has no indefinite article but is still indefinite.*

Determination

We introduced the concept of determination in ch. 5, when we surveyed the Hebrew parts of speech, and then mentioned it again in ch. 9. I am determined to treat the topic now.

All nominal words are either determined or undetermined. Determination is roughly the equivalent of definiteness. The reason I'm choosing to follow grammarians who use *determination* instead of *definiteness* is because the latter implies the presence of the article; but the article is not the only way to mark determination. There are three ways to mark determination: (1) the presence of the article, (2) the quality of being a proper noun or pronoun, or (3) to be in the construct state with a word that is determined (see ch. 11).

Proper nouns are determined because a name functions to identify an individual. All pronouns are determined because they refer back to a specific noun.

Common nouns may be determined by prefixing the article or by joining the noun to a following noun that is determined (this includes attaching it to a pronominal suffix; see ch. 11 on the construct state). First, we will look at the basic forms of the article.

Hebrew, just as Greek, differs from English in that it has no indefinite article; Hebrew nominals either have the article or they do not. Therefore, there is no need to call it a "definite article," though some grammarians do; it is simply the article. When a Hebrew word does not have the article, it may be translated with or without the English indefinite article. So the Hebrew noun דָּבָר may be translated into English as "word" or "a word."

All of the following discussion deals with the presence or absence of the article. The principles discussed apply to nominals determined by the construct state. You will get a chance to review this topic when I treat the construct in the next chapter.

The Forms of the Article

The article is always prefixed to a word and *never* stands alone. The basic form of the article is

קוֹל + הַ → הַקּוֹל   *haq | qôl*   the voice
דָּבָר + הַ → הַדָּבָר   *had | dābār*   the word

For *qôl*, the *qof* becomes doubled. For *dābār* with *dagesh lene*, the *dalet* in הַדָּבָר becomes *dagesh forte*.

In the first chapter we learned about certain letters that will not take a *dagesh forte*. When a noun begins with such a letter, Hebrew makes adjustments in the form of the article. Below is one possible example.

$$עַם \; + \; הַ \; \rightarrow \; הָעָם \quad hā\,|\,ʿām \quad \text{the people}$$

Notice that there is no *Ddagesh forte* in the עַ. To compensate for this loss, the *patakh* under the article has lengthened to *qamets*.

What about nominals (Nl) with both the article (T) *and* an inseparable preposition (Pp) and the conjunction (cj) *waw*? Any other prefixes attached to a noun with the article come before the article. Hebrew has the same word order as English: Pp + T + Nl. When you put הַ☉ + בְּ together, the ה drops out and the consonant of the Pp takes over the spot previously occupied by the ה. If there is a *waw* cj, it comes before the Pp. (Remember that Hebrew is read right-to-left and English is read left-to-right!)

FIGURE 10.2: Hebrew Nouns: Some Assembly Required

Hebrew						English					
שָׂדֶה	שָׂדֶה	+	+		+		+		+	N	(a) field
וְשָׂדֶה	שָׂדֶה	+	+		+	וְ	cj +		+	+	N	and (a) field
בְּשָׂדֶה	שָׂדֶה	+	+	בְּ	+		+	Pp	+	+	N	in (a) field
וּבְשָׂדֶה	שָׂדֶה	+	+	בְּ	+	וּ	cj +	Pp	+	+	N	and in (a) field
הַשָּׂדֶה	שָׂדֶה	+	הַ	+		+		+	T	+	N	the field
וְהַשָּׂדֶה	שָׂדֶה	+	הַ	+		+	וְ	cj +	+	T	+	N	and the field
בַּשָּׂדֶה	שָׂדֶה	+	הַ	+	בְּ	+		+	Pp	+	T	+	N	in the field
וּבַשָּׂדֶה	שָׂדֶה	+	הַ	+	בְּ	+	וּ	cj +	Pp	+	T	+	N	and in the field

Basic Functions of Determination

The functions of the article fall into two categories: semantic and structural. By **semantic** functions of the article, I mean that the article adds meaning; by **structural** functions, I mean that the article merely marks relationships between words. After this, I add a third category of the **undetermined** noun, i.e., a common noun without the article. The most important category is the list of semantic functions, so that is where we will spend the most time. Structural functions will merely be mentioned; we will treat them in coming chapters as we meet other parts of speech.

> **Teaching/Learning Tip:** This section on functions of determination is a little advanced. If this is more than you wish to deal with at this time, you may skip this as well as the exercises in *HRUW*. I think it is comprehensible, however, and there is good payoff for understanding texts.

I. Semantic Functions[1]

A. **Individualizing functions:** Distinguishing one member from others of a group.

1. **Simple identification:** To identify one from among a group (a.k.a. "specifying" use, very much like English *the*).

Ruth 3:8	הָאִישׁ	וַיֶּחֱרַד
	the man	And (it) startled
NIV	[In the middle of the night] something startled **the** man.	
Explanation	The man (Boaz) and not the woman (Ruth) was startled. Incidentally, the Hebrew verb translated "startled" in the NIV is in Hebrew a stative verb (see ch. 13, p. 166). There is no Hebrew word behind "something"; the grammatical subject of the verb in Hebrew is "the man."	

2. **Anaphoric:** Referring back to a previously mentioned thing.

Gen 2:10	הַגָּן	אֶת־	לְהַשְׁקוֹת	מֵעֵדֶן	יֹצֵא	וְנָהָר
	the garden	←	to water	from Eden	used to flow out	Now, a river
NIV	A river watering *the* garden flowed from Eden.					
Explanation	This is the same garden that was introduced in 2:8.					

This function includes **apposition** (see also below under II. Structural Functions). Sometimes nouns are described by other nouns, as opposed to adjectives. Look at the following sentence:

David **the king** also rejoiced greatly. (1 Chr 29:9 NIV)

The noun "the king" (1) follows closely the noun *David*, (2) refers to the same entity as *David*, (3) agrees in definiteness with the referent "David," and (4) has the same function in the sentence as *David* (the subject of the verb). The noun "the king" is said to be in apposition to *David*. As a test, the sentence would mean approximately the same thing if either *David* or *the king* was removed.

Nouns without the article (= anarthrous) can also stand in apposition.

---

1. I am indebted to the treatment of the article in Dan Wallace, *Greek Grammar beyond the Basics* (Grand Rapids: Zondervan Academic, 1996), 209–54.

3. **Demonstrative (a.k.a. Deictic):** More emphatic than simply definite (compare English *this* and *that*).

Deut 29:10	אֱלֹהֵיכֶם	יְהוָה	לִפְנֵי	כֻּלְּכֶם	הַיּוֹם	נִצָּבִים	אַתֶּם
	your God	the Lord	before	all of you	**the** day	standing	You (are)
NIV	All of you are standing *to*day in the presence of the Lord your God						
Explanation	"The day" means "this day"; idiomatically, "today."						

4. **Well-Known:** A common noun is sufficient to identify an individual because that is the individual's defining characteristic.

2 Sam 3:32	קוֹלוֹ	אֶת־	הַמֶּלֶךְ	וַיִּשָּׂא
	his voice	←	**the** king	and he lifted up
ESV	And **the** king lifted up his voice [and wept at the grave of Abner].			
Explanation	David is mentioned in v. 31. In v. 32 he is the called "the king" because everyone knows whom the author means.			

In addition, there are two subcategories.
   a. *Par excellence*: Not the only one of a kind, but the best example.

Job 1:6	בְּתוֹכָם	הַשָּׂטָן	גַּם־	וַיָּבוֹא
	in their midst	**the** adversary	also	and he came
NIV	And Satan also came with them.			
Explanation	The Hebrew text is treating the word as a noun with the article. There may be many deceivers, but this figure is the epitome. The NIV renders with the proper name to identify the one that the Hebrew epitomizes.			

   b. **Monadic:** Truly one of a kind.

Josh 10:13	הַשֶּׁמֶשׁ	וַיִּדֹּם
	the sun	And (it) stopped
NIV	So **the** sun stood still	
Explanation	The sun is conceived of as one of a kind.	

5. **Generic:** To mark a class of which there may be many members.

Eccl 2:19	סָכָל	אוֹ	יִהְיֶה	הֶחָכָם	יוֹדֵעַ	וּמִי
	a fool?	or	he will be	**the** wise	knows	and who

NIV84	And who knows whether he will be *a* wise man or a fool?

Explanation	English usually uses the indefinite article here but sometimes will use the definite article. Notice that the parallel word *fool* has no article in Hebrew. The article perhaps highlights being a member of the class of the wise as opposed to being an unnoteworthy simpleton.

Lev 16:28	בְּגָדָיו	יְכַבֵּס	אֹתָם	וְהַשֹּׂרֵף
	his clothes	shall wash	← them	And **the** one who burns

NIV	*The* man who burns them must wash his clothes.

Explanation	Verse 27 mentions the clothes burning up. Verse 28 is a change of subject (note the clause beginning with *waw* + nonverb) to the one who does the burning. It refers to the class of those burning the clothes.
	Also, here the article is prefixed to a participle acting as a noun. We will discuss this more in ch. 17.

6. **Collective:** The article with a singular noun used for a collective plural.

Exod 14:31	יְהוָה	אֶת־	הָעָם	וַיִּרְאוּ
	the Lord	←	**the** people	And they feared

NIV	**The** people feared the Lord.

Explanation	The verb has a plural subject, "And they (pl) feared," but the grammatical subject, "the people" is singular.

B. **Pronominal:** The article is equivalent to a personal pronoun in the context.

1 Sam 20:6	הַמִּשְׁפָּחָה	לְכָל־	שָׁם	·	הַיָּמִים	זֶבַח	כִּי
	the family	all of	there	(is being made)	the days	the sacrifice of	for

NIV	… because an annual sacrifice is being made there for **his** whole clan.

Explanation	The family referenced is none other than that of David, who is mentioned in the previous clause of the verse. Incidentally, the NIV rendering of "the days" as "annual" is a perfectly good idiomatic translation. The biblical books of Chronicles are in Hebrew דִּבְרֵי הַיָּמִים, woodenly, "The Matters of the Days," but more appropriately, "The Matters of the Years."

C. **Vocative:** To mark out the one addressed, rather than being a part of the clause.

1 Sam 23:20	רֵד	לָרֶדֶת	הַמֶּלֶךְ	נַפְשְׁךָ	אַוַּת	לְכָל־	וְעַתָּה
	come down	to come down,	**the** king,	your soul	the pleasure of	at all of	and now
ESV	Now come down, *O* king, according to all your heart's desire to come down.							
Explanation	The invitation is addressed to the king; the article marks the noun as addressee. Note that the Prn referring to a Voc is "you/your."							

II. Structural Functions

Frequently the article is used with nouns or other parts of speech (participle, infinitive, even entire clauses) to mark position. We will see examples when we get to those parts of speech.

A. **With nouns in apposition:** Sometimes nouns are described by other nouns, as opposed to adjectives. Look at 1 Chr 29:9 again:

> David **the king** also rejoiced greatly. (1 Chr 29:9 NIV)

The noun "the king" is in apposition to *David*. Since *David* is determined, *king* must also be determined to be in apposition. The article marks this structurally.

B. **With adjectives and participles:** The article usually has little to no semantic force, unless they are being treated as nouns, in which case refer to the determined functions.

C. **With infinitives and clauses:** There may also be a semantic force, and you may again consult the list of determined functions.

III. Functions of the Absence of the Article

A. **Indefinite:** Referring to a member of a class without identifying it from any other member.

Ruth 1:4	מֹאֲבִיּוֹת	נָשִׁים	לָהֶם	וַיִּשְׂאוּ
	Moabite	**wives**	for themselves	and they took
NIV	They married Moabite **women.**			
Explanation	This is the first mention of the two women. In the next clause they are named and therefore made definite, but at this point the author merely mentions two undefined members of the class of Moabite women.			

B. **Qualitative:** Emphasizing the defining characteristic of the class rather than any individual member; this function is nearly identical to the generic use with the article.

Jonah 3:3	לֵאלֹהִים	גְּדוֹלָה	עִיר־	הָיְתָה	וְנִינְוֵה
	to God	great	**a city**	was	And Nineveh
NIV	Now, Nineveh was **a very large city.**				
Explanation	The word *city* is the class to which Nineveh belongs. The adjective *great* makes clear that the quality is in view.				

C. **Definite:** When a noun without an article is still viewed as definite, then you should consult the functions under determined nouns. This is particularly common in poetry.

Gen 40:16	פִּתְרֹן inter- pretation	. (was)	טוֹב good	כִּי that	הָאֹפִים the bakers	שַׂר־ chief of	וַיַּרְא and he saw
ESV	When the chief baker saw that **the interpretation** was favorable						
NIV	When the chief baker saw that Joseph had given **a** favorable **interpretation**						
Explanation	פִּתְרֹן is undetermined. Yet the context refers back to Joseph's interpretation of the cupbearer's dream. So this is not indefinite or qualitative but must be definite (actually, anaphoric). The ESV preserves this in its translation. The NIV changes the structure of the Hebrew by adding the verb *given*; the Hebrew is a noun clause.						

Figure 10.3 is a summary of the above information. This figure is also found in the collection of Action Figures in the appendix to this work.

FIGURE 10.3: Summary of Functions of Presence and Absence of Article

Class	Function & Description
Semantic Functions	I. **Individualizing Functions:** Distinguishing one member from others of a group. A. **Simple Identification:** To identify one from among a group (a.k.a. "specifying" use, very much like English *the*). B. **Anaphoric:** Referring back to a previously mentioned thing. This function includes **apposition.** C. **Demonstrative (a.k.a. deictic):** More emphatic than simply definite (compare English *this* and *that*). D. **Well-Known:** A common noun is sufficient to identify an individual because that is the individual's defining characteristic.

(continued)

Semantic Functions (continued)	In addition, there are two subcategories.
	    a. *Par Excellence*: Not the only one of a kind, but the best example.
	    b. **Monadic:** Truly one of a kind.
	  E. **Generic:** To mark a class of which there may be many members.
	  F. **Collective:** The article with a singular noun used for a collective plural.
	II. **Pronominal:** The article is equivalent to a personal pronoun in the context.
	III. **Vocative:** To mark out the one addressed, rather than being a part of the clause.

Structural Functions	I. **With nouns in apposition:** Sometimes nouns are described by other nouns, as opposed to adjectives. II. **With adjectives and participles:** The article usually has little to no semantic force, unless they are being treated as nouns, in which case refer to the determined functions. III. **With infinitives and clauses:** There may also be a semantic force, and you may again consult the list of determined functions.
Absence of the Article	I. **Indefinite:** Referring to a member of a class without identifying it from any other member. II. **Qualitative:** Emphasizing the defining characteristic of the class rather than any individual member; this function is nearly identical to the generic use with the article. III. **Definite:** When a noun without an article is still viewed as definite, then you should consult the functions under determined nouns. This is particularly common in poetry.

Interrogative ה: The Question Marker

In English we form questions in a couple of different ways. First, we commonly reverse the word order of subject and verb or use an interrogative pronoun at the beginning of the question. Second, when speaking, we will usually raise the pitch of our voice at the end of a sentence, or, when writing, we will conclude the sentence with a question mark.

There is no doubt that Hebrew had voice inflection, but this is lost in writing; only stressed syllables are marked by the Masoretes. Spoken and written Hebrew, however, did have a prefixed ה to mark a question. Whereas the article is ה normally spelled with *patakh* plus *dagesh forte*, the interrogative particle is ה normally spelled with *hatef patakh*: הֲ. This particle is attached at the beginning of the question. It is never attached directly to an article, and only rarely does the conjunction *waw* precede the interrogative ה. Look at the following examples:

Gen 4:9	אָנֹכִי	·	אָחִי	הֲשֹׁמֵר
Interlinear	I		my brother	the keeper of?

NIV	Am I my brother's keeper?
Explanation	The הֲ at the beginning of the verse is not the article (note no *dagesh* in the *shin*) prefixed to a nominal word.[2]

Gen 18:14 Interlinear	דָּבָר	מֵיהוָה	הֲיִפָּלֵא
	anything	from the LORD	Is (it) too hard

NIV	Is anything too hard for the LORD?
Explanation	The interrogative הֲ at the beginning of the verse is prefixed to a verb.

Both the article and interrogative particle are spelled in a variety of ways. As a pre-Hebrew student, you will need to rely on additional resources to know the difference between them. To flowchart a question, I leave the sentence in its original order as much as possible, even though that may mean that the subject will not come first.

In figure 10.4 are flowcharts of the passages above. The subjects are bolded, and the verbs are underlined.

FIGURE 10.4: Flowcharting Questions

Function	Vs	Flowchart: Gen 4:7 (NIV)
Question	7	<u>Am</u> **I** ⇔ keeper? my brother's

Function	Vs	Flowchart: Gen 18:14 (NIV)
Question	14	<u>Is</u> **anything** ⇔ too <u>hard</u> for the LORD?

English typically forms yes-no questions by reversing subject and verb. Notice that for Gen 18:14 the underlining matches the Hebrew grammar because the Hebrew verb corresponds to the NIV "is . . . hard," while the flowchart follows the English grammar. The word *too* is an adverb; it is up to you if you want to indent it .25 inches under the word it modifies. Typically, I only do that if there is some significant exegetical point or there is a list of adverbial modifiers.

What about Aramaic?

The form of the article in Aramaic is quite different from that in Hebrew. The article is marked in Aramaic with the syllable אָ, *-ā'*, attached to the end of

---

2. The word שֹׁמֵר is actually a participle (Ptc) functioning as a noun (ch. 17) in the construct state (ch. 11, hence the translation's including "of").

nouns and certain other words. Sometimes it is spelled with a הinstead of an א. In Biblical Aramaic the functions are about the same as in Hebrew. In some later Aramaic dialects, the articular form of the noun becomes so normal that the article becomes meaningless.

The interrogative ה occurs in Hebrew and Biblical Aramaic alike. See Dan 2:26; 3:14. The targums also use this prefix, but sometimes it is spelled הא (often the texts do not have vowels written) as a separate word.

Advanced Information and Curious Facts

The Greek word for *father* occurs more than four hundred times in the NT. Three times in the NT, however, "father" appears in the phrase "*Abba* [ἀββά or ἀββᾶ]! Father!": Mark 14:36; Rom 8:15; and Gal 4:6. The Hebrew word for *father* is אָב; "*Abba*" is the Aramaic word, אַבָּא, which is אַב + the article at the end. The Greek ἀββά is a transliteration of the Aramaic, and the English *Abba* is a transliteration of the Greek. The Greek word for "Father" is πατήρ, (*patēr*).

Does it seem surprising that the three occurrences of *Abba* occur in Mark, whose work may have been associated with Peter and was perhaps written with a more Roman audience in mind, and in Paul's letters to the Galatians and the Romans? Why would this Aramaic word be used for these audiences and not Hebrew? Perhaps because Hebrew as a daily language was more limited to Judea and the Semitic language from previous centuries more widely known to more peoples was Aramaic. The term *Abba* was familiar to Jews and perhaps to some Gentiles in the Greco-Roman world (review ch. 2, if you would like).

So, why would Paul say to the Christians of Rome, "And by him we cry, '*Abba, Pater*'"? Why use Aramaic at all?

Many suggest that *abba* means "daddy" as opposed to "father," and that is why Jesus and Paul use it. The interpretation is that Paul is saying, "And by him we cry, 'Daddy, Father,'" as though we can speak to the Lord as a loving and gentle dad rather than as a strict father.

For a few reasons, I doubt this is the best answer:

(1) I cannot find in ancient Hebrew any word making a distinction between *father* and *daddy*, as in modern English. I am certainly willing to be corrected on the point, but finding a clear context will be a challenge.

(2) אָב is the only word in Biblical Hebrew that means "father." Modern Hebrew does have אַבָּא'לֶה (abba'le; cf. אִמָּא'לֶה, imma'le, "mommy"), but simple אַבָּא seems to be more common and is what Israelis use with their young children. אַבָּא'לֶה does not appear to be an ancient expression.

(3) Even in Aramaic, there are other words that might be metaphors for a father or teacher just as *father* might have extended uses for ancestor or teacher,

but no real word for a child's "daddy" instead of *father* is found in Jastrow's *Dictionary*.[3]

I suggest this simple answer. Since the churches of Rome and Galatia were struggling with proper relations between believers of Jewish and Gentile heritage, Paul uses *Abba* since this is how the Jews outside of Judea would refer to the Lord as Father in Aramaic, and he uses *Pater* since this is how the Gentiles would refer to the Lord as Father in Greek. In this way, Paul highlights that in Christ God is the Father of both (cf. Eph 2:11–22).

---

3. Jastrow never uses the gloss "dad" or "daddy." He does list two additional words that he also glosses with "father": first, הֹוֹרָ, meaning a "thrower" and then metaphorically for "instructor," "father," or "parent,"; second, חַנִיך (see also the entry and חֲנִיכָה) meaning the one "rubbing the infant's palate with a chewed fig" as an act of nurturing. See *Dictionary*, 1:340, 483.

CHAPTER 11

A TALE OF TWO STATES
Case Functions

Objectives

1. Compare English and Hebrew pronouns.
2. Define and identify English and Hebrew case systems.
3. Identify determination and the construct chain.
4. Analyze case functions.
5. Compare versions' interpretation of cases.
6. Flowchart the uses of the "particles of existence."

Tools Used: Grammatically tagged computer Hebrew OT or paper interlinear plus Davidson or Owens

Introduction

A well-known chorus is taken from Ps 118:24, "This is the day that the LORD has made; let us rejoice and be glad in it" (ESV). Often we sing this when we are feeling happy, especially when the weather outside is delightful. After all, the verse says, "let us be glad in *it*." The word *it* is a personal pronoun. Obviously, since it is neuter (meaning neither masculine nor feminine), it must refer back to a thing, namely, *day*. The day that the psalmist is talking about is when the Lord does the great work of making the rejected stone now to be the chief cornerstone.

You will remember, though, that in Hebrew there are only two genders, masculine and feminine. The word translated "it" by the English versions actually represents a masculine Hebrew pronoun. That means it must refer to an antecedent that is a masculine noun. Now the word "day" in Hebrew is masculine, but that is not the only option. The nearest antecedent is "the LORD." A legitimate way of translating the second line of the verse is, "let us rejoice and be glad in *him*!" One can make a case either way. The Lord is the agent bringing about the great work on that day. If we take the pronoun as referring to the Lord, then the cause and focus of our rejoicing and gladness is actually the Lord himself. In either case, "day" is the anticipated day of salvation. In the NT, this is equated with the coming of the Son. We can sing this song no matter the "weather" of our lives, knowing that salvation is from the Lord.

In this chapter, the main task is to understand Hebrew case usage. The term *case* simply refers to the role of a noun in a sentence. Pronouns serve as a good way to introduce noun cases, so that is where we will begin, covering both Hebrew and English pronouns plus English cases. Next, we will turn to the Hebrew cases themselves. We will treat these in two parts, the second part being the most exegetically significant. Finally, there are two little words used commonly in Hebrew, known as particles of existence and nonexistence, that English translations normally render idiomatically.

Personal Pronouns and English Cases

A pronoun (Prn) is a word that stands in place of (*pro-*) a noun. The noun for which it stands is called the antecedent. English has several kinds of pronouns; Hebrew has five kinds. They are summarized in the figure below. (Remember that English is always presented left to right and Hebrew right to left!)

FIGURE 11.1: Types of Pronouns in English and Hebrew

Pronoun Type	Description	English examples	Hebrew Equivalents
Personal	Pronouns with the grammatical person in the meaning	I, he, we	אֲנִי, הוּא, אֲנַחְנוּ
Reflexive	The object of the verb and refers to the same entity as the subject of the verb	myself, himself, ourselves	None[1] [Hebrew uses verb stems for this]
Interrogative	Asks questions	Who? What?	מִי, מָה
Demonstrative	Points to objects near or far	this, these; that, those	זֶה, אֵלֶּה
Relative	Introduces a relative clause	who, which, that	אֲשֶׁר
Indefinite	Refers to any member of a class	whoever, whichever someone a few	אֲשֶׁר אִישׁ, הָאִישׁ[2] מְעַט [Hebrew uses mostly nouns or nothing]

Personal pronouns have person as a lexical quality and therefore carry weight. While English nouns are not often inflected (i.e., they do not often add endings,

---

1. However, personal pronouns can be translated this way. See Lev 19:18.
2. This is the word for "man" or "the man"; it can be used to refer to an indefinite person (e.g., 1 Sam 9:9).

etc.) for case, personal pronouns (PPrn) are. So they serve as a good introduction into a discussion of cases.

Grammatical Qualities of English and Hebrew Pronouns

English Prns indicate person, gender (in third person only), number, and case. Person refers to identities of speaker (first person), addressee (second person), and topic of conversation (third person). Number may be singular or plural. Case refers to the function that a noun has in a sentence. Languages indicate case either by word order (as English does) or by adding endings to the word (as Greek and Latin do). Hebrew actually used to have case endings before the Bible was put into writing, but they were dropped and only remnants of them remain.

English has four cases: *subjective, possessive, objective,* and *vocative.* The vocative can be treated quickly. It is simply the case of address as in, *"Julie,* you are beautiful." The verb is *are;* the subject is *you; Julie* is not part of the clause and is therefore set off by a comma; further, the words *Julie* and *you* refer to the same person. Now we'll go to the three main cases.

The chart below illustrates case forms using PPrns. Notice that in the third-person singular, English Prns have gender. Just for fun I give the Prns for Elizabethan English (the English of the KJV) in parentheses.

FIGURE 11.2: English Personal Pronouns

Case	First Person		Second Person		Third Person	
	sg	pl	sg	pl	sg	pl
Subjective	I	we	you (thou)	you (ye)	he, she, it	they
Possessive Pronoun	My (my, mine)	our	your (thy, thine)	your	his, her, its	their
Possessive Pronoun	mine	ours	yours (thine)	yours	his, hers, its	theirs
Objective	me	us	you (thee)	you (you)	him, her, its	them

Personal pronouns (PPrns) in Hebrew and English share the same qualities: person, gender (for second and third persons in Hebrew, only third person in English), number, and case. Whereas English PPrns are all independent words, Hebrew PPrns come in two sets: **independent pronouns** and suffixed Prns, known as **pronominal suffixes** (PrnSf). The independent PPrns are, as their name implies, independent words and correspond to the English subject pronouns. PrnSfs are used for the English possessive and objective pronouns. Now we may expand our parsing chart to include PPrns:

			Verbal Qualities					Nominal Qualities			
PtSp	Word	Lex	Stem	Form	P	G	N	State	Det	Case	Suff
Nn						X	X	X	X	X	
V			X	X	X	X	X				
PPrn					X	X	X	Abs	D	X	
PrnSf								Abs	D	X	PGN

FIGURE 11.3: Parsing Chart

Just as with substantives, you will notice that PPrns have all the qualities of nouns. Because they are Prns, they are always in the absolute state (Abs) and are always determined (Det), so there is no need to label these on the chart. Because they are *personal* Prns, they have the quality of person (P). Really, though, this is due to their meaning rather than inflection. Since PrnSfs are never independent, their person, gender, and number (PGN) are in the "Suff" column in the same line as the word they are attached to.

Now let's look at four sentences.

S1. Jill loves the man's son.
S2. *She* loves the man's son.
S3. Jill loves *his* son.
S4. Jill loves *him*.

All four sentences have an active verb. S1 has no pronoun. S2, S3, and S4 have pronouns (in italics) substituted for each of the nouns in turn. The subject is the agent of an active verb. When the Prn is substituted for Jill in S2, the subject form is used; you wouldn't say "Her loved the man's son." The man is the possessor. In S2 this is indicated by a noun with the ending -'s; in S3, the possessive Prn *his* is used. In S4 the objective case (OC) Prn substitutes for the direct object (DO) of the sentences. Again, you wouldn't say "Jill loves he."

Now that we understand English cases to be simply the functions of nouns in sentences, we are ready to look more closely at Hebrew cases.

The First Three Noun Cases

Hebrew cases may be described similarly to English cases, but different names are used. The *vocative* (Voc) case is the same as in English. The *nominative case* (Nom) corresponds to the subject case (SC), the *genitive case* (Gen) corresponds to the possessive case, and the *accusative* case (Acc) corresponds to the objective case. Hebrew uses these cases for functions, which English renders with prepositions. For the Gen and Acc, I have included some key words to illustrate the functions. The Gen is the most complicated, so we will treat it last.

Nominative

1. **Subject Nom.** The substantive is the subject of an action or state. This is by far the most common use. In Hebrew noun clauses, the PPrn is simply the subject and the clause is disjunctive. Though English requires the same word in the subject case, in Hebrew verbal clauses PPrns are not needed. When they are present, they either indicate emphasis or mark a disjunctive clause.

   You [אַתָּה] are the man! (2 Sam 12:7 NIV)

   and that **you** [וְאַתָּה] are turning their hearts back again (1 Kgs 18:37 NIV)

2. **Predicate Nom.** The substantive is part of the predicate (the half with the verb) and refers to the same entity as the subject; most often this occurs in noun clauses, but certain other verbs may be present that also have this function.

   You are **the man** [הָאִישׁ]! (2 Sam 12:7 NIV)

   You and *the man* both refer to David.

3. **Nom Absolute.** The substantive is isolated at the beginning of a clause and is often referred to by a pronoun in the clause called a "resumptive pronoun." The clause after the Nom absolute is a complete clause. This function is also called a "pending case" (or *casus pendens*) or other names, since it can occur in any case,[3] i.e., a resumptive pronoun can be a subject Nom, a Prn suffixed to a noun (Gen case), or an object of a verb (Acc case). This use is not considered good grammar in English, so it requires a little explanation. Look at the following interlinear.

Gen 9:18	כְּנָעַן	אֲבִי	'	הוּא	וְחָם
	Canaan	the father of	(was)	he	now Ham
NIV	(Ham was the father of Canaan.)				
Explanation	By introducing the topic with *waw* + non-verb, a disjunctive clause, and then using the resumptive Prn "he" as the subject of the clause,[4] the author draws the reader's attention to a significant feature about Ham.				

3. See Paul Joüon and Takamitsu Muraoka, *A Grammar of Biblical Hebrew*, rev. ed. (Rome: Pontifical Biblical Institute, 2006), §156. For a clear explanation of this function, see Ronald J. Williams and John C. Beckman, *Williams' Hebrew Syntax*, 3rd ed. (Toronto: University of Toronto Press, 2007), §35.

4. Some grammarians say that the הוּא, the Prn "he," is actually functioning as the verb *to be*. This is not a correct understanding of Hebrew. This is simply a verbless clause (see ch. 6).

This is not to be confused with "fronting," which occurs when something other than a verb occurs first in the clause and there is no resumptive pronoun.

2 Sam 7:15	מִמֶּנּוּ from him	יָסוּר it shall turn aside	לֹא not	וְחַסְדִּי but my love
NIV	But my love will never be taken away from him.			
Explanation	This is a disjunctive clause (a nonverb is first; see ch. 20), but there is no resumptive Prn.			

4. **Nom in Simple Apposition.** Apposition occurs when two nouns are next to each other, refer to the same entity, and function the same way in the sentence (see ch. 10). *Apposition can occur with any case*, including objects of prepositions. Since their function "piggybacks" on that of the first noun, multiple examples are not needed; once again 1 Chr 29:9 clearly illustrates apposition in the Nom case.

> David **the king** also rejoiced greatly. (1 Chr 29:9 NIV)

David is the subject Nom of the verb; the phrase "the king" is in apposition. If you remove either word, the subject of the verb is still the same entity that "rejoiced."

Accusative

We mentioned that Hebrew usually marks case functions by word order. Hebrew does have a feature that marks the Acc. When a determined noun is in the Acc, Hebrew may precede the word with the particle אֵת. This particle may be joined to an Acc noun by *maqqeph* (אֶת־ with the short vowel). It may also have a pronominal suffix attached, in which case the vowel is a long *o* (e.g., אֹתִי or אוֹתִי, meaning "me"). The particle אֵת is not used for every determined Acc noun, and there does not appear to be any pattern as to when it is used. This particle is not translated into English except by word order to mark the direct object. We have already seen this in Gen 1:1: "In the beginning God created *the heavens* [אֵת הַשָּׁמַיִם] and *the earth* [וְאֵת הָאָרֶץ]" (NIV).

For the examples below, none of the Acc nouns are in prepositional phrases in Hebrew, even though almost all of them are in English.

1. **Acc of DO.** The most common function with no "key words."
   > They set up **sacred stones.** (2 Kgs 17:10 NIV)

2. **Acc of Simple Apposition** (no key word).
   > Elhanan son of Jair killed Lahmi **the brother** of Goliath the Gittite. (1 Chr 20:5 NIV; the brother = Lahmi [Acc of DO])

3. **Double Acc**
   a. **of Person-Thing** (the person and the thing are different entities).
      Let him go . . . and teach **them** the **law**. (2 Kgs 17:27 ESV)

   b. **of Object-Complement** (the object and the complement refer to the same entity).
      I appointed **you** as **a prophet** to the nations. (Jer 1:5 NIV)

4. **Adverbial Accusative**
   a. **of Time** (*at, during*)
      During the night [לַ֫יְלָה] Abram divided his men. (Gen 14:15 NIV)

   b. **of Place** (*at*)
      while he was sitting **at the entrance** [פֶּ֫תַח־] to his tent (Gen 18:1 NIV)

   c. **of Direction** (*to*)
      and all Lebanon **to the east** [מִזְרַח הַשֶּׁ֫מֶשׁ] (Josh 13:5 NIV; formally, "the rising of the sun")

   d. **of Manner** (*-ly* or other adverbial expression)
      Day after day [יוֹם], again and again I sent you my servants the prophets. (Jer 7:25 NIV; KJV renders "daily")

   e. **of Product** (*into*)
      He . . . made it **a molten calf** [עֵ֫גֶל]. (Exod 32:4 KJV)

      Compare NIV: He . . . made it **into** an idol cast in the shape of **a calf**.

   f. **of Material** (*from*)
      Then the LORD God formed a man **from the dust** [עָפָר] of the ground. (Gen 2:7 NIV)

   g. **of Instrument** (*with, using*)
      And all Israel stoned him **with stones** [אֶ֫בֶן]. (Josh 7:25 ESV)

      Compare the NIV, "Then all Israel stoned him."

   h. **of Contents** (*of, with*)
      Then I set bowls full **of wine** [יַ֫יִן]. (Jer 35:5 NIV)

      The "of" is not due to the Hebrew construct state (see below), but is simply the Adv Acc.

Vocative

The vocative is the case of direct address. The substantive is used as though in conjunction with a second-person verb.

1. **Voc of Address**

> I have a secret message for you, **O king**. (Judg 3:19 ESV)

Notice that the speaker ("I," the first person) speaks to an addressee ("you," the second person), and then addresses him as "O king." The NIV renders "Your Majesty," which is still in the Voc of direct address.

2. **Voc of Simple Apposition**

> As you say, **my Lord** [אֲדֹנִי], **O king** [הַמֶּלֶךְ], I am yours, and all that I have. (1 Kgs 20:4 ESV)

Compare NIV: "Just as you say, *my Lord the king.*"

Both "my Lord" and "O king" are in the Voc. Notice that the ESV took the article attached to *king* as marking the vocative (in fact, "O king" is a Voc in simple apposition).

The Construct Chain and the Genitive Case

In ch. 8 on prepositions, you learned that Hebrew has no word for the English word *of*; instead, Hebrew uses a grammatical construction. That construction is the "construct chain." Some people might suggest that the Gen means simply *of*. That is true—kind of; remember the difference between a gloss and a definition. In fact, the Hebrew Gen has a broader range of meaning than the English *of*. In any case, the interpreter of the English Bible must seek to figure out what *of* means any time it appears in the Bible. A formal translation would simply use the word "of"; to explain the meaning it is useful to paraphrase with something more precise. This is what we will learn here.

All Hebrew nouns are in one of two states: *absolute* (Abs), in which the noun is not bound to another form, and *construct* (Cst), in which the noun is bound to another following form. The two words so bound are said to be in a *construct chain. As a rule, the construct chain cannot be interrupted by anything*, though authors occasionally violate the rule for literary reasons. The "glue" that binds the words together is that they are pronounced as a unit. In writing, the first word loses its primary accent, often resulting in changes to the vowels. If you were learning full Hebrew, you would learn how to read these changes. As a pre-Hebrew student, you will have to rely on the work of others.

Here is how construct chains work. The chains can have several links, but to begin with we will consider only two-link chains. In a two-word construct chain the first word, the head noun (N^h), is in the construct state. The second word, the tail noun (N^t), is in the absolute state and is always in the Gen. (Note: not all absolute nouns are tails of a Cst noun; we are only talking about construct chains here.) The following diagram illustrates this graphically; remember that Hebrew reads from right to left and all English letters, even in diagrams, read from left to right.

FIGURE 11.4: State and Case

Nouns in Abs and in **Gen case**

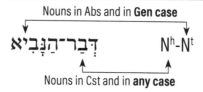

N^h-N^t

Nouns in Cst and in **any case**

Notice the following important points:

1. The N^h, דְּבַר, has the lexical form דָּבָר, meaning "word"; the Cst form means "word *of.*" Because of the shift in accent, the vowels have changed. Not all nouns alter vowels when they are in the Cst, but most do.

2. The N^t has the article and means "the prophet." The article may only be attached to the N^t. Whenever the N^t is determined, either because of the word being intrinsically determined or because of the article, each member of the chain is also determined; if the N^t is not determined, each member of the chain is undetermined. So, דְּבַר־הַנָּבִיא means "*the* word of *the* prophet"; דְּבַר־נָבִיא would mean "*(a)* word of *(a)* prophet."[5]

3. The example shows the words joined by *maqqeph*. This is optional and its presence or absence has no effect on the meaning.

4. *If there are three or more links in the chain, the middle items are all in the Gen, just like the* N^t. This may be graphically illustrated this way: N^h–N^{Gen}–N^t. The interpreter needs to determine based on word meaning and context the meaning of the Gen relationship, represented by the "–" between each pair.

5. *A PrnSf attached to a noun functions as a* N^t *that is determined.* For example, דְּבָרוֹ would mean "*the* word of—him," or "his word."

FIGURE 11.5: Terms and Nouns Bound Together

Quality	Head Noun	Tail Noun
Order	first	last
State	construct (Cst)	absolute (Abs)
Case	any	genitive
Translation	lexical meaning + "of"	lexical meaning
Article	no article	article optional

5. To say, "*the* word of *a* prophet," a construct chain could not be used. Instead Hebrew would use a לְ preposition: הַדָּבָר לְנָבִיא, in which the לְ functions to mark possession.

The Meaning of the Genitive Case

The Gen denotes a relationship between two nouns, often translated by the English word "of." The word "of" denotes a wide variety of nuances. Here are some things you need to know when you meet "of" in the English Bible when it translates a construct chain.

1. The most exegetically significant preposition in the English Bible is *of.* The reader who encounters the preposition *of* rendering the construct state should try to identify the function of the preposition as precisely as possible and be open to alternative possibilities.
2. The translation *of* is not the meaning of the Gen; *of* is only a gloss; the function labels will help you to clarify meaning.
3. Whenever the Gen is rendered with *of,* consider it as simply marked and as in need of analysis.
4. The quality of possession (see figure 11.6) is overused. Avoid the impulse to make this your first choice. Try to be more specific.

The Functions of the Genitive Case

I have found it helpful to think of the logical relationship between the two nouns as consisting of two dynamics: *direction* and *movement*. By *direction* I mean that either a given quality is with the N^t or separated from it. By *movement* I mean that a given quality may either be static or dynamic. In figure 11.6 below, the arrows ($\rightarrow$ and $\leftarrow$) indicate the direction, but movement must be inferred.

> **Teaching/Learning Tip:** The genitive functions take a while to get used to, but as mentioned above, *of* is the most exegetically significant English Pp. Taking time to think through these precisely will yield clarity in understanding versions and sometimes some real insights, especially when the versions simply read *of.*

Functions depend on word meaning and context. Remember to think about meaning from the perspective of the tail noun. The determination of the function depends on the meaning of the words in the chain and on context. Note that explained examples follow the figure.

FIGURE 11.6: Genitive Functions of the Construct State

Category	$N^h \rightarrow N^t$	Description	$N^h \leftarrow N^t$	Description
Possession	Gen of Possessor	N^t possesses N^h	Gen of Thing Possessed	N^t is possessed by N^h

(continued)

Category	$N^h \rightarrow N^t$	Description	$N^h \leftarrow N^t$	Description
Direction (a journey real or figurative)	Gen of Destination	N^t is the destination	Gen of Source	N^t is the place of origin
Relationship	Gen of Descendant	N^t is the descendant of N^h	Gen of Ancestor	N^t is the ancestor of N^h
Production	Gen of Product	N^t is the thing produced	Gen of Producer	N^t is makes the N^h
Agency (N^h is noun of action)	Subjective Gen	N^t is the one doing the implied action	Objective Gen	N^t is the one affected by the implied action
			Gen of Means	N^t is the instrument used to effect implied action
Action (N^{Gen} is noun of action/ state)	Gen of Purpose/ Result	N^t is actual result or intended purpose of N^h	Gen of Cause	N^t is caused by N^h
Adjectival	Attributive Gen	N^t functions as Adj describing N^h	Attributed Gen (= of Specification)	N^t is described by Adj^h
	Gen of Apposition	$N^t = N^h$ (= Explicative Gen)		
Partitive	Gen of Whole (partitive Gen)	N^t is the whole of which N^h is a part	Gen of Material	N^t is material of which N^h is made
	Gen of Measure	N^t is thing measured by quantity N^h	Gen of Degree/ Emphasis	N^t is plural form of N^h
Authority	Gen of Ruled	N^t is governed by N^h	Gen of Ruler	N^t governs N^h
(Dis)Advantage	Gen of Beneficiary/ Sufferer	N^t receives the benefit/harm of or from N^h	Gen of Benefactor/ Malefactor	N^t brings benefit/harm to N^h

Before we illustrate each of the functions listed in figure 11.6, we must add to this list two more categories.

First, **Gen Object of a Preposition**. Most grammarians do not think of the object of a Pp as a genitive, but that is the simplest way to construe it, and some prepositions are structured that way in Hebrew. For example, לְפָנֶיךָ, usually translated "before you," may be formally[6] translated as "to the face of you." In these instances, the Pp governs the genitive, and the function of the preposition is used instead of the functions in figure 11.6.

---

6. Recall from ch. 4 that we are using formal and formally to mean that the translation attempts to render into the target language (English) the grammatical structure of the source language (Hebrew and Aramaic in our case). These terms are more useful than literal and literally.

Second, **Gen of Simple Apposition**. This use functions in the same way that a Nom of Simple Apposition does, except that both nouns are in the Gen case. So in Josh 2:1 the Hebrew reads בֵּית־אִשָּׁה זוֹנָה, which can be rendered formally as "a house of a woman, a prostitute." "House of" is the N^h and "a woman" is the N^t and therefore in the Gen case. "A prostitute" is in apposition with "a woman" and is therefore in the Gen case as well. Since by definition an appositive (i.e., the noun in apposition) functions the same way in a sentence as the noun it refers to, the genitive function of the appositive will be the same as the tail noun of the construct chain. Compare the explanation of the Gen of Apposition below.

Here are some examples. Note the many nuances of the word "of" in English.

1. Gen of Possession
a. Possessor
So they went and entered *the house of a prostitute* [בֵּית־אִשָּׁה זוֹנָה] named Rahab. (Josh 2:1 NIV; formally, "a house of a woman, a prostitute")

b. Thing Possessed
The owner of the pit [בַּעַל הַבּוֹר] shall make restitution. (Exod 21:34 ESV)

2. Gen of Direction
a. Destination (dynamic)/Location (static)
Did God really say, "You must not eat from any *tree in the garden* [עֵץ הַגָּן]?" (Gen 3:1 NIV; cf. KJV: *"tree of the garden"*; the garden is the location)

It is too much for you *to go up to Jerusalem* [מֵעֲלוֹת יְרוּשָׁלַ͏ִם]. (1 Kgs 12:28; this is actually a PPhr with Pp + InfC + Nn. The NIV renders the prefixed Pp מִן idiomatically with *too* [of comparison; see ch. 8]; the point here is the phrase after the preposition: formally, *"the going up of Jerusalem"*; Jerusalem is the destination.)

b. Source/Origin[7]
that he may turn *man aside from his deed* [אָדָם מַעֲשֶׂה] (Job 33:17 ESV; i.e., *"a man of deed"*)

Many times: *"the man of God* [אִישׁ אֱלֹהִים]*."* This might be understood in several ways, but since it is most often a technical term for a prophet, it probably means a man sent from God.

---

7. This does not appear to be used geographically. To be from a place uses the Pp מִן, *from*. I understand expressions such as "Then Jephthah gathered all the *men of Gilead*" to mean that these were men who lived at Gilead rather than men who had come from Gilead. It is a subtle difference, but thinking about Hebrew idiom is useful.

3. **Gen of Relationship**
   a. **Descendant**

   The father of a righteous child [אֲבִי צַדִּיק] has great joy. (Prov 23:24 NIV)

   b. **Ancestor**

   The word of the LORD that came to Hosea *son of Beeri* [בֶּן־בְּאֵרִי].
   (Hos 1:1 NIV)

4. **Gen of Production**
   a. **Product**

   Woe to the one who quarrels with *his Maker* [יֹצְרוֹ]. (Isa 45:9 NASB; i.e.,
   "*the maker of him*")

   b. **Producer**

   We are all *the work of* your *hand* [וּמַעֲשֵׂה יָדְךָ]. (Isa 64:8 [Hebrew
   64:7] NIV)

5. **Gen of Agency**
   a. **Subjective**

   He was despised and *rejected by mankind* [וַחֲדַל אִישִׁים]. (Isa 53:3 NIV;
   cf. KJV "*rejected of men*"; i.e., *men* rejected him)

   b. **Objective**

   The Lord said to Joshua son of Nun, *Moses' aide* [מְשָׁרֵת מֹשֶׁה] (Josh
   1:1 NIV; formally "*the aide of Moses*"; i.e., he aided *Moses*)

   c. **Means/Instrument** (this category is simply impersonal agent and is a
   subcategory of the subjective Gen)

   with *those pierced by the sword* [מְטֹעֲנֵי חָרֶב] (Isa 14:19 NIV)

6. **Gen of Action**
   a. **Purpose/Result**

   The punishment that brought us *peace* [מוּסַר שְׁלוֹמֵנוּ] was on him. (Isa
   53:5 NIV; cf. KJV: "*the chastisement of* our *peace* was upon him")

   b. **Cause** (focus is on an action implied by a noun rather than on the agent
   or means)

   For I am *faint with love* [חוֹלַת אַהֲבָה]. (Song 2:5 NIV; formally, "sick
   of love")

   You will . . . remember no more *the reproach of* your *widowhood* [בֹּשֶׁת
   עֲלוּמַיִךְ]." (Isa 54:4 NIV; i.e., the reproach caused by your being a
   widow)

7. **Adjectival Gen**
   a. **Attributive**

   and *a throne of honor* [וְכִסֵּא כָבוֹד] (1 Sam 2:8 NIV; i.e., an honored position)

   a strong tower [וּמִגְדַּל־עֹז] (Judg 9:51 NIV; formally, "and *a tower of strength*")

   b. **Attributed**

   until you . . . perish quickly on account of *the evil of* your *deeds* [רֹעַ מַעַלְלֶיךָ] (Deut 28:20 ESV)

   c. **Apposition** (unlike simple apposition in which the two nouns are in the same case [see ch. 10], the Gen N^t may modify a N^h that is in another case)

   Then you shall return to *the land of* your *possession* [אֶרֶץ יְרֻשַּׁתְכֶם] and shall possess it. (Josh 1:15 ESV; meaning, the land which is your possession. Compare NIV, "and occupy your *own* land")

8. **Partitive Gen**
   a. **Wholative**[8] (a.k.a. partitive)

   Abel . . . brought . . . fat portions from some of *the firstborn of* his *flock* [בְּכֹרוֹת צֹאנוֹ]. (Gen 4:4 NIV; i.e., "the flock" is the whole; "the firstborn" are the part)

   b. **Material**

   The king made two *golden calves* [עֶגְלֵי זָהָב]. (1 Kgs 12:28 NIV; formally "*calves of gold*")

   c. **Contents**

   He had a string of donkeys . . . loaded with . . . *a skin of wine* [נֵבֶל יַיִן]. (2 Sam 16:1 NIV)

   d. **Measure** (i.e., of material measured)

   The 100 *talents of silver* [כִּכַּר הַכֶּסֶף] were used to cast the bases. (Exod 38:27 NIV; the "talent" was a unit of weight)

   e. **Degree/Emphasis** (subcategory of Wholative)

   the holy of holies [קֹדֶשׁ קֳדָשִׁים] (Exod 26:33 NASB; most English versions, including NIV, NIV84, ESV, NLT, and NET render "the Most Holy Place"; KJV, NRSV, and others do not include the word *place*)

---

8. I like the term *wholative*, which I took from Wallace, *Greek Grammar beyond the Basics*, 84–86. The Gen noun is the whole of which the N^h is a part.

9. **Gen of Authority**
   a. **Ruled**

   the king of Moab [מֶלֶךְ מוֹאָב] (Josh 24:9 NIV)

   b. **Ruler**

   that is, the whole *kingdom of Og* [מַמְלְכוּת עוֹג] in Bashan (Josh 13:12 NIV)

10. **Gen of Advantage/Disadvantage**
   a. **Beneficiary/Sufferer**[9] (the one who suffers good/harm)

   Blessed is *the one* . . . [אַשְׁרֵי הָאִישׁ] (Ps 1:1 NIV; more formally, "Oh, the blessings of the man")

   and talk about *the pain of those* you *hurt* [מַכְאוֹב חֲלָלֶיךָ] (Ps 69:26b [Hebrew 27b] NIV; formally, "*the pain of the pierced* of you")

   Pierced is an adjective used as a noun and the NIV, with many English versions, takes "pierced" as a metaphor for the sufferer of the pain. Incidentally, the "of you" would be a subjective Gen.

   b. **Benefactor/Malefactor** (the one who causes good/harm)

   The LORD favors those who fear Him, those who wait for *His loving-kindness* [לְחַסְדּוֹ]. (Ps 147:11 NASB; formally, "for *the lovingkindness of him*")

   I would have despaired unless I had believed that I would see *the goodness of the LORD* [בְּטוּב יהוה]. (Ps 27:13 NASB)

11. **Gen Object of a Preposition**: In these instances, the function is governed by the Pp.

Special Note: "Mountain of My Holiness" or "My Holy Mountain"?

The attributive Gen is a common way that Hebrew uses nouns to form adjectival ideas. For example, הַר קֹדֶשׁ (formally, "mountain of holiness") really means "holy mountain." It is easy to understand how adding the 1cs PrnSf, "my," to a Cst noun changes הַר, "mountain of" to הָרִי, "the mountain of me" or "my mountain." But, how does Hebrew say, "my holy mountain"? The problem is that it's not typical Hebrew to break the construct chain הַר קֹדֶשׁ to form הָרִי קֹדֶשׁ. The PrnSf is attached to the end of the chain: הַר קָדְשִׁי. Formally, this would be "the mountain of the holiness of me." But the meaning is "my holy mountain." Context decides what the Prn modifies.

---

9. I wish *maleficiary* were a word. ☺

Determining Noun Characteristics

If you were learning full Hebrew, you would learn how to identify gender, number, and state by reading and speaking in Hebrew. What about as a pre-Hebrew student? Looking up a Hebrew word in the *SNIVEC* will show you the lexical form and the gender, but it will not tell you the number and state in a given context. You must use one of the resources already mentioned. You may use an interlinear to see if the word *of* appears between the translation of two Hebrew words. The simplest way is to use a computer Bible with a tagged Hebrew text. Case and function are things you will have to figure out based on context. We have given numerous functions earlier in this chapter.

Prepositions and Case

In the previous chapter we noted that English prepositions take their objects in the objective case. In Hebrew we might say that as well, but, as we explained above, it is "tidier" to say that prepositions are in construct with their objects. In saying this, though, there is no need to ask how the Gen is functioning; the Pp governs the case function. Instead you look at the function of the preposition, as we saw in the last chapter.

Here is how it would look if you were to fill out a parsing chart for the expressions in the following sentences:

S1.   **A servant of a king** [עֶבֶד מֶלֶךְ (no article)] ran to tell him.
S2.   He heard **the word of the prophet** [דְּבַר־הַנָּבִיא (with an article)].
S3.   The fame of **the wisdom of Solomon** [חָכְמַת שְׁלֹמֹה (with a proper noun)] spread throughout the world.
S4.   They beat **his head** [רֹאשׁוֹ (with PrnSf; formally, "**the head of him**")].
S5.   **With pain** [בְּעֶצֶב] you shall give birth to children.

From the sentences above, here is the parsing. The roots given are as identified in Logos Bible Software.

FIGURE 11.7: Parsing Examples

| | | | Verbal Qualities | | | Nominal Qualities | | | | |
PtSp	Word	Lex	Stem	Form	P	G	N	State	Det	Case	Suff
Nn	עֶבֶד	עבד				m	s	Cst	U	Nom	
Nn	מֶלֶךְ	מלך				m	s	Abs	U	Gen	
Nn	דְּבַר־	דבר 2				m	s	Cst	D	Acc	

(continued)

		Verbal Qualities		Nominal Qualities			
Nn	נְבִיא הַנָּבִיא	m	s	Abs	D	Gen	
Nn	חכם חָכְמַת	f	s	Cst	D	Gen	
Nn	שָׁלוֹם שְׁלֹמֹה	m	s	Abs	D	Gen	
Nn	רֹאשׁ 1 רֹאשׁוֹ	m	s	Cst	D	Acc	3ms
Pp	בְּ בְּעֶצֶב			Cst			
Nn	עצב 2 בְּעֶצֶב	m	s	Abs	U	Gen	

Notice the following:
1. In the "Det" column, "D" stands for determined and "U" for undetermined.
2. The case of N^h is determined by its function in the sentence; the case of the N^t is always Gen, including a PrnSf.
3. The PrnSf doesn't get its own line, since it is not independent.
4. The Pp gets its own line but has no other features. For this reason, it might be ignored in parsing or simply added as "בְּ" in the "Lex" column.

Particles of Existence

Hebrew has an interesting way of saying that something "exists" or "does not exist." These are the particles יֵשׁ and אַיִן. Formally they mean "existence" and "nonexistence," respectively. They may be used in the absolute or construct state. As a pre-Hebrew student, there is not much you need to do with these, but if you come across one in an interlinear Bible, you will need to have some idea of what they are. Here are some examples.

Gen 18:24 Interlinear	הָעִיר	בְּתוֹךְ	צַדִּיקִם	חֲמִשִּׁים	יֵשׁ	.	אוּלַי
	the city	in the midst of	righteous	fifty	**the existence of**	(there is)	perhaps

NIV	What if **there are** fifty righteous people in the city?

Explanation	יֵשׁ is in the Cst.

Gen 39:5 Interlinear	וּבַשָּׂדֶה	בַּבַּיִת	לוֹ	יֶשׁ־	אֲשֶׁר	כָּל־	עַל	יְהוָה	בִּרְכַּת	וַיְהִי
	and in the field	in the house	to him	**(there) was**	which	all of	on	the Lord	the blessing of	and it was

NIV	The blessing of the Lord was on everything Potiphar **had**, both in the house and in the field.

Explanation	יֵשׁ is followed by a prepositional phrase. The לְ marks the possessor.

Gen 2:5 Interlinear	הָאֲדָמָה the ground	אֶת —	לַעֲבֹד to work	אַיִן *non-existence*	• (was)	וְאָדָם and man
NIV	And *there was no* one to work the ground.					
Explanation	אַיִן is in the Abs.					

Gen 7:8 Interlinear	טְהֹרָה purity	אֵינֶנָּה *the non-existence of it*	אֲשֶׁר that	הַבְּהֵמָה the beast	וּמִן and from
ESV	and of animals that *are not* clean				
Explanation	אֵינֶנָּה is in the Cst with a PrnSf referring back to the beast. Another translation might be, "and from the beasts which have no purity."				

Flowcharting Cases

When I introduced flowcharting to you, I gave the general principle that the only things on the clause line are subject, verb, indirect object, and direct object. Now that you have spent time working through all these case uses, how should you treat them in flowcharts? The answer is: however you find most helpful. There are no problems with the Nom and the Acc of DO; they are simply on the main line as we have seen. The question arises over the adverbial uses of the Hebrew Acc and over the Gen, which are translated by English prepositional phrases. As a general rule, I keep possessives in the line where their modifier is. They are so routine that giving each one a separate line is more of a distraction. To the other prepositional phrases, I do give a separate line and label the function.

If Vocatives begin or end a sentence, they get their own line and they are not indented. If the Voc stands in the middle of a sentence, I usually keep it in the order of the English text.

> **Teaching/Learning Tip:** The explanations that I offer also serve as examples of comments you might make for yourself in explaining a text in your notes or for a paper in a college course. Some of these comments are not suitable for preaching or teaching, however. You don't want to make your audience's eyes glaze over! Give them what they need from the fruit of your careful study.

Here are a few examples. Again, I have used different styles to point out different parts of speech; this is a pedagogical device and is not necessary in your work.

Function	Vs	Flowchart: Gen 2:7 (NIV)
Event Material Source	7	**The Lord God** formed → a man from the dust of the ground.
Explanation		"From the dust" is an Acc of material in Hebrew; it modifies the verb. "Of the ground" is in Hebrew a PPhr using מִן.

Function	Vs	Flowchart: Gen 14:15 (NIV)
Time Event Purpose		During the night **Abram** divided → his men to attack → them
Addition Event Means Extent Location	15	and **he** routed → them, pursuing → them as far as Hobah, north of Damascus.
Explanation		There are two clauses here. In the first, "During the night" is an Acc of time; "to attack" is a purpose phrase with an infinitive (see ch. 17).

Function	Vs	Flowchart: Deut 6:8 (NIV)
Command Comparison/ Purpose Place	20	[You] tie → them as symbols on your hands
Addition Command Place		and [you] bind → them on your foreheads.
Explanation		The PPhrs "on your hands" and "on your foreheads" include possessive PPrns; I left them on the same line as the nouns they modify. For commands, the implied Subj is *you*, which has been bracketed.

Function	Vs	Flowchart: Jer 1:5, NIV
Event Destination	5	I appointed → you ⬄ as a prophet to the nations.
Explanation		The double Acc of person-thing. The two accusatives are equated with the ⬄.

Function	Vs	Flowchart: Num 21:17b-c
Exhortation Address Exhortation	17	[You] Spring up, **O well!** [You] Sing about it,
Explanation		"O well" is in the Voc case and occurs at the end of a clause, so it gets its own line. Notice that I have inserted the implied "you" subject of the exhortation (see ch. 16 below).

Function	Vs	Flowchart: Job 17:3
Request	3a	Give me, **O God**, the pledge you demand.
Explanation		"O God" is in the Voc case and occurs in the middle of a clause, so I retained the English word order without the complication of moving the "O God" to a separate line. The Vocative again corresponds to the implied "you" subject of the request even though I did not insert it here.

What about Aramaic?

The pronouns work the same in Aramaic as in Hebrew.

The Nom, Acc, and Voc also work the same way in both languages.

The Gen also works the same way, except that Aramaic has three ways to form the Gen construction. All of these could be translated with two nouns joined with the Pp *of*; I have provided translations designed to duplicate the grammatical form of the Hebrew expressions.

Structure	Example	Explanation
N^{cst}–N^{abs} [± Art]	מִלַּת מַלְכָּא the matter of the king (Dan 2:10)	The use of the construct relationship just as in Hebrew.
N^1+Art–*dî*–N^2+Art	שַׁלִּיטָא דִּי מַלְכָּא the commander of the king (Dan 2:15)	A determined noun joined to another determined noun by the particle דִּי, which is often equivalent to the Hebrew RPrn שֶׁ (and אֲשֶׁר) but in this construction is functioning as the Pp *of*, unlike Hebrew. The demonstration of this is seen in that the two nouns refer to different entities.
N^h+PrnSf–*dî*–N^t+Art	שְׁמֵהּ דִּי־אֱלָהָא the name of God (woodenly: the name of him who [is] God) (Dan 2:20)	The N^h is in Cst with a PrnSf and thereby made Det; the PrnSf anticipates the following noun; the N^t is also Det. The particle דִּי is a RPrn here introducing an RC (ch. 12) and referring back to the PrnSf of the N^h.

The particle of existence in Aramaic is אִיתַי, which is a plural form of אִית (etymologically related to Hebrew יֵשׁ). Biblical Aramaic uses only the former. Both forms occur in other later Aramaic documents, along with יַת, a shortened form of אִית. These particles are made negative by the negative Adv לָא (Hebrew לֹא). In later Aramaic יַת and לָא were contracted to form the negative particle לֵיתָא, לֵית, לַיִת, and even abbreviated לֵי, all translatable as "there is/are not."

Advanced Information and Curious Facts

Hebrew Noun Endings

Hebrew uses endings to indicate the gender, number, and state of nouns. In case you are curious, figure 11.8 gives a summary of the endings by attaching them to two different nouns. סוּס is a masculine noun meaning *horse*; תּוֹרָה is a feminine noun meaning *law*.

FIGURE 11.8: Hebrew Noun Endings				
	ABSOLUTE STATE		**CONSTRUCT STATE**	
	Masculine	**Feminine**	**Masculine**	**Feminine**
Singular	סוּס	תּוֹרָה	סוּס	תּוֹרַת
Dual	סוּסַיִם	תּוֹרָתַיִם	סוּסֵי	תּוֹרָתֵי
Plural	סוּסִים	תּוֹרוֹת	סוּסֵי	תּוֹרוֹת

Since you are not learning full Hebrew, you do not need to memorize these endings (and the variations). The masculine singular (ms) is usually unmarked; i.e., it has no ending.

Immanuel

One of the well-known names for the Messiah is taken from Isa 7:14 and 8:8, "Immanuel." Matthew 1:23 quotes Isa 7:14 and then gives the meaning of the name, "God with us." Now that you know about Hebrew prepositions and that they can take PrnSfs, you can understand the Hebrew behind this name. In Hebrew *Immanuel* is actually two words: עִמָּנוּ אֵל. אֵל is the word for "God." עִמָּנוּ is the Pp עִם, "with," plus the 1cp PrnSf, "us." It is a verbless clause meaning "God is with us."

One more thing: Why do we sometimes see this word spelled Emmanuel, since the Hebrew has the letter *i*? Because the Greek spelling in the LXX and the NT is *Emmanouēl* (Ἐμμανουήλ), which was transliterated into Latin as *Emmanuel*, which English adopted.

CHAPTER 12

AN APT DESCRIPTION
Adjectives

Objectives
1. Analyze English and Hebrew adjectives.
2. Understand relative clauses.
3. Learn how to flowchart adjectives and relative clauses.

Introduction

A church I used to attend had an annual event at Christmastime: "the hanging of the greens." The running joke was that one of the prominent families, whose last name was Green, was always afraid to come!

Of course, what was meant was that we would get together to hang the green wreaths and green holly and green boughs for Christmas decorations. It is still interesting, though, how words work. The reason the joke works is because in the phrase "the hanging of the greens," the word *greens* fills a noun slot (a place where we expect to hear a noun). The name *Green* is a proper noun; the color green, though, is an adjective describing the decorations. The expression gets shortened to *greens* and behold: an adjective is transformed into a noun.

After the last chapter, this chapter on adjectives will seem like a vacation! Adjectives do about the same things in English (and in all languages) as in Hebrew. First, we will look at how adjectives work in both English and Hebrew. Then we will look at relative clauses because they function just like adjectives. Finally, we will look at flowcharting adjectives and relative clauses.

By the way, in case you were worried, the Greens always came and everyone enjoyed the event.

Adjectives

An *adjective* (Adj) is a word that modifies or describes a substantive. In talking about Adjs, there are two factors to consider: how they function and how they are structured (the arrangement of words).

English Adjectives

Adjectives function in three ways: attributively, predicatively, or substantivally. In the first two, the noun (Nn) is present; in the third, the noun is absent but understood. In the *attributive* use, the Adj describes a noun, and in the *predicative* use, the Adj ascribes a quality to a noun. In the *substantival* use, the Adj is substituted for a noun. In the following examples, the Adj is in bold type and the Nn it modifies (if any) is underlined.

S1. **Hot** coffee costs a lot.
S2. The **hot** cups are burning my hands.
S3. The cups are **hot**.
S4. **One** dollar still buys a cup of coffee.
S5. If I had a **one** in my wallet, I would buy a cup of coffee.
S6. I have some **ones** in my wallet.
S7. I'll buy some coffee during the time **out**.
S8. How many times **out** are left?
S9. By the way, I actually heard a **sports** announcer on TV say, "times out"!

Notice the following:
1. S1, S2 and S4 have attributive Adjs. The Adj is right next to the noun. In English the adjective normally precedes the noun.
2. S3 has a predicative Adj. Notice that a verb, *are*, separates the noun from its adjective. The noun and the Adj with an equative verb both refer to the same thing. Compare the predicate Nom use from the last chapter.
3. English does not pluralize attributive and predicative Adjs. Whether the noun is singular (S1) or plural (S2 and S3), the Adj does not change; i.e., it is not inflected.
4. In S5 and S6 there is no noun present; dollar bill(s) is understood. The Adj is substantival. When Adjs substitute for nouns, then they are inflected just like nouns.
5. S7 and S8 also have attributive Adjs. In certain expressions the Adj comes after the noun.
6. S9 is an interesting example of a noun, *sports*, being used as an Adj. Hebrew does this also.

Hebrew Adjective Parsing and Forms

Hebrew Adjs have the same kind of parsing information as nouns. Figure 12.1 supplements figures 5.2 and 9.2 with adjectives.

When we discussed Hebrew noun patterns, we noted how endings follow common patterns—most of the time. But there are many "irregular" nouns that don't follow the usual patterns. As a pre-Hebrew student, you will need to rely on computers to give you grammatical information. Adjectives, on the other hand, are quite regular, as you will see below.

FIGURE 12.1: Parsing Information for Nominals and Verbs

PtSp	Word	Lex	Verbal Qualities						Nominal Qualities			
			Stem	Form	P	G	N	State	Det	Case	Suff
V			X	X	X	X	X				
Nn						X	X	X	X	X	
Adj						X	X	X	X	X	

Adjectives Modifying Simple Nouns

Hebrew Adjs are similar to English Adjs. They have the same three functions, but there are some differences in grammatical construction. Three factors come into play in Hebrew constructions: the article (here we will once again use T instead of Art for the sake of brevity), the Adj, and the Nn. Further, the Adj and the Nn both have three qualities: gender, number, and definiteness. Here are the principles involved:

1. *Every Adj agrees with its Nn in gender and number.* We have already seen that gender in English is not often marked, but it is always present in Hebrew. Additionally, Adjs are inflected for gender.
2. *Every attributive Adj agrees with its Nn in determination.* This is one of the important ways that the Hebrew article is used differently from English. The article with an Adj is there to indicate the relationship to the noun rather than having any other meaning.
3. *Almost every predicative Adj disagrees with its Nn in determination.* Predicate Adjs occur mostly in noun clauses. When the Nn is determined and the Adj is not, English needs to insert the verb *to be* between them.

All of this leads to there being four possible positions (constructions) of adjectives, nouns, and articles. These positions mark the functions. Patterns with a black circle (·) following are nonroutine.[1]

FIGURE 12.2: Positions and Agreement of Adjectives with Common Nouns

Construction	Presence of Noun	Definite Determined Noun	Article before Adj	Function	Example	Pattern
Attributive	Y	Y	Y	Attributive	הַמֶּלֶךְ הַטּוֹב or מֶלֶךְ הַטּוֹב = the **good** king	T-Nn-**T-Adj** Nn-**T-Adj**[i]

(continued)

---

1. This construction is quite rare and looks like it contradicts the rule of agreement in determination. One example is Exod 12:15, "from the first day" (מִיּוֹם הָרִאשׁוֹן, the prefixed preposition is inconsequential). Another is

Construction	Presence of Noun	Definite Determined Noun	Article before Adj	Function	Example	Pattern
Predicate	Y	Y	N	Predicative	הַמֶּלֶךְ טוֹב or טוֹב הַמֶּלֶךְ = the king (is) **good**	T-Nn-**Adj** **Adj**-T-Nn •
Ambiguous	Y	N	N	Either Attributive or Predicative	מֶלֶךְ טוֹב or טוֹב מֶלֶךְ = a **good** king or a king (is) **good**	Nn-**Adj** **Adj**-Nn •
Isolated	N	—	Y or N	Substantival	טוֹב or הַטּוֹב = a **good** (man) or the **good** (man)	**Adj** T-**Adj**

Notice the following:

1. In the attributive Nn–T–Adj construction, the noun must still be determined, even if there is no article.
2. For the two predicative constructions, the subject (Subj) and predicate (Pred) differ in determination.
   a. The default word order is Subj–Pred. This means that the focus is on the noun, but there is no special emphasis on it.
   b. The Art–Nn–Adj order, e.g., הַמֶּלֶךְ טוֹב, answers the question, "Who is good?" or "What is the king?" with "The king is good," without drawing any special emphasis to either.
   c. The Adj–Art–Nn order, e.g., טוֹב הַמֶּלֶךְ, answers the question, "What is the king?" with, "Good is the king" with a marked focus (not necessarily emphasis) on the Adj.
3. In the ambiguous positions, only context can determine whether the Adj is attributive or predicative. Only rarely is the context unclear.
4. The isolated position occurs most commonly with the article. In these cases the Adj agrees in gender and number with the supposed antecedent.

Translating substantival adjectives is interesting because of the difference of English number. For example, a well-known chorus, "Blessed Be the Name of the Lord," uses Prov 18:10 as the refrain. Here is an interlinear version comparing versions:

Gen 41:26, "the seven good cows" (שֶׁבַע פָּרוֹת הַטּוֹבוֹת), however, a number of manuscripts have the T-Nn-T-Adj construction. If you are really curious, for a useful treatment see S. R. Driver, *A Treatise on the Use of the Tenses in Hebrew and Some Other Syntactical Questions* (Oxford: Oxford University Press, 1892), appendix IV on apposition and in appendix V, §209; though very good, it will be heavy reading for those who do not know Hebrew pretty well. Driver points out that when this structure is used, it is with set expressions, such as with יוֹם, "day," as in Exod 12:15 above, in which the noun is familiar enough that it was conceived to be definite in itself (p. 281).

FIGURE 12.3: Proverbs 18:10, Adjectives, and Versions

Hebrew Interlinear	וְנִשְׂגָּב	צַדִּיק	יָרוּץ	בּוֹ	יְהוָה	שֵׁם	•	עֹז	מִגְדַּל
	and he is saved.	the righteous	(he) runs	into it	the Lᴏʀᴅ;	the name of		(is) strength	tower of

NIV	The name of the Lᴏʀᴅ is a fortified tower; the righteous run to it and are safe.
KJV	The name of the Lᴏʀᴅ is a strong tower: the righteous runneth into it, and is safe.
ESV	The name of the Lᴏʀᴅ is a strong tower; the righteous man runs into it and is safe.

In the second clause, the subject, "the righteous," is singular. The KJV preserves this by using the singular verbs "runneth" and "is." The ESV preserves the singular number and the masculine gender by adding the word *man*. The NIV could have preserved the singular verb, "runs," but thought that the isolated position "righteous," with a generic meaning, should be understood to include plural people.

A key difference between nouns and Adjs is that whereas nouns have one and only one gender, Adjs must be able to take the endings of either gender. As a pre-Hebrew student, you are not learning the endings, but a couple of examples will help you understand. We will use the Adj טוֹב, meaning "good," and the nouns אִישׁ, "man," and מִשְׁפָּחָה, "family." In the following chart, the words are gray and the endings are black. The designations "m" and "f" stand for "masculine" and "feminine"; "s" and "p" stand for "singular" and "plural"; and "D" and "U" stand for "determined" and "undetermined."

FIGURE 12.4: Grammatical Agreement of Attributive Adjectives with Nouns

Hebrew	English	GN	Det
אִישׁ טוֹב	(a) good man	ms	U
אֲנָשִׁים טוֹבִים	good men	mp	U
הָאִישׁ הַטּוֹב	the good man	ms	D
הָאֲנָשִׁים הַטּוֹבִים	the good men	mp	D
מִשְׁפָּחָה טוֹבָה	(a) good family	fs	U
מִשְׁפָּחוֹת טוֹבוֹת	good families	fp	U
הַמִּשְׁפָּחָה הַטּוֹבָה	the good family	fs	D
הַמִּשְׁפָּחוֹת הַטּוֹבוֹת	the good families	fp	D

The attributive Adjs agree in gender, number, and determination with their respective nouns. I purposely chose words that would have endings to make that clear. Sometimes the endings are not identical, but the gender and number

still are. For example, דֶּרֶךְ is a feminine noun, even though it doesn't end in הֹ.
Nevertheless, "a good way" in Hebrew is דֶּרֶךְ טוֹבָה with the הֹ ending.

Adjectives Modifying Nouns in a Construct Chain

Since a construct chain is treated as a unit, it normally cannot be interrupted. If an Adj modifies one element of the chain, it is located after the chain
and follows the rules given above. The Adj may modify either element of the
chain. Study the following examples of attributive Adjs.

FIGURE 12.5: Grammatical Agreement of Adjectives with Nouns in a Construct Chain

Hebrew	English
בֶּן־הַנְּבִיאִים הַטּוֹב	the good son of the prophets **Explanation:** "Son" and "good" are both ms D, "prophets" is mp D.
בַּת־הַנְּבִיאִים הַטּוֹבִים	the daughter of the good prophets **Explanation:** Both "prophets" and "good" are plural and masculine; "daughter" is singular and feminine.
בֶּן־הַנָּבִיא הַטּוֹב	Either "the good son of the prophet" or "the son of the good prophet" **Explanation:** Because both Nns and the Adj agree in gender, number and determination, the Hebrew is ambiguous. The English must make a choice. Normally context makes clear which meaning is intended.

Adjectives and Comparison

The simple Adj is called the *positive*. The *comparative* indicates the member
of a group of items that has a certain quality to a greater degree. The *superlative*
indicates the member that has a certain quality to the greatest degree. The figure
below gives a few examples.

FIGURE 12.6: English Degrees of Comparison

Positive	Comparative	Superlative
big	bigg*er*	bigg*est*
fast	fast*er*	fast*est*
good	bett*er*	best

Hebrew expresses degrees differently from English. The comparative may be
expressed, as we saw in ch. 8 by the Pp מִן following an adjective. We learned in ch. 11
that Hebrew may also express a superlative with an expression that English renders with
of, as in "king *of* kings," meaning "the greatest king." The superlative may be expressed
by a simple Adj, by the phrase "from all/any of" (מִן־כָּל). It may also be expressed
by the repetition of Adjs, *"Holy, holy, holy* is the LORD of hosts" (Isa 6:3, ESV).

Payoffs from Being Able to Analyze Adjectives

Gender and number. When you find differences in number between versions, you can use the tools we have already mentioned repeatedly to get grammatical information. You are able to follow arguments in commentaries. Singular number gives a more specific, individual, or corporate perspective, while plurals give a more general perspective. Retaining this from Hebrew helps you see what the author is intending.

Distinguishing nonroutine word order from default word order. An Adj before a noun emphasizes the Adj. Oftentimes versions, whether formal or functional, do not retain Hebrew word order because the translation would be awkward. Being able to identify nonroutine word order gives you the ability to understand remarks in commentaries and at times to see for yourself where stress might be placed.

Making Relatives Your Friends

Sometimes the people we find most difficult to get along with are those we are closest to. Who fights more often or more vigorously than brothers? And the closer in age, the more they pick at each other. Ah, but if an outsider comes between them, they gang up together like the closest of friends. This is what I want to do with relative clauses—make them your friends!

> **Teaching/Learning Tip:** Do not confuse *who, what, which,* and *whose* with the interrogative pronouns that introduce questions! Or the relative *that* with the demonstrative pronoun *that,* or with the conjunction *that* that indicates purpose or result.

Let's begin with terms. Remember that a clause is an expression with a verb in it (as opposed to a phrase, which has no verb). A relative pronoun (RPrn) introduces a relative clause (RC) and relates it to a word in another clause. A RPrn does double duty. First, it has a grammatical function within the RC. Second, it often has an antecedent outside the RC. An RC is a subordinate clause. An RC consists of a RPrn + the clause that follows it. Examples of RPrns are: who, what, which, whose, that, whatever.

Sometimes the RPrn is omitted, as in "I *have* a car I *want* to sell." There are two clauses (both verbs are italicized). The second one describes the car. The sentence could be rewritten, "I have a car *that* I want to sell."

In the chapter on clauses, I told you that we would treat RCs here. The reason is because RCs have the same three functions as Adjs. The whole RC may function attributively, predicatively, or substantivally. When it functions substantivally, just like any Nn, the RC can be the subject or object of a verb, or object of a preposition. In all three functions, an RC serves to describe.

A Strategy

What we need is a plan for dealing with RCs. In the concluding section, you will see how to deal with them in flowcharts. Here is a strategy for dealing with them in sentence form.

> **Teaching/Learning Tip:** If you are working in a MSWord document, instead of circles, simply double-click the word and use the Borders command in the Paragraph box to make a box around the selected text. You can also insert curly brackets, {}, into the text. You can also draw arrows using the Shapes menu in the Illustrations box under the Insert tab. In *HRUW* we will use a different system.

1. Circle the RPrn and draw an open bracket.
2. Find the end of the RC and draw a closing bracket. Sometimes this step involves some interpretation.
3. See if you can draw an arrow from RPrn to a noun *outside* of the RC.
   a. If you can, the RC is acting like an Adj and is describing that noun.
   b. If you cannot, the RC is acting like a noun and you need to describe it as subject or object of a verb or preposition.
   c. If it is the object of a preposition, circle the preposition and underline the complete prepositional phrase.

Here is an example illustrating each step.

Step	Passage: Gen 11:5 (ESV)
1	And the Lᴏʀᴅ came down to see the city and the tower, [(which) the children of man had built. **Explanation:** I notice the RPrn *which* (it doesn't introduce a question), circle it, and draw an open bracket. The RPrn functions as the DO of the RC verb, "had built."
2	And the Lᴏʀᴅ came down to see the city and the tower, [(which) the children of man had built.] **Explanation:** The RC ends at the end of the sentence, so that is where I put the closing bracket.
3	And the Lᴏʀᴅ came down to see the city and the tower, [(which) the children of man had built.] **Explanation:** The RPrn refers back to both *city* and *tower*. Since I can draw an arrow to a word outside the RC, and since there is no verb *to be* between the RC and the antecedent, the RC is functioning adjectivally. In this case, there are two antecedents.

Here is another example, in which the RC has no antecedent and functions substantivally. Instead of drawing a circle, I've used MSWord as described in the tips box above to envelop the RPrn in a box.

PASSAGE: 1 Sam 28:8 (ESV)

And he said, "Divine for me by a spirit and bring up for me [whomever I shall name to you]."

Explanation: I notice the RPrn *whomever* (OC), envelop it, and draw brackets. The RPrn functions as the DO of the RC verb, "shall name." However, there is no antecedent (i.e., referent) outside the RC. Therefore the entire RC is functioning as a noun in the main clause, and is the DO of the verb "bring up."

To check our identification of a substantival use of the RC, substitute any noun for the RC to see if it makes sense. We might try, "Bob" or "lunch," yielding, "and bring up Bob"; "and bring up lunch." This checks out; the RC is functioning as a substantive.

Hebrew RCs work just the way English ones do, except they are simpler: there is only one RPrn, אֲשֶׁר. It may be translated by any of the English RPrns, depending on the context. Often there is within the RC (usually at the end) a resumptive pronoun or adverb that clarifies the antecedent of the אֲשֶׁר and may be omitted, just as in English. Study these two examples of interlinears.

The first example is Gen 7:19, which reads, "They rose greatly on the earth, and all the high mountains under the entire heavens were covered" (NIV). In Hebrew, "under the entire heavens" is an RC modifying "mountains":

Gen 7:19	הַשָּׁמָיִם	כָּל	תַּחַת	·	אֲשֶׁר	הַגְּבֹהִים	הֶהָרִים
	the heavens	all of	under	(were)	which	(the) high	the mountains
Explanation	The RC begins with אֲשֶׁר and ends with the verse. Within the RC, the RPrn אֲשֶׁר functions as the subject Nom of a noun clause in which the predicate is a Pp, "under all of the heavens." The RPrn has an antecedent, namely, "mountains." The RC is functioning attributively, describing the mountains.						

In the next example from Gen 42:38, the RC has a resumptive pronoun. The NIV reads, "But Jacob said, 'My son will not go down there with you; his brother is dead and he is the only one left. If harm comes to him on the journey you are taking, you will bring my gray head down to the grave in sorrow.'" In Hebrew, "you are taking" is an RC modifying the feminine noun דֶּרֶךְ.

Gen 42:38	בָהּ	תֵּלְכוּ	אֲשֶׁר	דֶּרֶךְ
	in it (her)	you are walking	which	the way
NIV	the journey you are taking			

(continued)

ESV	the journey that you are to make
Explanation	The ESV preserves the RPrn; the NIV doesn't. This is due to translation philosophy differences, the ESV wishing to represent each Hebrew word in some way and the NIV opting for simpler style. Both translations are good. The key thing to notice is the final PPhr בָּהּ. The PrnSf is 3fs agreeing with the gender and number of the antecedent דֶּרֶךְ. This is routine in Hebrew RCs. Neither translation renders this, because English does not use this construction. To translate it would produce something abnormal and might make some Bible students read into the PPhr some meaning that is not present in Hebrew.

Flowcharting Adjectives and Relative Clauses

Flowcharting Adjs is going to depend on how you want to do it. Basically, I treat them the same way I treat possessive pronouns: since they have one main function (namely, describing), I usually keep them in the same line as the noun they modify. If there are lists of Adjs modifying one noun, I might indent them .25 inches under the word they modify. The idea is to do whatever you find most helpful to make the grammar clear and avoid unnecessary work. Flowcharting RCs follows the example of all subordinate clauses: indent about one inch and draw a line to what the RC modifies. Note: in the function column, there is a blank line for the functions of the main clauses. You will learn how to label them in ch. 13. In anticipation of this, I have scattered some labels as we have been going and included them in keys to the exercises for this chapter.

Ellipses (. . .) mark that material has been moved, and a circumflex (ˆ) marks the material that has been moved.

Function	Vs	Flowchart: Gen 29:2 (NIV)

(_____)
Place
Possessor
	2	The stone . . . was ⟺ large
		          ˆover the mouth
		               of the well

Explanation		"Large" is a predicate Adj; it sits on the same line as the subject and rest of the predicate. In Hebrew, the phrase is גְדוֹלָה (large) וְהָאֶבֶן (and the stone). The noun has the article, making it the subject, and the Adj does not, marking it as predicative.

Function	Vs	Flowchart: Gen 27:34 (NIV)

Time
(_____)
Manner
Description
Addition
Description
	34	When Esau heard his father's words,
		     he burst out
		                    with a . . . cry
		                          ˆloud
		                               and
		                          bitter

Explanation	The Hebrew has a noun followed by two Adjs joined by the conjunction *waw*. It is simpler to keep them in line; I indented them for illustrative purposes, because there was more than one. The function label for attributive Adjs is "Description"; they are indented under "cry" because that is what they modify.

Function	Vs	Flowchart: Josh 24:32 (NIV)
Sequence (_____)		And Joseph's bones, . . . were buried
Description Origin		^which the Israelites had brought up from Egypt,
Location Location Partitive	32	at Shechem in the tract of land
Description Price Source		that Jacob bought for a hundred pieces of silver from the sons of Hamor,
Apposition		the father of Shechem

Explanation	The RC is subordinate and indented one inch. The arrows point to the antecedents. Both the PPhrs are adverbial and are therefore indented under the verb each modifies.

What about Aramaic?

There is not really any difference between Hebrew and Aramaic, except for vocabulary. Instead of the Hebrew RPrn אֲשֶׁר and שֶׁ◌, Aramaic uses שֶׁ◌ and דִּי.

Advanced Information and Curious Facts

Deuteronomy 6:4 is the beginning of the famous "Shema" passage (named after the first Hebrew word in the verse). It is a verbless clause (see ch. 6). I give the text in interlinear format without supplying a verb, and I have rendered God's name, traditionally rendered LORD, as Yahweh to avoid confusion with the noun Lord. Below the interlinear I give two versions, NIV and KJV.

Deut 6:4	אֶחָד one	יְהוָה Yahweh	אֱלֹהֵינוּ our God	יְהוָה Yahweh	יִשְׂרָאֵל O Israel	שְׁמַע Hear
NIV	Hear, O Israel: The LORD our God, the LORD is one.					
KJV	Hear, O Israel: The LORD our God is one LORD.					

The problems are (1) whether to translate the last four Hebrew words as one clause or two, and, (2) if one clause, where the verb should be placed. If it is two clauses, then it should be rendered, "Yahweh *is* our God; Yahweh *is* one." This makes sense, but the Greek translations of both the LXX and the NT (see Mark 12:29, for example) render this as one clause, as indicated by the fact that the Greek includes the verb *is* only at the end of the sentence.

Both the NIV and KJV follow the Greek in rendering this as one clause, but there is a difference between them with respect to the placement of the verb. The KJV has taken the first phrase, in particular, "Yahweh," as the subject nominative and the second Yahweh as a predicate nominative. At first read, this seems well enough. But remember that both the LXX and NT render the name Yahweh with the Greek *kyrios*, "Lord, lord, master." Most modern versions follow that same practice. In Hebrew, the term is not the title "Lord" but the actual name of God, "Yahweh." Taking the KJV and replacing "Lord" with "Yahweh" yields "Yahweh our God is one Yahweh." I suppose we can make sense out of this, but it is awkward.

The NIV understands the Hebrew (and the Greek) a bit differently: the first phrase is a nominative absolute (see ch. 11) as indicated by the comma; then follows the subject nominative, Yahweh, and the predicate. Again replacing "the Lord" with "Yahweh" in the NIV yields: "As for Yahweh our God, Yahweh is one." Incidentally, this rendering also agrees with how the LXX translators understood the verse, and therefore the NT, since the Greek has the verb at the end.[2]

So what's the difference? Not a lot; it is a matter of emphasis. The KJV rendering makes the predicate Adj "one" less prominent. The NIV brings out the thrust of the Hebrew (and Greek) more simply and clearly: the Nom Abs draws attention to the subject in the clause as the covenant God of Israel ("our"). Then the main clause makes the assertion: Yahweh is one, or unique. This is the great truth of the Shema passage.

---

2. On LXX grammar, see John William Wevers, *Notes on the Greek Text of Deuteronomy* (Atlanta: Scholars Press, 1995), 114.

CHAPTER 13

WHERE THE ACTION IS
Overview of Verbals

Objectives
1. Define the parts of speech comprising verbals.
2. Identify the qualities English and Hebrew verbs indicate.
3. Describe two ways that Hebrew verbs can take a DO.
4. Explain some general features of Hebrew verbals, including word order.
5. Use tools to identify verbs and understand parsing.
6. Flowchart main clause functions.

Tools Used: Interlinear Bible

Introduction

The heart of any language is the verb. It describes the action related to the actors. In this chapter we will begin with some terminology common to verbs in any language. Then we will turn to general features of Hebrew verbs.

There has been much research done in the last several decades on the nature of the Hebrew verbal system, and research is continuing. Some of the traditional models are beginning to be replaced, but traditional language is still common. Therefore, you need to learn both traditional descriptions because you will frequently come across these in your reading, and newer terminology, because it is more precise and is becoming more current. Finally, we will deal with labeling main clause functions. Let's begin with some terminology.

Essential Concepts

As we introduced in ch. 5, there are two main types of verbal forms, *finite verbs* and *nonfinite verbs*. Some writers use the word *verb* to mean finite verbs as opposed to nonfinite. The term *verbal* is used to refer to both finite and nonfinite verbs.

A *verb* is a word that depicts an action or a state of being. I will call action verbs "dynamic";[1] examples are *run, see, love*. A verb depicting a state of being is

---

1. Some grammarians call them "fientive," but I think "dynamic" is more understandable.

called a stative verb. The most common example is *be*, but others are *become* and *remain*. Look at these examples with the verbs or verb phrases italicized:

FIGURE 13.1: Identifying Stative Verbs		
Example	**Analysis**	**Type of Action**
The book *is* heavy.	*Be* + Adj	Stative
The man *was running*.	*Be* + Present Participle	Dynamic (Present Progressive)
Dinner *is* eaten.	*Be* + Past Participle	Stative
Dinner *was eaten*.	*Be* + Past Participle	Stative or Dynamic (Past Passive)
He *has eaten*	*Have* + Past Participle	Dynamic (Present Perfect)

Verbs that govern a direct object (DO) are called *transitive verbs*; verbs that do not take a DO are called *intransitive verbs*. Some verbs can do either. Look at the following examples:

S1.   Paul ate a sandwich.
S2.   Paul ate.
S3.   Paul is full.

In S1 the verb is *ate* and *sandwich* is what was eaten, the DO. Therefore, *ate* is a transitive verb. In S2 there is no DO; and in this sentence, *ate* is intransitive. In S3 *is* is a stative verb; the adjective *full* is called a predicate Adj.

A *finite verb* has a grammatical subject. It is *limited* (hence the term *finite*) by that grammatical subject. We will treat Hebrew finite verbs in chs. 14–16. As we learned in ch. 6, a *clause* is an expression having a subject and finite verb (predicate).

A *nonfinite verb* is not limited by a grammatical subject, though it may modify a subject. Nonfinite verbs, therefore, cannot form clauses but rather form *phrases* (not everyone makes a distinction between the terms clause and phrase, but it is useful, and we will practice that here). There are two types of nonfinite verbs, infinitives and participles, which we will treat in ch. 17.

Parsing the English Verb

As native speakers, we may not realize it, but English verbs actually tell us many things: (1) person, (2) number, (3) tense, (4) voice, (5) aspect, and (6) mood.

The (1) *person* and (2) *number* of the verb match those of the subject. This is obvious in languages that are highly inflected, i.e., in languages that change the "shape" of a verb by adding prefixes, suffixes, or infixes (collectively known as afformatives). English, however, is not a highly inflected language. So, we often use pronouns to indicate whether the grammatical subject is the speaker (first person), the one spoken to (second person), or the one spoken about (third person), and whether or not these are singular or plural.

(3) The word *tense* refers to the time frame of the action with respect to the speaker. It may be past, present, or future. (4) *Voice* is the description of how the action relates to the subject. For an *active voice* verb, the subject is the agent (doer) of the action; for a *passive voice* verb, the grammatical subject is the patient (receiver) of the action. English indicates voice by the presence or absence of the helping verb *to be*. (5) *Aspect* is how the action is portrayed. For example, an action might be simple, as in "Billy played," or progressive, as in "Billy was playing."

(6) *Mood* is generally understood as the relation of the action to reality. The *indicative mood* is the mood of "reality"; that is, events are portrayed as real. The *subjunctive mood* is the mood of "probability"; that is, events are portrayed as having some condition upon which accomplishment depends. Spoken English in America does not use the subjunctive very much anymore, except with "modal" verbs indicating probability, such as *can, may, should, could, ought*, etc. The *imperative mood* is the mood of "volition"; that is, the fulfillment of the event depends upon the will, or volition, of someone other than the speaker.

Parsing the Hebrew Verb

We have already mentioned that the Hebrew verbal system is comprised of both finite and nonfinite forms. There are three traditional categories of finite forms: the perfect (ch. 14), the imperfect (ch. 15), and the volitional forms (ch. 16). Hebrew finite verbs convey all the information that English verbs convey by using two main features: a system of *afformatives* and a system of *stems*.

To begin, figure 13.2 is reproduced from ch. 5:

FIGURE 13.2: Parsing Information for Nominals and Verbals

			Verbal Qualities					Nominal Qualities			
PtSp	Word	Lex	Stem	Form	P	G	N	State	Det	Case	Suff
Nn						X	X	X	X	X	
V			X	X	X	X	X				

Besides the root, you may remember that verbs share with nouns the qualities of gender and number (G, N). Unique to verbals is stem and form, and unique to finite verbs is person (P). Hebrew inflects (changes the "shape" of) verbs by using afformatives and stems. In the next chapters, you will get some idea of how that happens. For now, I will simply summarize what information the afformatives and stems provide.

Dynamic and Stative Verbs

One feature of Hebrew verbs (unlike English verbs) is the existence of stative verbs. Hebrew has verbs that indicate state in the *qal* stem. These verbs can appear in the *hiphil* stem to make them dynamic. For example, גָּדַל in the *qal* stem is stative, meaning "he was/became great" (note that to form this in English, we must use the verb be/became + the Adj *great*). In the *hiphil* stem the verb הִגְדִּיל means "he made [something] great," and it is no longer stative. Hebrew dynamic verbs may be transitive (taking a DO) or intransitive (not taking a DO). Stative verbs do not take a DO.

Personal Afformatives

Afformatives are prefixes, suffixes, infixes, or a combination. Personal afformatives indicate a number of things.

1. **Person**—first, second, third person
2. **Number**—singular, plural
3. **Gender**—masculine, feminine, common

   The person, gender and number (PGN) agree with that of the grammatical subject. In Hebrew the default gender is masculine. If the subject is "people," a group composed of both men and women, the grammatical gender used to refer to them is the masculine. Sometimes, even when the plural subjects are all women, a masculine personal ending is used, especially in the plural.
4. **"Tense"**—Hebrew traditionally has two "tenses," perfect and imperfect.
5. **Mood**—indicative, subjunctive, imperative, though in a manner different from English. We will use the terms *real*, corresponding to most of the English indicative mood, and *irreal*, corresponding to English future tense and subjunctive and imperative moods.

Stem Afformatives

The stems in Hebrew indicate:

1. **Voice**—active, passive, reflexive (in which the grammatical subject acts on itself). The doer of the action is the "agent," and the receiver of the action is the "patient."
2. **Intensity**—simple, intensive/plurative, causative (but these will require a little further explanation).

Close-Up on Hebrew Tenses

The word *tense* normally means "time." The English verbal system is dominated by time. The Hebrew verbal system includes time but also aspect, and Hebrew may feature one over the other in various circumstances. English verbs do indicate time and aspect in a way quite unlike Hebrew. English uses auxiliary verbs; Hebrew uses afformatives and word order. Many commentators and grammarians use the word *tense* in reference to the form or "shape" of the Hebrew word, that is, the verb form with the various afformatives it may take. I use the word *form* to include all verbals, both finite and nonfinite forms.

I will present the Hebrew verb under five verb forms. Unfortunately, there are different names for the Hebrew tenses. Some grammarians use names based on time. Others use names based on aspect, thinking that "perfect" tense forms represent completed action and "imperfect" forms represent incompleted action. Due to difficulties with these names, other scholars gave them names based on the shape of the verb. This took two forms. Some named two forms calling them "prefixed" and "suffixed" conjugations; others wanted to identify more than two forms and used transliterated forms based on the Hebrew root *qtl* either with or without the vowels.[2] Because different authors use different terminology, you need to know how the different systems compare. Figure 13.3 constitutes a list of the five verb forms we will treat and the various systems of naming.

FIGURE 13.3: Various Names Used for Hebrew Tense Forms

Form Names	Alternate Form Names	Aspect Names	Time Names
qatal = qtl	Suffixed	Perfect (Pf)	Past
weqatal = wqtl	*waw*-relative + Suffixed	ו consecutive + Perfect	
yiqtol = yqtl	Prefixed	Imperfect (Imp)	Future
[weyiqtol] [= wyqtl]	Simple *waw* + Prefixed	ו conjunctive + Imp	[Future]
wayyiqtol = wayyqtl	*waw*-relative + Prefixed	ו consecutive + Imp ו conversive + Imp ו sequential + Imp	Preterite
qotel	Participle	Progressive	Present

The *weyiqtol* form is in brackets because it has the same range of meanings as *yiqtol* and we will treat them together. I avoid the "Time Names." However, I agree with scholars that teach that Hebrew is a time-prominent verbal system, at least in the sense that the time component disallows certain expressions.[3] There are advantages to the other naming systems at different times, and I use them interchangeably.

---

2. The vowels that are included, e.g., *qatal*, also indicate the stem. Since stem is not significant when talking about tense forms, some grammarians chose to leave them out.

3. For example, it jolts the brain to hear the sentence "Tomorrow I ate" with the temporal Adv "tomorrow" followed by a *qatal* verb form.

So, what about time in Hebrew verbs? Hebrew verbs often indicate time relative to the context. Basically, Hebrew verbs with prefixed 1 have a time that is relative to a previous verb. Hebrew verbs without prefixed 1 have their time determined by adverbial time expressions.

Time in Hebrew is complicated and still debated by scholars. In this course, it is enough to rely on English translations for time and trust the translators and commentators. Mood and relative time can be combined in chart form.[4]

FIGURE 13.4: Hebrew Verb Forms, Mood, and Relative Time

FORM	TIME RELATIVE TO PREVIOUS VERB			
	Sequential	Simultaneous	Anterior	Background
qatal (ch. 14)		Real & Irreal	Real	Real
weqatal (ch. 14)	Irreal			
yiqtol (ch. 15)			Irreal	Irreal
wayyiqtol (ch. 15)	Real			
qotel (ch. 17)		Real & Irreal		

The meaning of these time relationships is as follows:

1. **Sequential**—action after the previous modal verb, either chronologically or logically.

   But I will establish [V1] my covenant with you, and *you will enter* [V2, וּבָאתָ, *weqatal*] the ark. (Gen 6:18 NIV; a chronological sequence)

2. **Simultaneous**—action at the same time as the previous verb

   But the LORD came down [V1] to see the city and the tower the people *were building* [V2, בָּנוּ, *qatal*]. (Gen 11:5 NIV)

3. **Anterior**—action before the previous verb

   God saw [V1] all that he *had made* [V2, עָשָׂה, *qatal*], and it was very good. (Gen 1:31 NIV)

4. For this treatment I am indebted to Galia Hatav, "Teaching the Biblical Hebrew Verbal System," *Hebrew Higher Education* 12 (2007): 5–52, and her *The Semantics of Aspect and Modality: Evidence from English and Hebrew* (Philadelphia: Benjamins, 1997), whose work I am adapting and simplifying in this and the next few chapters. For a different approach to the Hebrew verbal system, please see John A. Cook, *Time and the Biblical Hebrew Verb: The Expression of Tense, Aspect, and Modality in Biblical Hebrew*, Linguistic Studies in Ancient West Semitic 7 (Winona Lake, IN: Eisenbrauns, 2012).

4. **Background**—circumstance existing before the previous verb
Adam and his wife were both naked, and they felt [V1] no shame. Now the serpent was [V2, הָיָה, *qatal*] more crafty than any of the wild animals the LORD God had made. (Gen 2:25–3:1 NIV)

Close-Up on Hebrew Stems

There are seven major verb stems in Hebrew (and a number of minor stems). Some of them, however, are simply the passive forms of the active stems. The most common stem is called the *qal* stem. *Qal* is an actual Hebrew word meaning "light" or "simple" and is used because this stem simply adds personal afformatives to the root without any changes inside the root. The lexical form is the 3ms (third person masculine singular) because it is marked by having no personal afformative; it is "simple."

The other stems are called "derived" stems by modern grammarians because they are formed by adding some feature to the simple root before attaching the personal afformatives. The name of each of the derived stems is not descriptive as the word *qal* is, but simply an example. Modern grammarians have also created another system of naming using descriptive terms rather than examples. Since both are used, learning both is helpful.

The names of the stems and their general functions are given in figure 13.6 below. I use as a model the Hebrew root קטל, which means "kill"; the meaning is unfortunate for use as a model, but this root is useful because it has no "weak" letters that cause deviations from the normal patterns of word formation. And please note: the glosses provided are somewhat artificial. Meaning in the stems is determined by use not by etymology, a principle we will repeat.

FIGURE 13.5: Names and Forms of the Hebrew Stems

Classical	Pattern	Modern	Explanation
qal	קַל	Q or G	"Q" is used for stem name *qal*, of course. Some scholars use "G," from a German word, *Grundform*, meaning "base form." We will use Q.
niphal	נִפְעַל	N	Stem is characterized by a prefixed n, or "N."
piel	פִּעֵל	D	These stems are characterized by a doubled (hence the "D") second root letter. The active one has an "e-i" class vowel (*tsere*)
pual	פֻּעַל	D passive (Dp)	under the *ayin*; the passive has an "a" class vowel (*patakh*).
hiphil	הִפְעִיל	H	These stems are characterized by a prefixed ה, or "H." Again the active one has an "e-i" class vowel following the *ayin* and the
hophal	הָפְעַל	H passive (Hp)	passive has a *patakh*.
hithpael	הִתְפַּעֵל	HtD	This stem has a prefixed syllable הִת, "Ht," plus a doubled (D) second letter.

The category "Plurative-Factitive" requires some explanation. Traditionally, grammarians summarized the D-stem function as intensive. More recently, scholars have refined this in numerous ways. *Plurative* refers to repeated actions or results; *factitive* refers to being made into a state of being.[5]

FIGURE 13.6: Overview of Intensity and Voices of Stems

Voice	Simple	Plurative-Factitive	Causative
Active	Q-*qal* קָטַל "he killed"	D-*piel* קִטֵּל "he made killed"	H-*hiphil* הִקְטִיל "he made (someone) kill"
Passive	N-*niphal* נִקְטַל "he was killed"	Dp-*pual* קֻטַּל "he was made killed"	Hp-*hophal* הָקְטַל "he was made to kill"
Reflexive	N-*niphal* נִקְטַל "he killed himself"	HtD-*hithpael* הִתְקַטֵּל "he was made to kill himself"	

Two Ways Verbs Take a Direct Object (DO)

You learned that Hebrew nouns and prepositions can take pronominal suffixes (PrnSfs). For example, דָּבָר means "word," and דְּבָרוֹ means "his word." לוֹ is a prepositional phrase meaning "to him." Hebrew verbs can also take a PrnSf. This is one of two ways that Hebrew can mark the DO. The other way is to introduce a definite DO with the particle אֵת (or אֹת when the DO is a PrnSf). This particle is never translated with an English word. In the examples below the DO is in gray type.

בָּרָא אֶת הַשָּׁמַיִם	He created →	the heavens.
קָטַלְתִּי אֹתוֹ	I killed →	him.
קְטַלְתִּיו	I killed →	him.

In the first example, the particle אֵת marks הַשָּׁמַיִם as the DO. In קָטַלְתִּי אֹתוֹ, the PrnSf is attached to the other form of the particle אֵת. In קְטַלְתִּיו, the PrnSf is attached directly to the verb. Note three important things:

1. The PrnSf has no effect on the meaning of the verb.
2. The PrnSf attached to a verb functions as the DO.

---

5. If you are really curious, see Benjamin J. Noonan, *Advances in the Study of Biblical Hebrew and Aramaic: New Insights for Reading the Old Testament* (Grand Rapids: Zondervan Academic, 2020), 102–4.

3. The PrnSf is never reflexive. For example, the form קְטָלוֹ, in which the verb is 3ms and the PrnSf is also 3ms, might be translated "he killed him." The question is, can the PrnSf ("him") ever refer to the grammatical subject ("he") so that it might be understood to mean "he killed himself" with the English reflexive Prn? No, it can't. Hebrew does not have reflexive Prns, though sometimes PrnSfs may be translated reflexively. Instead, it expresses this reflexive idea by using certain verb stems (see figures 11.1 and 13.6) or stative verbs.

Retrieving and Using Information

Getting stem information for Hebrew verbs is now pretty simple. If you were learning full Hebrew, you would learn how to identify the stems from sight. With what you have learned so far, you can use books such as Davidson, *The Analytical Hebrew and Chaldee Lexicon*, or John Joseph Owens, *Analytical Key to the Old Testament*. Of course, the computer Bible programs are immeasurably faster. The point is that identifying the stem is simple by using these tools. Note, however, that scholars may occasionally disagree about some forms.

By using these resources, you can sometimes figure out the meaning of the verb in its different stems. But there are only a few verbs in the OT that appear in all seven stems. For example, קטל does not. The meanings I gave are only theoretical to illustrate a point. The actual meaning, as always, must be determined from context. An interesting example of a verb that does appear in all seven stems is ילד. Figure 13.7 lists the stems and the frequency of ילד in each. Then it provides glosses of the word in each stem followed by a brief explanation of the agents of the action. In the last column I offer just a few examples.

Stem	Gloss	Agency	Examples
FIGURE 13.7: ילד in Seven Stems			
G (239x)	Bear children	The action of the mother (but also used of the father)	Gen 3:16[6]
N (39x)	Be born	The "action" of the child	Gen 4:18
D (10x)	Help at birth	The action of the midwife	Exod 1:16
Dp (27x)	Be born	Child born (with help of midwife?)	Gen 4:26[7]

(continued)

---

6. This verb is used with a man as the agent in Gen 10:24 and similar passages, but see Jer 30:6 where men as agents of ילד in the *qal* stem is seen as ridiculous.

7. This *pual* (Dp) verbal form is quite common. The problem is that in English the meaning is indistinguishable from the *niphal* form. However, due to the fact that childbirth put mothers' lives at such risk, they normally occurred with an attending midwife (see R. K. Harrison and Edwin M. Yamauchi, "Childbirth," *Dictionary of Daily Life in Biblical and Post-Biblical Antiquity*, ed. Edwin M. Yamauchi and Marvin R. Wilson, 4 vols. [Peabody, MA: Hendrickson, 2014], 1:280). Perhaps the difference between the N and the Dp meanings is that the Dp portrays the normal procedure with a midwife and the N focuses solely on the infant without portraying the midwife one way or the other.

Stem	Gloss	Agency	Examples
H (176x)	Beget	The action of the father	Gen 11:27
Hp (3x)	Be born	Child begotten (by a father?)[8]	Gen 40:20; Ezek 16:4, 5
HtD (1x)	Register	The action of an official recorder of births	Num 1:18

Most of these meanings are pretty simple to figure out, such as the *niphal* being the passive of the *qal*. Some of them, such as the *hithpael*, make sense but are not predictable.

An Important Warning about Stems and Meaning

Figure 13.7 is actually an oversimplification. Notice that the *qal* is used of the mother's role, but it is not exclusive to her. The father's role is described by both the *qal* and the *hiphil* stems. One cannot determine the meaning of a word solely on the basis of identifying the stem. Meaning is determined by usage.

If you were learning full Hebrew, you would learn more about the functions of the stems. Figure 13.7 above gives you only the general functions.

The *SNIVEC* gives you this information in a reliable format. Take for example the entry for G/K 3086 on p. 1409:

FIGURE 13.8: Verb and Stem Information in *SNIVEC*

3086 ¹חָרַשׁ *ḥāraš*, v. [27] [⟶ 3045, 3046?, 3088, 3093, 3096, 3098, 4739]. [Q] to plow; engrave; plan, plot; [Qp] to be inscribed; [N] to be plowed; [H] to plot against:—plow (6), plot (3), be plowed (2), plowed (2), plowing (2), craftsman (1), devises (1), farmer (1), inscribed (1), plan (1), planted (1), plots (1), plotting (1 [+2021 +8288]), plowman (1), plowmen (1), plows (1), tools (1)

The superscript "¹" (with ¹חָרַשׁ) indicates that this is the first in a list of roots with the same root letters; "v." means it is a verb; the numbers in brackets after the "⟶" are other words derived from this root. Then the definitions are given for each of the stems in which the verb appears: G = *qal*; Gp = *qal passive*; N = *niphal*; H = *hiphil*. The entry concludes with a list of translations and frequencies for each.

What You Can and Cannot Do

1. You are *not* qualified to determine the meaning of a word based on the general functions of the stems. Leave this to the experts.
2. You *can* find out what stem a given verb is by using books and computer tools mentioned in this chapter.

---

8. In the three occurrences of this stem, the root ילד is found only in the expression, "on the day of birth."

3. You *can* now understand what the *SNIVEC* (and other study tools) is telling you in the dictionary sections to the Hebrew and Aramaic words.
4. You *can* learn the meaning of a given verb in a given stem using lexicons and wordbooks.
5. You *can* sort verbal roots according to stem when you do word studies and take the stem into account when determining meaning.

"Now, about Word Order You I Will Tell!"

If you are a Star Wars fan, perhaps you can hear Yoda's voice speaking the title to this section. In Yoda-speak, the subject and verb tend to come last. When we hear it, we laugh, because, though we understand the meaning, the sentence sounds funny. Normally word order in an English clause is subject-verb-object (SVO). Normal Hebrew word order is verb-subject-object (VSO).[9] Deviations from this order are common. What we mean is that whenever a sentence is not VSO, it may be "marked" for a special purpose.

Hebrew constructions are best classified according to how they begin. You want to pay particular attention to the following constructions ("cj" means "conjunction"):

1.	ן	+ verb
2.	ן	+ nonverb
3.	other cj	+ verb
4.	other cj	+ nonverb
5.	no cj	+ verb
6.	no cj	+ nonverb

Because you know the Hebrew alphabet and the cj *waw*, you can identify which structure a Hebrew clause has by consulting an interlinear OT. In the coming chapters we will look at these structures with respect to the verbal forms, and in the last unit we will look at them with respect to narrative and poetry.

Flowcharting and Labeling Main/Independent Clauses

In ch. 6 on clauses you learned how to tell the difference between main/independent clauses and subordinate clauses. In ch. 7 on conjunctions you learned that the functions for dependent clauses are indicated by the subordinating conjunction. Now you need to know how to label main/independent clauses.

---

9. For a different conclusion on Hebrew word order, see that advocated by Cook, *Time and the Hebrew Verb*, §3.3.1, 235–37. He follows several writings (see Cook for details) of Holmstedt: default is SV for real action and VS or X-VS (where X signifies some fronted element) for irreal action. For an explanation of *real* and *irreal*, see Flowcharting and Labeling Main/Independent Clauses below.

Bill Mounce in *GRU* calls these "Foundational Expressions." I will build from his list and offer brief explanations.

Foundational clauses can be organized around two main categories that correspond roughly to the moods mentioned above. Actions whose reality is assumed by the writer/speaker are called *real*, corresponding to the indicative mood of English. Actions whose reality has to do with necessity or possibility are called *irreal*, corresponding to the English subjunctive and imperative moods. The major difference is that whereas English has a future tense in the indicative mood, in Hebrew, expressions in future time are regarded as *irreal* because they have not yet occurred and are therefore only possible. Some grammarians and commentators use the term *modal* for *irreal*. I prefer *irreal* because it is broader than *modal*. It is important to understand that *irreal* does not necessarily mean that a statement is *unreal* or untrue or that it won't happen; it merely means that a particular event has not yet happened.

FIGURE 13.9: Real Main/Independent Clause Functions

Label	Explanation	Examples (NIV)
Assertion	A statement of simple existence of a fact; usually in present time	• The Lord **is** my strength and my defense. (Exod 15:2) • I do not seal my lips, Lord, as you **know.** (Ps 40:9) • the Lord your God is **giving you** (Josh 1:11)
Event	Report of an event as having happened; past time	• In the beginning God **created** the heavens and the earth. (Gen 1:1) • Hannah **was praying** in her heart. (1 Sam 1:13)
Anticipatory	A future event including predictions and promises	• After the boy is weaned, I **will take** him. (1 Sam 1:22) • He **will guard** the feet of his faithful servants. (1 Sam 2:9)
Exclamation	Emphatic assertion; often an "incomplete" sentence	• **Alas, Sovereign Lord** (Jer 1:6)
Rhetorical Question	A question intending to make a point rather than find out information. A rhetorical question therefore assumes a reality (many linguists classify rhetorical questions as irreal)	• Joshua said, "**Why have you brought this trouble on us?** The Lord will bring trouble on you today." (Josh 7:25)

FIGURE 13.10: Irreal Main/Independent Clause Functions

Label	Explanation	Examples (NIV)
Habitual/ Gnomic	An action is viewed as repeated. The time frame may be past, present or future. The term *gnomic* means a general, proverbial truth.	• Now Moses **used to take** a tent and pitch it outside the camp some distance away, calling it the "tent of meeting." (Exod 33:7) • That is why a man **leaves** his father and mother and **is united** to his wife. (Gen 2:24)
Command/ Request	The speaker is trying to impose his will on another. A command is offered by a superior to an inferior; a request (a.k.a. a prayer) is offered by an inferior to a superior. In English the second-person subject is implied.	• Then the officials said to Baruch, "You and Jeremiah, **go** and **hide**. • **Don't let** anyone **know** where you are." (Jer 36:19) • **Show** me your ways, Lord, **teach** me your paths. (Ps 25:4)
Exhortation	Statement by a superior encouraging others to do or be something. Sometimes the speaker is included. Exhortation has the first person as the subject.	• Saul said, "**Let us go down** and pursue the Philistines by night and plunder them till dawn, and **let us not leave** one of them alive." (1 Sam 14:36)
Obligation	A "must" statement. Hebrew has also third-person imperatives that in English are often translated "may" or "let" with the grammatical subject listed second.	• Has anyone built a new house and not yet begun to live in it? **Let him go** home. (Deut 20:5, meaning "he **must go**" or "**may** he **go**")
Permission	A "may" statement with the subject having permission to do something, but the action is not viewed as having yet ended.	• We **may eat** fruit from the trees in the garden. (Gen 3:2)
Question	A question intending to find out information does not assume anything in existence and is therefore irreal (the answer may be real).	• Then they asked Baruch, "Tell us, **how did you come to write all this? Did Jeremiah dictate it?**" (Jer 36:17)
Desire	A statement whose reality is in doubt by the speaker, but he is not trying to impose his will on another.	• All the Israelites ... said to them, "**If only we had died** in Egypt! Or in this wilderness!" (Num 14:2)

A Word on Conditional Sentences

Conditional sentences are made up of two clauses, an "if" clause and a "then" clause. The "then" part, called the apodosis, is the main clause and can have any of the above main clause functions. The "if" part, called the protasis, is a subordinate clause (see chs. 6 and 7). These may be possible conditional statements or impossible, known as "contrary to fact." Here is an example of each with the conditional clause indented above the main clause:

Potential Condition:	If the anointed priest sins, . . . he must bring to the Lord a young bull. (Lev 4:3)
Contrary-to-Fact Condition:	If we had not delayed [but we did], we could have gone and returned twice. (Gen 43:10)

What about Aramaic?

The Aramaic verbal system has not been studied nearly as thoroughly as the Hebrew system.[10] For our purposes, Aramaic works in much the same way as Hebrew with a few notable differences from the matters discussed in this and the following chapters. Word order in Biblical Aramaic varies greatly and in Aramaic during the first millennium BC seems to have shifted from VSO to SVO; basic word order in Biblical Aramaic seems to be VSO.[11] The most obvious difference is in the stems. The chart below compares the major Hebrew and Aramaic stems. The primary difference is that there is no *niphal* in Aramaic. Stems may be summarized by form (e.g., Q = *qal*, D = doubled second root letter, H = prefixed *he*) just as in Hebrew, but there are new patterns that are used. BA = Biblical Aramaic, TA = Talmudic Aramaic, Ar = both BA and TA, and BH = Biblical Hebrew. I use the customary stem names based on the patterns with the root פְּעַל, but I use the root קְטַל as a model.

FIGURE 13.11: Comparison of Aramaic and Hebrew Stems

Voice	Q		D		H	
Act	BH: *qal* Ar: *peal*	קָטַל קְטַל	BH: *piel* Ar: *pael*	קִטֵּל קַטֵּל	BH: *hiphil* Ar: *haphel*[12]	הִקְטִיל הַקְטֵל, אַ-, שַׁ-, סַ-

---

10. For a survey and evaluation, see Noonan, *Advances in the Study*, §7.4, 193–99. Two detailed and notable recent studies are John A. Cook, *Aramaic Ezra and Daniel: A Handbook on the Aramaic Text*, ed. W. Dennis Tucker Jr., Baylor Handbook on the Bible (Waco, TX: Baylor University Press, 2019), and Tarsee Li, *The Verbal System of the Aramaic of Daniel: An Explanation of the Context of Grammaticalization* (Leiden: Brill, 2009).

11. This follows Randall Buth's dissertation, "Word Order in Aramaic from the Perspectives of Functional Grammar and Discourse Analysis" (PhD diss., University of California, Los Angeles, 1987), as summarized in Noonan, *Advances in the Study*, 194–95. Again, though, scholars are divided on this.

12. There are several letters that can be used as prefixes, ה, א, שׁ, and ס, but for the most part they have no difference in meaning from each other.

Voice	Q		D		H	
Pass	BH: *niphal* BA: *peil* Ar: *hithpeel*	נִקְטַל קְטִיל הִתְקְטֵל	BH: *pual* BA: *hithpaal* Ar: *hithpaal* pual	קֻטַּל הִתְקַטַּל הִתְקַטַּל קֻטַּל [rare]	BH: *hophal* BA: *huphal* TA: *peal*	הָקְטַל הֻקְטַל הִתְקְטַל
Reflex	BH: *niphal* Ar: *hithpeel* *ethpeel*	נִקְטַל הִתְקְטֵל אֶתְקְטֵל	BH: *hithpael* Ar: *hithpaal* *ethpaal*	הִתְקַטֵּל הִתְקַטַּל אֶתְקַטַּל	BH: *histaphal* [13] Ar: *histaphal* *ettaphal* *eštaphal* *estaphal*	הִשְׁתַּחֲוָה הִשְׁתַּקְטַל אֶתַּקְטַל אֶשְׁתַּקְטַל אֶסְתַּקְטַל

Remember that the letters *p* and *ph* represent the two sounds of the letter *pe*. For the reflexive stems Aramaic prefixes the syllable *hith-* (or *ith/eth* [אִת/אֶת] or even *nith-* [נִת] in some dialects) to the root in the Q and D stems. For the H reflexive, the prefixed syllable is *hišta-* (with some variants).

Final Reminders

In this and the coming chapters, you will be learning many things, but you must not forget that this is not a full Hebrew course. Even a student who completes a two-year course in Biblical Hebrew is not knowledgeable enough to engage in exegesis completely independent from the work of professionals. However, you are in a position to make more detailed observations of the text and better understand commentators and translations.

Some readers will be satisfied studying only ch. 13 and not going into the details of chs. 14–17. Each reader will set their own learning goals. I encourage you, though, to keep moving through the details (ch. 17 I think is especially helpful). I hope you sense that there are payoffs all along the way. But chs. 20 and 21 are the target of this course and will enable you to gain a new depth of understanding of Scripture.

Advanced Information and Curious Facts

One Bible verse well known to many parents is Prov 22:6: "Train up a child in the way he should go; even when he is old he will not depart from it" (ESV). Putting this in a flowchart yields:

---

13. This stem occurs in only one word in Hebrew, the root חוה/חוו, "to bow down, worship," which occurs about 170 times in the OT. Older grammarians instead identify this as a *hithpael* stem from the root שׁחה, and some resources you use may identify it as such.

Function	Vs	Prov 22:6 (ESV)		
Command		[You]	Train	up a child
Sphere				in the way
Description				he should go;
	6			
Time				even when he is old
???		he	will not depart	
separation			from it.	

I've labeled all the clauses except the last main clause. This is the key. Many people see the future tense, "will not depart," and read this as a promise. This is a grammatical possibility, as you can see from the explanation of the anticipatory label in figure 13.9. Parents with straying children might cling to this verse as some sort of promise from God that eventually their child will come back to the Lord. When that doesn't happen, the parent may be heading toward a crisis of faith. Are God and his word trustworthy?

However, this understanding of the proverb may be incorrect in at least a couple of ways. First, this text is specifically speaking about the child trained properly and staying true to the way of the Lord. It says that a person so trained when he is a child will not stray from the truth when he is an adult. It is not promising that a rebellious adult will turn back to the Lord after he has already departed from the right way. Second, "future promise" is not the only possible function that this verb can have. In the next chapters we will learn that this tense (imperfect) is mostly used to mark irreality. It might have any of the other functions. Most likely the function is gnomic. The gnomic function is proverbial; that is, it is a statement that is generally true. In the explanation, I said that these are often translated with the English present tense. This is one that is not, except in the little used Young's Literal Translation, which reads, "Even when he is old he turneth not from it."

How do you tell what function is best here? As always, context. The most important context for the book of Proverbs is that of genre, or the type of literature. Because details on genre are beyond the scope of this book, after you complete this study you need to read a book like *How to Read the Bible for All Its Worth* by Fee and Stuart, 4th ed. (Grand Rapids: Zondervan, 2014). They describe the Hebrew term *proverb* as meaning "a *brief, particular* expression of a truth. The briefer a statement is, the less likely it is to be totally precise and universally applicable" (p. 241; italics theirs). To read Proverbs as a collection of universally true promises instead of as a collection of generally true maxims is to read them in a way different than the author intended, that is, to misread them. The grammar you have studied this far bears this out. For confirmation of this interpretation based on the conjunction *and*, see the exegetical insight by Gordon P. Hugenberger in Gary D. Pratico and Miles V. Van Pelt, *Basics of Biblical Hebrew*, 2nd ed. (Grand Rapids: Zondervan, 2007), 162–63. Hugenberger makes another important observation on the Hebrew text behind the English "in the way he should go." He points out that there is no firm basis for supplying the English word *should*: "[T]he Hebrew merely has עַל־פִּי דַרְכּוֹ, which is formally, "according to *his way*" (p. 162). The upshot of this understanding is that the verse in fact serves as a warning to parents! If parents let their children act according to their own way rather than disciplining their children, then even when they are old they will not turn away from that path.

CHAPTER 14

WHEN THE PERFECT COMES
Perfect Forms

Objectives
1. Explain what is an "event" and the different ways it can be conceived.
2. Identify the two constructions of the perfect and understand their possible meanings.
3. Know that verbs can take pronominal suffixes as objects.
4. Use tools to identify verb form.

Tools Used: Grammatically tagged computer Hebrew interlinear or paper interlinear plus Davidson or Owens

Introduction

In the last chapter you were introduced to the Hebrew verbal system. The first finite verb form is called the perfect "tense" (Pf). Remember that though the word "tense" refers to the time frame of the action, in Hebrew verb "tenses" are more precisely referred to as "tense forms" because the forms also mark aspect.

In this chapter you will learn (1) the two constructions of the Pf, (2) how Pf verbs are inflected and how those relate to the subject of the verb, (3) two ways that the direct object (DO) is indicated, (4) how to use tools to find out this information, and finally and most importantly, (5) the main functions of the two constructions.

The Two Perfect Constructions

You will recall from the last chapter that scholars refer to this form by different names. The term *perfect* (Pf) was intended to be a description of the perfective aspect, namely, a completed action, typically translated by the English past tense. We will see, however, that the Pf can be used in any time frame. The other terms are *suffixed* and *qatal* or *qtl*.

The two constructions are simply whether or not the verb has a prefixed *waw*. Without *waw* the verb is called *qatal*; with the *waw* it's called *weqatal*. Since the *qatal* form often portrays past time action and the *weqatal* form often portrays future time action, earlier grammarians thought the *waw* converted the past time to future and therefore called it *waw conversive.*[1] Sometimes the time was not changed; that *waw* was then called *waw conjunctive.* More recent studies understand the functions of *waw* more precisely, and it is better simply to use the terms *qatal* and *weqatal.*

Inflecting the Perfect Tense

The personal endings on verbs indicate person, gender, and number (PGN). Gender may be masculine (m), feminine (f), or common (c). Gender is distinguished only in second and third persons. The first-person verbs do not distinguish gender. It is as if the assumption was that the listener would know who is speaking, so it was thought unnecessary to indicate the gender of the speaker. Therefore, we call it "common." One more thing, the third-person plural form is also common. So, כָּתְבוּ,[2] "they wrote," may refer to masculine or feminine subjects.

Figure 14.1 shows how the personal endings attach to the root. The black letters are the personal prefixes and suffixes; the gray letters are those of the root. The gray vowels are a function of the stem, not the personal ending. The shading in the English translations corresponds to the shading of the Hebrew. The suffixes indicate PGN but also mark the verb form as "perfect," which is why the –ed ending is in black type. Realize that the translation is only one of the several possible, as you will learn.

FIGURE 14.1: Personal Endings for the Pf of the Qal Stem

PGN	Hebrew √ קטל	Translation Pronoun + Lexical Mng
3ms	קָטַל	he killed
3fs	קָטְלָה	she killed
2ms	קָטַלְתָּ	you (ms) killed
2fs	קָטַלְתְּ	you (fs) killed
1cs	קָטַלְתִּי	I killed
3cp	קָטְלוּ	they killed
2mp	קְטַלְתֶּם	you (mp) killed
2fp	קְטַלְתֶּן	you (fp) killed
1cp	קָטַלְנוּ	we killed

---

1. In fact, this conversion may have arisen in imitation of the apparent conversion of the future *yiqtol* to a past *wayyiqtol.* If so, this lends weight to the time component built in to the Hebrew verbal system.

2. Notice the metheg (see ch. 3) next to the *qamets* indicating that this is to be pronounced *kāṭəḇû* and not *koṭbû.*

Notice:

1. Because it is the simplest, the dictionary form of most verbs is the *qal* stem, Pf, third person, masculine gender, singular number. With the abbreviations we are using here, that can be shortened to "G Pf 3ms."
2. The Hebrew personal endings are a function of the tense form, not the stem. What that means is that these same personal endings are used for all the stems. That is really good news for you when you learn full Hebrew!
3. The tense names *qatal* and *weqatal* include any combination of PGN. The personal ending is completely unimportant for the name of the tense.

So, how do these personal endings relate to a subject? First, since a verb includes PGN information, a single verb can make a complete sentence. For example, to say "he ate" requires only one Hebrew word, אָכַל. In this sentence the identity of the subject is not expressed, but that the subject is 3ms is marked by the fact that there is no ending added. To translate it, English must add the pronoun *he*. Hebrew can also add the pronoun, but it is not required and would add some nuance of emphasis or focus on the subject pronoun.

Second, when the subject is expressed, it more commonly follows the verb; remember that normal word order for a Hebrew verbal clause is verb-subject-object (VSO). To specify the subject as in "Abram and Sarah went," Hebrew would say הָלְכוּ אַבְרָם וְשָׂרָה, formally, "they went Abram and Sarah." The writer is reporting to the reader that both Abram and Sarah went. Since Abram and Sarah are the ones spoken about, the person of the verb is third. Since the subject of the verb is plural, the number of the verb is plural (there are many exceptions to this, but this is the norm). Since the compound subject is both masculine and feminine and the gender of the Pf 3p ending is common, just like the pronoun *they*, so there is no problem for our English minds. To translate, English includes the pronoun only when the subject is not expressed. When the subject is expressed, the pronoun must be dropped. So, for הָלְכוּ אַבְרָם וְשָׂרָה, it is wrong to translate, "they went Abram and Sarah." Since the subject is expressed, it takes the place of the English pronoun: "Abram and Sarah went." In situations in which there is no common form to use with subjects including men and women, the default gender is masculine. Because in English today our culture is sensitive about using masculine pronouns to refer to anyone, male or female, many recent translations are rendering masculine Hebrew expressions as gender neutral either with "one" instead of "he" or even changing singulars to plurals. For example, in Ps 8:4–6, the pronouns referring to generic people, including "son of man," are masculine in Hebrew. The ESV and NASB preserve these in English as well. In order to make clear that these expressions can refer generically to a man or a woman, the NIV converts the pronouns to "them/their" and instead of "son of man" it renders "human beings." The NIV is not wrong in translating this way. "Son of man" is a routine way to refer to a human. The NASB/ESV rendering, however, tends to make Christian readers limit the meaning of "the Son of Man" to Jesus unnecessarily. This becomes an issue in Heb 2:6–8 and translators and commentators differ. Translation, like much of life, often involves tradeoffs.

Now you can understand one more feature of the *Lexham Hebrew-English Interlinear Bible*. Here is Gen 1:1:[3]

FIGURE 14.2: Lexham Hebrew-English Interlinear Bible for Gen 1:1

הָאָרֶץ:	וְאֵת	הַשָּׁמַיִם	אֵת	אֱלֹהִים	בָּרָא	בְּרֵאשִׁית
אֶרֶץ · הָ	וְ · אֵת	שָׁמַיִם · הַ	אֵת	אֱלֹהִים	בָּרָא	רֵאשִׁית · בְּ
the · earth	and · [obj]	the · heaven^bc	[obj]	God	create^a	in · beginning
the · earth	and · [obj]	the · heaven	[obj]	God	(he) create	in · the · beginning (of)^l
A · NC-SA	C · PO	A · NCMPA	PO	NCMPA	VaP3MS	P · NC

Notice that in the column for בָּרָא, the second, third, and fourth rows give in turn the root, ברא, the lexical meaning, "create," and the inflected meaning "(he) created." The reason the pronoun is there is to alert you to the fact that the PGN is 3ms (which is also indicated in the parsing information in the last row; "3MS" means third person, masculine, singular). The parentheses are there to make clear that the subject, אֱלֹהִים, is expressed and the pronoun *he* ought not to be translated.

Using Tools to Gather Information

Using the same tools you are now familiar with, you can complete a parsing chart for verbs. I give a couple of noun examples just for comparison. In your work, you will probably not be filling many of these out, but you could. It is a handy way to collect information, especially if you are using books, such as Davidson, instead of a computer Hebrew OT. You will get a chance to practice in *HRUW*.

FIGURE 14.3: Parsing Information for Nominals and Verbals

			Verbal Qualities					Nominal Qualities			
PtSp	Word	Lex	Stem	Form	P	G	N	State	Det	Case	Suff
Nn	דָּבָר	דָּבָר				m	s	Cst	[?]	[?]	
Nn	דְּבָרָיו	דָּבָר				m	p	Cst	[?]	[?]	3ms

(continued)

---

3. Christo van der Merwe, *The Lexham Hebrew-English Interlinear Bible* (Bellingham, WA: Lexham, 2004), Gen 1:1.

				Verbal Qualities				Nominal Qualities	
V	קָטַל	קטל	G	Pf	3	m	s		
V	נִקְטַלְתִּי	קטל	N	Pf	1	c	s		
V	גֵּרַשְׁתִּיו	גרש	D	Pf	1	c	s		3ms
V	וַהֲשִׁבֹתִיךָ	שׁוב	H	ו + Pf	1	c	s		2ms

You'll notice that I've used "Pf" and "ו + Pf" instead of *"qatal"* and *"weqatal."* The reason is purely practical: "ו + Pf" fits in my chart better.

The Functions of the Perfect Forms

We mentioned above three qualities about action that languages indicate in some way: mood (the relationship of the action to reality), time, and aspect (the portrayal of the progress of the action). In Hebrew, the main function of Hebrew verbs is portrayal of the aspect. The tense forms also correspond to the two moods that we saw in ch. 13 (figures 13.9 and 13.10). In the rest of this chapter, I will first describe the mood and time of the two forms, then the aspects of each. Then I will provide a figure that relates Hebrew and English verb uses.

Mood and Aspect of *Qatal* and *Weqatal*

The *qatal* does not include the quality of mood but may be either real or irreal as indicated in the text by other words or context. It is mostly used, however, for *real* functions. The *weqatal* form almost always indicates irreal functions.

To understand aspect, we need to start with the components of an event. Think of an event as having a beginning, a middle in progress, and an end. Graphically:

FIGURE 14.4: Anatomy of an "Event"

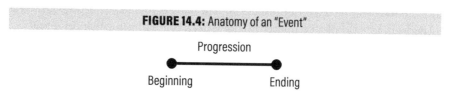

Verb forms in Hebrew indicate one of two classes of verbal aspects: perfective and imperfective. Perfective aspect refers to completed action; imperfective aspect refers to uncompleted action.

These two aspects can be further specified into the components of an event. These are based on context and word meaning. Figure 14.5 gives the names of these aspects, a description, and then a graphic representation built from this basic anatomy. The gray portions of the graphic represent those elements of an event that may be included but are not the focus.

FIGURE 14.5: Seven Aspects of an Event

Class	Aspect	Description	Representation
Perfective	Constative	Portrays the event as a whole without regarding its progression	
	Instantaneous	Event has no progression; beginning = ending	
	Ingressive (Inceptive)	Focus on the beginning of the event; progress not really in view	
	Resultative (Telic)	Focus on the ending of the event; progress not really in view	
Imperfective	Iterative (Habitual, Customary)	Focus on the progress of a repeated event	
	Continuous	Focus on the progress of a constant action or state without viewing beginning or ending	
	Perfective	Portrays both the beginning and the continuing action or resulting state	

Aspect in the *Qatal* Form

The *qatal* is perhaps the most flexible form in terms of how it portrays action. What this means is that Hebrew uses the one form to portray any of the seven aspects. The unaffected meaning (i.e., the intrinsic meaning of the form unaffected by word meaning or context) of the *qatal* is perfective. However, that meaning can be affected by word meaning or context to indicate one of the other aspects, either real or irreal. Here are examples of the *qatal* representing each aspect.

1. **Constative**

    In the beginning God *created* [בָּרָא] the heavens and the earth. (Gen 1:1 NIV)

    The seven days are viewed as a totality.

2. **Instantaneous**

    I *raise* [הֲרִימֹתִי] my hand to the LORD, the Most High God. (Gen 14:22 NET)

    The event happened at the instant of speaking. Cf. the NIV84 "I *have raised*" (the NIV still renders with an English present perfect: "I *have sworn*"), which readers might interpret as though Abram raised his hand and then some result or state continues.

3. **Ingressive**

> In the eighteenth year of the reign of Jeroboam son of Nebat, Abijah *became king* [מָלַךְ] of Judah. (1 Kgs 15:1 NIV)

The starting year of the reign makes it clear that this is ingressive.[4]

4. **Resultative**

> Just then David's men and Joab *returned* [בָּא] from a raid and brought with them a great deal of plunder. (2 Sam 3:22 NIV)

The return, or arrival, was the culmination of their journey.

5. **Iterative**

> And Tobiah *sent* [שָׁלַח] letters to intimidate me. (Neh 6:19 NIV)

It is likely that these letters were sent in a series instead of in one bunch.

6. **Continuous**

> But the LORD came down to see the city and the tower the people *were building* [בָּנוּ]. (Gen 11:5 NIV)

Since the building was never completed (v. 8), the ending is not in view.[5]

7. **Perfective**

> When Abram heard that his relative [Lot] *had been taken captive* [נִשְׁבָּה], he called out the 318 trained men. (Gen 14:14 NIV)

The being taken captive (Pf) was prior to the Abraham's hearing about Lot, and Lot was still in captivity when he heard it. English renders this with a perfect tense; here it is past perfect.

Aspect in the *Weqatal* Form

The *weqatal* can portray actions with any of these aspects as well, but such action is always irreal. Most of the time, *weqatal* actions will be future time and these seem to be conative (i.e., attempted with no indication of being completed). I don't need to repeat examples illustrating the aspects, but I will give two examples of the iterative use to show that for irreal aspects, time frames can vary.

---

4. The Lexham interlinear makes this explicit: "(he) began to reign." Cf. the constative use of the exact form in the very next verse giving the three-year duration of his reign.

5. The NIV takes the *qatal* as encapsulating the process and renders with the English past progressive. Compare the NET, which prefers an ingressive nuance: "that the people *had started building.*"

A future-time example:

> For I [the LORD to those with him] have chosen him [Abram], so that he will direct his children and his household after him *to keep* [וְשָׁמְרוּ, *weqatal*] the way of the LORD by doing what is right and just, so that the LORD will bring about for Abraham what he has promised him. (Gen 18:19 NIV)

The action is sequential after the verb "he will direct." The idea is that his children should habitually keep the way of the LORD. Note that the NIV doesn't translate וְשָׁמְרוּ as a finite verb but as an infinitive indicating purpose.

A past-time example:

> And Peninnah had children, but Hannah had no children. Now this man *used to go up* [וְעָלָה] year after year from his city to worship. (1 Sam 1:2b-3 ESV)

The ESV rightly indicates the habitual nature of the action made explicit by the phrase "year by year." The NIV reads simply "*went up*" relying on "year by year" to mark the iterative nature of the action.

A Working Table

Figure 14.6 seeks to combine all the information on the tense and aspect function covered in chs. 14–15 in a format that enables readers of English versions to explain differences between translations and to better understand issues discussed in scholarly literature.

The table comes in two parts based on English grammar: the indicative mood and the subjunctive mood. As we said in ch. 13, the subjunctive is the mood of probability. We will build the chart gradually, with only the *qatal* and *weqatal* forms (a.k.a. Pf and ׳cs[i.e., *waw* consecutive]+Pf, respectively). Then we will add to this in ch. 15 and complete it in ch. 17.

FIGURE 14.6: Indicative and Nonindicative Structures and Functions

INDICATIVE MOOD (REALITY)

Time	English Tenses	Examples	Aspect	Pf	׳cs+Pf	Imp	׳cs+Imp	Ptc
Past (Real & Irreal)	Simple Past	he <u>ate</u>	Constative, Instantaneous, Resultative	X X X				
	Emphatic Past	he <u>did eat</u>	Constative	X				
	Past Perfect	he <u>had eaten</u>	Perfective	X				

(continued)

Time	English Tenses	Examples	Aspect	Pf	וcs+Pf	Imp	וcs+Imp	Ptc
Past (Real & Irreal) (continued)	Contrary-to-Fact Condition	(if) he had eaten	Constative	X				
	Contrary-to-Fact Assertion	(then) he would have eaten	Constative			X		
	Customary Past	he used to eat	Iterative			X		
	Progressive Past (Historic Present + היה)	he was eating	Continuous			X		
	Ingressive Past	he began eating	Ingressive			X		
	Historic Future (In Subordinate Clauses)	he would (was going to) eat	Conative			X		
Present (Real & Irreal)	Simple Present (incl. Stative, Gnomic, Habitual)	he eats	Constative. Instantaneous. Resultative. Habitual	X X X X	X			
	Emphatic Present	he does eat	Constative	X				
	Present Perfect	he has eaten	Perfective	X	X			
	Performative	He (hereby) eats	Instantaneous	X				
	Progressive Present	he is eating	Continuous			X		
Future (Irreal)	Simple Future	he shall eat	Constative			X		
	Conditional Assertion	(then) he will eat	Constative					
	Immediate Future	he is about to eat	Constative			X		
	Rhetorical/Dramatic Future	he eats (perfected aspect)	Constative	X				
	Future Perfect	he will have eaten	Constative	X				
	Anterior Future	he will have eaten	Constative					
	Progressive Future (+ יהיה)	he will be eating	Progressive					

SUBJUNCTIVE MOOD (POTENTIALITY)

Time	English Tenses	Examples	Aspect	Pf	וcs+Pf	Imp	וcs+Imp	Ptc
Future (Irreal)	Condition (Protasis)	(if) he eats/eat/should eat	Constative	X	X			
	Possibility	he might eat	Constative			X		
	Purpose/Result	in order that/so that he might eat	Constative			X		

Time	English Tenses	Examples	Aspect	Pf	ıcs+Pf	Imp	ıcs+Imp	Ptc
Future (irreal) (continued)	Capability	he can eat	Constative					
	Permission	he may eat	Constative					
	Obligation/ Propriety	he ought to eat	Constative		X			
	Command/ Prohibition	Eat!/Do not eat!	Constative		X			
	Desire/Intention	he wants/ intends to eat	Constative					
	Request/Wish	please, eat!	Constative					

A Plan of Attack

In chs. 13 and 14 we have noticed three qualities of verbs: mood (real or irreal), time (i.e., relative time), and aspect (the seven aspects from figure 14.5). What can you do to understand meaning better? First, you can use your tools to identify Hebrew tense forms and see mood possibilities; second, rely on translations and commentators for time and sequencing of Hebrew verbs; and third, study the context and use figure 14.6 to identify possible aspects. Here are steps to follow:

1. *Determine the verb form.* Use a grammatically tagged computer Hebrew OT or interlinear, or else use an interlinear Bible plus Davidson or Owens as needed. For now, the verb form is *qatal* or *weqatal*.
2. *Examine the context to determine the mood and aspect.* Use figure 14.6 to locate the verb form and time frame. This can be repeated for each version compared.
3. *Based on your findings, briefly describe the action of the verb in the clause.*

As an example of how to use figure 14.6, look again at Gen 9:9–11 (NIV):

> [9] I now establish my covenant with you and with your descendants after you [10] and with every living creature that was with you—the birds, the livestock and all the wild animals, all those that came out of the ark with you—every living creature on earth. [11] *I establish* [וַהֲקִמֹתִי] my covenant with you: Never again will all life be destroyed by the waters of a flood; never again will there be a flood to destroy the earth.

1. **Get the Hebrew grammatical information.** A quick look at an interlinear reveals that the verb "establish" in v. 11 is a *weqatal* form.
2. **Identify how the translation renders.** The NIV renders this as a simple present tense. Consulting figure 14.6, you look down the *weqatal* (ıcs+Pf) column in the present time section; the possible aspects are constative, stative, habitual, and continuous.

3. **Evaluate the version with respect to the context.** NIV is taking the *weqa-tal* as instantaneous, completed at the moment of speaking.

You can repeat the last two steps to compare versions.

1. The KJV renders this same phrase with "and I will establish," as future. Studying the *weqatal* column in the future-time section for the KJV reveals eight possibilities, but without subordinating cjs, modal auxiliary verbs (could, would, etc.), or a command, the subjunctive/volitional forms are not indicated. Neither is this a contingent assertion. So only two possibilities are left: simple future with constative aspect or immediate future with ingressive aspect.

2. Of these two possibilities, the immediate future fits the context best—God is not going to establish his covenant in some distant future. This meaning is about the same as the NIV. The NIV seems to bring out the meaning more clearly.

What about Aramaic?

More research on Aramaic is needed, but here are three key differences.

The vowels and personal endings for the verb are different, קְטַל (*qəṭal*) instead of the Hebrew קָטַל (*qāṭal*).

Aramaic does not have a *waw* consecutive. So, *waw* + Pf functions just as the Pf; the *waw* is simply conjunctive.

The default form for past tense is the participle.[6] The continuous past is formed by the *qəṭal* form of the root *to be* (היה) + the Ptc. Aramaic forms the continuous present by אִיתַי + the Ptc.

Advanced Information and Curious Facts

One of the goals of this study is to understand why versions differ. Paying close attention allows us to pick up little nuances. A simple example is found in the well-known passage of Isaiah's vision in Isa 6. Isaiah 6:3 reads (NIV):

And **they were calling** to one another:

"Holy, holy, holy is the LORD Almighty;
    the whole earth is full of his glory."

---

6. See Noonan, *Advances*, 140, citing the work by Tarsee Li, *Verbal System of the Aramaic of Daniel: An Explanation in the Concept of Grammaticalization*, Studies in Aramaic Interpretation of Scripture 8 (Leiden: Brill, 2009).

For the bolded verb the NASB reads "**And** one **called out** to another." This is different from the NIV in two ways: (1) the NIV verb is plural while the NASB is singular, and (2) the NIV is a progressive past while the NASB is simple past. Why, and what's the difference?

Checking an interlinear reveals that the Hebrew verb is *weqatal* and singular. The NIV progressive rendering brings out that aspect characteristic of this verb form. The context makes this past time rather than the usual future time. The NASB retains the singular but does not make explicit the continuous aspect. The NASB translators may have assumed that the "one . . . to the other" sufficiently brought that out. The difference is simply in the picture Isaiah is painting. The continuous aspect portrays the scene more vividly.

CHAPTER 15

THERE'S NOTHING WRONG WITH . . .

Imperfect Forms

Objectives

1. Explain the Hebrew imperfect.
2. Identify three constructions of imperfects.
3. Use tools to identify verbs and understand parsing.

Tools Used: Grammatically tagged computer Hebrew interlinear and reverse interlinear (recommended) or paper interlinear plus Davidson or Owens

Introduction

Imperfect (Imp) is the second category of Hebrew finite verbals. As we mentioned in ch. 13, the term *imperfect* means that the action of the verb is portrayed as incomplete. This is only a generalization. After getting an idea of the shape of this form, we will look at its various functions.

The Imperfect Form and Its Constructions

Names for the Imperfect Tense Form

The three names typically used for this verbal form correspond to the three names for the Pf: (1) *imperfect*, from the aspect; (2) *prefixed*, because afformatives are attached to the beginning of each verb; and (3) *yiqtol*, because it describes the shape of the Imp (see figure 13.3).

Once again it is important to identify the presence or absence of the *waw* conjunction. So, in addition to *yiqtol*, there is *weyiqtol*. This *waw* is called a "conjunctive *waw*" in order to distinguish it from the *waw* consecutive.

Inflecting the Suffixes of the Imperfect Tense

Even though the Imp is often called "prefixed," half of the Imp forms also have suffixes. Figure 15.1 below gives the forms of both the Pf and the Imp for comparison. The black letters are the personal prefixes and suffixes; the gray letters are those of the root; the gray vowels are a function of the stem, not the personal ending. For comparison I give one possible translation of the forms.

FIGURE 15.1: A Comparison of Pf and Imp Person Markers

English	PGN	Pf	Imp	PGN	English
he killed	3ms	קָטַל	יִקְטֹל	3ms	he will kill
she killed	3fs	קָטְלָה	תִּקְטֹל	3fs	she will kill
you killed	2ms	קָטַלְתָּ	תִּקְטֹל	2ms	you will kill
you killed	2fs	קָטַלְתְּ	תִּקְטְלִי	2fs	you will kill
I killed	1cs	קָטַלְתִּי	אֶקְטֹל	1cs	I will kill
they killed	3cp	קָטְלוּ	יִקְטְלוּ	3mp	they will kill
			תִּקְטֹלְנָה	3fp	you will kill
you killed	2mp	קְטַלְתֶּם	תִּקְטְלוּ	2mp	you will kill
you killed	2fp	קְטַלְתֶּן	תִּקְטֹלְנָה	2fp	you will kill
we killed	1cp	קָטַלְנוּ	נִקְטֹל	1cp	we will kill

Notice the following:
1. All of the Imp forms have prefixes; none of the Pf forms do.
2. Notice that while the Pf 3p is common in gender, the Imp distinguishes the 3mp and the 3fp.
3. Notice also that the 3fp and the 2fp are identical. These forms are not common in the Hebrew Bible (probably a statistical accident in biblical literature rather than in real-life speech in biblical times), and there is rarely any confusion. Context is normally clear.

Waw Consecutive and the Imperfect

There is a special form of the Imp. Some grammarians call it "preterite" (abbreviated Pret) meaning "past time." Others call it *wayyiqtol*. Most call it *waw* consecutive plus the imperfect (וcs+ Imp) as opposed to *waw* conjunctive with the imperfect (וcj + Imp).

In the vast majority of instances, this verbal construction refers to a past event, but this is not always the case. Grammarians have identified additional nuances. The most important thing for you to understand about this form is that it is used to describe sequential actions. That is, a series of *wayyiqtol* forms produces a narrative of events in chronological (or logical) order.

Gathering Parsing Information

Parsing works the same way as in the last chapter. In the examples below, I begin with a noun and a Pf form for comparison.

FIGURE 15.2: Parsing Information for Nominals and Verbals

PtSp	Word	Lex	Stem	Form	P	G	N	State	Det	Case	Suff
Nn	דְּבָרָיו	דָּבָר				m	p	Cst	[?]	[?]	3ms
V	וַהֲשִׁבֹתִיךָ	שׁוב	H	ו + Pf	1	c	s				2ms
V	יִמְשֹׁל	משׁל	G	Imp	3	m	s				
V	וְיִשְׁכֹּן	שׁכן	G	וcj + Imp	3	m	s				
V	וַיְקַדֵּשׁ	קדשׁ	D	וcs + Imp	3	m	s				
V	וַיַּנִּחֵהוּ	נוח	H	וcs + Imp	3	m	s				3ms

The Functions of the Imperfect Forms

There are three forms covered in this chapter: *yiqtol* (Imp), *weyiqtol* (וcj+Imp), and *wayyiqtol* (וcs+Imp = וcs+Pret). In terms of functions, however, *yiqtol* and *weyiqtol* (with וcj) function in similar ways. The form *wayyiqtol* is distinct. The result is that, as we talk about functions, we only need to discuss *yiqtol* and *wayyiqtol*. Before we get to functions, however, there are two special forms that require our attention.

The Special Words וַיְהִי and וְהָיָה

The construction וַיְהִי is very common in the Hebrew Bible (784 times). This is parsed as a Q וcs + Imp 3ms from the root הָיָה. The construction וְהָיָה is a Q ו+Pf 3ms from the same root (402 times).

These forms are used in two ways: (1) as a main clause or (2) as a temporal clause. As a main clause, it has the meaning "become." It is more commonly used as a marker for an adverbial time phrase. The KJV usually renders וַיְהִי, "and it came to pass," and וְהָיָה as the future tense, "and it shall come to pass." A couple of examples with וַיְהִי will illustrate sufficiently.

Gen 19:26b	מֶלַח	נְצִיב	וַתְּהִי
	salt	pillar of	and she became
NIV	And she became a pillar of salt.		

The first word is וַתְּהִי. The subject, of course, is the wife of Lot. Clearly, the meaning of the sentence is that she *became* a pillar of salt, the resultative (or perhaps perfective) aspect, not that she was one, constative. In this case, וַתְּהִי should be treated as any other 1cs+Imp form.

	יְהוָה	וַיֹּאמֶר	יְהוָה	עֶבֶד	מֹשֶׁה	מוֹת	אַחֲרֵי	וַיְהִי
Josh 1:1	the Lᴏʀᴅ	and (he) said	the Lᴏʀᴅ	the servant of	Moses	the death of	after	and it was
NIV	After the death of Moses the servant of the Lᴏʀᴅ, the Lᴏʀᴅ said							
KJV	**Now** after the death of Moses the servant of the Lᴏʀᴅ **it came to pass,** that the Lᴏʀᴅ spake							

Notice here that וַיְהִי does not mean "become" and that it is followed by a time phrase. There is nothing wrong with the KJV translation; people simply don't talk like that anymore. The NIV is more idiomatic by leaving וַיְהִי untranslated. In fact, the NIV more precisely brings out the adverbial function of this clause. The main clause is "the Lᴏʀᴅ said." We will come back to this form in ch. 20 on prose.

Mood and Aspect of *Yiqtol* and *Wayyiqtol*

The mood of the *yiqtol* is irreal. *Wayyiqtol* has about the same range of meaning as *qatal*, i.e., it usually portrays (1) real action, and (2) it can portray irreal action, but that is a function of context rather than verb form.

The aspect of the *yiqtol* (and *weyiqtol*) form is primarily iterative or continuous. It portrays aspect similarly to the *qatal*, the chief difference being that *yiqtol* portrays irreal mood. The *wayyiqtol* is sequential like *weqatal* but portraying action in the real mood.

Figure 15.3 expands on the forms from figure 14.6 by adding our two new forms. Remember that this figure is an approximation; you must not use it to argue with scholars about a particular use. We will complete the figure in ch. 17.

You can use the information in this figure as you did in the last chapter. Take, for example, Gen 3:16b. The NIV translates it like the other versions:

> Your desire will be for your husband,
>   and *he will rule* over you.

For the second half, the NET reads differently:

> but *he will dominate* you.

FIGURE 15.3: Nonvolitional Structures and Functions

INDICATIVE MOOD (REALITY)

Time	English Tenses	Examples	Aspect	Pf	ↄcs+Pf	Imp	ↄcs+Imp	Ptc
Past (Real & Irreal)	Simple Past	he ate	Constative	X				X
			Instantaneous	X				X
			Resultative	X				X
	Emphatic Past	he did eat	Constative	X				X
	Past Perfect	he had eaten	Perfective	X				X
	Contrary-to-Fact Condition	(if) he had eaten	Constative	X				
	Contrary-to-Fact Assertion	(then) he would have eaten	Constative		X	X		
	Customary Past	he used to eat	Iterative		X	X		
	Progressive Past (Historic Present + היה)	he was eating	Continuous		X	X		
	Ingressive Past	he began eating	Ingressive		X			
	Historic Future (In Subordinate Clauses)	he would (was going to) eat	Conative		X	X		
Present (Real & Irreal)	Simple Present (incl. Stative, Gnomic, Habitual)	he eats	Constative	X				X
			Instantaneous	X				X
			Resultative	X				X
			Habitual	X	X	X		X¹
	Emphatic Present	he does eat	Constative	X				
	Present Perfect	he has eaten	Perfective	X	X			X
	Performative	He (hereby) eats	Instantaneous	X				
	Progressive Present	he is eating	Continuous		X	X		
Future (Irreal)	Simple Future	he shall eat	Constative		X	X		
	Conditional Assertion	(then) he will eat	Constative			X		
	Immediate Future	he is about to eat	Constative		X			
	Rhetorical/Dramatic Future	he eats (perfected aspect)	Constative	X				X
	Future Perfect	he will have eaten	Constative	X				
	Anterior Future	he will have eaten	Constative			X		
	Progressive Future (+ יהיה)	he will be eating	Progressive					

---

1. This is not common and not expected, since the *wayyiqtol* usually represents completed action. How-

SUBJUNCTIVE MOOD (POTENTIALITY)

Time	English Tenses	Examples	Aspect	Pf	۱cs+Pf	Imp	۱cs+Imp	Ptc
Future (Irreal)	Condition (Protasis)	(if) he <u>eats/eat/ should eat</u>	Constative	X	X	X		
	Possibility	he <u>might eat</u>	Constative		X	X		
	Purpose/Result	in order that/so that he <u>might eat</u>	Constative		X			
	Capability	he <u>can eat</u>	Constative			X		
	Permission	he <u>may eat</u>	Constative			X		
	Obligation/ Propriety	he <u>ought to eat</u>	Constative		X	X		
	Command/ Prohibition	<u>Eat!/Do not eat!</u>	Constative		X	X		
	Desire/Intention	he <u>wants/ intends to eat</u>	Constative			X		
	Request/Wish	<u>please, eat!</u>	Constative			X		

What kind of "rule" is envisioned? The NET Bible, note 49, says,

> The translation assumes the imperfect verb form has an objective/indicative sense here. Another option is to understand it as having a modal, desiderative nuance, "but he *will want to dominate* [italics added] you." In this case, the LORD simply announces the struggle without indicating who will emerge victorious.

A quick glance at an interlinear reveals that the verb under consideration is *yiqtol*. Glancing at the chart you can see that in their note, they are suggesting that the *yiqtol* be understood as expressing desire. How do scholars decide which use? Context. We will come back to this verse in ch. 18 on word studies.

What about Aramaic?

Continuing from the note in ch. 14, remember that Aramaic does not have a *waw* consecutive. So, *waw* + Imp functions just as the Imp; the *waw* is simply conjunctive.

---

ever, see Prov 8:35: "For those who find me [*qotel*] find [*qatal*] life **and receive favor** [*wayyiqtol*] from the Lord" (NIV). The *wayyiqtol* might also be normalized as the present perfect "and has received favor." Cf. KJV, "and shall obtain favour," which might be seen as an anterior future, "shall have obtained favour." See also Prov 11:2, 8; 12:13; etc.

The vowels and personal endings for the verb are different: יְקְטֵל (*yiqṭul*) instead of the Hebrew יְקְטֹל (*yiqṭōl*).

Again, Aramaic does not have a *waw* consecutive. So, in *waw* + Imp the verb always functions simply as an Imp; the *waw* is simply conjunctive. There is no *wayyiqtol* form in Aramaic.

The *yiqṭul* form is very similar to Hebrew *yiqtol*. Aramaic forms the continuous future by the *yiqṭul* forms of the root *to be* (היה) + Ptc.

Advanced Information and Curious Facts

Here is one more glance at Isa 6:3, including a review of the genitive case from ch. 11 by continuing the discussion from the previous chapter on Isa 6:3 (NIV):

And they were calling to one another:

"Holy, holy, holy is the LORD Almighty;
the whole earth is **full of** his glory."

Virtually all translations render "full of his glory." However, the Hebrew for "full of" is מְלֹא, which is actually a noun in the construct state meaning "fullness of." A quick look at an interlinear shows that the tail noun, the Gen case, is not "glory" but rather "all of." "All of" is followed in turn by the Gen "earth." Both of these Gens may be understood as a partitive (i.e., "wholative") Gen. A more precise rendering of the Hebrew would be "the fullness of all of the earth is his glory." Since "fullness" and "all" both refer to completeness, we might paraphrase "the totality of the earth and its contents." It's not that the earth is filled with his glory, some metaphysical substance that fills the earth somehow not visible to humans, but that the earth and everything in it, all that is visible to humans, is itself the glory of the Lord and evidence of his praiseworthiness.

CHAPTER 16

WHERE THERE'S A WILL, THERE ARE . . .

Volitional Forms

Objectives

1. Explain that Hebrew has three volitional verbs.
2. Identify how Hebrew places volitional forms in sequence to form subordinate clauses.
3. Label the functions of volitional verbs.
4. Identify and explain the two types of Hebrew prohibitions.
5. Flowchart volitional and subordinate clauses.

Tools Used: Interlinear Bible

Introduction

You have already been introduced to the meaning of volitional verbs (ch. 13). Volition has to do with the will. Because these actions depend on the will of another, the fulfillment of these actions is in doubt and they are future by nature. In English, these actions are put in the subjunctive and imperative moods. In Hebrew, these actions fall under the irreal mood. We have already seen that some nonvolitional forms are used to represent irreal action. In this chapter we will learn the rest of the irreal functions that are performed by volitional verbs, the last category of finite verbs.

We will begin with the names and "shapes" of volitional verbs and their functions. Next you need to understand the way Hebrew strings together various verb forms using the *waw* conjunction to indicate meaning. Scholars call this "consecution of tenses." We will conclude with parsing information and flow-charting verbal sequences.

Volitional Forms

There are three types of volitional verbs, the cohortative (Coh), imperative (Imv), and jussive (Juss). The one most familiar to you, of course, is the imperative. This is the verb form whose chief function is to indicate a command in the second person.[1] The simplest way to explain the Coh and Juss is that they serve purposes similar to the Imv for the first and third persons, respectively.

FIGURE 16.1: Hebrew and English Methods of Expressing Volitional Moods

Person	Hebrew Forms	English Forms
1st	• Coh • *weqatal*	I/We **will** go, **let** me/us go
2nd	• Imv (pos.) • Imp + אַל/לֹא (neg.)	**Go**! **Do not** go!
3rd	• Juss • *yiqtol*	**Let** him/them go, he/they **must** go

As for the forms themselves, the Imv has the most distinctive form. It looks like the Imp forms with the prefixes removed. For example, תִּקְטֹל is the G Imp 2ms for "you will kill"; the Imv 2ms is simply קְטֹל. (By the way, it is not really necessary to write the "2" for the person of the Imv, since the Imv is only the second person. It's okay to do it, though.) The only variation is that the 2ms may add ה to the end of the verbal form. This long form is often called an emphatic form. Here are the basic forms for the G Imv. You may notice some changes in vowel pointing. If you want to know why, you will need to learn full Hebrew.

FIGURE 16.2: Comparison of Qal Imperfect and Imperative Forms

PGN	Imp	Imv	Imv (Long)
2ms	תִּקְטֹל, *tiqṭōl*	קְטֹל, *qaṭōl*	קָטְלָה, *qoṭlâ*
2fs	תִּקְטְלִי, *tiqṭəlî*	קִטְלִי, *qiṭlî*	
2mp	תִּקְטְלוּ, *tiqṭəlû*	קִטְלוּ, *qiṭlû*	
2fp	תִּקְטֹלְנָה, *tiqṭōlnâ*	קְטֹלְנָה, *qaṭōlnâ*	

The Coh and Juss frequently look just like the Imp form. The only difference is that ה may be added to the cohortative verb just like the long form of the Imv 2ms. Compare the following:

FIGURE 16.3: Comparing the Imperfect with the Long Cohortative Form

Parsing	Hebrew	English
Q Imp 1cs *or* Q Coh 1cs	אֶקְטֹל	"I will kill" "let me kill"

---

1. Note that even though the English word *cohort* implies a plural, "cohortative" is used for both singular and plural for this Hebrew verb form.

Parsing	Hebrew	English
Q Coh 1cs	אֶקְטְלָה	"let me kill"
Q Imp 3ms *or* Q Juss 3ms	יִקְטֹל	"he will kill" "let him kill"
Q Juss 3ms	יִקְטְלָה	"let him kill"

So how does Hebrew indicate when a form without the emphatic ה should be understood as volitional? They put it at the beginning of the clause. In Gen 33:12, Esau says,

Gen 33:12	נֵלֵךְ let us journey
NIV	Let us be on our way (Q Coh 1cp)

In the priestly blessing of Num 6:24, we read

Num 6:24	וְיִשְׁמְרֶךָ and may he keep you	יְהוָה the Lᴏʀᴅ	יְבָרֶכְךָ may he bless you
NLT	May the Lord bless you (D Juss 3ms + 2ms PrnSf) and protect you (Q Juss 3ms + 2ms PrnSf)		

Volitional forms may appear with or without the conjunctive *waw*, as in "and may he keep you" in Num 6:24 above. It may be preceded by the negative, as in Gen 18:30 below. After the author narrates, "And he said," we read the direct speech of Abraham:

Gen 18:30	לַאדֹנָי to the Lord	יִחַר may it be hot	אַל־נָא not
NIV	**May** the Lord not **be angry** (Q Juss 3ms)		

The word אַל means "not"; the particle נָא is perhaps a marker of emotion or emphasis. The verb חָרָה means "to be hot." This is an idiom; the full expression is, "may the nose be hot."[2] The point is that the ל Pp before Adonai is possessive.

Just like the other finite verb forms, the volitional forms may add PrnSfs to the end. In Isa 6:8, when the Lord asks, "Whom shall I send? And who will go

---

2. This expression was their way of using a body part that physically participates in an emotional response to refer to the emotion. It may seem strange at first, but we do the same thing in English with expressions like "That makes my blood boil!"

for us?" Isaiah answers, "Here am I. Send me!" The form for "Send me!" is one word in Hebrew: שְׁלָחֵנִי. The נִי suffix means "me."

Volitional Functions

The function of volitional forms requires little explanation. We will start with the Imv because it is the most familiar. Then we will cover Juss and Coh. Finally, there is a special note on second-person prohibitions, which are not made with the Imv. In these cases, function is determined by context.

Main Imperative Functions

1. **Command**—a directive from a superior to an inferior (note: this does not include prohibitions! See below.)

    The LORD had said to Abram, "**Go** [לֶךְ] from your country, your people and your father's household." (Gen 12:1 NIV)

2. **Request**—a directive by an inferior to a superior (a.k.a. prayer)

    Vindicate me [שָׁפְטֵנִי], LORD, for I have led a blameless life (Ps 26:1 NIV)

3. **Advice**—a directive in which no superiority is in view (though one may still be superior to the other, in offering advice that distinction is not pressed)

    [Jethro says to Moses when he is overwhelmed by judging the people's disputes] **Listen** [שְׁמַע] now to me and I will give you some advice. (Exod 18:19 NIV)

4. **Interjection**—a directive used to draw the listener's attention

    See [רְאֵה], I set before you today life and prosperity. (Deut 30:15 NIV)

Main Jussive Functions

1. **Command**—a directive from a superior concerning an inferior (note: this may take a negative; compare the Imv and see below)

    And God said, "**Let there be** [יְהִי] light," and there was light. (Gen 1:3 NIV)

    Go down and bring Aaron up with you. But the priests and the people **must not force** [אַל־יֶהֶרְסוּ] their way through. (Exod 19:24 NIV)

In both cases, the speaker, God, is not directly addressing the parties that are being commanded. In Gen 1:3, the command concerns the light, but light does not yet exist to hear the command. The hearers are not specifically identified. In Exod 19:24 the Lord's (negative) command concerns the priests and the people, but the Lord is speaking to Moses.

2. **Request**—a directive by an inferior to a superior (a.k.a. prayer or benediction), including both positive and negative requests

> **May the** LORD **cut off** [יַכְרֵת] all flattering lips. (Ps 12:3a ESV)

> **May he** [the LORD] **never leave us** [אַל־יַעַזְבֵנוּ] nor forsake us. (1 Kgs 8:57b NIV)

3. **Permission**—a request by an inferior to a superior

> "**Let** your servant **return** [יָשָׁב־נָא].... **Let him cross over** [יַעֲבֹר] with my lord the king." (2 Sam 19:37 [Hebrew 38] NIV)

English does not have this construction. The English expression "let me..." is actually a second-person Imv. This function is the result of the fact that for the sake of politeness, speakers often referred to themselves in the third person. In 2 Sam 19:37, the "servant" is the speaker, Barzillai.

Main Cohortative Functions

1. **Request**—a directive used when the fulfillment of the action depends on the power of another

> May the Lord not be angry, but **let me speak** [וַאֲדַבְּרָה]. (Gen 18:30 NIV)

2. **Resolve**—a directive used when the speaker has the ability to fulfill the action

> I [the LORD] **will go down** [אֵרְדָה־נָּא] and see if what they have done is as bad as the outcry that has reached me. (Gen 18:21 NIV)

3. **Exhortation**—used only with the first-person plural, an encouragement for two or more to participate in an action

> **Let's call** [נִקְרָא] the young woman and ask her about it. (Gen 24:57 NIV)

Prohibitions

Unlike English, Hebrew does not form a prohibition (negative command), such as "Do not steal," by placing a negative particle before an Imv form. Instead, a negative particle (more precisely an adverb) is placed immediately before a verb in the second-person Imp (*yiqtol*) form. When we discussed adverbs, I said that negative particles were adverbial and that Hebrew had two forms, אַל and לֹא. There has been a lengthy discussion over whether they mean anything different or not, and if so, what is that difference. Here is the current consensus:

1. **General Prohibition** (לֹא + Imp)—prohibition of an action in general

> **You shall not steal** [לֹא תִגְנֹב]. (Exod 20:15 NIV)

2. **Specific Prohibition** (אַל + Imp)—prohibition of a specific action immediately in view

> [Lot said,] "But **don't do** [אַל תַּעֲשׂוּ] anything to these men, for they have come under the protection under my roof." (Gen 19:8 NIV)

These are summarized in Figure 16.4.

FIGURE 16.4: Summary of Volitional Functions and Forms

FUNCTION	FORM				
	Imv	Juss	Coh	לֹא + Imp	אַל + Imp
Command	X	X			
Prohibition				General	Specific
Request	X	X	X		
Advice	X				
Interjection	X				
Permission		X			
Resolve			X		
Exhortation			X		

Parsing

You already know how to get the information from printed and electronic tools. Figure 16.5 shows how these forms compare using the parsing chart.

FIGURE 16.5: Parsing Information for Nominals and Verbals

PtSp	Word	Lex	Stem	Form	P	G	N	State	Det	Case	Suff
Nn	דְּבָרָיו	דָּבָר				m	p	Cst	[?]	[?]	3ms
V	וַהֲשִׁבֹתִיךָ	שׁוב	H	ו + Pf	1	c	s				2ms
V	וַיַּנִּחֵהוּ	נוח	H	ו cs+Imp	3	m	s				3ms
V	אֵלְכָה	הלך	G	Coh	1	c	s				Emph
V	בַּקְשׁוּנִי	בקשׁ	D	Imv	2	m	p				1cs
V	וְהַעֲלֵהוּ	עלה	H	ו + Imv	2	m	s				3ms
V	וַאֲדַבְּרָה	דבר	D	ו + Coh	1	c	s				
V	יִחַר	חרה	G	Juss	3	m	s				

Sequencing of Volitional Forms

In ch. 7 on the *waw* conjunction, you read that Hebrew is paratactic; that is, it prefers to coordinate clauses instead of subordinate clauses, and the ו is considered to be a coordinating conjunction. However, you also read that Hebrew had certain constructions by which it can convey subordinate relationships using the *waw* conjunction. Now you are ready to understand this.

What we are looking at here is a series of two or more clauses joined by *waw* in which the first clause is volitional (Coh, Imv, or Juss). If the series is more than two clauses long, then you must treat each pair in turn. It is beyond the study of pre-Hebrew for you to learn about the constructions in detail. You will need to rely on translations. However, a couple of examples may be helpful so that you can understand why translations differ.

When a volitional form has a prefixed ו (V2) to join it to a preceding clause (V1), it may function either as an independent clause or as a subordinate clause. The identity of the function is determined by context. Here are just two examples:

FIGURE 16.6: Volitional Forms in Sequence

V2 Function	Description	Example
Independent-Sequential	V2 has the same volitional force as V1, V2 simply happens afterward.	God blessed them and said, "Be fruitful [Imv] and increase [ו + Imv] in number and fill [ו + Imv] the water in the seas, and let the birds increase on the earth." (Gen 1:22 NIV)
Dependent-Purpose	V2 gives the intended outcome of the action of V1.	I will go down [Coh] to see [ו + Coh, cf. NASB "and see"] whether they have done altogether according to the outcry that has come to me. (Gen 18:21 ESV)

Flowcharting

There are two new things to learn: how to flowchart commands and how to flowchart subordinate clauses formed from ו + volitional form. In modern English imperatives, the subject, the Prn "you," is left out. If you wish, you can insert "[you]" to fill the subject slot so you can align verbs. When a ו + volitional form is subordinate, it should be indented just as explicit subordinate clauses. Here are a couple of examples to illustrate.

What about Aramaic?

There simply has not been much recent research on Biblical Aramaic,[3] so it is difficult to say much here. We can make the following points, however.

---

3. Noonan, *Advances*, 142.

FIGURE 16.7: Flowcharting Volitional Forms		

Function	Vs	Flowchart: Gen 27:7 (NIV)
Command (Imv)		[you] *Bring* me → some game
Addition Command (ו + Imv)		*and* [you] *prepare* me → some tasty food
Purpose (ו + Coh)		*to eat,*[4]
Result (ו + Coh) Place		*so that* *I may give* you → my *blessing* in the presence of the LORD
Time		before I die.

Function	Vs	Flowchart: 1 Chr 16:31 (NIV)
Command		*Let* the heavens *rejoice,*
Command		*let* the earth *be glad;*
Command		*let* them *say* among the nations,
Assertion		••[5]"The LORD reigns!"

1. The Aramaic Imv functions much like the Hebrew Imv.
2. The clause-initial Imp form can also be a volitional. For example, the *yiqtul* form in Dan 4:14 (Aramaic 4:11), תְּנֻד, "Let them flee," is jussive (NASB, "let the beasts flee"; the verb is actually a 3fs with a singular subject, which the NASB takes as a collective and renders as a plural). The targums, which are Aramaic translations, commonly render Hebrew *yiqtol* forms with Aramaic *yiqtul* forms.
3. The Aramaic *yiqtul* and *weyiqtul* have basically the same range of meaning as the Hebrew *yiqtol* and *weyiqtol*. However, the Aramaic *weyiqtul* can also function as a purpose/result clause, which the Hebrew *weyiqtol* does not (instead the Hebrew *weqatal* can have this function, as mentioned in the chapter).
4. The Aramaic *uqtal* form (the Aramaic parallel to the Hebrew *weqatal*) is simply sequential and does not carry the same modal or volitional force as the Hebrew.

---

4. Formally, "and [so that] I shall eat."
5. I use bullets to mark the beginning and ending of direct discourse. When the entire discourse is only one line, I insert both bullets next to each other to mark the quote as completed.

Advanced Information and Curious Facts

Amy Grant, a Christian singer who became quite popular in the 1980s and still works in the Christian music industry, produced a popular Christian song titled "El Shaddai." Most people know that El Shaddai is traditionally translated "God Almighty." One of the lines continues with the Hebrew phrase, "Erkamka na Adonai." This phrase is based on Ps 18:1 (Hebrew 18:2), אֶרְחָמְךָ יהוה. The verb is אֶרְחָמְךָ. The ךָ ending is the 2ms object suffix. The "na" syllable in the verse is the Hebrew particle נָא mentioned in ch. 16. The Hebrew Bible does not include it; the song writer cleverly added it for a needed syllable. The NIV translates this form, "I love you." However, because it is first in the clause, the verb form is a Coh. This form strengthens the emotion of the verb in a way that simply cannot be brought out easily in an English translation. But it needs to be brought out in teaching and preaching. "I will love the LORD"; no mere future tense, but the word is a verb carrying an intense act of the will. May we all vow desperately to love our LORD!

CHAPTER 17

TO INFINITIVES AND BEYOND!

Infinitives & Participles

Objectives

1. Define participles and infinitives.
2. Explain how English can translate various nonfinite verbs in Hebrew.
3. Explain parsing of participles and infinitives in Hebrew.
4. Identify how English translations interpret Hebrew nonfinite verbs.
5. Flowchart English versions and compare with data in traditional and reverse interlinear Bibles.

Introduction

Finite verbs, you remember, are limited (hence the term *finite*) because they have the quality of person. In other words, they have a grammatical subject built into the verb form; those are the afformatives you saw on the perfect, imperfect, and volitional forms. This chapter deals with the nonfinite verbal forms, which are forms not limited by person. The nonfinite forms are sort of a hybrid of a verb and a noun, but they are properly treated with verbs because they have a stem. Also, participles may function like verbs so that they convey aspect. Infinitives sometimes function in the place of finite verbs. When they function as nonfinite verbs, they form phrases, not clauses. When they function as verbs, they form clauses.

In Hebrew there are two types of nonfinite verbal forms, infinitives and participles. In the chapter title, I listed infinitives first just to be clever; we will treat the participle first, because it is the most familiar, and then infinitives.

A word of encouragement: before you finish this chapter, you may have a sense of being overwhelmed. Don't be intimidated. I am going to give you plenty of examples so that you can understand the principles involved, but you don't need to understand all the details. Focus on the functions of each form so that you can understand what commentators are talking about.

Participles

A participle (Ptc) is a verbal Adj. This means that it has qualities of both verbs and Adjs.

Like a verb, a Ptc

1. implies some action, though the focus is on the participant, whereas in a finite verb the focus is on the action with a specific grammatical subject;
2. has a verbal stem;
3. has voice, active or passive. The Qal stem has two forms, the active (PtcA) and passive (PtcP). The other stems only have one, and the voice is determined by the stem;
4. may take a DO and be modified by adverbial expressions; and
5. the negative is indicated with אֵין.

Like an Adj, a Ptc

1. has the qualities of gender, number, and state;
2. may be determined or undetermined;
3. may have case functions;
4. may have a PrnSf; and
5. may function as a noun.

Figure 17.1 summarizes the information contained in participle forms. You will notice that I have marked the qualities under the purely nominal qualities (state, determination, and case) with an X in brackets: [X]. This is to indicate that these qualities are present when the Ptc is acting as an Adj. They are not present when the Ptc is acting as a pure verb.

FIGURE 17.1: Parsing Information for Nominals and Verbals

PtSp	Word	Lex	Verbal Qualities					Nominal Qualities			
			Stem	Form	P	G	N	State	Det	Case	Suff
V			X	X	X	X	X				
Nn						X	X	X	X	X	
Adj						X	X	X	X	X	
Ptc			X	X		X	X	[X]	[X]	[X]	

Forms of the Participle

Because participles do not have the quality of person, they do not have personal afformatives. They do have the characteristics of their stem. For the *qal*, the "simple" pattern, active participles (PtcA) are pronounced with a long *ō* (*holem*) or *ô* (*holem waw*) after the first root letter. Passive participles (PtcP) are pronounced with *û* (*shureq*) after the second root letter. Some grammarians call the Ptc, whether active or passive, the "*qotel*" form, corresponding to the names *qatal* for the Pf and *yiqtol* for the Imp. I will use both terms.

Because Ptcs function like Adjs, they do take the same endings as Adjs. Figure 17.2 gives the forms for the *qal* PtcA and PtcP. The roots are in gray type and the gender and number endings are in black type. Characteristic vowels of the *qal* Ptc are also in black.

FIGURE 17.2: Forms for the Qal Participle				
Q	**ACTIVE**		**PASSIVE**	
	Absolute	Construct	Absolute	Construct
ms	קֹטֵל	קֹטֵל	קָטוּל	קְטוּל
fs	קֹטֶלֶת , קֹטְלָה	קֹטֶלֶת , קֹטְלַת	קְטוּלָה	קְטוּלַת
mp	קֹטְלִים	קֹטְלֵי	קְטוּלִים	קְטוּלֵי
fp	קֹטְלוֹת	קֹטְלוֹת	קְטוּלוֹת	קְטוּלוֹת

Of course the Ptcs in the other stems have their own "shapes." The *holem* in the paradigm above is characteristic of the *qal* PtcA. The *niphal* has a prefixed *nun* (נ); the rest have a prefixed *mem* (מ). If you study full Hebrew, you will learn these. As an English-only student using interlinear Bibles, simply noting the grammatical information is sufficient.

Adjectival Uses of the Participle

As a verbal Adj, a Ptc may function either like an Adj or a verb. The Ptc in the predicate position (review ch. 12 on Adjs) and the "verbal" Ptc have the same construction. The difference is that a predicate Adj describes the state of the subject and is always in a noun clause; the passive Ptc is especially suited for this. The verbal Ptc describes an action in which the subject is engaged; the active Ptc is suited for this. When a Ptc is used adjectivally, it can function in any of the three ways an Adj can function: attributively, predicatively, or substantivally. The function of the Ptc is determined by grammatical structure in just the same way the function of an Adj is determined. Figure 17.3 is reproduced from figure 12.2, except that I have substituted the Ptc מֹשֵׁל, "ruling," for the Adj "good." In the chart below, as we've done before, we will use T instead of Art for the article.

FIGURE 17.3: Positions and Agreement of Adjectives						
Construction	Presence of Noun	Definite Noun	Article before Ptc	Function	Example	Pattern
Attributive	Y	Y	Y	Attributive	הַמֶּלֶךְ הַמֹּשֵׁל or מֶלֶךְ הַמֹּשֵׁל [rare][1] = the ruling king	T-N-T-Ptc N-T-Ptc

---

1. This is an extremely rare construction. Here are some examples with my wooden translations. See

Construction	Presence of Noun	Definite Noun	Article before Ptc	Function	Example	Pattern
Predicate	Y	Y	N	Predicative	הַמֶּלֶךְ מֹשֵׁל or מֹשֵׁל הַמֶּלֶךְ = the king (is) ruling	T-N-Ptc Ptc-T-N
Ambiguous	Y	N	N	Either Attributive or Predicative	מֶלֶךְ מֹשֵׁל or מֹשֵׁל מֶלֶךְ = a ruling king or a king (is) ruling	N-Ptc Ptc-N
Isolated	N	—	Y or N	Substantival	מֹשֵׁל or הַמֹּשֵׁל = a ruler or the ruler	Ptc T-Ptc

In the examples below, I used *The English-Hebrew Reverse Interlinear Old Testament* in Logos.[2] Remember that the reverse interlinear scrambles the Hebrew word order to align with English word order; subscript numbers indicate the Hebrew word order. I will decode some of their abbreviations then transfer that information to the parsing charts we have been using.

Attributive Adjectival Ptc

Both active and passive Ptcs may be used attributively. Just as with Adjs, the attributive Ptc will agree with the noun it modifies in gender, number, and determination, and it will follow the substantive. Furthermore, since it is attributive, it must also agree in case. Here are a couple of examples.

1. PtcA; Exod 24:17a (ESV)

Now	the	appearance	of	the	glory	of	the	Lord	was	like	a	devouring	fire
₁	→	מַרְאֵה ₂	→	→	כְּבוֹד ₃	▶4	·	יְהוָֹה ₄	·	כְּ ₅	▶6	אֹכֶלֶת ₇	אֵשׁ ₈
ו		מַרְאֵה			כְּבוֹד			יהוה		כְּ		אֹכֶלֶת	אֵשׁ
C		NC-SC			NC-SC			NPMSA		P		VaR-FSA	NC-SA

Gen 49:17, שְׁפִיפֹן עֲלֵי־אֹרַח הַנֹּשֵׁךְ, "a serpent on a path, the one biting," and Isa 47:8, עֲדִינָה הַיּושֶׁבֶת, "O voluptuous one, the one sitting," for examples in poetry. For examples in prose, see Judg 21:19, לִמְסִלָּה הָעֹלָה, "of a road, the one going up," and 1 Sam 25:10, עֲבָדִים הַמִּתְפָּרְצִים, "servants, the ones breaking away."

2. All interlinear references are from McDaniel and Collins, *The ESV English-Hebrew Reverse Interlinear Old Testament.*

EXPLANATION OF INTERLINEAR		
Word 6 = fire	NC-SA	Noun, common, s Abs [no Art]
Word 7 = devouring	VaR-FSA	Vb, Q [active], Ptc, f, s, Abs [no Art]

			Verbal Qualities					Nominal Qualities			
PtSp	Word	Lex	Stem	Form	P	G	N	State	Det	Case	Suff
Nn	אֵשׁ	אֵשׁ				f	s	Abs	U	Gen	
Ptc	אֹכֶלֶת	אכל	G	PtcA		f	s	Abs	U	Gen	

Note the agreement of the Ptc with its noun in G, N, state, Det, and case (remember: I view objects of prepositions as being in the Gen, whose function is determined by the preposition). Note also its position right after the noun, as indicated by the subscript number 7 coming right after 6, of course! The English word "a" represents no separate Hebrew word, and the symbol "▶6" means that the translation "a" is combined with word number 6, the bold arrow indicating that there is an intervening word or words.

2. PtcP; Gen 49:21 (NIV)

Naphtali	is	a	doe	set	free
נַפְתָּלִי	.	→	אַיָּלָה	שְׁלֻחָה	←
נַפְתָּלִי			אַיָּלָה	שׁלח	
NP-SA			NCFSA	VaS-FSA	

			Verbal Qualities					Nominal Qualities			
PtSp	Word	Lex	Stem	Form	P	G	N	State	Det	Case	Suff
Nn	אַיָּלָה	אַיָּלָה				f	s	Abs	U	Nom	
Ptc	שְׁלֻחָה	שׁלח	Q	PtcP		f	s	Abs	U	Nom	

EXPLANATION OF INTERLINEAR		
Word 2 = doe	NCFSA	Noun, common but feminine here, s Abs [no Art]
Word 3 = set free	VaS-FSA	V, Q, PtcP, f s Abs [no Art]

Again, note the agreement of the Ptc with its noun in G, N, state, Det, and case. Case is not regularly grammatically marked in Hebrew, so this is not given in the parsing. Instead, it is determined by inspection. Note also the position of the Ptc, word 3, right after the noun, word 2.

Predicate Adjectival Ptc (In Clauses with *Be* and in Noun [Verbless] Clauses)

Recall from ch. 6 that a verbless clause has no expressed verb, but the concept of a form of the English verb "be" is understood. The Ptc can function just the same way. Remember that there is no semantic difference whether the verb "be" is included or not. Its inclusion is primarily to specify time.

Predicate Ptcs are typically passive. These indicate a state, a completed action. Just like Adjs, they agree with the noun they modify in gender and number, but they are *always* indefinite. The ***absence*** of the article here is as a function marker, namely, to mark the predicate position. It has virtually no semantic significance. See ch. 12 on the article. Most often, predicate Ptcs are located before their noun, giving predicate-subject (Pred–Subj) word order. Since they are part of a noun (verbless) clause, however, the subject may come first (Subj–Pred). The case will always be Nom.

1. Subj–Pred order: This is the default word order, meaning that there is no emphasis. This answers the question, "Who or what is characterized this way?"; 1 Sam 21:8 [Hebrew 21:9] (NIV).

Because	the	king's	mission	was	urgent
כִּי 29	▶31	מֶלֶךְ־הַ 32 33	דְּבַר 31	הָיָה 30	נָחוּץ 34
כִּי 2		מֶלֶךְ־הַ 1	דְּבָר	היה	נחץ
C		A NC-SA	NC-SC	VaP3MS	VaS-MSA

		Verbal Qualities				Nominal Qualities			
PtSp	Word	Lex	Stem	Form	P	G	N	State	Det	Case	Suff
Nn	דְּבַר	דָּבָר				m	s	Cst	D	Nom	
Ptc	נָחוּץ	נחץ	Q	PtcP		m	s	Abs	U	Nom	

The predicate Ptc is "urgent," word 34 in the verse. The subject noun (subject Nom) is "mission," word 31. In Hebrew, this Nn is in Cst with "king's," which has the article, making it determined. Recall that when the tail noun is Det, every member of the Cst chain is Det.

Notice that the Nn and Ptc agree in G, N, and case but disagree in state and Det. The disagreement in state is not important. The disagreement in Det is relevant. The Det state marks the noun as subject Nom, while the U state marks the Ptc as the predicate Nom.

Also, its predicate Ptc follows the noun. What is it that is urgent? The mission (of the king). In this example the verb *to be* (הָיָה) is present to specify the time frame as past.

2. Pred–Subj order: This is not default word order, i.e., the word order is marked; it answers the question, "What is the character of the subject?" Here is Gen 29:33.

Because	the	Lord	heard	that	I	.	am	not	loved,
←	שְׂנוּאָה ₁₃	→	וָ ₁₅	.	אָנֹכִי ₁₄	כִּי ₁₂	שָׁמַע ₁₀	יְהוָה ₁₁	→	כִּי ₉
כִּי ₂	יהוה	שמע	כִּי ₂	אָנֹכִי	וְ	שׂנא			
C	NPMSA	VaP3MS	C	RP1-S	C	VaS-FSA			

EXPLANATION OF INTERLINEAR		
Word 13 = am not loved	VaS-FSA	V, G Passive, Ptc, f, s, Abs [no Art]
Word 14 = I	RP1-S	PPrn, 1st person, s

Incidentally, in the third line of data, the "2" in "כִּי ₂" refers to a second lexical entry for כִּי[3] instead of referring to the word order given in the second line.

Substantival Ptc

Even though a Ptc forms a phrase instead of a clause, English commonly must translate the substantival Ptc as a relative clause, "the one who/he who X-s," unless English has an acceptable way of saying, "the X-er." For example, הַשֹּׁמֵר might be translated either "the one who/he who keeps" or "the keeper."

Both active and passive Ptcs may function like a noun. They can fill any noun slot—Nom, Gen, or Acc—with any of the case functions. In other words, they should be treated just like nouns. Therefore, I don't need to give you examples for all the noun uses. Here is one illustration, from Exod 22:6 [Hebrew 22:5] (NIV), in which the substantival Ptc is functioning as a subject Nom.

---

3. This numbering is according to Swanson, *Dictionary of Biblical Languages with Semantic Domains: Hebrew (Old Testament).* Remember that different lexicons may use different numbering. In fact, they may even group words differently, which can result in different word counts between resources.

the	one who started	the	fire	must	make	restitution
הַ־₁₈	אֶת₂₀ מַבְעִר₁₉	הַ־₂₁	בְּעֵרָה₂₂	→	יְשַׁלֵּם₁₇	←
הַ	אֶת בער₁	הַ	בְּעֵרָה		שלם	
A	VcR-MSA PO	A	NCFSA		VbI3MS	

Compare a traditional interlinear:[4]

אֶת־הַבְּעֵרָה	הַמַּבְעִר	יְשַׁלֵּם	שַׁלֵּם
[obj] · the · fire	the · one who started₂	he shall make restitution	surely₁
PO · A · NCFSA	A · VcR-MSA	VbI3MS	VbF---A

The complete Ptc phrase is translated "the one who started the fire." Notice that English changed the construction into a relative clause. Another way to translate this would be "the fire starter," but that is awkward. Within the Ptc phrase, the Ptc takes a DO, *fire*, just like a verb. The entire phrase functions as a noun in the Nom. There is no antecedent to the Ptc; it is simply functioning as the subject of the verb phrase "shall make full restitution." Below are two options for flowcharting. The first follows the English of the NIV. The second keeps all the words grouped according to Hebrew grammar, and I have added brackets to indicate the grouping.

Function	Vs	Flowchart: Exod 22:6 [H 5] (NIV Reverse Interlinear)
Assertion		The one … must make → restitution
Description		^who started → the fire
Assertion		[The one who started the fire] must make → restitution

Notice that the most important difference between the two is that the second one identifies the function simply as an assertion, without drawing any special attention to the description. This is a good observation to make so that you can distinguish those sentences that specifically mark descriptive clauses for the reader's attention.

Verbal Uses of a Participle and Noun Clauses

Now we come to the verbal uses of the Ptc. Structurally the verbal Ptc is identical to the predicate Ptc. A verbal Ptc may be either active or passive, but

---

4. Van der Merwe, *Lexham Hebrew-English Interlinear Bible,* loc. cit.

clear cases are much more commonly active. The difference is in the relationship to a referent. Whereas the predicate Ptc functions like an Adj and describes an action drawing attention to a participant, the verbal Ptc functions like a finite verb and relates to a grammatical subject. When making flowcharts, treat verbal Ptcs as finite verbs.

The verbal PtcA indicates continuous or progressive aspect and may be either real or irreal. The verbal PtcP indicates a completed state and is therefore constative. The time frame for the verbal Ptc may be past, present, or future, and the time is determined by context. If there is need to specify time, the speaker or writer includes a form of to be (הָיָה). Here are some examples of the verbal Ptc used in different time frames:

1. **Past Time**

> When Moses' father-in-law saw all that he was doing [עֹשֶׂה; Q PtcA ms] for the people (Exod 18:14 ESV)

The Ptc is part of an RC modifying the word "all." The main verb is "saw," a *wayyiqtol* form, which is past time. The Ptc piggybacks on the past time of the main verb indicating progressive action. The ESV rightly brings this out with the English progressive, "was doing." The Ptc is describing an action in progress currently with respect to the speaker.

> We were brought [מוּבָאִים; Hp Ptc mp] here because of the silver. (Gen 43:18 NIV)

The PtcP is the main clause, which in Hebrew is preceded by a lengthy PPhr. Upon their return to Egypt to regain Simeon, left in Joseph's custody, Joseph's brothers had been brought back to the house of Joseph, and no reason had been given to them. They were fearful that they might suffer punishment. מוּבָאִים reveals the completed action in the past and the current resulting state.

2. **Present Time**

> And what is my sin before your father, that he seeks [מְבַקֵּשׁ, D Ptc ms] my life? (1 Sam 20:1 ESV)

The attempts on David's life are repeatedly in progress.

> Your servants are given [נִתָּן, N Ptc ms] no straw [formally, "straw is not given to your servants"], yet we are told, "Make bricks!" (Exod 5:16 NIV)

The PtcP describes a current state of affairs, which are repeated actions, but the state is ongoing.

3. **Future Time**

> Then the Lord said to him, "<u>Know</u> [Imv] for certain that for four hundred years your descendants <u>will be</u> strangers in a country not their own, and they <u>will be enslaved</u> and <u>mistreated</u> there. But I *will punish* [דָּן; G PtcA ms] the nation they serve as slaves." (Gen 15:13–14 NIV)

The previous underlined clauses clearly set up a future time frame. The *will punish* (PtcA) is future, based on context. Usually the future time of the PtcA is imminent but in this case is four hundred years in the future.

> What is left will *hang* [סָרוּחַ, G PtcP ms] over the sides of the tabernacle. (Exod 26:13 NIV)

The building of the tabernacle is future, made explicit with verb יִהְיֶה. The PtcP describes what will be the accomplished state in the future.[5]

4. **Conditional Ptc**

The quality of conditionality is built into a Ptc. Even the articular Ptc can have this nuance. For example, in Gen 26:11 Abimelek declares concerning Isaac,

> *Anyone who harms* [הַנֹּגֵעַ; formally, *the one harming*] this man or his wife shall surely be put to death. (NIV)

The Ptc (with the Art) implies the condition, "*If anyone harms*"
The Ptc without the Art can function the same way.

> *Whoever sheds* [שֹׁפֵךְ] human blood, by humans shall their blood be shed. (Gen 9:6 NIV)

The first word of the verse is simply the Ptc without the Art; there is no separate Hebrew word behind the English "Whoever"; the NIV is taking the Ptc as an indefinite pronoun, which also implies a conditional notion. In fact, the NLT specifies this: "If anyone takes a human life."

---

5. Francis I. Andersen and A. Dean Forbes, *The Hebrew Bible: Andersen-Forbes Phrase Marker Analysis* (Bellingham, WA: Lexham, 2009), label this as a pure verbal Ptc. The presence of the verb *be* might also allow categorization of the Ptc as a predicate adjective.

Summation of Verbal Participles

Now we can complete the chart of nonvolitional functions from figure 15.3:

FIGURE 17.4: Nonvolitional Structures and Functions

INDICATIVE MOOD (REALITY)

Time	English Tenses	Examples	Aspect	Pf	ıcs+Pf	Imp	ıcs+Imp	Ptc
Past (Real & Irreal)	Simple Past	he ate	Constative	X			X	
			Instantaneous	X			X	
			Resultative	X			X	
	Emphatic Past	he did eat	Constative	X			X	
	Past Perfect	he had eaten	Perfective	X			X	
	Contrary-to-Fact Condition	(if) he had eaten	Constative	X				
	Contrary-to-Fact Assertion	(then) he would have eaten	Constative			X	X	
	Customary Past	he used to eat	Iterative			X	X	
	Progressive Past (Historic Present + היה)	he was eating	Continuous			X	X	X
	Ingressive Past	he began eating	Ingressive			X		
	Historic Future (In Subordinate Clauses)	he would (was going to) eat	Conative			X	X	
Present (Real & Irreal)	Simple Present (incl. Stative, Gnomic, Habitual)	he eats	Constative	X			X	
			Instantaneous	X			X	
			Resultative	X			X	
			Habitual	X	X	X	X[6]	X
	Emphatic Present	he does eat	Constative	X				
	Present Perfect	he has eaten	Perfective	X	X		X	
	Performative	He (hereby) eats	Instantaneous	X				
	Progressive Present	he is eating	Continuous			X	X	X

(continued)

---

6. This is not common and not expected, since the *wayyiqtol* is characterized by representing completed action. However, see Prov 8:35: "For whoever finds me [*qotel*] finds [*qatal*] life **and obtains favor** [*wayyiqtol*] from the LORD" (ESV). The *wayyiqtol* might also be normalized as the present perfect "and has obtained favor." Cf. KJV, "and shall obtain favour," which might be seen as an anterior future, "shall have obtained favor." See also Prov 11:2, 8; 12:13; etc.

Time	English Tenses	Examples	Aspect	Pf	וcs+Pf	Imp	וcs+Imp	Ptc
Future (Irreal)	Simple Future	he shall eat	Constative		X	X		X
	Conditional Assertion	(then) he will eat	Constative			X		
	Immediate Future	he is about to eat	Constative		X			X
	Rhetorical/Dramatic Future	he eats (perfected aspect)	Constative	X			X	
	Future Perfect	he will have eaten	Constative	X				
	Anterior Future	he will have eaten	Constative			X		
	Progressive Future (+ יהיה)	he will be eating	Progressive					X

SUBJUNCTIVE MOOD (POTENTIALITY)

Time	English Tenses	Examples	Aspect	Pf	וcs+Pf	Imp	וcs+Imp	Ptc
Future (Irreal)	Condition (Protasis)	(if) he eats/eat/should eat	Constative	X	X	X		X
	Possibility	he might eat	Constative		X	X		
	Purpose/Result	in order that/so that he might eat	Constative			X		
	Capability	he can eat	Constative			X		
	Permission	he may eat	Constative			X		
	Obligation/ Propriety	he ought to eat	Constative		X	X		
	Command/ Prohibition	Eat!/Do not eat!	Constative		X	X		
	Desire/Intention	he wants/ intends to eat	Constative			X		
	Request/Wish	please, eat!	Constative			X		

Infinitives

An Inf is a verbal noun, meaning that it has both verbal and nominal qualities. Infinitives are not inflected for person, gender, or number. For forms, see the "Advanced Information and Curious Facts" section at the end of this chapter.

Like a verb, an infinitive
  1. implies some action;

2. has a verbal stem, though the focus is on the process rather than on the participant;
3. may also take a DO and be modified by other adverbial phrases; and
4. may take a negative, but the negative particle is בִּלְתִּי or לְבִלְתִּי.

Like a noun, an infinitive
1. functions as a noun in any case; and
2. can be the object of a preposition or be the head noun in a construct chain.

Figure 17.5 summarizes the parsing information for Infs with comparisons to other forms. Not only do they have no personal ending like verbs, they also don't have gender and number as nominals do. Just as with the Ptc, the Inf has noun qualities when it is acting like a noun, so state, Det, and case are marked with an X in brackets.

FIGURE 17.5: Parsing Information for Nominals and Verbals

PtSp	Word	Lex	Verbal Qualities					Nominal Qualities			
			Stem	Form	P	G	N	State	Det	Case	Suff
Nn						X	X	X	X	X	
V			X	X	X	X	X				
Ptc			X	X		X	X	[X]	[X]	[X]	
Inf			X	X				[X]	[X]	[X]	

Overall, the uses of Hebrew Infs are pretty simple. The trick with them is that there are two separate types of Infs. We'll treat the infinitive construct (InfC) first, because it is similar to English. The second type is the infinitive absolute (InfA). English has no formal equivalent to the Hebrew InfA, so translations must use other parts of speech.

Uses of the Infinitive Construct

InfC as a Noun

The InfC can function in any role that a noun plays. This means that it can appear in any case. Furthermore, it may function as the head noun in a construct chain! It may take a PrnSf, and that PrnSf is often either the subjective Gen or the objective Gen, as context dictates. An InfC may also be the object of a preposition. Because noun functions have already been covered, just a few examples will suffice.

1. **Nom**

> *To do* [עָשֹׂה] what is right and just is more acceptable to the LORD than sacrifice. (Prov 21:3 NIV)

The entire Inf phrase is "to do what is right and just." This entire phrase serves as the subject of the noun clause. Incidentally, *acceptable* in Hebrew is a Ptc used predicatively.

FLOWCHARTING INF PHRASE AS A SUBJ (USE BRACKETS TO JOIN THE INFPH)

To do what	(is)	right	(is)	more acceptable
		and		
		just		
				to the LORD
				than sacrifice*

* It is traditional to take English *than* as introducing a clause in this case, "than sacrifice is," in which case "sacrifice" is the subject and corresponds to the InfPhr. However, English grammarians have also accepted *than* as functioning as a Pp, in which case "sacrifice" is the object of the Pp, and that is what has been done here (see *Concise Oxford English Dictionary*, "than"). This works well because it is simpler and is parallel to the Hebrew מִזֶּבַח, formally, "from sacrifice." For the comparative use of מִן, see ch. 8.

---

2. **Gen**

> Better what the eye sees *than the roving* [מֵהֲלָךְ] of the appetite. (Eccl 6:9 NIV)

The InfC is the Gen object of the Pp מִן. The entire Inf phrase is "the roving of the appetite." Notice here that the InfC is in a construct chain with "the appetite." The Gen function is subjective; i.e., the appetite is doing the roving. Note also that the מִן is used comparatively.

3. **Acc**—including the *complementary* use

> Before I finished *praying* [לְדַבֵּר] in my heart (Gen 24:45 NIV)

The DO of *finished* is the Inf phrase "praying in my heart"; the Inf phrase "completes" (i.e., it's complementary to) the main verb. The PPhr "in my heart" modifies the InfC. Note also that the InfC has the Pp לְ. You can flowchart this verse in two ways just using English, depending on which way you take the Inf:

FLOWCHARTING INFC AS A DO (TREAT VERB + INF SEPARATELY)

Before	I	had finished	→ praying
			in my heart

FLOWCHARTING INFC AS A COMPLEMENTARY INF (TREAT VERB + INF TOGETHER)

Before	I	had finished praying
		in my heart

Flowcharting as a DO has the advantage of making the PPhr more clearly modifying the Inf than the verb phrase (V + Inf). In terms of meaning, the praying was in his heart (i.e., silently) and not that the finishing of his praying was in his heart.

InfC as an Adverb

The InfC commonly functions adverbially when it is the object of a preposition, mainly the inseparable prepositions. Figure 17.6 summarizes the functions and constructions. In the boxes I have placed "key words" that might be used to translate the construction.

FIGURE 17.6: Prepositions and Adverbial Infinitive Functions

FUNCTION	PREPOSITION			
	לְ	בְּ	כְּ	Other
Time		when	when, as	
Means		by		
Manner	by	by		
Cause				because, since
Concession	(as) though			although
Purpose	to, in order that			
Result	so that			

1. **Time**

   Her husband is known in the gates *when he sits* [בְּשִׁבְתּוֹ] among the elders of the land. (Prov 31:23 ESV)

   Compare the NIV, "*where he takes his seat.*" A reader might infer from the NIV rendering that this is used adjectivally to describe the gate. This InfC + Pp בְּ, formally, "in his sitting," is adverbial, and the ESV makes this more parallel to the Hebrew. Note also that the 3ms PrnSf is a subjective Gen. Which rendering do you think best captures the best perspective of the proverb? Is there any difference in meaning?

   Both of these English translations render the InfPhr with an English subordinate clause, which is better English than the formally equivalent "in his sitting."

   Flowcharting with the English subordinate clauses is simple enough, and this can be done with all these adverbial uses:

2. **Means**

   By warfare and *exile* [בְּשַׁלְחָהּ] you contend with her. (Isa 27:8 NIV)

The InfC follows the Pp בְּ indicating the instrument or means of the action of the main verb. If you can substitute "using" for the preposition, the function is means.

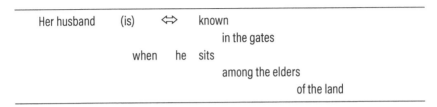

3. **Manner**

    If you play the fool *and exalt yourself* [בְּהִתְנַשֵּׂא] (Prov 30:32 NIV)

Compare the ESV, "*exalting yourself*." The Inf phrase is giving the manner in which "playing the fool" is done. By translating with *and* the NIV opens up the possible interpretation that two separate actions are involved, as though it meant, "If you play the fool, or if you exalt yourself." This is clearly not the intent. The ESV brings out the adverbial nature of the Inf phrase but does not choose which adverbial function is best.

4. **Cause**

    Because *you rage* [הִתְרַגֶּזְךָ] against me and because your insolence has reached my ears, I will put my hook in your nose. (Isa 37:29 NIV)

The InfC is the object of the Pp יַעַן ("because of"). The InfC has a PrnSf that is a subjective Gen.

5. **Concession**

    I will shoot three arrows to the side of it, *as though* I *were shooting* [לְשַׁלַּח] at a target. (1 Sam 20:20 NIV)

The action of the shooting is a pretense. Note the לְ Pp.

6. **Purpose**

    Do not wear yourself out *to get rich* [לְהַעֲשִׁיר]. (Prov 23:4 NIV)

There may be times when it is worthwhile to weary yourself, but to do so for the purpose of getting rich is not wise.

7. **Result**

    They burned all the palaces and *destroyed* [לְהַשְׁחִית] everything of value there. (2 Chr 36:19 NIV)

The result of all the burning was that everything of value was destroyed.

Uses of the Infinitive Absolute

The infinitive absolute (InfA) is a verbal noun, just like the InfC. Unlike the InfC, the InfA is never in construct with a following noun (hence the term *absolute*). The InfA has three classes of functions. In addition to functioning like (1) a noun or (2) an adverb just like the InfC, the InfA may also function as (3) a finite verb, substituting for any of the five finite verb forms we've studied, except the participle.

Here are just a few examples.

InfA as a Noun (In Any Case)

But see, there is . . . *slaughtering* [הָרֹג] of cattle. (Isa 22:13 NIV)

The InfA phrase is simply "slaughtering cattle," with the InfA (rendered with a gerund) taking a DO. The entire InfPhr is functioning as a Nom noun (a predicate Nom, to be more precise). Notice that the InfA takes a DO; the NIV adds the word *of* for the sake of English style, but this is not a construct chain.

InfA as a Finite Verb

Advanced Information:[7] Cohen demonstrates that the use of the InfA in place of a finite verb is present throughout the OT but becomes more frequent in later Hebrew. In the books written in the First Temple period (destroyed in 586 BC), the bulk of the uses are for general commands. The InfA is ideal for this purpose, since it is not limited to a particular subject or verb because it lacks limiting grammatical features. In the books written in the Second Temple period (516 BC–AD 70), the InfA for finite forms is much more common for all forms. One purpose they serve in replacing finite forms can be to mark the conclusion of one series from a following series.[8]

1. **Substitute for the 1cs + Imp (*wayyiqtol*)**

   They blew their trumpets and *broke* [וְנָפוֹץ] the jars that were in their hands. (Judg 7:19 NIV)

The InfA follows a *wayyiqtol* form and has the same function in the English translation. The *wayyiqtol* sequence resumes in the next clauses. The *waw* + InfA is used to close off the series of *wayyiqtol* forms in v. 19 before v. 20, which begins a new string with a *wayyiqtol* form.

---

7. For this analysis, see Ohad Cohen, *The Verbal Tense System in Late Biblical Hebrew Prose*, Harvard Semitic Studies 63 (Winona Lake, IN: Eisenbrauns, 2013), 253–72.

8. See Cohen, *Verbal Tense System*, 261n16, where he discusses Esth 2:2–3, concluding with a sequential InfA. At first glance, v. 4 appears to continue the list, but the Hebrew syntax makes v. 4 not parallel to vv. 2–3. Better is to understand v. 4 as a secondary clause, the main ones being vv. 2–3.

2. **Substitute for the Pf (*qatal*)**

   Yea, the hind also calved in the field, and *forsook* [וְעָזוֹב] it. (Jer 14:5 KJV)

The InfA follows a *qatal* form and has the same function. The KJV does not catch the correct use of the *qatal* "calved" (it should be gnomic, translated with an English simple present tense). Most modern translations render these as one clause. Compare the NIV, "Even the doe in the field *deserts* her newborn fawn."

Advanced Information. One might be tempted to think that since the *waw* is prefixed, the *waw* + InfA is equivalent to the *wayyiqtol* instead of the *qatal*. I think Cohen's study, referenced above and below, suggests that the *waw* is not consecutive but simply conjunctive.[9]

3. **Substitute for the Imp (*yiqtol*)**

   Fields will be bought for silver, and deeds *will be signed* [וְכָתוֹב], *sealed* [וְחָתוֹם] and *witnessed* [וְהָעֵד]. (Jer 32:44 NIV)

Three occurrences of an InfA follow a *yiqtol* form, all with the same function in relation to the main verb, "will be bought."

Adverbial InfA—Emphasis

1. **Emphasis of the certainty of its main verb**—InfA preceding main verb of same root

   You have *indeed* defeated [הַכֵּה הִכִּיתָ] Edom. (2 Kgs 14:10 NIV)

The InfA precedes the finite verb of the same root (נכה). The NIV renders the InfA with an adverb.

2. Emphasis of the intensity of the main verb—InfA following main verb of same root

   But if you are going to deal with me like this, then kill me *immediately* [הָרְגֵנִי הָרֹג]. (Num 11:15 NET)

The InfA follows its finite verb of the same root. The NET translates with the adverb *immediately* to bring out the intensity of the action. The NIV has "please go ahead and kill me," rendering the intensity with "please go ahead and."

Adverbial InfA—Complementary

   He scraped it out into his hands and went on, *eating* as he went [וְאָכֹל]. (Judg 14:9 ESV)

---

9. For Hebrew students who want to research the topic in more detail, I accept the research of Cohen, *Verbal Tense System*, 16–19, 24–28, and Jan Joosten, *The Verbal System of Biblical Hebrew* (Jerusalem: Simor,

The ESV understands this semi-independent use of the InfA as simultaneous action.

Summary and Flowcharting

This chapter has covered a lot of ground, but congratulations! You have finished all the grammar! If you are feeling overwhelmed at this point, remember, you don't have to know all the details—you are not learning full Hebrew. All you need to understand is the main functions of Ptcs and Infs in order to understand references in commentaries.

FIGURE 17.7: Summary of Main Functions of Nonfinite Verbals

Major Function	Participle	Infinitive Construct	Infinitive Absolute
Substantival	• As a noun in any case with a focus on the ***participant*** • May govern a Gen • May govern a DO	• As a noun in any case with a focus on the ***action*** • May govern a Gen • May govern a DO	• As a noun in any case with a focus on the ***action*** • May ***not*** govern a Gen • May govern a DO
Adjectival	• Attributively • Predicatively		
Verbal	• Real or irreal action simultaneous to the verb in the previous clause		• for *qatal* • for *weqatal* • for *yiqtol/weyiqtol* • for *wayyiqtol*
Adverbial		• Time • Means • Manner • Cause • Concession • Purpose • Result	• Emphasis of certainty • Emphasis of intensity • Complementary of simultaneous action

First, let me summarize the functions of the nonfinite forms:

Second, as for flowcharting, simply chart the Ptc or Inf according to its function in the text. If it is acting like a finite verb, chart it that way; as a noun, then like a noun. If it has an adverbial function, the English translation will usually change the Inf construction to a subordinate clause introduced by a subordinating conjunction and you make the flowchart as you learned in ch. 7.

2012), 25–31, 161–92, that the *wayyiqtol* functions differently in that it sets a new reference time. But this is far beyond what we are trying to accomplish in this book.

What about Aramaic?

Aramaic infinitives and participles basically function the same way as they do in Hebrew, but Aramaic Ptcs have some differences from Hebrew.

Aramaic Ptcs are commonly used for the present tense, just as in Hebrew (e.g., Dan 2:8). Perhaps the major difference between Ptcs in Aramaic and Hebrew is that Aramaic Ptcs are normal also for the simple past. In Dan 4 Nebuchadnezzar the king recounts the story of how he turned into an animal. In v. 7 (H v. 4) there are three Ptcs referring to the simple past. The NASB reads, "Then the magicians . . . and diviners *came in* and I *related* the dream to them, but they *could not make* its interpretation *known* to me." All three of the English verbs in the NASB are simple past. In Aramaic they are all Ptcs.

One difference is that the Hebrew construction of the article + the singular Ptc for a generic person is relatively common in Hebrew (more common is a singular Ptc without the Art). Aramaic typically translates these with an RC, as English translations often do. For an example in prose, see Gen 26:11: "Anyone who harms" (NIV; formally, "the [one] harming"), whereas in Targum Onkelos the Aramaic begins the clause with the RPrn דּ + the Imp, "The one who would do harm." For an example in poetry, see Prov 6:29: "he who sleeps" (NIV; formally, "the [one] entering"), where Targum Proverbs has "whoever *who* (מאן) + *who* (דּ) + Pf" in the sense of "whoever has entered."

The typical way general statements with indefinite subjects are formed in Aramaic is with plural Ptcs without an expressed subject[10] or the article. Here are two examples from Biblical Aramaic with the English rendering of the Ptcs in italics.

A formal translation of Ezra 6:3 would be "a place where [they are] *sacrificing* sacrifices." The NIV has "a place *to present* sacrifices"; cf. the ESV: "the place where sacrifices *were offered*."

A formal translation of Dan 3:4 would be "To you [they are] *saying*, O peoples." The English versions differ greatly: "This is what you *are commanded to do*" (NIV), "You *are commanded*" (ESV, NRSV), "To you *the command is given*" (NASB), "To you . . . *the following command is given*" (NET), "To you *it is commanded*" (KJV), "*Listen to the king's command*" (NLT). Here is an analysis of translation decisions about the active Ptc "saying": (1) passive verb with "you" as the subject" (NIV, ESV, NRSV), (2) rendering with the passive verb "given" and the subject noun "command" (NASB, NET), (3) passive verb with the impersonal "it" as subject (KJV), and (4) retain the active but render it with the command "listen to" and "the king's command" (NLT).

---

10. See Wm. B. Stevenson, *Grammar of Palestinian Jewish Aramaic*, 2nd ed. (Oxford: Clarendon, 1962), §21.13.

No theology rests on this use of the Aramaic Ptc. However, it does serve to illustrate how challenging translating is.

Advanced Information and Curious Facts

What Is a Tanak?

In ch. 4 we introduced the Hebrew term *Tanak*. In fact, there is a book titled *Tanakh* (for the spelling with *kh* at the end, remember from ch. 1 that there are many different systems of transliteration). Remember that Tanak must not be confused with *Torah*. *Torah* is a word meaning "law, instruction." Most commonly the word refers to the Torah *par excellence*, namely the Mosaic writings, Genesis through Deuteronomy, the Pentateuch. *Tanak*, on the other hand, is an acronym. The three consonants, T, N, K stand for three Hebrew words:

Torah	→	Law
Nevi'im	→	Prophets
Ketuvim	→	Writings

In other words, Tanak refers to the three parts of the Jewish canon, the Christian OT.

I refresh your memory, because the last term, *Ketuvim*, is from the root כתב, "to write": כְּתוּבִים. You may recognize the *shureq* as the sign of the *qal* PtcP. This is one more example of a Ptc being used as a noun. Formally, it means "things written." More idiomatically, we say "Writings." Oh, and that book, *Tanakh*? Its full title is *Tanakh: The Holy Scriptures—The New JPS Translation according to the Hebrew Text*. This *Tanakh* is a translation of the Hebrew Bible done by Jewish scholars. You might find it interesting to read.

Is Gen 1:1 a Main Clause or Subordinate?

We have studied Gen 1:1 several times. The first word in Hebrew is a prepositional phrase, בְּרֵאשִׁית, "in (the) beginning." The Hebrew pointing has no article. Yet a definite beginning seems to be in view. The *Lexham Hebrew-English Interlinear Bible*, along with some commentators, parses רֵאשִׁית in the Cst state rather than the absolute state and suggests the translation "in the beginning of." But if this is correct, what is the tail noun for רֵאשִׁית? Some suggest the pointing of the G Pf 3ms verb בָּרָא, "he created," be changed to בְּרֹא, which would be followed by a subjective Gen and two direct objects. The result would be a long construct chain made definite by the tail noun, *God*. A formal translation would be, "In the beginning of God's creating the heavens and the earth." In fact, the *Tanakh Translation* renders, "When God began to create the heavens and the earth."[11]

---

11. Reprinted from *Tanakh: The New JPS Translation According to the Traditional Hebrew Text*

In an unpointed text, ברא could be either the Pf or the InfC. Obviously the Masoretes preserved a tradition that the verb should be finite and רֵאשִׁית should be in the absolute state. The note to this verse in *The Jewish Study Bible* explains that Rashi, a famous eleventh-century Jewish commentator, suggested reading this as a temporal clause. They explain further that other ancient creation stories begin similarly, including Gen 2:4.[12]

The difference between these is significant. In the traditional interpretation, Gen 1:1 is the first act of creation; matter is brought into existence. In the other view, God created, narrated in vv. 2 or 3 and following, from previously existing unstructured matter, described in v. 1. Here is Wenham's analysis:

> First and fundamental is the observation that the absence of the Article in ברֵאשִׁית does not imply that it is in the construct state. Temporal phrases often lack the Article (e.g., Isa 46:10; 40:21; 41:4, 26; Gen 3:22; 6:3, 4; Mic 5:1; Hab 1:12). Nor can it be shown that רֵאשִׁית may not have an absolute sense. It may well have an absolute sense in Isa 46:10, and the analogous expression מֵרֹאשׁ in Prov 8:23 certainly refers to the beginning of all creation. The context of ברֵאשִׁית standing at the start of the account of world history makes an absolute sense highly appropriate here. The parallel with Gen 2:4b disappears, if, as argued below, the next section of Genesis begins with 2:4a, not 4b. As for the alleged parallels with Mesopotamian sources, most of those who acknowledge such dependence point out that better parallels with extrabiblical material may be found in Gen 1:2–3 than in 1:1. The first verse is the work of the editor of the chapter; his indebtedness to earlier tradition first becomes apparent in v 2.[13]

By learning the things in this course, you are able to follow the lines of reasoning in this comment. This should give you confidence to understand the issues involved. If you are determined and curious, you can even investigate some of the arguments further for yourself.

(Philadelphia: Jewish Publication Society of America, 1985) with the permission of the publisher. For a discussion of the various views, see Gordon J. Wenham, *Genesis 1–15*, Word Biblical Commentary (Dallas: Word, 2002), 11–13.

12. *The Jewish Study Bible* (Oxford: Oxford University Press, 2004), 13.

13. Wenham, *Genesis 1–15*, WBC, 12.

CHAPTER 18

WHAT DO YOU MEAN?
Hebrew Word Studies

Objectives
1. Perform a full word study.
2. Perform a shortcut word study.
3. Avoid common pitfalls in using biblical tools.

Tools Used
- Computer resources that display Hebrew grammatical information and include a quality wordbook
- Or use paper resources: at *least* three English translations (in addition to NIV, NASB), *The Interlinear Bible: Hebrew-Greek-English* by Jay P. Green, ed. (*IBHGE*), *The Strongest NIV Exhaustive Concordance* (*SNIVEC*), *The Hebrew-English Concordance to the OT with the NIV* (*HECOT*), *Mounce's Complete Expository Dictionary of Old & New Testament Words* (*MCED*) or equivalent

Introduction

One Sunday you have a special speaker in church. The speaker uses the verse on his organization's logo as the central passage in his sermon: "Where *there is* no vision, the people perish" (Prov 29:18 KJV).[1] He makes use of this passage to spur your congregation to plan for church growth: if you have no goals and no plan, you will not grow. You agree with his point, but when you follow along in your NIV, you read, "Where there is no revelation, people cast off restraint." What catches your eye is that *revelation* in the NIV implies something different to you than the point the preacher was making. The issue is that you need to know the meaning of this word translated "vision" in the KJV.

Out of all the things covered in this book, the topic of word studies is probably the one people will use most often. Word studies are fun. They are interesting. Preachers usually have people's attention when they explain (briefly!) the background to a word's meaning. However, there are pitfalls to be avoided. In this chapter, you will learn a procedure for doing your own word studies.

---

1. Remember that the KJV (as well as NASB) italicize English words that are added for sense where the original languages have no explicit words.

Many authors write about proper practice, and they all follow the same basic procedures. I will mention in footnotes a few of those writers to whom I am most indebted. The last part of the chapter identifies common pitfalls to avoid.

Performing Proper Word Studies

One way to think about the idea of context in Bible study is as a target with a bull's eye, as in figure 18.1. At the center is the word in the passage we are studying, the immediate context. Next closest is the context of that book and other books by that author. Then other books in the same genre (e.g., poetry, prophecy, law, history). Farther removed is all the OT. Beyond that there is some ancient Hebrew literature outside the Bible. Ancient translations of Scripture, such as the LXX, are even further removed from our immediate context but still very important. Finally, the largest context is cognate languages (see ch. 2).

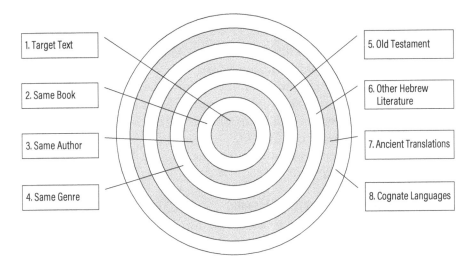

As you move out from the center you increase the number of possible contexts for your word. The more examples you have toward the center, the less you need to extend your search outward.

Of course the best research includes all levels of context. As a pre-Hebrew student, you can do very little with levels 6–8. You will have to rely on the experts for that research. The good news is that you can do quite a lot with levels 1–5. In keeping with the overall purpose of this book, the aim of this chapter is to empower you to study a word on your own before you turn to the experts. Why? Because (1) word-study books may not cover your passage specifically and therefore do not help in your particular case, and when they do cover your word (2) you will be better able to recognize careful research in commentaries and word-study books you may read.

The Process

First, I explain the process. Second, I give a full example by completing a Word-Study Guide. Next, we will look at common mistakes to avoid. Finally, you will see a shortcut version of a word study. MS Word versions of the full- and short-form documents are available by creating an account under Instructor Resources at zondervanacademic.com. For the abbreviations used below, please see the list of tools at the beginning of this chapter.

Step 1: Identifying the Word

1. *Write a clear question you want to answer from the text.* You don't have time to study every word, so you need to choose words carefully. Your word needs to be significant and have enough occurrences to arrive at a valid range of meanings. Duvall and Hays[2] recommend that you study words that are
   - crucial to the passage;
   - repeated in the pericope or the book;
   - figures of speech; or
   - unclear, puzzling, or difficult (clue: if versions differ in how to translate a word, it is probably a difficult word).
2. *Identify the Hebrew word you are investigating.* Determine the G/K and the Strong's numbers for your word. You learned how to use the *SNIVEC* in ch. 7. You may also start with the *IBHEG* to find the Strong's number or use the conversion table in the *SNIVEC*.
3. *Frame the question.* You want to answer the question, "What does the word *X* mean in this target text?"

Step 2: Determine the Range of Meaning

It is very important here to remember the distinction between a "gloss" and a "definition." A gloss is the nearest equivalent of the original word in a translation. A definition is a description of what the word means. The *SNIVEC* dictionary section gives you glosses. In our example the *MCED* gives you definitions. What you need to do is write brief definitions and list every passage, except the target text, under those definitions.

4. *Find all the occurrences of your word.* If you are using the *SNIVEC*, look up the G/K number in the dictionary section and write down the frequency of the word. Look up the concordance entry for each translation of your word (it may help to jot them down) by using the appropriate dictionary in the back of the *SNIVEC*. In each concordance entry find and record all the passages that have your G/K number. A much more efficient tool is the *HECOT*; you simply

2. J. Scott Duvall and J. Daniel Hays, *Grasping God's Word: A Hands-On Approach to Reading, Interpreting, and Applying the Bible*, 4th ed. (Grand Rapids: Zondervan Academic, 2020), 170.

look up the word by the G/K number and all the entries are collected for you, no matter how the NIV translated the word. Computer Bibles are even faster.

5. *Look up each occurrence (except your passage) and write a brief definition based on context.* You may list multiple passages under one definition, but be sure to list all occurrences. Try to answer such questions as:
   - Is there a contrast or a comparison that seems to define the word?
   - Does the subject matter or topic dictate the word's meaning?
   - Does the author's usage of the same word elsewhere in a similar context help you decide?
   - Does the author's argument in the book suggest a meaning?
   - Does the historical-cultural situation tilt the evidence in a certain direction?

Step 3: Meaning of the Word in the Target Text

Based on the context of the target text, choose one of the definitions that fits best and draw some preliminary conclusions. Then compare with word-study books. To finish up, draw a final conclusion and answer the question posed at the beginning.

6. *Draw preliminary conclusions.* Based on your understanding of the word in your context, choose the definition from your analysis in the previous step that best fits your target text. If you think it means something else in your context, add that as a separate category.
7. *Verify with experts.* Look up the word in *MCED* or any other resources.
8. *Final conclusions.* Summarize your conclusions, taking into account what you've gleaned from the wordbooks.

Word-Study Guide: Full Version Example

I heard a missionary quoting from Prov 29:18: "Where there is no vision, the people perish" (KJV) to support the goals of his organization. Many, from churches to secular businesses, use this quotation to give biblical support to the idea that organizations or individuals must have a vision of a desired goal, or else they will not succeed. (I suspect this understanding is why the second half of the verse is rarely mentioned: "but he that keepeth the law, how happy is he"—it just doesn't seem to fit.)

The word *vision* is what we will study because it is crucial to the passage. In particular, I want to find out if the speaker understood the word properly. He understood it to mean "plan." But the NIV translation "revelation" suggests that the word might be interpreted as revelation from God. Which is it? Are there other possibilities? Which is the most probable? Complete a chart comparing how various translations render the word.

Looking up the word "revelation" in *SNIVEC*, I see that it is G/K number 2606 (חָזוֹן). By using the conversion table (p. 1630), I learn that the Strong's number is 2377. I write these down on my Word-Study Guide (WSG).

I frame the question on the Word-Study Guide.

Step 1: Identifying the Word

1. **Question to answer:** Does the word vision mean "a plan for the future," or does it mean something different?

WSG 1: Comparison of Versions[3]			
Formal	**Functional**	**Free**	**Paraphrase**
NASB: vision	NIV: revelation	NLT: divine guidance	MSG: see what
KJV: vision	NET: prophetic vision	NCV: word from God	God is doing
Translations ESV: prophetic vision	NAB: vision	TEV:	LB: divine vision
NRSV: prophecy	JB: vision	GNB: God's guidance	
RSV: prophecy	NEB:		

2. G/K# 2606; Strong's # 2377[3]
3. Frame the question: What does the word translated "vision" in the KJV version mean in Prov 29:18?

Step 2: Range of Meaning

4. Find all the occurrences of the word
   - Number of occurrences: 35
   - Distribution of occurrences:

Remember to list Hebrew verb meanings grouped by stem (G, N, D+Dp, H+Hp, HtD).

WSG TABLE 2: Distribution of Occurrences of the Word (optional)		
Category		**Passages**
In same book		none
Other books by same author		none
Rest of OT	Law	none
	History	1 Sam 3:1 1 Chr 17:15 2 Chr 32:32
	Poetry	Lam 2:2
	Prophets	Hos 12:10 Obad 1:1 Mic 3:6 Nah 1:1 Hab 2:2, 3 Isa 1:1; 29:7 Jer 14:14; 23:16 Ezek 7:13, 26; 12:22, 23, 24, 27; 13:16 Dan 1:17; 8:1, 2, 13, 15, 17, 26; 9:21, 24; 10:14; 11:14

---

3. On p. 48 above, we noted that the versions fit on a continuum from formal to functional. For the purpose of comparing versions it is useful to identify four categories: formal, functional, free , and paraphrase. The "free" category exhibits a greater degree of difference from the "formal" category.

Note: Computer Bible programs will have this distribution information readily available, though perhaps in a different form. Here is an example from Logos:

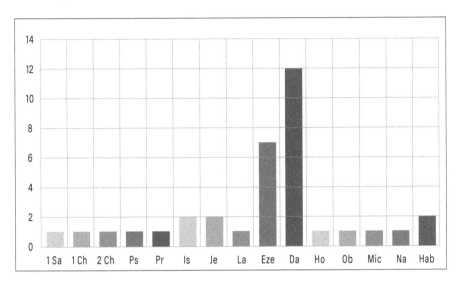

5. Definitions

WSG 2: Definitions (Based on Reading Each Passage)	
Definitions	**Passages**
a. Miraculous divine revelation from God; (1a) Specific messages genuinely from God	1 Sam 3:1; Lam 2:2; 1 Chr 17:15; Ezek 7:13, 26; 12:23, 27; Dan 8:1, 2, 13, 15, 17, 26; 9:21; 10:14; Hab 2:2, 3
(1b) Specific messages genuinely from God recorded in written form	Obad 1; Nah 1:1
(2) General reference of messages to biblical writing prophet	2 Chr 32:32; Ps 89:19; Isa 1:1; Dan 9:24; 11:14(?); Hos 12:10; Micah 3:6
(3) Dream intended to be interpreted by prophet of God	Dan 1:17
(4) False vision; genuineness claimed by people lying about it	Jer 14:14; 23:16; Ezek 12:22, 24; 13:16; 11:14(?)
b. Normal dream of the night, a symbol of unreality	Isa 29:7
c. Planning based on human forethought	NONE

Step 3: Meaning of the Word in the Target Text

6. Preliminary conclusions on the meaning in your passage.

In all but one case, the word G/K 2606 is used of miraculous, divine revelation from God, including the references to prophecies by false prophets who make the same claim. In one case, Isa 29:7, the meaning seems to be a normal dream without any miraculous element implied. In Prov 28:19, the second half of the verse contrasts "vision" with the law, presumably the law of Moses. Since this is clearly miraculous revelation, the meaning in Prov 28:19 is likely miraculous, prophetic revelation from God.

7. Verify with experts (notes from wordbooks).

This word is not treated in the main word-study section of *MCED*. There is a Hebrew-English Dictionary section that gives brief definitions (note: not merely glosses!). The conclusion there agrees with mine, adding something that I didn't notice: "with a possible focus on the visual aspects of the message" (p. 932).

8. Conclusions
    o Meaning of target word in target passage:
       Miraculous revelation from God
    o Effect of the meaning of target word on the meaning of target passage:
       Since there were no references where the word meant planning for the future, that meaning can be eliminated, and the speaker did not properly apply the passage.

Troubleshooting Word Studies

Verbs

> **Teaching/Learning Tip:** Looking up passages from your word study can serve as an excellent source of sermon/lesson illustrations. You don't need to try to impress people with pronunciations and technical information. You can simply make statements such as, "This is the same word used in passage X and Y," so that your audience gets to benefit from your research.

Remember when you are studying verbs, different stems have different meanings. You may need to separate your list of passages by verbal stem. You also learned that prepositions may alter the meaning of a verb, so you may need to identify those passages that are followed by certain prepositions. Computer programs will help to identify the form, and some actually sort them automatically. Mostly, though, you will have to rely on experts. As a pre-Hebrew student, you need to be aware of your limitations. Note that for verbs in *HECOT*, a code by each NIV verse indicates the verbal stem. Learn to use the code (printed at the bottom of each page).

For a key to all the abbreviations, see the "Word-Study Books" section in the bibliography in ch. 19.

Rare and Common Words

Both rare and common words are worthy of your study. You can usually get a good sampling if you have twenty to fifty occurrences. The problem with choosing a word that is rare is that you don't have enough contexts for a good sampling. The rarer the word, the more important it is to include the outer rings of the "Context Target." This also means, however, that you will be more dependent on the work of others (as you progress to the outer circles in figure 18.1). That's okay though.

Words that are common give you too large of a number to be manageable. If a word occurs say, five hundred times, you usually don't have time to study every context. What you can do, though, is focus on the occurrences in your genre or time period. Even when you do this, though, you will need to rely more on the work of others because you aren't looking at every context. Sometimes, if your question is worded appropriately, you can go through enough verses to find a context that answers your question clearly. Also, don't be afraid to say, "I don't know the answer."

Avoiding Word-Study Pitfalls

Duvall and Hays do a nice job of describing eight pitfalls to avoid.[4] I have summarized and arranged these below with examples.

FIGURE 18.3: Word-Study Pitfalls

Fallacy	Description
English-Only	Studying an English word rather than an original language word. **Example:** This is the error made in the Prov 29:18 example above.
Root	Determining the meaning of a word by the parts (or the root) that make it up. **Example:** Some say the root used for the word for priest (כהן) is one who builds a bridge, and therefore a priest is a bridge builder between God and man. Even if this etymology were correct (scholarship suggests that it isn't), this would not help us to understand what a biblical priest is.

(continued)

---

4. Duvall and Hays, *Grasping God's Word*, 166–70.

Fallacy	Description
Time Frame	Neglecting the change of a word's meaning over time, especially after the time of the Bible. **Example:** A prophet now means someone who predicts the future. But in the OT, prophets were spokesmen for God, and the predictive element takes a comparatively minor role.
Overload	Making a word contain all of the meanings in its range of meaning every time it occurs. **Example:** This can be a problem with those who use the Amplified Bible, which gives multiple translations of key words. E.g., in Gen 1:2: "The Spirit of God was moving (hovering, brooding) over the face of the waters."
Word Count	Neglecting the fact that a given word may have more than one meaning and determining the meaning based on that which occurs most often. **Example:** It is a mistake to say, "Since שָׂנֵא commonly means 'to hate,' Jacob hated Leah (Gen 29:30 KJV), and the NIV rendering, 'not loved' is wrong."
Word-Concept	Thinking that understanding a word's meaning equals understanding the whole concept. **Example:** Studying חָזוֹן, the word in Prov 29:18, even properly, does not mean you understand everything the Bible says about the concept of prophecy.
Selective Evidence	Looking only at passages that support your point. **Example:** To say that בָּרָא, "to create," in Gen 1:1 means to create out of nothing neglects passages where it is used in the sense of creating out of something. So in Gen 5:1 we read that God created (בָּרָא) man, which refers to the event in which "God formed [יָצַר] a man *from the dust* of the ground" (Gen 2:7 NIV, italics added).[5]

Word-Study Guide: Shortcut

Sometimes you are feeling a time pinch, but there are one or more key terms in your passage that you need to study. There are two options.

1. You may skip looking up all the contexts and just classify the glosses in the dictionary section of the *SNIVEC* or information from a computer Bible. Once you have a short list of passages, you ought to look up at least one in

---

5. This example comes from John H. Walton, *Chronological and Background Charts of the Old Testament*, rev. ed. (Grand Rapids: Zondervan Academic, 1994), 95.

each category. Obviously, this process is inferior because you may misunderstand the meaning of the gloss if you don't look up the passages.

2. You can go straight to the word-study books *after* you have identified the G/K number. This process is also inferior because you don't make the study your own. If you only have one wordbook, you are relying even more heavily on a smaller amount of research than if you could check other wordbooks, but it is better than nothing. Finally, looking up the other passages can give you some great illustrations.

The form below is abbreviated from the form used above. The only part completed that differs is that the definitions chart is derived only by listing the glosses used in a translation. I used the NIV. Remember that by following this simplified procedure, you may not be able to answer your question, but it can be of help in deriving a range of meaning. Comparing multiple versions on your passage will probably be of greater help.

One more thing: please never use an English dictionary to define a biblical word! Remember "The Vow" from ch. 5?

Step 1: Identifying the Word

1. Question to answer:

| | **WSG 1:** Comparison of Versions | | | |
	Formal	Functional	Free	Paraphrase
	NASB:	NIV:	NLT:	MSG:
	KJV:	NET:	NCV:	LB:
Translations	ESV:	NAB:	TEV:	
	NRSV:	JB:	GNB:	
	RSV:	NEB:		

2. Strong's # _____   G/K# _____
3. Frame the question: What does the word translated _____ in the ____ version mean in the passage _____?

Step 2: Range of Meaning

1. List all the translations and frequencies of the word in the ESV (or base version you are using)
   ○ Number of occurrences _____
   Remember to list Hebrew verb meanings grouped by stem (G, N, D+Dp, H+Hp, HtD).

WSG 2: Definitions (Cite Version)		
Definitions (NIV)	**Passages**	
1. vision, visions (29)	2 Chr 32:32; Isa 1:1; 29:7; Jer 14:14; 23:16; Ezek 7:13, 26; 12:22, 23, 24, 27; 13:16; Dan 1:7; 8:1, 2, 13, 15, 17, 26; 9:21, 24; 10:14; 11:14; Hos 12:10; Mic 3:6;	Ps 89:19; Lam 2:9; Obad 1; Nah 1:1
2. revelation (4)	1 Chr 17:15; Hab 2:2, 3	Prov 29:18;
3. had a vision (1)	Dan 8:1	
4. many visions (1)	1 Sam 3:1	

2. Definitions from wordbooks (see bibliography of approved wordbooks below).

WSG 2: Definitions (Cite Wordbook Used)	
Definitions	**Example Passages**
1.	
2.	
3.	
4.	
5.	

WSG 2: Definitions (Other Wordbooks)	
Definitions	**Example Passages**
1.	
2.	
3.	
4.	
5.	

Step 3: Meaning of the Word in the Target Text

1. Conclusions
   a. Meaning of target word in target passage:

b. Effect of the meaning of target word on the meaning of target passage (How does the meaning answer the question you began to answer?):

> **Teaching/Learning Tip:** This is a good time to take stock of how far you've come in your study. If you are studying by yourself, reflect, preferably in writing. If you are studying with a group, each member can express to the group what they sense they have gained so far and how they will put things into practice in ministry.

Advanced Information and Curious Facts

Here is a sequel to Gen 3:16. The immediate context is the first half of the verse, "your desire will be for your husband" (NIV). The NET note 48 on this reads,

> **tn** *Heb* "and toward your husband [will be] your desire." The nominal sentence does not have a verb; a future verb must be supplied, because the focus of the oracle is on the future struggle. The precise meaning of the noun תְּשׁוּקָה (*téshuqah* [the NET transliterates vocal Shewa with *é*], "desire") is debated. Many interpreters conclude that it refers to sexual desire here, because the subject of the passage is the relationship between a wife and her husband, and because the word is used in a romantic sense in Song 7:11 HT[6] (7:10 ET). However, this interpretation makes little sense in Gen 3:16. First, it does not fit well with the assertion "he will dominate you." Second, it implies that sexual desire was not part of the original creation, even though the man and the woman were told to multiply. And third, it ignores the usage of the word in Gen 4:7 where it refers to sin's desire to control and dominate Cain. (Even in Song of Songs it carries the basic idea of "control," for it describes the young man's desire to "have his way sexually" with the young woman.) In Gen 3:16 the Lord announces a struggle, a conflict between the man and the woman. She will desire to control him, but he will dominate her instead. This interpretation also fits the tone of the passage, which is a judgment oracle. See further Susan T. Foh, "What is the Woman's Desire?" *WTJ*[7] 37 (1975): 376–83.

Take a minute to reflect on how well you would have understood this note before you started this course. If you can read these comments and understand them, then you are achieving the goals for this study. Celebrate!

---

6. HT means "Hebrew Text"; ET means "English Text."
7. *WTJ* means *Westminster Theological Journal*.

CHAPTER 19

TOOLS OF THE TRADE
Books in Paper and Electronic Form

Objectives
1. Learn how to use a commentary.
2. Learn about tools to supplement this book.
3. Develop a buying strategy.

Introduction

Once after coming back from a used bookstore with a few bargains (*treasures*, really, is what they were!), one of my wife's well-meaning relatives asked her, "Does he really need all those books?"

What kind of a carpenter doesn't own a hammer (or multiple ones!)? If you want to be a Bible student, you need to view books as tools just as important as a hammer is to a carpenter. These days, of course, carpenters don't use hammers nearly as much as they use air guns. In the same way, the tools for the trade of Bible study are much better, as you have seen in this course. Don't be afraid to invest a little. For the price of a compressor and air gun, you can have quite a nice collection of tools that will enhance your personal Bible study and your ability to minister to others.

Using Commentaries

If you have never used a commentary, you will be amazed. Your first thought might be, "Well, they've done all the work for me. I don't have to!" This is living on borrowed opinions—or dying on them. Commentaries are wonderful tools, when used properly. Like anything else, there are good ones and bad. Here are a few guidelines on choosing and using them.

There are different types of commentaries. They may be categorized by type, or their purpose. *Exegetical* commentaries seek to explain the meaning of the Bible text. The better ones not only explain the commentator's understanding of the text but also give alternative views and reasons for or against various interpretations. *Homiletical* commentaries also explain the meaning of the text, but in less detail. Their primary aim is to guide preachers in sermon preparation. This may include sermon illustrations and outlines. *Devotional* commentaries are relatively weak in the explanation of the meaning of the text, spending most space on applying the biblical text to life. Because many authors for these books are often not Bible scholars, their exegesis is usually less carefully done. To study a passage, you should use the exegetical commentaries primarily.

Commentaries may also be categorized by level of detail, that is, what knowledge the author assumes the reader will have. I classify them into three levels. A *level one* commentator assumes the typical reader does not know biblical languages. When original language terms are used, they are always in transliteration, usually in a simplified form without all the diacritical marks that you have learned here. The more reliable commentators do know the original language and will still treat the difficult passages in some detail. A *level two* commentator expects that some readers may know biblical languages and usually places words and grammatical discussions on the original languages in footnotes. A *level three* commentator assumes that readers know biblical languages and interacts with the original languages in the text, often without translation or transliteration. (They might also assume that the reader knows German, French, and Latin!) Do not be afraid to use these. Usually English-only readers can benefit from this level of work. You as a pre-Hebrew student will be able to benefit even more.

Here are some common-sense guidelines:

1. *Complete your own study of your passage before turning to the commentaries.* While you are making your own observations, write down any questions you may have, including both ones you have answered (use commentaries for verification) and ones you were not able to figure out (use commentaries for information).
2. *Select at least three commentaries for your passage.* People have been writing commentaries on the Bible for over two thousand years. Making a selection can be difficult.
   a. *Tend to use the more modern commentaries.* Don't necessarily avoid the older ones (those written more than fifty years ago or so); many of them are still valuable. Modern commentators often use them as well and can save you time since they have worked through that material. Still, the older ones are often worth mining, especially particular authors such as Franz Delitzsch, J. A. Alexander, E. W. Hengstenberg, S. R. Driver.
   b. *Tend to use exegetical commentaries, including those from among levels two and three.*
   c. *Get suggestions from published bibliographies and from fellow Christians who read good commentaries.* I give two sources for bibliographies below.
   d. *Get to know publishers and authors.* This is a slow process, but valuable. In particular, you want to know the theological starting points of the commentator. Evangelical scholars hold firmly to the Scriptures as the authoritative word of God; nonevangelical scholars do not. You may disagree with authors' starting points, but you can still learn things from them.

3. *Take notes from your reading of commentaries.*
   a. *Always record the author and title of each commentary* you use as well as the page number for each note you take. This includes during sermon and lesson preparation; it is a good habit to have. Not only do you want to avoid plagiarism (a moral issue), you want to be able to find that reference again if needed (a practical issue).
   b. *Record notes in verse-by-verse order, not commentary order.* You may even want to go phrase-by-phrase. Notes are *summaries* of what the commentator says. Be selective. Write only those things you think are valuable to your understanding of the passage.
   c. *Take notes that answer the questions you have.* Some commentaries seem to be shallow and only deal with the simple matters. Good commentators help you answer the questions you have and may even help you raise more questions. All such questions may be good for asking students or using as sermon or lesson points.
   d. *Evaluate commentators' reasons for interpretations* to help you decide which interpretation you think is best, where they disagree. You cannot merely take a majority vote.
   e. *Note where your interpretations agree or differ.* Have an attitude of respect for the experts, but remember that they are not infallible.

Many commentaries do not discuss the grammar of every word. When they do, it is because the grammar is important for understanding the passage. They can't afford the space to discuss routine matters, and they assume that those who know the biblical languages understand such matters, and those who do not understand the biblical languages could not follow along anyway. This is why what you have learned in this study can help you to understand the commentaries better. You are both able to make some of your own observations and better able to follow the problems scholars encounter in the text.

Tools

Below is a categorized list of a few tools for OT study. I have tried to be brief by choosing to focus on resources dealing with the topics we have covered in this book. I do not give a list of commentaries. Instead, I list a couple of bibliographic resources that you can consult.

Computer Bibles
Because Bible programs vary so much in content, cost, and design, and because they are continually being upgraded, I am not going to comment on any of them. You should go to their websites to compare costs and features that will fulfill your needs both now and in the future. Some online programs are free. In your

evaluation, you need to identify what electronic books are included. The less expensive programs contain mainly (or only) works that are public domain. These are usually too old to help you very much, and certainly not for serious study. Here are some of the more recognized resources listed alphabetically with their web addresses.

Accordance. At www.accordancebible.com. (Mac)
Biblesoft PC Study Bible. At biblesoft.com. (PC)
Bibleworks. At www.bibleworks.com. (PC; no longer producing but still supporting licensed users)
Gramcord. At www.gramcord.org. (PC)
Logos Bible Software. At www.logos.com. (PC, Mac). *Wordsearch* is now part of Logos.

To this list we add here:
Greenwood, Kyle. *Dictionary of English Grammar for Students of Biblical Languages.* Grand Rapids: Zondervan Academic, 2020. This work gives definitions and illustrations of English grammatical terms that are also relevant in discussions of Greek and Hebrew grammar. Entries are arranged alphabetically.
Williams, Michael. *The Biblical Hebrew Companion for Bible Software Users: Grammatical Terms Explained for Exegesis.* Grand Rapids: Zondervan, 2015. Williams provides definitions and illustrations to make sense out of technical terminology regarding Hebrew grammar found in computer and paper resources. Topics are arranged alphabetically.

Bibliographies

Dallaire, Hélène, Knut Heim, and Richard Hess, "Annotated Old Testament Library–2021." This document is available online at https://denverseminary.edu/the-denver-journal/2021/. There is a NT counterpart. These are very valuable articles.
Duvall, J. Scott, and J. Daniel Hays. *Grasping God's Word: A Hands-On Approach to Reading, Interpreting, and Applying the Bible.* 4th ed. Grand Rapids: Zondervan Academic, 2020. This book actually teaches how to interpret the Bible. The bibliography on pp. 510–46 is classified according to type of work and includes commentaries on every book of the Bible. The list is reliable.
Klein, William, Craig L. Blomberg, and Robert L. Hubbard. *Introduction to Biblical Interpretation.* 3rd ed. Grand Rapids: Zondervan Academic, 2017. This is another book on interpretation in much more detail. It has an extensive bibliography on pp. 637–81. The entries are annotated, i.e., the authors give brief insights into the nature of each work.

Longman, Tremper, III. *Old Testament Commentary Survey*. 5th ed. Grand Rapids: Baker Academic, 2013. This book is completely devoted to bibliography of works for OT studies. It goes beyond commentaries, covering all types of works for studying the OT. Entries are briefly annotated. In addition, Longman indicates the level of reader the work is appropriate for (layperson, minister, scholar) and grades it for quality on a 1–5 scale.

Basic Introductions to the Old Testament Studies

Arnold, Bill T., and Bryan E. Beyer. *Encountering the Old Testament: A Christian Survey*. 3rd ed. Grand Rapids: Baker Academic, 2015. Survey of the OT in book-by-book format.

Dillard, Raymond B., and Tremper Longman, III. *An Introduction to the Old Testament*. 2nd ed. Grand Rapids: Zondervan Academic, 2007. In-depth treatment of special introduction (authorship, date, outline, etc.) for each book of the OT.

Hill, Andrew E., and John Walton H. *The Old Testament Today: A Journey from Ancient Context to Contemporary Relevance*. 2nd ed. Grand Rapids: Zondervan Academic, 2014. Survey of the OT in book-by-book format.

Patzia, Arthur G., and Anthony J. Patrotta. *Pocket Dictionary of Biblical Studies: Over 300 Terms Clearly and Concisely Defined*. Downers Grove, IL: IVP Academic, 2002. Dictionary of technical terms used in biblical and theological studies.

Schultz, Samuel. *The Old Testament Speaks: A Complete Survey of Old Testament History*. 5th ed. San Francisco: Harper & Row, 1999. Surveys the OT chronologically.[1]

Soulen, Richard N., and R. Kendall Soulen. *Handbook of Biblical Criticism*. 4th ed. Louisville: Westminster John Knox, 2011. Dictionary of technical terms used in biblical and theological studies.

Walton, John H. *Chronological and Background Charts of the Old Testament*. Rev. ed., Grand Rapids: Zondervan, 1994. Helpful collection of charts on many topics of OT studies.

Old Testament Literature

Chisholm, Robert B. *Interpreting the Historical Books: An Exegetical Handbook*. Handbooks for Old Testament Exegesis. Grand Rapids: Kregel: Academic & Professional, 2006. Treatment of how to study narrative literature of the OT. (The entire series is good.)

---

1. On a personal note, Schultz's book was the first college-level work on biblical studies I ever used, and it opened a new world of Bible study for me and resulted in my professional Bible teaching career.

Fee, Gordon D., and Douglas Stuart. *How To Read the Bible for All Its Worth*. 4th ed. Grand Rapids: Zondervan Academic, 2014. Treatment of how to study all types of literature in both testaments.

Lucas, Ernest C. *A Guide to the Psalms & Wisdom Literature*. Exploring the Old Testament. Downers Grove, IL: IVP Academic, 2003. Treatment of how to study poetic literature of the OT. (The entire series is good.)

Waltke, Bruce K., and Cathi J. Fredricks. *Genesis: A Commentary*. Grand Rapids: Zondervan Academic, 2001. I'm including this commentary because it is a model of how to deal with OT narrative texts.

Interlinear Bibles and Specialty Bibles

Abegg, Martin A., Jr., Peter Flint, and Eugene Ulrich. *The Dead Sea Scrolls Bible: The Oldest Known Bible Translated for the First Time into English*. San Francisco: Harper, 1999. This is an English translation of the biblical manuscripts of the Hebrew Bible. Translations are arranged in OT order, and variations in fonts allow you to see quickly where the DSS Bible manuscripts differ from the MT.

The Apostolic Bible. Apostolic Press, 2004. Modern translation of the LXX into English under the auspices of the Greek Orthodox Church. It is available in e-text at http://septuagint-interlinear-greek-bible.com/ downbook.htm, free and printable online in Adobe format. A hard copy edition is available. The translation is based on the 1709 edition of the LXX published by Lambert Bos, which ultimately derives its text from Codex Vaticanus. Words are coded to Strong's numbering system.

The Apostolic Bible Polyglot. Apostolic Press, 2004. The Greek and English text of the LXX plus the English translation is available on CD or online at http://septuagint-interlinear-greek-bible.com/. It can be downloaded for a fee.

Brenton, L. C. *The Septuagint with Apocrypha: Greek and English*. Repr., Peabody, MA: Hendrickson, 1986. A nineteenth-century English translation of the Septuagint (not the Hebrew!) in parallel columns with the Greek text. Available in print and online. The translation was done by one person using the Greek texts available in the nineteenth century.

Green, Jay P., ed. *The Interlinear Bible: Hebrew-Greek-English*. 1 vol. ed. Peabody, MA: Hendrickson, 2005. Traditional interlinear using the same text base as the KJV. Includes Strong's numbers above most words.

Kohlenberger, John R., III. *The Interlinear NIV Hebrew-English Old Testament*. Grand Rapids: Zondervan Academic, 1993. Traditional interlinear using the *BHS* as its text base.

McDaniel, Chip, and C. John Collins. *The ESV English-Hebrew Reverse Interlinear Old Testament.* Bellingham, WA: Logos, 2006. The ESV with the Hebrew MT arranged beneath. This includes parsing information.

The New English Translation of the Septuagint. Corrected printing. Oxford: Oxford University Press, 2009. Modern English translation of the Septuagint done by committee using the latest research available. This is also available online. For information, see http://ccat.sas.upenn.edu/nets.

Tov, Emanuel, and Computer Assisted Tools for Septuagint Studies. *The Parallel Aligned Hebrew-Aramaic and Greek Texts of Jewish Scripture.* Bellingham, WA: Logos, 2003. The MT text with the LXX arranged beneath.

van der Merwe, Christo. *The Lexham Hebrew-English Interlinear Bible; Bible. O.T. Hebrew.* Bellingham, WA: Lexham, 2004. Interlinear with the Hebrew first and the English arranged beneath each word. This includes parsing information.

Concordances

Kohlenberger, J. R., and E. Goodrick. *The Strongest NIV Exhaustive Concordance of the Bible.* Rev. ed. Grand Rapids: Zondervan, 2004, based on the NIV84. The newest edition on the NIV2011 was published in 2015. This series by Zondervan also has produced exhaustive concordances for other versions including the KJV, NASB, and NRSV. In my opinion, these concordances are the best available for any English version.

Kohlenberger, J. R., and E. Goodrick. *The Hebrew-English Concordance to the Old Testament.* Grand Rapids: Zondervan, 1998. Concordance arranged by Hebrew word based on the G/K numbers rather than English translation. The English translation used is NIV84. Very useful!

The Lexical Concordance of the Apostolic Bible. Apostolic Press, 2004. CD-ROM. Concordance to *The Apostolic Bible Polyglot* of the LXX. It is available on CD or online at http://septuagint-interlinear-greek-bible.com/. It can be downloaded for a fee.

Wigram, George V. *The New Englishman's Hebrew Concordance.* Rev. by Jay P. Green. Carol Stream, IL: Tyndale House, 1995. Concordance arranged by Hebrew word based on the Strong's numbers rather than English translation.

Parsing Tools (Not Counting Computer Software)

Davidson, Benjamin. *Analytical Hebrew and Chaldee Lexicon.* 1871; Repr., Sydney: Wentworth, 2016.

Owens, John Joseph. *Analytical Key to the Old Testament*. 4 vols. Grand Rapids: Baker Academic, 1989–92.

Word-Study Books and Tools

Many of these books are considered to be advanced. In the past, the user had to know Hebrew to use them because entries are not coded to numbers. But you are now able to identify roots and lexical forms. Furthermore, a good computer Bible can make it possible for you to go directly to the right entry in an electronic version of a technical work.

Botterweck, G. J., and H. Ringgren, eds. *Theological Dictionary of the Old Testament*. 17 vols. Grand Rapids: Eerdmans, 1974–2021. Technical and up-to-date treatment of theologically significant OT Hebrew words. Vol. 17 is an index volume. A more reliable treatment of words than is the Greek counterpart to the NT. Abbreviated *TDOT*.

Brown, F., S. R. Driver, and C. A. Briggs. *The New Hebrew-English Lexicon of the Old Testament*. Peabody, MA: Hendrickson, 1979. Technical treatment of all OT Hebrew words. Outdated but still valuable. Coded to the Strong's numbering system. Also covers Aramaic. Abbreviated **BDB**.

Clines, David A., ed. *Dictionary of Classical Hebrew*. 9 vols. Sheffield: Sheffield Academic, 1993–2016. Vol. 9 is an index volume. Technical treatment of all OT Hebrew words. Includes Hebrew literature beyond the OT. Abbreviated *DCH*.

Harris, R. L., et al., eds. *Theological Wordbook of the Old Testament*. 2 vols. Chicago: Moody, 1980. Less technical treatment of theologically significant OT Hebrew words. It uses its own numbering system and is also cross-referenced to Strong's numbering system. Abbreviated *TWOT*.

Holladay, William Lee, and Ludwig Köhler. *A Concise Hebrew and Aramaic Lexicon of the Old Testament*. Leiden: Brill, 2000. This is an abridgment of Köhler, *HALOT*. Abbreviated *CHALOT*.

Jenni, Ernst, and Claus Westermann, eds. *Theological Lexicon of the Old Testament*. Translated by Mark E. Biddle. Peabody, MA: Hendrickson, 1997. Very thorough work treating theologically significant OT Hebrew words. One feature that makes it even more valuable is that at the beginning of every entry article, in addition to the Strong's number are cross-references to where the word is treated in BDB, *HALOT*, *TDOT*, *TWOT*, and *NIDOTTE*. Abbreviated *TLOT*.

Koehler, Ludwig, Walter Baumgartner, M. E. J. Richardson, and Johann Jakob Stamm. 5 vols. *The Hebrew and Aramaic Lexicon of the Old Testament*. Leiden: Brill, 1994–1996. Technical work treating all OT words, including Aramaic. The electronic edition was published in 1999. Abbreviated *HALOT.*

Mangum, Douglas, Derek R. Brown, Rachel Klippenstein, and Rebekah Hurst, eds. *Lexham Theological Wordbook.* Lexham Bible Reference Series. Bellingham, WA: Lexham, 2014. Only available in Logos. This work is a unique hybrid between a Bible dictionary and a theological wordbook. Entries are arranged by English word, though limited to theologically significant topics. The entries begin with an article on the topic similar to a Bible dictionary. After this, entries distinguish individual Hebrew and Greek words, like a theological wordbook. Entries are searchable, however, by English, Hebrew, or Greek words. Abbreviated *LTW.*

Mounce, William D, ed. *Mounce's Complete Expository Dictionary of Old and New Testament Words.* Grand Rapids: Zondervan Academic, 2006. Popular-level treatment of theologically significant words from both Testaments. It is reliable and up to date. Many words are treated with articles; other words are treated with only brief definitions. This supersedes the old *Vine's Complete Expository Dictionary of Old and New Testament Words.* Abbreviated *MCED.*

Swanson, James. *Dictionary of Biblical Languages With Semantic Domains: Hebrew (Old Testament).* Bellingham, WA: Faithlife, 1997. Thorough treatment of all the words of the OT. There is also a separate Aramaic publication. The electronic version makes it very easy to use. Entries are alphabetical with G/K numbers. Each entry lists numbered definitions with a gloss in bold type followed by an expanded definition in regular type. Abbreviated *DBLH* and *DBLA.*

Van Gemeren, W., et al., eds. *New International Dictionary of Old Testament Theology and Exegesis.* 5 vols. Grand Rapids: Zondervan, 1996. Very thorough treatment of theologically significant Hebrew words of OT. Keyed to G/K numbering system. Abbreviated *NIDOTTE.*

A Buying Strategy

There are so many great study tools out there! Where should you start? Duvall and Hays in *Grasping God's Word,* mentioned above, offer a sensible strategy for filling your tool chest. Remember that many works are available in electronic format. You should consider a Bible program that allows you to buy more books to add on later.

Phase 1: Cover All Your Bases

If you have the following types of books, a Bible school teacher will be able to cover almost all needs. For specific recommendations, see the bibliographies mentioned above. I have listed various types of tools beginning with what I think is the greatest priority.

1. Concordance
2. Commentary on the whole Bible (preferably at least a two-volume work)
3. Bible dictionary
4. Bible wordbook
5. Bible handbook
6. Dictionary of theology
7. Atlas

Phase 2: Plan for Growth

When you preach or teach on a new book of the Bible, buy something on that book. Begin by buying at least one reliable commentary on each book of the Bible as you study. You may get more for your money if you buy commentary sets. Because they are often done by different authors, the quality of volumes within sets may vary. Occasionally buy additional reference books after you look them over to see how useful they will be for you. The more serious student that you are, the greater the need you will have to keep detailed works handy. Building a church library is an excellent idea, but someone will need to take charge of that as a ministry so that the library can be both usable and used.

Advanced Information and Curious Facts

I want to show you that reading the English translations of the Septuagint (LXX) and of the Dead Sea Scrolls from the bibliographies can pay off. In Heb 1:6, the author quotes from the OT: "Let all God's angels worship him" (NIV). The job of the interpreter is to study first what the OT meant in its original context, then see how the NT author used it, noting any significant twists. For this quotation, the identity of where it comes from is the first issue. Some say it comes from the end of Ps 97:7, which reads, "worship him, all you gods!" (NIV). However, the wording is not exactly the same as in Hebrews. The first difference is that the verb as quoted in Heb 1:6 is third-person plural, whereas in Ps 97:7 it is a 2mp imperative. The second difference is that the plural noun in Heb 1:6 is *angels*, while that in Ps 97:7 is *gods*. This problem is not insurmountable, since the word *gods* (אֱלֹהִים) can be used to mean "angels." In fact, using Brenton's translation, we can see that the LXX translates this into the Greek word "angels." Still, it would be nice to find a better alternative.

The NIV footnote gives the cross-reference Deut 32:43 and adds, "see Dead Sea Scrolls and Septuagint." If you look up this passage in the *DSSB*,[2] mentioned

---

2. Abegg, Flint, and Ulrich, *The Dead Sea Scrolls Bible*, 193.

in the bibliography above, you can read a translation of a Hebrew Bible from the Qumran community. Figure 19.1 compares the first part of Deut 32:43 in the KJV, NIV plus footnote, Brenton's LXX, and the *DSSB*. In the center I've placed the quotation according to Heb 1:6 with the key words in italic type.

FIGURE 19.1: Comparison of Heb 1:6 and Deut 32:43	
Deut 32:43 (KJV)	Rejoice, O ye nations, with his people: For he will avenge
Deut 32:43 (NIV with Footnote)	Rejoice, you nations, with his people, *and let all the angels worship him*, for he will avenge
Heb 1:6 (NIV)	*Let all God's angels worship him*
Deut 32:43 (LXX)	Rejoice, ye heavens, with him, *and let all the angels of God worship him; rejoice ye Gentiles*
Deut 32:43 (DSSB)	Rejoice, O *heavens, together with him; and bow down to him all you gods,* for he will avenge

The KJV of Deut 32:43 and the main text of the NIV do not contain the italicized phrase because the Hebrew text that the translators used (the Masoretic Text) did not have it. This phrase is included in the footnote to the NIV because it is found in the LXX, which the author of Hebrews seems to be quoting. The LXX reading was not something the translators just plopped in willy-nilly; it is supported by a Hebrew manuscript of Deuteronomy among the DSS. The exact words as recorded by the author of Hebrews are found here, though the quotation is abbreviated.

There is more to research for this passage, but at least we can be reasonably confident that the original context is Deut 32. Now we are ready to interpret. This chapter is a song that Moses recited before the assembly of Israel about the Lord's judgment on the wicked. In the LXX, the song concludes at verse 43 with a call for the heavens to rejoice and for the angels of God to worship "him." Our author identifies the speaker as the Father and "him" as the Son, the object of worship. In doing this, our author is also attributing to the Son the great deeds of the Lord mentioned in Deut 32. The point is clear: since the angels worship the Son, he is clearly superior to them, because of his great deeds.

CHAPTER 20

IF IT'S NOT POETRY, IT'S . . .
Hebrew Prose

Objectives
  1. Explain conjunctive and disjunctive clauses as devices in Hebrew narrative.
  2. Use adjusted flowcharting.
Tools Used: Paper or electronic interlinear Bible

Introduction

You have already learned that in verbless clauses either the subject or the predicate noun may be placed first in the clause, or "fronted." The routine word order is Subj–Pred. This clause answers the question, "Whom does the predicate describe?" If the predicate is fronted, Pred—Subj, the clause answers the question, "How would you describe the subject?"

You have also learned that normal word order in a Hebrew verbal clause is VSO (verb-subject-object). Many grammarians refer to this normal order as "unmarked"; i.e., there is nothing unusual in the construction of the sentence and the verb takes its place as the primary focal point. What you want to pay attention to are deviations from the norm. Fronting may be done to (1) set a time frame, (2) emphasize the fronted element, or (3) form a disjunctive clause.

In this chapter, you will learn about how clauses work in Hebrew narrative. Narrative literature in the OT constitutes the story parts. Narrative is found most commonly in the historical books, of course, but it is also found in all the other sections of the OT. Describing all the details of the interpretation of this kind of literature is beyond the scope of this book.[1] What you can do is grasp the big picture of narrative literature and then see how what you've learned in these previous chapters can give you insights that are normally lost in translation.

There are three principles to keep in mind when studying Hebrew narrative. First, all narrative has three basic elements: setting, characterization, and plot.

---

1. For further reading, see the books listed in ch. 19 under the heading Old Testament Literature. Fee and Stuart cover OT narrative in ch. 5. Robert B. Chisholm, *Interpreting the Historical Books: An Exegetical Handbook*. Handbooks for Old Testament Exegesis (Grand Rapids: Kregel: Academic & Professional, 2006), is more advanced.

Second, the player behind the scenes is the narrator. He is the one describing the setting and characters and relating the story. We want to observe what the narrator is trying to make visible to our mind's eye. Third, one task of the interpreter is to find the section breaks between and within stories—to pay attention to the story line and to what the author points out. Hebrew can do this with conjunctive and disjunctive clauses. This aspect of Hebrew narrative is frequently lost in English translation. But since you are now equipped to use a traditional interlinear, that information will no longer be lost on you!

In this chapter you will learn the functions of conjunctive and disjunctive clauses. Then you will learn how to work with embedded speech. The last section illustrates how to incorporate these features into a flowchart.

Conjunctive and Disjunctive Clauses

When the conjunction *waw* connects one clause to another, it may introduce a conjunctive clause or a disjunctive clause. Simply put, a *conjunctive clause* is a clause that begins with *waw* + finite verb. We treated these in the chapters on the verb. A *disjunctive clause* is one that begins with *waw* + nonverb or with no conjunction at all. Conjunctive clauses may be either independent/main or dependent.

Terminology overlaps a little here, so it is important to keep things straight. A *waw* is considered to be a *coordinating* conjunction. The function of the clause it introduces, however, may be either a main/independent clause or a subordinate clause.

One of the characteristics of narrative in the OT is the abundance of direct speech. Reading narrative is sort of like watching a play. The main difference is that a play is meant to be acted and watched while a narrative is the work of a narrator and is meant to be read. The conjunctive and disjunctive clauses in narrative literature are the words of the narrator, not the recorded speech.

Conjunctive Clauses

The standard construction for a conjunctive clause in Hebrew narrative is the *wayyiqtol* verb form. This structure is considered unmarked. A series of *wayyiqtol* clauses builds a sequence or series of activities. A negative clause in such a sequence is usually expressed by וְלֹא + Pf. Occasionally the negative will be expressed by וְלֹא + Imp, with one of two senses: (1) customary past (e.g., "he *used to* not go into town") or (2) past progressive (e.g., "he *was* not *going* into town"). Scholars are divided over whether וְלֹא introduces a disjunctive clause (a strict application of the definition) or not. I agree with the position that it does not discontinue the narrative, because that would mean there is no way to negate a sequential clause.[2]

You learned in ch. 15 that וַיְהִי is a common verb form in the Hebrew Bible

---

2. I refer the curious to Aaron D. Hornkohl, "Biblical Hebrew Tense–Aspect–Mood, Word Order and Pragmatics: Some Observations on Recent Approaches," in *Studies in Semitic Linguistics and Manuscripts*,

and that it may function in one of two ways: either to mark a temporal clause or as a main clause. The construction וַיְהִי + a temporal clause often introduces a new narrative or scene; וַיְהִי + a subject is used as a main verb and translated, "And [subject] was/became."

In a series, *wayyiqtol* can have any of the following semantic notions:[3]

FIGURE 20.1: Eight Basic Functions of *Wayyiqtol* Clauses

Function	Description
Introductory	Begins a scene or narrative by providing background for following story
Initiatory	Begins the story proper
Sequential/ Consequential	Describes events in temporal or logical sequence *(most common use)*
Flashback	Interrupts story to refer to prior action that now becomes relevant
Focusing	Draws attention to an individual in the event just described, gives more detailed account of the event or aspect thereof, or provides specific example
Resumptive	Resumptive-(con)sequential follows a supplementary, focusing, or flashback statement Resumptive-reiterative repeats a portion or paraphrase of a previous statement
Complementary	Completes preceding statement by describing an action that naturally or typically accompanies what precedes
Summarizing/ Concluding	Summarizes or marks the conclusion of a narrative

Disjunctive Clauses

A disjunctive clause may be either a verbal clause or a noun clause. The key factor is how the clause begins. In short, it begins with *waw* + a nonverb. A nonverb includes any nonfinite verb such as a noun, pronoun, participle, or particle, except the negatives לֹא and אַל, as we mentioned above.

A disjunctive clause functions to break up a sequence of events. Using Bible study tools, you should be able to identify disjunctive clauses. Once you find one, what do you do? You may use figure 20.2 to determine how versions have rendered a given disjunctive clause.[4] These differences may show up in words, punctuation, or chapter and verse divisions.

---

ed. N. Vidro, R. Vollandt, E. M. Wagner, J. Olszowy-Schlanger, Studia Semitica Upsaliensia 30 (Uppsala: Uppsala Universitet, 2018), 45; he does not establish this but assumes it.

3. This chart is a summary taken from Robert B. Chisholm, Jr., *A Workbook for Intermediate Hebrew: Grammar, Exegesis, and Commentary on Jonah and Ruth* (Grand Rapids: Kregel: Academic & Professional, 2006), 263. See also his *Interpreting the Historical Books*, which is a practical presentation of how to analyze narrative literature.

4. This chart is a reformatting of information in Chisholm, *A Workbook for Intermediate Hebrew*,

FIGURE 20.2: Functions of Disjunctive Clauses			
Function	**Description**	**Function**	**Key Words**
Initial	Marks beginning of new section		*now*
Concluding	Marks the end of a section		
Adverbial	Also called "circumstantial," this clause provides information about the action of a main clause	Time-simultaneous	*while, when*
		Manner	*by*
		Concession	*although*
		Cause	*because*
		Description	—
Parenthetic	Information parenthetic to main clause (meet needs of reader)		*now*
Contrastive	Contrasts with main clause		*but*
Focusing	Draws reader's attention as a witness to the events (particularly when introduced by וְהִנֵּה)		*Look!,* *Take note!*

What about Embedded Speech?

Embedded speech, also called direct discourse, is quoted speech. Quoted speech is the words of someone other than the narrator. It is embedded in the narrative. Note, however, that sometimes the narrator becomes an actor (e.g., 1 Sam 3:4, assuming that Samuel himself is responsible for this part of the books of Samuel). This is especially common in the prophets (e.g., Isa 6:5). The narrator speaks to the reader; the actors speak to each other.

The grammar for embedded speech is the same as simple narrative (on poetry, see the next chapter). However, each speech act begins a new unit and therefore interrupts the narrative, which makes them offline from the narrative structure. As offline expressions, the speech acts are intended to be focal points for the reader.

Once again, I refer you to Chisholm, *Interpreting the Historical Books*, 57–68. Chisholm treats the narration as I have explained above. For embedded speech, however, he analyzes direct discourse (i.e., quoted speech) by discourse types and speech function. This makes sense, because most recorded speech acts are pretty short, and there is therefore little narrative development.

Chisholm's types and functions go outside of what we are doing here because they are not linked to Hebrew syntax. Instead, they are based on the narrative

---

264, in Allen P. Ross, *Introducing Biblical Hebrew* (Grand Rapids: Baker Academic, 2001), 156–57, and in Gary Pratico and Miles V. Van Pelt, *Basics of Biblical Hebrew Grammar*, 3rd ed. (Grand Rapids: Zondervan Academic, 2019), §24.7.

context (setting, plot, characters). I think it is valuable to include a summary of his analytics here so that you can work through complete texts. Figure 20.3 lists and describes the types and functions explained by Chisholm.

FIGURE 20.3: Chisholm's Discourse Types and Speech Functions for Embedded Discourse

Discourse Types	• Predictive discourse	Speaker describes what will happen
	• Narrative discourse	Speaker rehearses what has happened
	• Hortatory discourse	Speaker urges, commands, exhorts listeners
	• Expository discourse	Speaker explains or argues a case
	• Procedural/Instructional discourse	Speaker explains how to do something
Speech Functions	• Informative	Simple information designed to inform listeners
	• Persuasive-dynamic	Intended to change hearers personally (emotionally, educationally, attitudinally)
	• Expressive	Speaker verbalizes feelings without concern to affect others
	• Evaluative	Speaker expresses judgment on quality of something
	• Performative	Speaker's speech is the act; for example, a decree
	• Relational	Speaker seeks to enhance personal relationships

Thinking about speech acts in these ways will help you to understand more accurately what the speaker is saying. I will use these labels in an example below. You or your teacher may wish to ignore them for now. But if you wish to use them, this will get you started. I do recommend that you obtain and use Chisholm's work for a more extensive explanation.

A Strategy

1. Flowchart your passage from your English version, adding a fourth column titled "Hebrew Clause Structure–Function." For narrative analysis, we will not do all the grammatical analysis but instead will focus on the narrative features.
2. Use a traditional interlinear Bible to discover all the clauses, both verbal and nominal, in your passage. Match each with your English translation.
3. Label the beginning of each clause according to conjunction and the following word.
4. Use figure 20.4 to identify the function of the clause.
5. Optional: Identify the embedded speech types and functions using figure 20.3.

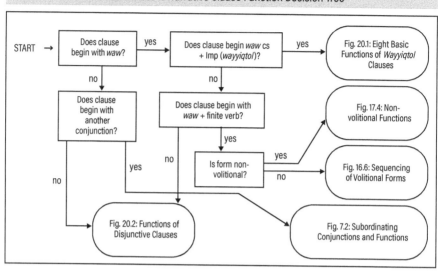

FIGURE 20.4: Narrative Clause Function Decision Tree

Below is an example of how a completed flowchart might look based on Ezek 37:1–15. I have placed all the recorded speech in bold font and indented with bullets to mark the beginning and ending of each speech act and the level of embedding; remember that two bullets means that the entire quotation is completed in one line. I have also included the speech functions in bolded font. Afterward, there are a few observations.

First, note these symbols and abbreviations:

ٱ	= a clause beginning with *waw*
cj	= a clause beginning with a conjunction other than *waw*
Ø	= a clause beginning with no conjunction
NV	= nonverb

For best results, create the table with landscape orientation. Be sure to use figures 20.1–4 from this chapter. At first, they will seem cumbersome, but after a surprisingly short amount of practice, you will find that many things are routine and you'll only need the functions for nonroutine uses.

Flowcharting Hebrew Clause Structure

What good is this? What can you do with it? Here are a just a few things to note:
1. I included v. 15 because it has a form that marks a new unit. You can actually tell this from the English. There are cases, though, in which the English doesn't make this clear. At least now you know what to look for and what commentators may discuss.

FIGURE 20.5: Narrative Analysis Applied to Ezek 37:1-15

Function	Vs	Passage: Ezek 37:1-15 (NIV)	Clause Structure	Function
Event	1	The hand of the LORD was on me,	Ø + Pf	Initial
Event		and he brought me out by the Spirit of the LORD	ıcs + Imp	Initiatory
Event		and set me in the middle of a valley;	ıcs + Imp	Sequential
Assertion		it was full of bones.	ı + NV	Parenthetic
Event	2	He led me back and forth among them,	ı + Pf	Past Progressive
Event		and I saw a great many bones on the floor of the valley,	ı + NV רבה	Focusing
Assertion		bones that were very dry.	ı + NV	Focusing
Event	3	He asked me,	ıcs + Imp	Sequential
Address		· **"Son of man,**		
Question		· **can these bones live?"**	**Predictive**	**Informative**
Event		I said,	ıcs + Imp	Sequential
Address		· **"Sovereign LORD,**		
Assertion		· **you alone know."**	**Expository**	**Informative**
Sequence	4	Then		
Event		he said to me,	ıcs + Imp	Sequential
Command		· **"Prophesy to these bones and say to them,**	**Hortatory**	**Persuasive**
Content		· **'Dry bones,**		
Command		**hear the word of the LORD!**	**Hortatory**	**Performative**
Assertion	5	**This is what the Sovereign LORD says to these bones:**	**Expository**	**Performative**
Immediate Fut		· **I will make breath enter you,**	**Predictive**	**Informative**
Addition		**and**		
Result		**you will come to life.**	**Predictive**	**Informative**

(continued)

Function	Vs	Passage: Ezek 37:1-15 (NIV)	Clause Structure	Function
Simple Future	6	I will attach tendons to you	Predictive	Informative
Addition		and		
Simple Future		make flesh come upon you	Predictive	Informative
Addition		and		
Simple Future		cover you with skin;	Predictive	Informative
Simple Future		I will put breath in you,	Predictive	Informative
Addition		and		
Result		you will come to life.	Predictive	Informative
		Then		
Result		you will know	Predictive	Persuasive
Content		that I am the Lᴏʀᴅ.'"	Expository	Relational
Event	7	So I prophesied	ו + Pf	Inceptive Past
Description		as I was commanded.	RC	Past Perfect
Addition		And		
Time		as I was prophesying,		
Event		there was a noise,	וcs + Imp	Sequential
Description		a rattling sound,	ו + NV הנה	Focusing
		and		
Event		the bones came together, bone to bone.	וcs + Imp	Sequential
Event	8	I looked,	ו + Pf	Inceptive Past
Addition		and		
Assertion		tendons and flesh appeared on them	ו + NV הנה	Focusing
Addition		and		
Assertion		skin covered them,	וcs + Imp	Sequential
Contrast		but		
Assertion		there was no breath in them.	ו + NV	Contrastive

Function	Vs	Passage: Ezek 37:1-15 (NIV)	Clause Structure	Function
Sequence	9	Then		
Event		he said to me,	ʾcs + Imp	Sequential
Command		• "Prophesy to the breath;	Hortatory	Informative
Command		prophesy, son of man,	Hortatory	Informative
		and		
Command		say to it,	Hortatory	Informative
Content		• 'This is what the Sovereign Lᴏʀᴅ says:	Performative	Informative
Command		Come, breath, from the four winds,	Hortatory	Informative
Addition		and		
Command		breathe into these slain,	Hortatory	Informative
Purpose		• • that they may live.'"	Predictive	Informative
Event	10	So I prophesied	ʾ + Pf	Inceptive Past
Description		as he commanded me,	RC	Past Perfect
Addition		and		
Event		breath entered them;	ʾcs + Imp	Sequential
Event		they came to life	ʾcs + Imp	Sequential
Addition		and		
Event		stood up on their feet	ʾcs + Imp	Sequential
Assertion		—a vast army.	Ø + NV	Focusing
Sequence	11	Then		
Event		he said to me:	ʾcs + Imp	Sequential
Assertion		• "Son of man, these bones are the people of Israel.	Expository	Informative
Assertion		They say,	Expository	Informative
Content: Assertion		• 'Our bones are dried up	Expository	Expressive
Addition		and		
Assertion		our hope is gone;	Expository	Expressive
Assertion		• we are cut off.'	Expository	Expressive

(continued)

Function	Vs	Passage: Ezek 37:1-15 (NIV)	Clause Structure	Function
Command	12	**Therefore prophesy**	Hortatory	Persuasive
		and		
Command		**say to them:**	Hortatory	Persuasive
Content		· 'This is what the Sovereign LORD says:	Performative	Informative
Address		My people,		
Immediate Future		· I am going to open your graves	Predictive	Persuasive
		and		
Immediate Future		bring you up from them;	Predictive	Persuasive
Immediate Future		I will bring you back to the land of Israel.	Predictive	Persuasive
	13	Then		
Result		you, my people, will know	Predictive	Persuasive
Content		That I am the LORD,	Expository	Relational
Time		when I open your graves	Expository	Persuasive
Addition		and		
Time		bring you up from them.	Expository	Persuasive
Simple Future	14	I will put my Spirit in you	Predictive	Persuasive
Addition		and		
Result		you will live,	Predictive	Persuasive
Addition		and		
Simple Future		I will settle you in your own land.	Predictive	Persuasive
Sequence		Then		
Result		you will know	Predictive	Persuasive
Content		that I the LORD have spoken,	Expository	Persuasive
Addition		and		
Content		I have done it,	Expository	Persuasive
Exclamation		· · declares the LORD.'"	Expository	Performative
Event	15	The word of the LORD came to me:	ʔcs + Imp	Initial

2. The nonbold areas represent the narrator. There are several places in which the structure is disjunctive, though it is not represented as disjunctive in the English translations. For example, v. 8 has four clauses. The first one is ו + Pf. The English is a simple past. But using the figures helps us to understand that the narrator is trying to increase the vividness with a progressive aspect. The second is ו + הִנֵּה (nonverb). Here the author is trying to focus the reader's attention. This important activity includes the third clause, which is sequential to the second. The fourth clause is also disjunctive. The presence of the negative makes it clear that contrast is in view.

3. In the embedded discourse, the speech acts begin with the Lord asking a question. The purpose, though, is not to elicit information but to inform Ezekiel by engaging him in discussion about the vision. When the bones, which are Israel in captivity, speak (v. 11), their speech expresses their emotions about their "dead" and hopeless status. At the end when the Lord speaks in vv. 12b–14, the purpose of his predictions is to encourage the dry bones: as a result of what the Lord is about to do, they ought to take courage, and their hope is as sure as their certitude that the Lord keeps his word and has in effect accomplished it. The deed is as good as done. The purpose is that his people will know that he is the Lord (v. 13).[5]

4. You should be willing to disagree with any of the labels that I have selected. That's part of the fun of interpreting using these tools and techniques.

Advanced Information and Curious Facts

Paraphrasing. Many people confuse paraphrasing with summarizing. A summary is briefer than the original and focuses on highlights. By the term *paraphrase*, on the other hand, I mean a statement longer than the original. The aim is to make explicit that which is less obvious in the original. It represents the fruit of study.

Often in sermons and lessons on narrative, preachers and teachers will paraphrase in order to be more vivid. Paying attention to the clause structure can guide preaching and teaching of narrative literature and aid you in producing a paraphrase that more accurately brings out the intended meaning of the authors of the biblical text.

For example, in Ezek 37:8 there are four clauses. The first clause, "I looked" in the NIV, is the simple past. Most translations render it this way. A reader might think the major point is that Ezekiel saw because the first and the next sentences change the grammatical subject from Ezekiel to the objects in the vision. The ESV and NET Bible (and some other translations) render "As I watched,"

---

5. This phrase, "then they will know that I am the LORD," is repeated many times in Ezekiel where the "they" sometimes refers to Israel and other times refers to the nations. This is a major theme of the book and offers a theme for a sermon or series, if you are interested.

which subordinates the opening clause to what follows, in which case the *weqatal* (ו + Pf) clause in v. 8, "I saw," is perhaps ingressive, "I began seeing," rather than a simple past.[6]

The second clause begins with *and* followed by the new subject. The ESV has "and behold." Checking an interlinear shows that the clause begins with וְהִנֵּה, and figure 20.2 identifies the function as focusing. The narrator is drawing attention to the appearance of tendons, flesh, and skin on the bones.

The fourth clause in v. 8 begins with the word "but" and draws an important contrast. Checking an interlinear reveals that this is the simple ו + NV (וְרוּחַ). Figure 20.2 on disjunctive clauses and figure 7.1 on the *waw* both allow for a contrastive meaning. However, it is not an explicit contrasting adverb. The translation is based on context.

Here is a suggested paraphrase of v. 8 to bring out the vividness that the Hebrew author does:

> As Ezekiel was prophesying, and these bones were coming together, he suddenly began seeing tendons and muscle start to appear on the bones and then skin covering them. Even after all of this amazing restoration, however, there is still no breath in the body; they are not yet alive. Something more is needed.

The contrast heightens the suspense in the story for the reader to discover the "something needed."

---

6. An observation not for the faint of heart: in v. 4 the Lord commands Ezekiel to prophesy a message. The final verb in v. 5, "and you will come to life," is the first of seven *weqatal* verbs continuing through v. 6, all of which are the normal sequential future and translated as such. Then Ezekiel narrates his obedient response to the command in v. 7, but the account begins with another *weqatal* form, as does v. 8, where we would expect a *wayyiqtol*. These two forms are both translated as sequential simple past tenses as though resuming the past time *qatal* form in v. 5, "This is what the Sovereign LORD says to these bones." Perhaps these are progressive past tenses (see figure 17.4). This would have the effect of making the account more vivid.

CHAPTER 21

IT MAY NOT RHYME, BUT IT'S STILL . . .

Hebrew Poetry

Objectives
1. Define Hebrew poetry.
2. List some characteristics of Hebrew poetry.
3. Count lines in Hebrew poetry.
4. Count meter in Hebrew poetry.
5. Use flowcharting adjusted for poetry.

Tools Used: Interlinear Bible

Introduction

> When poetry I think about,
>> It sometimes turns me inside out.
> Word order often strange,
>> The lines of odd arrange.
> But worst of all to me it seems
>> Is when the poet writes his themes
> In a fashion without rhyme—
>> To be sure it's quite appalling![1]

When I and those like me, who are unlearned in sophisticated literature, think of poetry, we think that there simply must be rhyme. How else would you recognize a poem? Of course, many poems rhyme, but that is not the essence of poetry, even in English. Hebrew poetry has far less rhyming than English. Because Hebrew has more inflections than English, rhyming would be a simple matter; there would be little challenge to it. Understanding Hebrew poetry can enhance our understanding and appreciation of the poetic sections of the OT.

In this chapter you will not learn all you need to know about interpreting Hebrew poetry, but in keeping with our theme, you will learn how to use tools,

---

1. This poem is offered with my apologies to all true poets out there.

in particular an interlinear Bible, to study one of the main features of Hebrew poetry. First you will learn what Hebrew poetry is. Then I will give you a three-step strategy for studying poetry. Finally, I will take you through some examples from Proverbs and Psalms to fine-tune your flowcharting technique.

What Is Hebrew Poetry and How Do You Identify It?

About one-third of the OT is written in poetry. Poems occur in the Pentateuch (e.g., Exod 15:1–18) and in the historical books (e.g., 2 Sam 1:19–27) as well as in the poetic books. Poetry is a major feature of the prophets (Joel 1:2–20). But just what is poetry, and how can you recognize it when you see it? Poetry is the type of literature that uses a concentration of literary devices to embellish the author's message in a way that is memorable.[2]

Identifying Hebrew poetry is a task you must leave to others. Thankfully, modern versions, such as the NIV, delineate poetry into stanzas. You can use such a translation to recognize poetic passages. At times there may be some disagreement, so comparing versions is also a good idea.

Even though Hebrew poetry is often delineated in English translations, much is lost in translation. Only an advanced knowledge of Hebrew can enable a reader to comprehend the full beauty of Hebrew poetry. However, as a pre-Hebrew student, you are now skilled in the use of an interlinear such that you can appreciate more of what is there. James E. Smith has conveniently summarized five major features of Hebrew poetry:[3]

1. *Alliteration:* The repetition of similar sounds at the beginning of words or in stressed (accented) positions within a verse. The purpose seems to be to bind together the words, lines, or verses that contain the alliteration.[4]
2. *Paronomasia:* Play on the sound and meaning of words.
3. *Acrostic Structure:* Consecutive verses (or half verses or stanzas) beginning with successive letters of the alphabet.
4. *Terseness:* Much said in few words. In particular, it is common in poetry that function words, such as the article and conjunctions, are left out; the writer expects the reader to figure out the meaning.
5. *Imagery:* Use of an image to both convey information and evoke emotion.

Of these five features, imagery is least likely to be lost in English, though even here more functional translations tend to alter or simplify the Hebrew imagery. The skills developed in this book will allow you to follow discussions

---

2. Ernst R. Wendland, *Analyzing the Psalms: With Exercises for Bible Students and Translators,* 2nd ed. (Winona Lake, IN: Eisenbrauns, 2002), 62.

3. James E. Smith, *The Wisdom Literature and the Psalms* (Joplin, MO: College Press, 1996), 17–18.

4. So says Wilfred G. E. Watson, *Classical Hebrew Poetry: A Guide to Its Techniques,* Journal for the Study of the Old Testament Supplement Series 26 (Sheffield: JSOT Press, 1986), 227.

by others. In fact, you may observe some things for yourself (for example, look at your interlinear and explain why Lam 1 has twenty-two verses).

Another important feature of Hebrew poetry is parallelism. **Parallelism** is the joining together of related ideas to form a complete thought. Repeated elements may be related phonologically (sound), lexically (meaning), or syntactically (word order). Noticing sound in pronunciation requires more sensitivity than we have developed, though some reading this book may be able to pick up on this. You can, however, observe lexical and syntactic qualities. The parallel elements may be adjacent lines, what Wendland calls "connected (or near) parallelism," or they may be unconnected lines in the same passage, "disconnected (or distant) parallelism." Disconnected parallelism is something you can observe without using the tools and techniques taught in this book, and I will leave this topic for other studies in how to interpret the Bible. We want to look at connected parallelism.

A Strategy for Reading Hebrew Poetry

Students of Hebrew poetry are indebted to Robert Lowth, who in the middle of the 1700s observed that there are three basic types of parallelism: synonymous, antithetic, and synthetic. In recent years, scholars have added categories. Longman gives a list and explanation of Lowth's three categories and four more recent additions.[5] The treatment below divides these seven into two groups, one based on structure and one based on meaning. These will form the last two parts of a three-step process for studying Hebrew poetry: line count, structure, and meaning. Line count is simply identifying how many lines go together to form a unit. Structure is the arrangement of words and encompasses four categories: simple, chiastic, repetitive, and pivot. Meaning involves Lowth's three categories with some fine-tuning with Longman. As we go through these three steps, remember that the goal is to figure out how one line (line b) relates to the previous line (line a).

Step 1: Determine the Line and Beat Count

The first task is to determine the number of parallel lines and the rhythm. These are two separate tasks but they work together. We will treat them in turn.

Line Count

The Latin term *colon* (pl. *cola*) means "line." The number of lines in a thought unit is determined by the lexical (i.e., meaning) content of the lines. As you read, look for thoughts that are closely connected in some way. The number of lines normally forming a thought unit ranges from one to four. Identifying the lines can often be done by following a modern a modern translation, and I will begin with examples taken from the NIV. However, we will see below that an interlinear Bible works much better.

---

5. Tremper Longman, III, *How to Read the Psalms* (Downers Grove, IL: IVP Academic, 1988), 99–104.

Just as narrative has an "unmarked" form, so does poetry. The unmarked form is the bicolon, or two-liner, with an "a" line + "b" line. For example, look at Prov 8:1–2 (NIV):

1a	Does not wisdom call out?
1b	Does not understanding raise her voice?
2a	At the highest point along the way,
2b	where the paths meet, she takes her stand;

In this example I want to focus in on verse 1. I have numbered each line by its biblical verse number (1, 2) and line (with lowercase letters a, b). Notice that v. 2 clearly moves on to a new pair. In other words, v. 1 has two lines and is therefore a bicolon. Pretty simple, eh?

When the poet wants to draw special attention to a line, the lines vary from the bicolon. The variations from the bicolon usually serve to indicate some special discourse function, perhaps to give additional emphasis or reveal beginning or ending of stanzas. Psalm 1:1 includes an example of a tricolon, a three-liner (NIV). The four lines of the verse may be simply labeled 1a, b, c, d. However, we can also label the lines in a way that draws attention to the structure:

1a	Blessed is the one
1b(1)	who does not walk in step with the wicked
1b(2)	or stand in the way that sinners take
1b(3)	or sit in the company of mockers

Clearly 1b(1)–(3) are parallel and related to each other in such a way that they are distinct from 1a.

Two very long lines can be broken up into a tetracolon, a four-liner, as in Ps 5:7 shown below. Again, the four lines might just simply be labeled 7a–d (this is true for every verse and will not be mentioned again). They may also be labeled as below.

7a(1)	But I, by your great love,
7a(2)	can come into your house;
7b(1)	in reverence I bow down
7b(2)	toward your holy temple.

Notice that 7a(1)–(2) form a unit and 7b(1)–(2) form another. The reason this is better than the simple 7a–d is because the second line of each pair is not parallel but complementary; the second line completes the thought of the first line.

The line number considered to be strongly marked is the monocolon, a single line with no parallel. Psalm 11:1 serves well here:

1a	*In the Lᴏʀᴅ I take refuge.*
1b(1)	How then can you say to me:
1b(2)	"Flee like a bird to your mountain."

The NIV correctly indents in such a way that 1b(1) and 1b(2) go together, the second line being complementary. Line 1a stands as a monocolon.

Beat Count

Related to the identification of lines is counting the beats in each line. The details of all of this are debated by scholars, but there are some things you as an English-only user can observe for yourself and you can follow the scholars that discuss rhythm.

Rhythm can be observed a little simplistically by counting the number of stressed syllables, or beats, in the lines. Remember from chs. 3 and 4 that the Masoretes, the preservers of the Hebrew text, included accent marks. Virtually every word in the Hebrew Bible has an accent (some more than one). These serve as punctuation, as series of musical notes, and as marks of word stress. Sometimes words are joined together by the *maqqeph*, a mark similar to a hyphen. In such cases, the word-group counts as one stressed syllable. Using this information, we can count the "beats" or major stresses of each line.

Let's look at the first two verses of Ps 22. In the chart below is the Masoretic Text (MT) and the same in transliteration. Where there is a *maqqeph* in Hebrew I have added a hyphen in the transliteration. In the final column is the "beat count" (Ct), in which I count the number of stressed syllables. After this, we'll make some observations and draw some inferences about the poetry.

Notice that Hebrew vv. 2–3 = English vv. 1–2, and I have given letters to each line. Below the chart is a wooden translation. Hyphens (-) join multiple English words when they represent a single Hebrew word. An equals sign (=) marks the *maqqeph*.

MT	Vs	Transliteration	Ct
אֵלִי אֵלִי לָמָה עֲזַבְתָּנִי	2a	*'ēlî 'ēlî lāmâ 'ăzabtānî*	4
רָחוֹק מִישׁוּעָתִי דִּבְרֵי שַׁאֲגָתִי:	2b	*rāḥôq mîšû 'ātî dibrê ša 'ăgātî*	4
אֱלֹהַי אֶקְרָא יוֹמָם וְלֹא תַעֲנֶה	3a	*'ĕlōhay 'eqrā' yômām walō' ta 'ăne*	5
וְלַיְלָה וְלֹא־דוּמִיָּה לִי:	3b	*walaylâ walō'-dûmiyyâ lî*	3

> [1] My-God, my-God, why have-You-forsaken-me?
>   Far from-my-deliverance [are] the-words-of my-groaning
> [2] O-my-God, (A) I-cry-out daily, (B) but-not do-You-answer,
>   (A') And-nightly, (B') but-no=rest [is] to-me. (author's translation)

Observations and Inferences

Verse 2(E1) There are two lines in this verse, a bicolon. The last word of the first line is "have-You-forsaken-me." This word is used for separation, a leaving behind. The first word of 2b is "far."

This arrangement forms a figure of speech known as a hysteron-proteron ("last-first") referring to the last word of line a *and the first word of line* b. *The juxtaposition of these two words heightens the emotion of the separation that the psalmist feels.*

Verse 3(E2) Both vv. 2 and 3 begin with a vocative referring to God. But whereas the vocative in v. 2 is the short form for God, אֵלִי (*ēlî*), repeated twice, v. 3 begins with a single occurrence of the lengthened and more commonly used form אֱלֹהַי (*ĕlōhay*), "my God."

English versions count this as a bicolon. Each line has two clauses, to which I have assigned letters in the translation for easy reference. Not counting the vocative "O-my-God," clauses (A) and (B) have two words each. (A) consists of a verb and a time element, "daily." (B) is "but-not" plus a verb, "do-You-answer."

(A') (read as "A prime") contains only one word, a time element, "nightly," which parallels the time element in clause (A). Its verb is assumed from (A), "I-cry-out," making it a third verbal clause, but it looks like a noun clause (see the next paragraph).

Clause (B') is the most intricate. It has three words, but the first two are joined by a *maqqeph* and count as one beat. It is a noun clause (or verbless clause), meaning that a form of the verb *to be* is assumed (see ch. 6). This structure of *to be* plus the preposition לְ (*l*), "to," is a normal way for Hebrew to say "X has Y," where X is the object of the preposition. The noun "rest" in (B') is parallel to the verb "answer" in (B).

The temporal parallel in (A) and (A') heightens the constancy of the psalmist's crying to the Lord. In the (B)::(B') parallel, the "answer" in (B) is the (unfulfilled) cause *and the "rest" in (B') is the (unfulfilled)* **result**.

Step 2: Identify the Structure

The second task is to identify the structure. The structure is largely determined by the syntax (word order). Each line has identifiable grammatical elements: nouns, verbs, prepositional phrases, etc. We want to note the arrangement both within a line and between lines.

1. **Simple parallelism:** The elements of line b are in the same order as the elements of line a. This structure is unmarked.

Line	Prov 10:1 (NIV)			
1a	A wise son	brings	joy	to his father,
1b	but a foolish son	brings	grief	to his mother.

In flowcharting poetry, keep all the elements of each clause on the same line, rather than indenting clauses above or beneath the Subj–V–IO–DO line as you did in narrative. In this verse, the parallel elements in each line are obviously in the same order.

2. **Chiastic parallelism:** The elements of line b appear in reverse order from those of line a. The chiastic parallelism is marked; the center element(s) is normally the focal point.

Line	Ps 76:1 (NIV)		
1a	A: God is renowned	B: in Judah;	
1b	B′: in Israel		A′: his name is great.

For this example, I have labeled the elements of line 1a as A and B and the corresponding elements of line 1b as A′ and B′. If you draw a line connecting A to A′ and B to B′, the resulting shape is similar to the Greek letter *chi* from which we get the term *chiasm*. These lines form this chiastic pattern. The focal point is the two "A" elements. The problem is that most often English translations do not maintain Hebrew chiastic structure. To analyze structure reliably you need to check an interlinear. A quick glance shows that the NIV of v. 1 preserves the chiasm that is present in the Hebrew.

X
The Greek letter *chi*

Now look at Ps 76:2 [Hebrew 76:3], which reads, "His tent is in Salem, his dwelling place in Zion" (NIV), apparently simple A—B—A′—B′ parallelism. An interlinear shows otherwise:

סֻכּוֹ [B] His tent	בְשָׁלֵם [A] in Salem	וַיְהִי is	2a
בְצִיּוֹן [A′] in Zion	וּמְעוֹנָתוֹ [B′] and his dwelling place		2b

Clearly v. 2 is chiastic, just like v. 1. The focal point is on the dwelling place and tent of the Lord. In conjunction with v. 1 above, focusing on the fame of God, we can understand that the terms "tent" and "dwelling place" are not intended to draw our attention to physical structures but to the very presence of God himself. This subtlety is brought out in the identification of the chiastic structure of the elements of the two lines.

3. **Repetitive parallelism:** Line b repeats all or part of line a and adds to it. This is a subset of simple parallelism.

Line	Ps 29:3–5 (NIV)		
3a	The voice of the LORD	is over the waters;	
3b	the God of glory	thunders,	
3c	the LORD	thunders	over the mighty waters.
4a	The voice of the LORD	is powerful;	
4b	the voice of the LORD	is majestic.	
5a	The voice of the LORD	breaks the cedars;	
5b	the LORD	breaks in pieces the cedars	of Lebanon.

These verses give two examples: v. 3 is a tricolon; vv. 4–5 form a tetracolon. The repetition is obvious. Notice the additional element in lines 3c and 5b, which are the final lines of both the tricolon and the tetracolon.

4. **Pivot parallelism:** The NIV of Ps 119:105 reads, "Your word is a lamp for my feet, a light on my path." In the chart the word order is rearranged to match the Hebrew. The hyphens are used to join English words in groups that correspond to each Hebrew word, and English words supplied with no Hebrew base are in parentheses.

Line	Ps 119:105 (NIV rearranged)		
105a	a-lamp	for-my-feet (is)	Your-word
105b	a-light	on-my-path.	

The final element in line 105a below is not repeated in line 105b, but it functions in both clauses. Pivot structure is the opposite of repetitive and a subset of chiastic. Because it is located at the center, the pivoting element is the focus of the parallel.

Step 3: Determine the Logic

This step involves applying line labels describing logical relationships between lines (cola). The norm in poetry is the absence of conjunctions marking relationships between lines; the writer expects the reader to figure this out. Lowth's three categories of parallelism serve well as the major classes of meaning. Within these, especially the third class, we can make more specific identifications between lines.

1. **Synonymous:** Line b says basically the same thing as line a but in different words that add nuance.

Line	Ps 3:1 (NIV)		
1a	LORD,	how many	are my foes!
1b		How many	rise up against me!

Structurally line 1a is a noun clause and line 1b is a verb clause. Nevertheless, the line meanings are synonymous. The added nuance is the general "foes" to the more vivid "rise up against me."

2. **Antithetic:** Line b makes the same point as line a, but in contrasting terms, such as with antonyms or negative adverbs. A key word is *but*, which is usually marked by the conjunction *waw* in Hebrew.

Line	Prov 10:3 (NET)			
3a	The LORD	satisfies	the appetite	of the righteous,
3b	*but* he	thwarts	the craving	of the wicked.

The parallelism is brought out nicely by the NET. To accomplish this, they changed the negative statement in the Hebrew in 3a to a positive statement. A formal translation of line 3a would be "The LORD does not let the appetite [נֶפֶשׁ] of the righteous go hungry." The NIV of 3a, "The LORD does not let the righteous go hungry," retains the negative in the Hebrew but includes the word rendered "appetite" in the NET in the verb "let . . . go hungry," which makes the parallelism less obvious, since there is no separate word for the Hebrew נֶפֶשׁ. Both translations are good; they each made different decisions to render the verse.

3. **Synthetic:** Line b completes the thought of line a.
   Line 18b completes the thought of 18a; notice that 18b is only two phrases. Lines 18b–19b form a structural tricolon, all of which relate synthetically to 18a. The additions may be features of time, cause, or completion.

Line	Ps 116:18-19 (NIV)		
18a	I will fulfill	my vows	to the Lᴏʀᴅ
18b	in the presence	of all his people	
19a	in the courts	of the house of the Lᴏʀᴅ—	
19b	in your midst,		Jerusalem.

Figure 21.1 helps to clarify these logical relationships. Ernst Wendland has provided a detailed list of logical relationships between lines.[6] Figure 21.1 is adapted from his list, including his explanations. His examples come from the book of Psalms, but they apply to all Hebrew poetry. Remember: line a is always the reference point or "base"; we want to describe how subsequent lines relate to this base line. However, the logical relationships may occur in either order, e.g., cause-effect or effect-cause.

After you consider the logic of the adjacent lines, you apply these categories to larger blocks until the entire poem is treated.

FIGURE 21.1: Meaning in Hebrew Poetic Parallelism

Class			Line a	Line b	Explanation	Example
Synonymous			Base	Restatement	**b** is very similar in meaning to **a**	61:1
			Base	Amplification	**b** is similar to **a**, but adds a significant feature	61:3
			General	Specific	**b** is more specific than **a**	60:12
Contrastive			Base	Contrast	**b** makes same point as **a** by contrast	145:20
Synthetic	Time		Base	Sequential	**b** occurs after **a**	105:23
			Base	Simultaneous	**b** occurs during **a**	105:26
			Base	Circumstantial	**b** is subordinated to main event **a**	31:22
	Cause		Reason	Result	**b** happens because **a** happens	116:2
			Ground	Conclusion	**b** is the conclusion based on evidence of **a**	48:8
			Reason	Request	**b** is a request based on **a**	82:8
			Means	Request	**b** is a request that an action be done by means of **a**	79:11
			Means	Result	**b** happens by means of **a**	17:4
			Base	Purpose	**b** is the purpose for which **a** was done	78:71
			Request	Purpose	**b** is the purpose for the requested action in **a**	24:7

---

6. Wendland, *Analyzing the Psalms*, 67–99.

Class		Line a	Line b	Explanation	Example
Synthetic (continued)	Cause (continued)	Real Condition	Result	**b** will happen if **a** happens	7:12
		Unreal Condition	Result	**b** would have happened if **a** had happened, but **a** did not happen	66:18
		Concession	Result	**b** happens unexpectedly in spite of **a**	118:18
	Completion	Base	Attribution	**b** describes **a**	53:4
		Base	Location	**b** gives location for **a**	116:18-19
		Base	Manner	**b** is the manner in which **a** was done	55:20, 21
		Base	Response	**b** is a reply to what was said in **a**	118:2-4
		Base	Content	**b** gives content of **a**	30:6
		Base	Comparison	**b** is compared to **a** in likeness or degree	118:9
		Base	Addition	**b** adds content to **a**	68:31
		Base	Alternative	**b** is an alternative to **a**	1:1

Putting It Together

Let's look at some examples. Figure 21.2 is a figure similar to one I used in an adult Bible school class at a small country church (I didn't give them the "Logic" column). I collected several proverbs from the lesson that had similar forms and treated them together with the NIV text. I had the class members complete some of the blanks. The columns below are more detailed than the examples above. Feel free to vary your technique as you see fit.

	FIGURE 21.2: Prov 28: 5, 7, 10 (NIV)				
Vs	Subject (What they do ...)	(... to what)	Verb	Object	Logic
5a	Evildoers		do not understand	what is right,	Base
5b	but those who seek	the LORD	understand	it [justice] fully.	Contrast
7a	A discerning son		heeds	instruction,	Base
7b	but a companion of gluttons		disgraces	his father.	Contrast
10a	Whoever leads along an evil path	the upright	will fall	into their own trap,	Base
10b	but the blameless		will receive	a good inheritance.	Contrast

Now some observations may be based on what items are parallel. These are good questions to ask your students.

1. In v. 5: How are "evildoers" to be understood in view of the parallelism?
   They are those who do not seek the Lord.
2. In v. 7: What is the relationship between heeding instruction and being a companion with gluttons?
   The contrast is between who or what one spends time with and what one allows to influence oneself.
3. In v. 7: What disgraces one's father?
   Being a fool who pursues only his own desires.
4. In v. 10: Define what it means to be blameless.
   To live righteously and lead others in the same good path.

Here is another example taken from Ps 13 (*The Interlinear Bible*), excluding the title. The verse numbers follow the Hebrew. I have preserved Hebrew word order. As above, the hyphens join English word groups that represent a single Hebrew word; the double hyphen (=) represents two or more Hebrew words that are joined by the *maqqeph* (remember this from chapter 2). The elements of each line are aligned, but they do not always match grammatically. I bolded the verbs, including the pronoun, when it is included in the verb form. I will give a brief analysis and then make a few observations.

FIGURE 21.3: Sample Analysis of Ps 13

Vs	Elements			
2a	Until=when,	O-Jehovah,	**will-You-forget-me**	forever?
2b	Until=when,	**will-You-hide**	your-face	from-me?
3a	Until=when	**shall-I-set**	counsel	in-my-soul?
3b	(having-)sorrow	in-my-heart	daily?	
3c	Until=when	**shall-be-lifted-up**	my-enemy	over-me?
4a	**Look!**			
4b	**Answer-me,**	O-Jehovah,	my God!	
4c	**Make-gleam**	my-eyes,		
4d	Lest=**I-sleep**	in-death;		
5a	Lest=**say**	my-enemy,		
5b	**I-have-beaten-him;**			

(continued)

Vs	Elements		
5c	My-foes	**rejoice**	
5d	when	**I-am-shaken.**	
6a	But-I	in-your-mercy	**have-trusted;**
6b	**Shall-rejoice**	my-heart	in-your-salvation.
6c	**I-will-sing**	to-Jehovah,	
6d	for	**He-has-rewarded**	me.

Step 1: Determine the line count. The translation retains Hebrew word order. I analyzed the text as follows: v. 2 is a bicolon, v. 3 is a tricolon, and v. 4 is a tetracolon. Verse 5 might be viewed as a tetracolon or as two bicola; I chose the latter, since the four clauses function differently. I took v. 6 as a tetracolon in which 6a–c and 6d relate to the 6a–c group. I have lined up parallel items as best I can; sometimes it's not as tidy as we might like, but that's okay.

Step 2: Identify the structure. Structurally, 2ab is simple parallelism. In 3abc, 3a and 3c are simple parallelism; 3b might be analyzed as a monocolon, but the tricolon involves a chiasm. Lines 4a–d are simple; so are 5a–d. Lines 6a–b form a chiasm.

Step 3: Determine the logic. The first level of examination considers the adjacent lines. Then relate adjacent groups until the entire psalm is covered. To do this, first determine whether the lines are synonymous, antithetic, or synthetic. Then use figure 23.1 to get the specific relationship. You may analyze lines differently, but below are my suggestions.

Cola	First Level Logic	Additional Level Logic		
2a-b	Synonymous: base-amplification	2ab-3abc: Synonymous: general-specific	2a/3c-4a/5d: Synthetic: Cause: reason-request[7]	2a/5d-6a/d: Contrastive: base-contrast[8]
3a-b	Synthetic: Completion: base-description			
3ab-c[9]	Synonymous: general-specific			

(continued)

---

7. I viewed 2a–3c as a description of the psalmist's fear over his circumstances. That fear causes him to turn to the Lord in prayer, 4a–5d.

8. The key word here is at the beginning of v. 6, "but." Verses 2–3 express the psalmist's fear, vv. 4–5 the resulting prayer, and v. 6 the psalmist's faith in God to deliver in spite of circumstances.

9. I understand 3a and b to be more closely related as a unit. Verse 3c, then, relates to the pair, 3ab.

Cola	First Level Logic	Additional Level Logic		
4a-b	Synonymous: base-amplification	4ad-5ad: Synthetic: Cause: request-purpose	2a/3c-4a/5d: Synthetic: Cause: reason-request *(continued)*	2a/5d-6a/d: Contrastive: base-contrast *(continued)*
4ab-c	Synonymous: general-specific			
4abc-d	Synthetic: Cause: request-purpose			
5a-b	Synthetic: Completion: base-content			
5c-d	Synthetic: Time: base-circumstance			
6a-b	Synonymous: general-specific[10]			
6ab-c	Synonymous: general-specific			
6abc-d	Synthetic: Cause: result-reason			

Once you have completed all this analysis, you can convert all this shorthand to your own commentary to make understandable to others the fruit of your research. The footnotes below the chart provide an abbreviated explanation of this.

After this, reading commentaries will be much more rewarding than simply following what one or more others say. You will have some insights to evaluate their comments.

A Final Word

If you have finished all twenty-one chapters, congratulations! Your skills in using tools and techniques to study the OT should have grown significantly. You are much further along the road to greater independence in understanding the OT.

No matter how much you feel you did or did not understand, there is always more to learn. Don't let this fact be discouraging; let it spur you on to continue growing. The genius of Scripture is demonstrated in the fact that the basic message of the gospel is simple enough that even the unlearned person can understand it; but the message of Scripture is so profound that no one this side of heaven will ever comprehend it fully. You are studying the words of the infinite God of the universe.

---

10. I understood lines a and b to have similar meaning; i.e., I took the promise to rejoice as a more specific description of the current trust he has.

Using these tools and techniques does not make Bible study easier or faster, but it does make it better and more rewarding. I hope you will never again be satisfied with regular Bible study. I hope you will appreciate more the preparation that goes into good sermons and commentaries. I hope you will encourage others to join with you in studying God's Word. May we all grow in our understanding of and submission to this Word.

APPENDICES

APPENDIX 1

HEBREW SONGS

The Hebrew Alef Bet Song

Lee M. Fields

The first time through has only two simple chords. The second time through has a little embellishment. Plus, there is a fun ending. See if you can harmonize with some friends!

Praise Ye the Lord, the Almighty (in Hebrew)

Lee M. Fields   Joachim Neander; Catherine Winkworth, trans.

Praise Ye the Lord, the Almighty

I've translated the English lyrics of this hymn into Hebrew. Catherine Winkworth's words were:

> Praise ye the Lord, the Almighty, the King of creation!
> O my soul praise him for he is thy health and salvation!

All ye who hear unto his temple draw near;
Join me in glad adoration!

Below I give the Hebrew in Hebrew letters and a back-translation into English.

			הָעוֹלָם	מֶלֶךְ	שַׁדַּי	הַלְלוּ־יָהּ
			creation	the King of	the Almighty	Hallelujah
וִישׁוּעָתֵךְ	שְׁלוֹמֵךְ	הוּא	כִּי	אֹתוֹ	נַפְשִׁי	הַלְלִי
and thy salvation	thy health	he (is)	for	him,	O my soul,	Praise,
			בֵּיתוֹ	אֶל	כׇּל־הַשֹּׁמְעִים	קׇרְבוּ־נָא
			his temple	unto	all who hear,	Draw near,
			אָמֵן	הִתְחַבְּרוּנִי	שִׂמְחָה	בִּתְחִלַּת
			Amen!	join me!	gladness	In adoration of

Notes

1. The first three lines begin with imperatives; the fourth ends with one. The poetry would be better if the imperative began the fourth line also, but I thought the syllables fit the music better this way. Besides, the last two lines form a chiasm.

2. I used הָעוֹלָם for "creation, universe." Hebrew does have a word for creation, בְּרִיאָה, but it is not found in the OT. הָעוֹלָם most commonly has a temporal meaning: "eternity, a long time." In rabbinic literature, both of these words, בְּרִיאָה and עוֹלָם, are found. In the rabbinic prayers, מֶלֶךְ הָעוֹלָם, "king of the age," i.e., "of the universe," is a common designation for God. Jastrow, *Dictionary*, 1052, cites passages in which "this age," i.e., the earth in present existence, is contrasted with "the age to come," i.e., the age of the Messiah. A spatial sense may be found in the sense of "creation" in the OT in Ps 41:13, rendered "from everlasting to everlasting" in NIV, NASB, and ESV, where a formal rendering is "from the age to the age" and might be understood spatially. Even-Shoshan sees the physical world as the meaning of הָעוֹלָם in Eccl 3:11, "He has also set *eternity* [הָעוֹלָם] in the human heart" (NIV).[1] This meaning corresponds to the NT "this age" (e.g., 1 Cor 2:8), so it seemed appropriate for the translation of this hymn.

3. In the second line, all the pronouns are feminine because the speaker uses נֶפֶשׁ, a feminine noun, to address himself. נֶפֶשׁ is most commonly translated "soul" but is frequently used to refer to a person, an inner person, and often means the equivalent of "self."

4. In the last line, the Gen "gladness" is attributive, meaning "in glad adoration."

---

1. Even-Shoshan, *Dictionary* (in Hebrew), 1353–54. We translate his entry: "The earth [תֵּבֵל] and its fullness, the heavens and the earth and all their host, existence [יְקוּם]."

WORD-STUDY GUIDES

Word-Study Guide: Full Version

Step 1: Identifying the Word

1. Question to answer:

WSG 1: Comparison of Versions			
	Formal	Functional	Free	Paraphrase
Translations	NASB: KJV: ESV: NRSV: RSV:	NIV: NET: NAB: JB: NEB:	NLT: NCV: TEV: GNB:	MSG: LB:

2. G/K# _____; Strong's # _____
3. Frame the question: What does the word translated _____ in the _____ version mean in _____?

Step 2: Range of Meaning

4. Find all the occurrences of the word
   ○ Number of occurrences:
   ○ Distribution of occurrences:

   Remember to list Hebrew verb meanings grouped by stem (G, N, D+Dp, H+Hp, HtD).

   Note: Insert distribution chart from your computer Bible program as a substitute.

WSG TABLE 2: Distribution of Occurrences of the Word (Optional)	
Category	**Passages**
In same book	
Other books by same author	
Rest of OT Law	
History	
Poetry	
Prophets	

5. Definitions

WSG 2: Definitions (Based on Reading Each Passage)	
Definitions	**Passages**

Step 3: Meaning of the Word in the Target Text

6. Preliminary conclusions on the meaning in your passage.

7. Verify with experts (notes from wordbooks).

8. Conclusions
   - Meaning of target word in target passage:

   - Effect of the meaning of target word on the meaning of target passage:

Word-Study Guide: Shortcut

Step 1: Identifying the Word

1. Question to answer:

WSG 1: Comparison of Versions			
	Formal	**Functional**	**Free**	**Paraphrase**

	Formal	Functional	Free	Paraphrase
Translations	NASB: KJV: ESV: NRSV: RSV:	NIV: NET: NAB: JB: NEB:	NLT: NCV: TEV: GNB:	MSG: LB:

2. Strong's # _____   G/K# _____
3. Frame the question: What does the word translated _____ in the ____ version mean in the passage _____?

Step 2: Range of Meaning

4. List all the translations and frequencies of the word in the ESV (or base version you are using)
   - Number of occurrences: ____

   Remember to list Hebrew verb meanings grouped by stem (G, N, D+Dp, H+Hp, HtD).

WSG 2: Definitions (Cite Version)	
Definitions (NIV)	**Passages**
1.	
2.	
3.	
4.	

5. Definitions from wordbooks (see bibliography of recommended wordbooks ch. 18, pp. 251–2).

WSG 2: Definitions (Cite Wordbook Used)	
Definitions	**Example Passages**
1.	
2.	
3.	
4.	
5.	

WSG 2: Definitions (Other Wordbook)	
Definitions	**Example Passages**
1.	
2.	
3.	
4.	
5.	

Step 3: Meaning of the Word in the Target Text

6. Conclusions
   a. Meaning of target word in target passage:

   b. Effect of the meaning of target word on the meaning of target passage (How does the meaning answer the question you began to answer?):

APPENDIX 3

ACTION FIGURES

FIGURE 7.2: Subordinating Conjunctions and Functions

Word	Functions	Word	Functions
after*	Time—prior	except	Restrictive
although	Contrast, Concession	for example	Example
as	Comparison, Manner	hence	Result
as . . . as	Measure/Degree, Comparison	however	Contrast
		if	Condition
as . . . so	Comparison	in order that	Purpose/Result
as a result	Result	inasmuch as	Cause
as if	Manner	just as	Comparison
as long as	Extent, Cause	just as . . . so	Comparison
as soon as	Time	lest	Condition (negative)
as though	Manner	not only . . . but also	Addition
because	Cause	now	Result
before*	Time—subsequent	provided (that)	Condition
besides	Continuative	since	Time (inauguration), Cause
both . . . and	Addition		
consequently	Result	so	Cause, Result
even as	Comparison	so also	Comparison
even if	Concession	so . . . as	Comparison
even though	Concession	so that	Purpose/Result

FIGURE 7.5: Functions of Waw

	Functions	English Glosses	Explanation
Coordinating	1. Addition	and, also, while, both ... and	Connects words in a sentence to form a list, or sentences without any notion of sequence; this includes correlative uses
	2. Continuation	and, then, [untranslated]	Adds an expression to another with some notion of sequence
	3. Alternative	or, nor	May be inclusive or exclusive
	4. Contrast	but	The joining of a word or sentence to another from which it differs in some way
	5. Emphatic	indeed, even	Introduces an expression that restates the prior one without significant additional information
	6. Explanation	for	Specifies the meaning of a prior expression
	7. Hyphenating	and	Two words joined to form one idea (hendiadys), or two opposites joined to form a totality (merism)
	8. Introductory	now	Introduces a change of topic or focus
	9. Content	that	Introduces content after verbs of speaking; this actually marks the entire quotation as a substantive, the direct object of the verb of speaking or perceiving
Subordinating	10. Cause	because, for	Introduces the root or reason of a prior action
	11. Purpose/Result	so that, that, so, to	Introduces the intentional or likely outcome of a prior expression
	12. Condition	if, when	Introduces a circumstance necessary for the realization of a main clause

FIGURE 10.3: Summary of Functions of Presence and Absence of Article

Class	Function & Description

Semantic Functions	I. **Individualizing Functions:** Distinguishing one member from others of a group.
	  A. **Simple Identification:** To identify one from among a group (a.k.a. "specifying" use, very much like English *the*).
	  B. **Anaphoric:** Referring back to a previously mentioned thing. This function includes **apposition.**
	  C. **Demonstrative (a.k.a. deictic):** More emphatic than simply definite (compare English *this* and *that*).
	  D. **Well Known:** A common noun is sufficient to identify an individual, because that is the individual's defining characteristic.
	  In addition, there are two subcategories.
	    a. *Par Excellence*: Not the only one of a kind, but the best example.
	    b. **Monadic:** Truly one of a kind.
	  E. **Generic:** To mark a class of which there may be many members.
	  F. **Collective:** The article with a singular noun used for a collective plural.
	II. **Pronominal:** The article is equivalent to a personal pronoun in the context.
	III. **Vocative:** To mark out the one addressed, rather than being a part of the clause.

Structural Functions	I. **With nouns in apposition:** Sometimes nouns are described by other nouns, as opposed to adjectives. II. **With adjectives and participles:** The article usually has little to no semantic force, unless they are being treated as nouns, in which case refer to the determined functions. III. **With infinitives and clauses:** There may also be a semantic force, and you may again consult the list of determined functions.
Absence of the Article	I. **Indefinite:** Referring to a member of a class without identifying it from any other member. II. **Qualitative:** Emphasizing the defining characteristic of the class rather than any individual member; this function is nearly identical to the generic use with the article. III. **Definite:** When a noun without an article is still viewed as definite, then you should consult the functions under determined nouns. This is particularly common in poetry.

FIGURE 13.9: Real Main/Independent Clause Functions

Label	Explanation	Examples (NIV)
Assertion	A statement of simple existence of a fact; usually in present time	• The Lord **is** my strength and my defense. (Exod 15:2) • I do not seal my lips, Lord, as you **know.** (Ps 40:9) • the Lord your God is **giving you** (Josh 1:11)
Event	Report of an event as having happened; past time	• In the beginning God **created** the heavens and the earth. (Gen 1:1) • Hannah **was praying** in her heart. (1 Sam 1:13).
Anticipatory	A future event including predictions and promises	• After the boy is weaned, I **will take** him. (1 Sam 1:22) • He **will guard** the feet of his faithful servants. (1 Sam 2:9)
Exclamation	Emphatic assertion; often an "incomplete" sentence	• **Alas, Sovereign Lord** (Jer 1:6)
Rhetorical Question	A question intending to make a point, rather than find out information. A rhetorical question therefore assumes a reality (many linguists classify rhetorical questions as irreal).	• Joshua said, "**Why have you brought this trouble on us?** The Lord will bring trouble on you today." (Josh 7:25)

FIGURE 13.10: Irreal Main/Independent Clause Functions

Label	Explanation	Examples (NIV)
Habitual/ Gnomic	An action is viewed as repeated. The time frame may be past, present or future. The term *gnomic* means a general, proverbial truth.	• Now Moses **used to take** a tent and pitch it outside the camp some distance away, calling it the "tent of meeting." (Exod 33:7) • That is why a man **leaves** his father and mother and **is united** to his wife. (Gen 2:24)
Command/ Request	The speaker is trying to impose his will on another. A command is offered by a superior to an inferior; a request (a.k.a. a prayer) is offered by an inferior to a superior. In English the second-person subject is implied.	• Then the officials said to Baruch, "You and Jeremiah, **go** and **hide**. (Jer 36:19b) • **Don't let** anyone **know** where you are." (Jer 36:19c) • **Show** me your ways, Lord, **teach** me your paths. (Ps 25:4)
Exhortation	Statement by a superior encouraging others to do or be something. Sometimes the speaker is included. Exhortation has the first person as the subject.	• Saul said, "**Let us go down** and pursue the Philistines by night and plunder them till dawn, and **let us not leave** one of them alive." (1 Sam 14:36)
Obligation	A "must" statement. Hebrew has also third-person imperatives that in English are often translated "may" or "let" with the grammatical subject listed second.	• Has anyone built a new house and not yet begun to live in it? **Let him go** home. (Deut 20:5, meaning "he **must go**" or "**may** he **go**")
Permission	A "may" statement with the subject having permission to do something, but the action is not viewed as having yet ended.	• We **may eat** fruit from the trees in the garden. (Gen 3:2)
Question	A question intending to find out information does not assume anything in existence and is therefore irreal (the answer may be real).	• Then they asked Baruch, "Tell us, **how did you come to write all this? Did Jeremiah dictate it?**" (Jer 36:17)
Desire	A statement whose reality is in doubt by the speaker, but he is not trying to impose his will on another.	• All the Israelites . . . said to them, "**If only we had died** in Egypt! Or in this wilderness!" (Num 14:2)

FIGURE 17.4: Nonvolitional Structures and Functions

INDICATIVE MOOD (REALITY)

Time	English Tenses	Examples	Aspect	Pf	וcs+Pf	Imp	וcs+Imp	Ptc
Past (Real & Irreal)	Simple Past	he ate	Constative	X			X	
			Instantaneous	X			X	
			Resultative	X			X	
	Emphatic Past	he did eat	Constative	X			X	
	Past Perfect	he had eaten	Perfective	X			X	
	Contrary-to-Fact Condition	(if) he had eaten	Constative	X				
	Contrary-to-Fact Assertion	(then) he would have eaten	Constative		X	X		
	Customary Past	he used to eat	Iterative		X	X		
	Progressive Past (Historic Present + היה)	he was eating	Continuous		X	X		X
	Ingressive Past	he began eating	Ingressive		X			
	Historic Future (In Subordinate Clauses)	he would (was going to) eat	Conative		X	X		
Present (Real & Irreal)	Simple Present (incl. Stative, Gnomic, Habitual)	he eats	Constative	X			X	
			Instantaneous	X			X	
			Resultative	X			X	
			Habitual	X	X	X	X¹	X
	Emphatic Present	he does eat	Constative	X				
	Present Perfect	he has eaten	Perfective	X	X		X	
	Performative	He (hereby) eats	Instantaneous	X				
	Progressive Present	he is eating	Continuous		X	X		X
Future (Irreal)	Simple Future	he shall eat	Constative		X	X		X
	Conditional Assertion	(then) he will eat	Constative			X		
	Immediate Future	he is about to eat	Constative		X			X

---

1. This is not common and not expected, since the *wayyiqtol* is characterized by representing completed action. However, see Prov 8:35: "For those who find me [*qotel*] find [*qatal*] life **and receive favor** [*wayyiqtol*] from the LORD." The *wayyiqtol* might also be normalized as the present perfect "and has received favor." Cf. KJV, "and shall obtain favour," which might be seen as an anterior future, "shall have obtained favor." See also Prov 11:2, 8; 12:13; etc.

Time	English Tenses	Examples	Aspect	Pf	ו cs+Pf	Imp	ו cs+Imp	Ptc
Future (Irreal) (continued)	Rhetorical/Dramatic Future	he eats (perfected aspect)	Constative	X			X	
	Future Perfect	he will have eaten	Constative	X				
	Anterior Future	he will have eaten	Constative			X		
	Progressive Future (+ יהיה)	he will be eating	Progressive					X

SUBJUNCTIVE MOOD (POTENTIALITY)

Time	English Tenses	Examples	Aspect	Pf	ו cs+Pf	Imp	ו cs+Imp	Ptc
Future (Irreal)	Condition (Protasis)	(if) he eats/eat/ should eat	Constative	X	X	X		X
	Possibility	he might eat	Constative		X	X		
	Purpose/Result	in order that/so that he might eat	Constative		X			
	Capability	he can eat	Constative			X		
	Permission	he may eat	Constative			X		
	Obligation/ Propriety	he ought to eat	Constative	X		X		
	Command/ Prohibition	Eat!/Do not eat!	Constative	X		X		
	Desire/Intention	he wants/ intends to eat	Constative			X		
	Request/Wish	please, eat!	Constative			X		

FIGURE 16.4: Summary of Volitional Functions and Forms

FUNCTION	FORM				
	Imv	Juss	Coh	לֹא + Imp	אַל + Imp
Command	X	X			
Prohibition				General	Specific
Request	X	X	X		
Advice	X				
Interjection	X				
Permission		X			
Resolve			X		
Exhortation			X		

FIGURE 16.6: Volitional Forms in Sequence

V2 Function	Description	Example
Independent-Sequential	V2 has the same volitional force as V1, V2 simply happens afterward.	God blessed them and said, "Be fruitful [Imv] and increase [ı + Imv] in number and fill [ı + Imv] the water in the seas, and let the birds increase on the earth." (Gen 1:22 NIV)
Dependent-Purpose	V2 gives the intended outcome of the action of V1.	I will go down [Coh] to see [ı + Coh, cf. NASB "and see"] whether they have done altogether according to the outcry that has come to me (Gen 18:21 ESV)

FIGURE 17.7: Summary of Main Functions of Nonfinite Verbals

Major Function	Participle	Infinitive Construct	Infinitive Absolute
Substantival	• As a noun in any case with a focus on the *participant* • May govern a Gen • May govern a DO	• As a noun in any case with a focus on the *action* • May govern a Gen • May govern a DO	• As a noun in any case with a focus on the *action* • May *not* govern a Gen • May govern a DO
Adjectival	• Attributively • Predicatively		
Verbal	• Real or irreal action simultaneous to the verb in the previous clause		• for *qatal* • for *weqatal* • for *yiqtol/weyiqtol* • for *wayyiqtol*
Adverbial		• Time • Means • Manner • Cause • Concession • Purpose • Result	• Emphasis of certainty • Emphasis of intensity • Complementary of simultaneous action

FIGURE 20.1: Eight Basic Functions of *Wayyiqtol* Clauses

Function	Description
Introductory	Begins a scene or narrative by providing background for following story
Initiatory	Begins the story proper
Sequential/ Consequential	Describes events in temporal or logical sequence *(most common use)*
Flashback	Interrupts story to refer to prior action that now becomes relevant
Focusing	Draws attention to an individual in the event just described, gives more detailed account of the event or aspect thereof, or provides specific example
Resumptive	Resumptive-(con)sequential follows a supplementary, focusing, or flashback statement Resumptive-reiterative repeats a portion or paraphrase of a previous statement
Complementary	Completes preceding statement by describing an action that naturally or typically accompanies what precedes
Summarizing/ Concluding	Summarizes or marks the conclusion of a narrative

FIGURE 20.2: Functions of Disjunctive Clauses

Function	Description	Function	Key Words
Initial	Marks beginning of new section		*now*
Concluding	Marks the end of a section		
Adverbial	Also called "circumstantial," this clause provides information about the action of a main clause	Time-simultaneous Manner Concession Cause Description	*while, when* *by* *although* *because* —
Parenthetic	Information parenthetic to main clause (meet needs of reader)		*now*
Contrastive	Contrasts with main clause		*but*
Focusing	Draws reader's attention as a witness to the events (particularly when introduced by וְהִנֵּה)		*Look !,* *Take note!*

FIGURE 20.3: Chisholm's Discourse Types and Speech Functions for Embedded Discourse

Discourse Types	• Predictive Discourse	Speaker describes what will happen
	• Narrative Discourse	Speaker rehearses what has happened
	• Hortatory Discourse	Speaker urges, commands, exhorts listeners
	• Expository Discourse	Speaker explains or argues a case
	• Procedural/Instructional Discourse	Speaker explains how to do something
Speech Functions	• Informative	Simple information designed to inform listeners
	• Persuasive-dynamic	Intended to change hearers personally (emotionally, educationally, attitudinally)
	• Expressive	Speaker verbalizes feelings without concern to affect others
	• Evaluative	Speaker expresses judgment on quality of something
	• Performative	Speaker's speech is the act; for example, a decree
	• Relational	Speaker seeks to enhance personal relationships

FIGURE 20.4: Narrative Clause Function Decision Tree

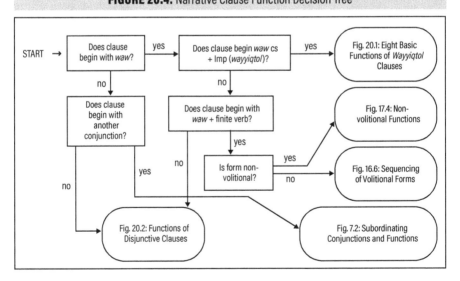

FIGURE 20.5: Narrative Analysis Applied to Ezek 37:1-15

Function	Vs	Passage: Ezek 37:1-15 (NIV)	Clause Structure	Function
Event	1	The hand of the LORD was on me,	∅ + Pf	Initial
Event		and he brought me out by the Spirit of the LORD	1cs + Imp	Initiatory
Event		and set me in the middle of a valley;	1cs + Imp	Sequential
Assertion		it was full of bones.	1 + NV	Parenthetic
Event	2	He led me back and forth among them,	1 + Pf	Past Progressive
Event		and I saw a great many bones on the floor of the valley,	1 + NV הנה	Focusing
Assertion		bones that were very dry.	1 + NV	Focusing
Event	3	He asked me,	1cs + Imp	Sequential
Address		· "Son of man,		
Question		· can these bones live?"	Predictive	Informative
Event		I said,	1cs + Imp	Sequential
Address		· "Sovereign LORD,		
Assertion		· you alone know."	Expository	Informative
Sequence	4	Then		
Event		he said to me,	1cs + Imp	Sequential
Command		"Prophesy to these bones and say to them,	Hortatory	Persuasive
Content		· 'Dry bones,		
Command		hear the word of the LORD!	Hortatory	Performative
Assertion	5	This is what the Sovereign LORD says to these bones:	Expository	Performative
Immediate Fut		· I will make breath enter you,	Predictive	Informative
Addition		and		
Result		you will come to life.	Predictive	Informative

(continued)

Function	Vs	Passage: Ezek 37:1-15 (NIV)	Clause Structure	Function
Simple Future	6	I will attach tendons to you	Predictive	Informative
Addition		and		
Simple Future		make flesh come upon you	Predictive	Informative
Addition		and		
Simple Future		cover you with skin;	Predictive	Informative
Simple Future		I will put breath in you,	Predictive	Informative
Addition		and		
Result		you will come to life.	Predictive	Informative
		Then		
Result		you will know	Predictive	Persuasive
Content		that I am the Lᴏʀᴅ.'"	Expository	Relational
		. .		
Event	7	So I prophesied	ו + Pf	Inceptive Past
Description		as I was commanded.	RC	Past Perfect
Addition		And		
Time		as I was prophesying,		
Event		there was a noise,	ו cs + Imp	Sequential
Description		a rattling sound,	ו + NV הנה	Focusing
Addition		and		
Event		the bones came together, bone to bone.	ו cs + Imp	Sequential
Event	8	I looked,	ו + Pf	Inceptive Past
Addition		and		
Assertion		tendons and flesh appeared on them	ו + NV הנה	Focusing
Addition		and		
Assertion		skin covered them,	ו cs + Imp	Sequential
Contrast		but		
Assertion		there was no breath in them.	ו + NV	Contrastive

Function	Vs	Passage: Ezek 37:1-15 (NIV)	Clause Structure	Function
Sequence	9	Then		Sequential
Event		he said to me,	1cs + Imp	Informative
Command		· **"Prophesy to the breath;**	**Hortatory**	**Informative**
Command		**prophesy, son of man,**	**Hortatory**	**Informative**
		and		
Command		**say to it,**	**Hortatory**	**Informative**
Content		· **'This is what the Sovereign LORD says:**	**Performative**	**Informative**
Command		**Come, breath, from the four winds,**	**Hortatory**	**Informative**
Addition		**and**		
Command		**breathe into these slain,**	**Hortatory**	**Informative**
Purpose		· · **that they may live.'"**	**Predictive**	**Informative**
Event	10	So I prophesied	1 + Pf	Inceptive Past
Description		as he commanded me,	RC	Past Perfect
Addition		and		
Event		breath entered them;	1cs + Imp	Sequential
Event		they came to life	1cs + Imp	Sequential
Addition		and		
Event		stood up on their feet	1cs + Imp	Sequential
Assertion		—a vast army.	Ø + NV	Focusing
Sequence	11	Then		Sequential
Event		he said to me:	1cs + Imp	Sequential
Assertion		· **"Son of man, these bones are the people of Israel.**	**Expository**	**Informative**
Assertion		**They say,**	**Expository**	**Informative**
Content: Assertion		· **'Our bones are dried up**	**Expository**	**Expressive**
Addition		**and**		
Assertion		**our hope is gone;**	**Expository**	**Expressive**
Assertion		· **we are cut off.'**	**Expository**	**Expressive**

(continued)

Function	Vs	Passage: Ezek 37:1-15 (NIV)	Clause Structure	Function
Command	12	Therefore prophesy	Hortatory	Persuasive
		and		
Command		say to them:	Hortatory	Persuasive
Content		· 'This is what the Sovereign LORD says:	Performative	Informative
Address		My people,		
Immediate Future		· I am going to open your graves	Predictive	Persuasive
		and		
Immediate Future		I will bring you up from them;	Predictive	Persuasive
Immediate Future		bring you back to the land of Israel.	Predictive	Persuasive
	13	Then		
Result		you, my people, will know	Predictive	Persuasive
Content		That I am the LORD,	Expository	Relational
Time		when I open your graves	Expository	Persuasive
Addition		and		
Time		bring you up from them.	Expository	Persuasive
Simple Future	14	I will put my Spirit in you	Predictive	Persuasive
Addition		and		
Result		you will live,	Predictive	Persuasive
Addition		and		
Simple Future		I will settle you in your own land.	Predictive	Persuasive
Sequence		Then		
Result		you will know	Predictive	Persuasive
Content		that I the LORD have spoken,	Expository	Persuasive
Addition		and		
Content		I have done it,	Expository	Persuasive
Exclamation		· · declares the LORD.'"	Expository	Performative
Event	15	The word of the LORD came to me:	1cs + Imp	Initial

FIGURE 21.1: Meaning in Hebrew Poetic Parallelism

Class		Line a	Line b	Explanation	Example
Synonymous		Base	Restatement	**b** is very similar in meaning to **a**	61:1
		Base	Amplification	**b** is similar to **a**, but adds a significant feature	61:3
		General	Specific	**b** is more specific than **a**	60:12
Contrastive		Base	Contrast	**b** makes same point as **a** by contrast	145:20
Synthetic	Time	Base	Sequential	**b** occurs after **a**	105:23
		Base	Simultaneous	**b** occurs during **a**	105:26
		Base	Circumstantial	**b** is subordinated to main event **a**	31:22
	Cause	Reason	Result	**b** happens because **a** happens	116:2
		Ground	Conclusion	**b** is the conclusion based on evidence of **a**	48:8
		Reason	Request	**b** is a request based on **a**	82:8
		Means	Request	**b** is a request that an action be done by means of **a**	79:11
		Means	Result	**b** happens by means of **a**	17:4
		Base	Purpose	**b** is the purpose for which **a** was done	78:71
		Request	Purpose	**b** is the purpose for the requested action in **a**	24:7
		Real Condition	Result	**b** will happen if **a** happens	7:12
		Unreal Condition	Result	**b** would have happened if **a** had happened, but **a** did not happen	66:18
		Concession	Result	**b** happens unexpectedly in spite of **a**	118:18
	Completion	Base	Attribution	**b** describes **a**	53:4
		Base	Location	**b** gives location for **a**	116:18–19
		Base	Manner	**b** is the manner in which **a** was done	55:20, 21
		Base	Response	**b** is a reply to what was said in **a**	118:2–4
		Base	Content	**b** gives content of **a**	30:6
		Base	Comparison	**b** is compared to **a** in likeness or degree	118:9
		Base	Addition	**b** adds content to **a**	68:31
		Base	Alternative	**b** is an alternative to **a**	1:1

SCRIPTURE INDEX

SUBJECT INDEX